Absolution

Absolution

Charlie Company
3rd Battalion, 22nd Infantry

by
Charles J. Boyle

Sergeant Kirkland's Press
Spotsylvania, VA

Copyright 1999
By Charles J. Boyle

Published & Distributed by

Sergeant Kirkland's Museum
and Historical Society, Inc.

8 Yakama Trail, Spotsylvania, VA 22553-2422
Tel.: (540) 582-6296; Fax: (540) 582-8312
E-mail: Civil-War@msn.com
www.kirklands.org

Manufactured in the USA

The paper in this book meets the guidelines for permanence and durability
of the Committee on Production Guidelines for Book Longevity of the
Council on Library Resources, Inc.

Library of Congress Cataloging-in-Publication Data

Boyle, Charles J., 1941-   Absolution: Charlie Company, 3rd
Battalion, 22nd Infantry / Charles J. Boyle. – 1st ed.

p.   cm.
ISBN 1-887901-30-2 (alk. paper)

1.Vietnamese Conflict. 1961-1975 — Personal narratives, American.
2. Vietnamese Conflict, 1961-1975 — Regimental histories — United States. 3.
Boyle, Charles J., 1941-   . 4. United States. Army, Infantry Regiment, 22rd. Battalion, 3rd. Charlie Company – History. I. Title.
DS559.5.B695   1999
959.704'342—dc21   99-23812
                                                    CIP

First Edition
1 2 3 4 5 6 7 8 9 10

Cover painting by
James D. Nelson, Machine gunner, Co. C, 2nd Battalion, 22nd (Mechanized) Infantry, 25th Infantry Division.
Jacket design and page layout by Ronald R. Seagrave
Text edited by Pia S. Seagrave, Ph.D.

Dedication

For All of the Gallant Men of
Charlie Company, 3rd Battalion, 22nd Infantry
and
Our Fallen Brothers

<u>Name</u>	<u>Killed</u>
George Allen Fogerty	11-12-66
Anthony T. Martin	11-22-66
Franklin Eugene Brooks	12-10-66
Robert R. Martinez	12-23-66
Harvey R. Parker	01-05-67
Douglas J. Sullivan	01-08-67
Gary Lee Lininger	01-16-67
Dennis Michael Thompson	02-21-67
Thomas James Poteet	04-03-67
Alton Shedd	05-19-67
Teddy Gene Tally	05-26-67
Edward S. Yamashiro	06-07-67
Elbert Thomas Williams	07-14-67
William Brian Monahan	07-14-67
Fred K. Kama	09-06-67
Jaime Cambrellan	10-15-67
Ralph Paul Costanzo	10-15-67
Joseph Vincent Zelinski	11-19-67

Kevin Anthony Porter	11-21-67
Phillip Jackson Dickens	12-14-67
Roger Dale Haste	12-22-67
John Wesley Beckett	01-02-68
Robert Eugene Bowman	01-02-68
Eldon Garamillo	01-02-68
Ralph Lee Rotter	01-02-68
Alton Lamotte Watkins, Jr.	01-02-68
David Ronald Smith	01-02-68
Bobby Joe Winkler	01-02-68
Ronald Edsel Ballard	01-02-68
Kenneth Braxton Carpenter	01-02-68
Fred C. Dubose, III	01-02-68
Victor David Tomczyk	01-02-68
James Jerome Lind	01-02-68
William H Scheiber, Jr.	01-27-68
James Richard Holt	02-05-68
Andrew Paul Crawford	02-06-68
Wallace Lee Giesen	02-06-68
Norman Earl Rose, III	02-06-68
Jackie Glen Smith	02-06-68
Howard Lerot Painter	02-10-68
Albertis Williamson	02-10-68
William L. Watson	02-24-68
Jay Cee Dyer	02-26-68
Jimmy Francis Lehman	03-03-68
Joseph Edward Hartz	03-06-68
Charles H. Rampley	03-07-68
Jimmy Ray Pierce	03-17-68

Stephen Floyd Booth	03-07-68
Warren Robert Orr, Jr.	05-12-68
Alonzo L. Dixon	05-12-68
Angel Luis Sanchez	05-22-68
Alonzo Carlton Collier	05-25-68
Glenn N. Nishizawa	05-31-68
Samuel Tony Hill	05-31-68
Stephen William Shaw	06-17-68
Jose H. Ramirez	06-24-68
John Michael Golden	06-25-68
Fred A. Chitwood, Jr.	08-21-68
Kenneth Wayne Reid	08-23-68
Robert Joseph Dorshak	08-25-68
Cornelius F. Murphy, Jr.	08-25-68
Leland Eugene Radley	08-25-68
Dennis Clayton Boone	09-12-68
Frank J. McManus	09-17-68
James Patrick Rawlins	09-17-68
James Burl Hansard	10-23-68
Henry Lewis Nix	11-12-68
Grady Ray Nelson	11-23-68
Eric Doran Jenkins	11-27-68
Jimmy John Lacosse	11-28-68
Larry Don Welsh	01-07-69
Leo Robert Mullen	01-07-69
Danny Ray Scott	01-07-69
Craig Seimon Olson	01-07-69
James Keith Merrell	01-07-69
William Francisco, Jr.	01-10-69

Randall J. Wicklace	01-16-69
David Paul Jacobs	03-05-69
Larry Steven Weil	05-14-69
Landus S. Taylor, Jr.	05-31-69
David Allen Strong	07-23-69
Ricky Wayne Church	08-15-69
Lanny Mayes Hanby	10-14-69
John Edwin Hill	04-07-70
Harry Daniel Jajola	04-07-70
Dale Arthur Erdman	04-07-70
Michael Paulson	04-07-70
Sylvester Ellis	05-06-70
Bruce Edward Hahn	05-06-70
Chatwin A. Strother	05-29-70
Wesley Eugene Melton	06-18-70
Joseph James Gagne	09-20-70

Table of Contents

Preface

Truth, crush'd upon the earth, shall rise again;
"The Battlefield"
William Cullen Bryant, 1784-1878

For those who lived and fought the war in Vietnam, it comes as no surprise that sorrows and regrets are the final consequences of battle. If war is hell, then Vietnam was fuel for the furnace. Between 1960 and 1975, hundreds of thousands of young men, most of them barely teenagers, were torn by conscription from their unworried lifestyles. In a matter of days, they were thrust into the barbarity of a civil war. Inadequately trained for jungle warfare, and initially armed with a defective weapon, they acquired their "killer skills" by instinct and imagination. Transformed by necessity, these genteel sons quickly became the brutal gladiators that their government expected them to be. For the foot soldier in Vietnam, death by any means was the ultimate objective. "What's your body count?" commanders asked their soldiers each evening at tattoo, as if the war was a sport, and as if a scorecard named the winner.

From that shortsighted viewpoint -- to search and destroy -- emerged a legion of men, struggling with an even greater battle, personal and private. It was a moral conflict that only those who have taken another life can comprehend. Exacerbating their dilemma, a powerful and biased news media created a myth that quickly spread across America. They created the illusion that the Vietnam-era soldier was a misfit: a perverse example of a military machine gone awry, wreaking havoc and destruction upon innocent civilians. The sources of the myth are well-known, their lies laid bare now.

After the fighting was done, someone coined a new phrase: "the only war we ever lost," they said. They passed that false legacy on to the Vietnam veteran, too. They would have you believe that the soldier lost the war, when, in fact, he lost nothing but his youth and his innocence.

Vietnam was handed to the Communists after the battle had been won. The soldier did not lose the war. Instead, spineless men in high places found that an abdication of the war effort suited their political purposes. Regrettably, all of this and more than thirty years of national loathing have burned emotional scars deep into the soul of the Vietnam veteran, an inner pain that no parade, no granite edifice of regret, can ever heal.

The men who pulled the trigger in the name of democracy, who left their flesh, their blood, and more than fifty-eight thousand of their buddies lying on that Asian battlefield, deserve better. *Absolution* is a true story of that war and of the warrior at his best. It is a long-awaited vindication of a generation of men haunted by an undeserved burden of shame and humiliation. It is a commemoration for their gallant service, their love of country, and their obedience to orders.

Absolution is not about the author; rather, it is about the men, the fearless men of the 3rd Battalion, 22nd Infantry, 25th Infantry Division. All of the characters are based upon real people; all of the episodes are true. The names are genuine, except in cases where pointless embarrassment might result. Pseudonyms are used for those men killed in action, so as to spare their families any further grief. The men who fought alongside them will know the names, know that their stories were true, and understand the equivocation.

Of the tales of thousands of men who served in the 22nd Infantry, each is a story of bravery and honor. There were few exceptions. It is impossible to tell every soldier's story; thus, *Absolution* seizes upon the boldness of their individual tales, and wraps each episode around the characters of a few. The dates and times of battles are accurate; the incidents of killed and wounded are factual. Some scenes, however, are compressed chronologically so as to lend comprehensibility and velocity to the story.

The 3rd Battalion, 22nd Infantry, "The Regulars," as they were called, was formed from groups of basic trainees at Fort Lewis, Washington. They arrived off the coast of Vietnam in October, 1966. The unit initially occupied a base camp called "Bear Cat" in the Delta, or southern part, of Vietnam. Considered to be the "rice bowl of the Orient," the Delta was a hotly-contested area and the Regulars quickly learned the frustrations and pain of battle.

In the summer of 1967, the unit moved north of Saigon to establish a base camp at Dau Tieng, near the southern edge of the vast Michelin rubber plantation. The camp was in the heart of war zone "C," not far from the Cambodian border, and astride the infamous Ho Chi Minh Trail.

From there, the battalion encountered its first big battle at a place called "Soui Tre." In March, 1967, they, along with the 2nd battalion (mechanized), fought off wave after wave of attacking Vietcong. From a soldier's point of view, the Regulars gave a good account of themselves, killing 647 enemy soldiers in that engagement.

Again, at the battle of Fire Support Base Burt, on the night of January 1, 1968, four regiments of North Vietnamese and Viet Cong attacked these two battalions. Through sheer tenacity and raw courage, these infantrymen killed over 400 of the enemy. The battle so impressed one young soldier that he later produced *Platoon*, one of the firsts in a series of movies about the war.

During the Tet offensive of 1968, the 3rd Battalion became critically engaged in a ferocious battle at the village of Ap Cho, a hamlet nestled astride the main supply route between Saigon and Cui Chi. The enemy was so solidly entrenched in tunnels and concrete bunkers that 14 days of frontal assaults were necessary to dislodge them.

Shortly after midnight on Good Friday evening, the 12th of April, 1968, North Vietnamese soldiers again attacked the 3rd battalion. The Regulars killed 153 enemy in some of the most intense fighting an infantryman could ever endure. It was hand-to-hand combat, bayonet for bayonet, all night long. Throughout the years 1969 through 1971, the battalion fought many more battles, large and small, with similar success.

Absolution is based upon these true episodes of battle. The reader will be astonished by the courage and character of the men of the 22nd Infantry, and, for that matter, the sacrifice of all American fighting men in Vietnam. *Absolution* destroys the myth and abolishes the burden of shame unjustly heaped upon these men. They did what their country asked them to do. They never lost a battle, and they didn't "lose the war." They were some of the finest fighting men that ever served America. It is a pity that it took so long to honor them, to absolve them. Vietnam was a very peculiar moment in history. Not much has changed since a simple shepherd boy threw a stone and killed a one-eyed Cyclops.

Charles J. Boyle

Acknowledgments

The names of the men and women to whom I owe an enormous debt of gratitude for helping me write this book would fill the pages, without the story. Nevertheless, my obligation to them is too great to even consider writing a page without my sincere expression of thanks. To my brothers, David and John, who read the early manuscripts and with great sensitivity, guided me throughout the writing, thanks for your wise counsel and moral support. To my sisters, Rose, Patricia, and Madeline, who also read the early drafts, I thank you for your balanced criticisms and kindly praise. To my "big" sister Nancy, thank you for teaching me to dress and feed myself, helping me to learn to read and write, and critiquing my fourth grade essays. I love you all, as only a brother can. To Sisters Mary John Bosco, and Mary Ivo, thank you for frequent inspiration.

Chief among those who deserve special credit and thanks are Jerry J. White, for insisting that I write this story (without his persistent encouragement, this book may have only been a fleeting abstraction); James A. Asher, for his courage as a soldier, his friendship, and his unyielding support for this writing; Awbrey Norris, my wise and gentle mentor, who sent me into my future, watched over me all the while, and who still promotes my career; Eddie Runge, my companion at war and "best-buddy," ever since; Ken Green, who helped me through the hard times and still does; Bill Schwindt, who had so much to do with bringing me home; and Beverly Ann Jagoda Boyle, forever my friend. To Donald, Jacqueline, and Sandra: thank you, my children.

My special thanks go to the three best Lieutenants a Commander could ever hope to know: Dennis R. Adkins, Michael D. Balser, and Michael Donnelly. They were my heroes, every day.

My profound thanks to these distinguished men and women, for their service then, their friendship now, and their contributions to this book: Mike (Stinger 96) Adkinson, Charlie Brown, Curtis Herbert Chancey, Wayne (Crash) Coe, James Dice, John Eberwine, Bob (Frenchy) Gibeault, Roy K. Flint, Greg Hall, Horacio Dos Santos, Nick Dragon,

Gordon Kelly, John Martz, Dr. Ira Mersack, Jim and Sharon Nelson, Mike Pectol, Steve (Mississippi) Rye, Patrick Shine, Joe (Stinger Top Gun) Skarda, Fr. James Tobin, Dr. David Warden, and Wanda Wilson. You men and women will, of course, deny any contribution to this effort, but I know better. Thanks.

A story is only someone's imagination, his hope, his dream, until an editor and a publisher decide to lay it in ink. In that regard, I must express deep appreciation to Mr. Ronald R. Seagrave, Director, Sergeant Kirkland's Press, and to all of the members and associates of Sergeant Kirkland's Museum and Historical Society. They took more than one chance on me. Particularly praiseworthy in all of this is Dr. Pia S. Seagrave, wife, mother, professor, and the editor who validated my meager prose. In more ways than I can count, she made this book better than it really is.

Finally, there are the men and women of the 22nd Infantry, and the countless others who have touched my life before, during, and after Vietnam. I cannot name you all, but be assured, my friends, you are nestled warm and snug at the center of my heart. Thank you all.

Chapter One
Lamentations

It was nearly midnight in his part of the world, a world colored with the red blood of dying soldiers, their painful screams reverberating across the tropical landscape. Dennis shook his head, freeing himself from the repulsive abstraction and turned his attention to more realistic matters.

Punching a hole in another can of warm beer -- his third or fourth now -- he felt a good buzz coming. He took a drag on a cigarette, swallowed a mouthful of the vinegary brew, and blew a cloud of purple cigarette smoke across the room.

The spooks are about gone now; I can almost think again... almost. Focus, damn it, focus. Get on with the job. Couple of months and I'll be out of here. Just got to get through Ap Cho.

A man of average height, Dennis was gifted with a muscular body -- a first-rate physique, some said. Top in his class in physical fitness tests at Officer Candidate School, he'd broken every record, in every event, and, as far as he knew, these achievements still stood a year later.

His once thick auburn hair was short and dirty now, but Dennis no longer cared. His prominent jaw, coupled with deep-set blue eyes and rosy cheeks, belied his true age of twenty-six. He looked and acted much younger. Except for that empty stare he'd recently acquired, Dennis hadn't changed all that much. Like every fighting man in Vietnam, he had naturally acquired this common form of evading the realities of war. "Death is in the eyes," some barracks philosopher had told him. "...best to hide it in your own."

With his right hand, his long fingers wrapped around the perspiring beer can. He squeezed it carefully, in and out, intrigued by the popping sound that it made. With his free hand, he unconsciously played with a book of matches, cradling a Winston cigarette between the fingers.

"If it doesn't kill you," his Tactical Officers had warned, "Vietnam will make a man out of you. It looks good on your record, too."

Good for my record? Damn, I should be home, college, anywhere but this Godforsaken place. I'd love to have my arm around sweet Beverly Ann, right about now, watching the Lions beat the hell out of Green Bay.

A guttural murmur echoed from a corner of the tent, forcing Dennis from his preoccupation with "golden days." Raising his brow at the sound, he never lifted his eyes from the beer can. He knew the man too well. *That damn First Sergeant Rudolph Krznarovich. Pissed ... fighting his third war now, and not very happy about it. He should have retired, two wars back.*

Although the normally short-tempered First Sergeant was present in the headquarters this night, as were others, he remained unusually quiet. The savvy old soldier was prudent enough to let these gloomy deliberations unfold by themselves.

Dennis, wholly absorbed in reshaping the beer can, finally crushed it in a quiet gesture of anger and despair. "Fuck it, it don't mean nothing," he said.

Dennis' mind began to focus exclusively on the morning's battle and its aftermath. It was a fiasco, a failure, an outright disaster. The leadership had failed them as it usually did, causing needless death. There was more death to come, he was sure.

Creeping doubts about the nature and effectiveness of his own tactics began to overwhelm him. Licking a mixture of rust and foam from the top of the can, knowing its ultimate effect, he gulped the rest of it down without drawing a breath.

Composed now against the perpetual flutter that had taken root in his stomach, he stood, walked to the open flap of the large tent, and threw the empty can outside into a trash barrel. Dennis cursed, stared into the darkness for a while, then directed his attention back inside the tent.

As usual, their meager workplace was badly cluttered. Everything in it lay smothered under a thick ruby powder, deposited there by passing cargo trucks and armored vehicles. A rancid odor of smoldering human waste saturated the air in the hovel as it did every building and hut at Dau Tieng. An inescapable aroma, it impregnated everybody's clothing, tainted the food, and, during sleep, its stench thickened in their nostrils.

Unconsciously licking his lips to rid himself of the taste, Dennis remarked, "Can't even dig a respectable shit house in this damned swamp; you've got to burn the crap."

Drawing himself up to his full height, he carefully addressed the First Sergeant: "OK, Top, let me get at it; I need your desk and typewriter."

First Sergeant Krznarovich slammed the center desk drawer shut, perhaps to acknowledge Dennis' presence, or to dispute his authority. "Yes, Sir. You can type, goddamn it?"

"About as good as anybody else around here, Top, I guess."

Nodding his assent, the graying soldier pulled his towering bulk upright, then stepped gracefully aside. He pulled open the top drawer of an ancient and battered file cabinet that wobbled freely alongside the desk, then mindlessly began fumbling with papers. Except for the idle purring of the lantern, it was the only sound in the unnerving silence -- an uncanny sort of quiet -- that seemed to force a mood of its own. Their incivility was mutually understood. Only through caustic exchanges like this, could they cope with the affairs of dead men.

"The first few hours after a bloodletting are like that. Everybody gets a little mean after a bad fight, after one of your boys goes belly up," Dennis had been told by someone he could barely remember. *Maybe it was Lieutenant Billy Potter -- before he nipped his turd.*

Yeah, it was sandy-haired Billy Potter all right. Puffy-eyed, angry and drunk, slamming his fist onto the bar as he ranted and his eyes filled with a salty wet mist.

Dennis remembered their last conversation.

"I despise the people, the ones that make this war. Don't you, Dennis?" Potter had asked.

"Yeah, I guess so," Dennis replied into his beer can.

"You guess so? Is that all you can say, 'I guess so?' What the fuck are you doing here anyway, Riley?"

"I've got my reasons, man. I came to fight the war – to kill some Communists. Hell, man, I came for the adventure, I guess."

It was still early in Dennis' tour when Potter had counseled him. He had not yet come to understand the passions that consumed men like Billy Potter, so he patronized. Lieutenant Potter was a good soldier and a tough leader, but he'd turned sour on the war.

Poor Billy; he didn't understand this war, either. Well, he knows the answers now. Let's see, Billy got killed.... Hell, I can't even remember, don't want to remember. He was right about one thing, though. I am mad and I feel pretty damn bad about Charlie Martin. Then there was Jimmy Hollister, too, and all the others. Did I set Charlie up last September on that ambush? Maybe I should have attached him to another squad?

"Aw, fuck it," Dennis said.

The few men gathered there glanced at him, some nodding their approval. They liked "good" profanity from an officer; it made it seem like he was one of them. It answered nothing and Dennis didn't know why he had said it. Still, the filthy curse gave him some pleasure and helped immunize him against further outbursts. He shut his eyes for a moment and thought about home and his mother.

The rising squeal of a rusty file drawer speeding shut served to snap him back to the task at hand. "Thanks," he said to the top enlisted man, noticing the neatly-placed paper and carbons in the dilapidated old typewriter. First Sergeant Krznarovich grunted his acknowledgment as Dennis took command of his well-worn swivel chair.

Good, the letter is already started. Now all I have to do is fill in the words. Dash off a proper and dispassionate letter to the dead boy's parents. Find some simple, clever, reasonable -- not too cold -- convincing way to explain and to make them accept, not blame any of us, that their nineteen-year-old son got blown away last week at Ap Cho.

Not too hard for a practiced dissembler like me. On second thought, maybe I should try telling the truth for once. Tell his folks how he kicked and screamed for twenty-minutes before he finally gurgled out his last breath. Tell them how Jimmy Hollister lay all afternoon in his own urine and feces, and how it seemed to mix so easily with his vomit and blood. Hell, that crap represents the only evidence that Jimmy ever lived and a ravenous Army of tropical insects now feasts on his body fluids at the spot where he died. I ought to tell them how I had to pry Jimmy's death grip off my shirt and how I almost snapped a couple of his fingers doing it and how I can still feel him -- our parting touch -- Jimmy and me.

Forget the commiseration, like Billy Potter would have had it. I'll tell them how, through his tears and his mucus, he choked and he wailed and he begged for just one more chance to live. I'll tell them how one of his buddies, Eddie Runge, I think it was, had to punch a hole in his belly with a bayonet to release the captured gasses threatening to burst his bloated body while we dragged it through that village under a scorching Asian sun.

I'll tell them how I just left his stiff and naked carved-up carcass laying on a cement slab alongside four of his other dead buddies over at Graves Registration with large tags tied on their big toes. They're lucky they won't be

*able to view him cause it'll have to be a closed coffin affair for sure. He's such
a mess.*

"Write the fucking letter, Lieutenant," First Sergeant Krznarovich
said as he slid another rusty can of beer toward Dennis.

Dennis' heart jumped. Embarrassed, he looked around and saw that
the tent was empty now. Only he and the First Sergeant remained to con-
clude the day's business.

*Thank God. Sure wouldn't do for the men to see me jumping through
my ass for Top.*

He cloistered himself against the First Sergeant's barbed distraction
and stared at the typewriter.

*I'm fooling myself; I'll never write such terrible things, anyway. This
letter is only a formality, just another Army requirement. Besides, it would
be a damn sick explanation of how Jimmy died, written for me, not for them.
Then, it wouldn't all be a lie.*

Dennis swiveled in the chair. "Do you think the Army has officially
notified them yet, Top? I don't want mine to be the first letter they get."

The First Sergeant stood back a few feet from the desk, rolling a big
cigar around in his mouth. He finally removed it and stared at Dennis.

"What the hell you think, Lieutenant?" he said. "Yeah, they've been
told by now. The fuckers pull up at daylight, usually bring a minister to
do the talking. They can't tell the parents nothing about how their boy
died, how the hell would they know this early in the game? They usually
stay a few minutes, wring some hands, pass out some Kleenex, then run
like hell. You're the Company Commander, Lieutenant. You do the honors."

"Yeah, great ... lucky me. Maybe the first shock will have passed by
the time my letter gets there and he'll be buried already. What do you
think?"

"Don't count on it, Lieutenant Riley," the First Sergeant said, blowing a huge cloud of cigar smoke straight at Dennis.

Waving his hand into the haze, Dennis feigned a coughing spell,
then lit his own cigarette. "Hell, Top, they'll never write back and if they
do, I'll just send the letter on to higher headquarters. Let them handle it."

Staring again at the trace of rust on the rim of the beer can as the
foam sputtered to conceal it, Dennis wondered if all the beer in Vietnam
came in rusty cans and was served warm, and he wished he could have
one with Charlie, Jimmy, and the other guys right then.

"I knew him real good, Top. He came over with us."

"Aw, hell, Sir. If you can't get started, here's a couple of old letters you can copy." First Sergeant Krznarovich threw some papers onto the desk; his towering mass leaning forward. "It don't make a good goddamn what you say, just fill in the blanks with his name. Christ, Lieutenant, you'll never be able to satisfy his folks anyway. I'll do it for you if you ain't up to it."

There was just enough feeling in his voice to grab Dennis' attention and he oozed out of his mournful reverie.

Hell of a thing, an enlisted man chewing out an officer....

"Thanks, Top, but this one's mine."

Coming alert now, sucking beer past the rusty rim and starting to peck aimlessly at the keys, Dennis softly said: "I'll get it out in a little bit. I really can't type, you know. I'll have to do it with two fingers. I'll just do like you said, Top. Fill in the blanks. What the hell, it's only a letter. Give me another beer."

Chapter Two
Death Notifications

Headquarters
Department of the Army
Company C
3rd Battalion, 22nd Infantry
APO San Francisco, 96268

7 February 1968

Mr. and Mrs. Kevin R. Hollister
1437 Fielding Avenue
Uniontown, Arkansas 72309

Dear Mr. and Mrs. Hollister,

   I regret to inform you that your son, Private First Class James R. Hollister, was killed in action on 5 February 1968, near the village of AP Cho, in the province of Hau Nghia, Republic of Vietnam. You have probably been informed of Jimmy's death by now, but I, too, want to convey my deepest sympathy to you and your family. Perhaps knowing the circumstances of his death will help you during this difficult time.

   I knew Jimmy well. We had trained together at Fort Lewis, Washington, before shipping to Vietnam. He was a member of our third platoon with duty as a rifleman and sometimes a Machine Gunner.

   We all respected Jimmy for his patriotism and I especially admired him for his sensitive attitude toward others. He had confided to me often his most deeply-held belief: that we were helping the world's poorest and contributing to the cause of freedom by our service in South Vietnam. Jimmy spoke frequently about his family, and he was not ashamed to express his feelings; he loved each of you with matchless affection.

   From our first day in country, Jimmy displayed a courage and skill seldom found in one so young. Always positive in his outlook, he set an example for everyone, including me. His enthusiasm constantly inspired the men of Charlie Company.

In the late morning hours on the fifth day of February, 1968, we were patrolling near the village of Ap Cho, along the main Military Supply Route between Saigon and the Cui Chi base camp. Charlie Company was the lead element in the battalion as we approached the village. Our mission was to search for and to eliminate enemy positions that had assembled there, trying to stop our supply convoys.

Shortly after 9:20 a.m., we were taken under fire by a large enemy force using small-arms, machine gun, and rifle grenade fire. Jimmy's platoon was on the left flank of our attack formation. While conducting this assault, he encountered an enemy machine gun position and was killed instantly. Our platoon corpsman, a superb and experienced soldier, was with him when he died, as was I. Be assured that Jimmy did not suffer. He died as he lived, serving his fellow man.

At our first opportunity, we removed his body from the battle zone to a rear area. There, Father James Tobin, a Catholic Priest, administered the Last Rites of his church. Although Jimmy was not Catholic, it seemed appropriate since there was little else we could do for him. A nondenominational memorial service was held the next day and attended by everyone.

We all share your loss and feel your grief, even as you read this letter. After the service we pledged to memorialize Jimmy by praying for his soul and modeling our lives after his. We want to keep his courageous spirit alive and within us, as we continue these unpleasant tasks.

Jimmy has been awarded the Purple Heart for wounds received in action and has been recommended for the Silver Star for his valorous performance that morning. I realize that these laurels are of little comfort to you, yet I hope they serve as a reminder of the absolute admiration and high esteem in which we held him.

He was a very special American -- a fine soldier. I can pay him no loftier compliment. He has brought great credit upon himself, Charlie Company, and the United States Army, but most particularly, he reflected the superb nature of his heritage.

Jimmy's personal effects are being inventoried now and they will be forwarded by special handling as soon as possible. If I may be of any assistance, please do not hesitate to write. Know that our prayers are with you and your family constantly. May the peace of Jesus Christ bring comfort to you all.

Sincerely,
Dennis J. Riley

1LT, Infantry
Commanding

Feeling somewhat acquitted and satisfied with his composition, Dennis smiled at First Sergeant Krznarovich. Without expression, the top soldier unfolded a metal chair, lit a fresh cigar, and sat eyeball-to-eyeball across the desk from Dennis. He peered for an instant into Dennis' face, shifted, then scanned the carbons quickly.

"Damn, you can really sling some crap. Good stuff, Lieutenant, good stuff. Get you another beer, Son. You've got some more of them to write tonight."

Throughout the night, under the watchful eye of the First Sergeant, Dennis carefully typed nearly identical letters to the parents and loved ones of the four others who had died that week, making each as personal as possible, but superficial in detail. He didn't like writing these letters and was always unsatisfied with their content. Having glossed over the actual circumstances of Jimmy Hollister's death and those of the rest of them, he felt good about not telling their parents what was really happening at Ap Cho. Experience and instinct told him not to reveal much of anything in these letters.

"Practice has made me the master of shallow prose, Top."

"Shallow prose, my ass. Hell, Potter would be proud."

Reviewing the letters, but displeased now with their cold and hollow explanations, Dennis wondered how many more he'd have to write. Taking a huge swallow of beer, a chill tingled his spine and he imagined someone else at the typewriter, with himself as the subject -- someday soon, perhaps.

Folding the letters neatly, Dennis laid them down and leaned forward across the desk. "I can only guess how they'll react to all this. The parents, the sweethearts -- how do you think they'll feel, Top?"

"Like shit."

"Talk about shallow prose, Top."

"Fuck it. This is war, Son. Don't get hooked on feelings."

Dennis addressed the envelopes by hand. He sealed and dropped them into the large canvas mailbag hanging by a nail on the center tent post, then stood stiffly by the bag for a moment. *At least from my handwriting they'll know I'm a real person, not just some typist.* Instinctively, he snapped a sharp salute, then abruptly spun toward the First Sergeant who stood and waved his own quick good-bye. Dennis smiled. "All right, Top."

Their morbid duties complete, they sat facing each other, drinking beer long after the lantern flame flickered out. Their silence was broken only by the occasional popping of tin lids and the frequent flicker of Zippo lighters as they consumed many cigarettes. They said nothing. Words could not satisfy their needs. Barely able to see his mentor in the dark, Dennis warmed inside, knowing that the older man approved of his writing -- of him, and that he endorsed his empathetic mushiness.

"I feel redeemed."

"Yeah, Boy, you did good. Now go get some fucking sleep."

"Good-nigh, ya old fart ... thanks."

Dennis stepped into the clammy night air and staggered blind toward his tent, vomiting a little along the way. He gulped a swallow of warm water from his plastic canteen, rinsing his mouth, then spit it onto the ground. Jerking open the mosquito netting, he fell, exhausted, onto his cot.

He lay back on the nylon poncho liner that served as a bed sheet and immediately shifted to one side to escape the wetness of his sweat. The shift created momentary coolness, yet the quilt now felt sticky against his flesh. The alcohol dulled his mind and, in a few moments, he drifted into an endless sea of pallid faces.

Chapter Three
Return to Battle

"Chopper leaving at six o'clock, Lieutenant Riley," the First Sergeant said as he shook Dennis awake. "Get your hung-over ass out of bed. You've got thirty minutes to get to the pad. The Battalion Commander's having a goddamn hissy fit about you being away from the company for so long, even if he did send you here. ...radio says you're going back into Ap Cho this morning. You OK, Lieutenant? Need anything?"

Dennis sat upright on the cot and rubbed his eyes. "Yeah, Top, I think I need a transfer to hell out of here, maybe to a mess kit repair unit. I was hoping that someone would have taken that bastard village by now."

"Fat chance, Lieutenant. It belongs to Charlie Company. Move it, now." The First Sergeant turned as if he were about to leave the tent.

"OK, OK, Top," Dennis replied. "I'll be at the helipad by six. Call the Company and tell them I'll be in by six-thirty. Can you get a dufflebag full of beer and sodas? Put some ice on it? Our boys could use something to cheer them up after yesterday."

"Anything else, your fucking Lordship? Jesus, cold beer, cheer them up? What the hell will this modern Army think of next? OK, Lieutenant, you got it." First Sergeant Krznarovich stomped out of the tent.

"I'll need a ride to the pick-up point," Dennis yelled after him "... and thanks, Top, for everything."

Large Chinook helicopters served as supply ships and Dennis didn't like flying in them. Few infantrymen did. A Chinook was too big a target and the tail sections had a nasty habit of disintegrating in flight. When operating well, however, it was a real workhorse and this particular aircraft was loaded to the ceiling with cases of ammunition rations watercans, spare parts for weapons and hundreds of other tools used for making war. Cupping his hands and shouting above the whine of the warming engines, Dennis interrupted the Crew Chief as he checked cargo straps and tie-downs.

"Where are you taking this ammo dump? Got enough stuff here to outfit the Chinese Army. Think it'll get off the ground?"

The soldier stopped what he was doing, coiled several thick straps into a neat roll, then faced Dennis. "Down to Cui Chi. There's been a battalion of 'leg' infantry wrapped around the axle south of there. They're up against North Vietnamese Regular troops, I hear. They're out of everything ... ammo mostly. We pulled this stuff from all over. Dau Tieng's our last hit. They're supposed to attack again this morning, but they ain't got much --"

The crewman bent forward abruptly, covering his flight helmet with his hands, trying to monitor a call from the pilot. Immediately, the rear cargo door shuddered, slowly sealing them in. A wave of fear threatened to envelope Dennis for just a moment, then, distracted by the aircraft's movement, he regained control. "Back to Ap Cho ... damn."

The powerful bird lifted reluctantly from the Dau Tieng base camp at the southern edge of the Michelin rubber plantation. Either the pilot chose to fly at treetop level or, loaded as it was, it couldn't do any better. Flying fast and low offered some protection from ground fire, but it gave little flexibility for crash maneuvers should something mechanical go wrong. Dennis watched closely the actions of the crew members. One was napping already and the other had rediscovered his page in a pornographic paperback. They appeared calm, even relaxed.

Guess I'll follow their lead, I've got no influence over the flight, anyway. I hope this bird stays in the air. We sure need the supplies. Even the Crew Chief knows about our battalion, "...wrapped around the axle," at Ap Cho. Third Battalion, Twenty Second Infantry ... a hard luck outfit if there ever was one. Nearly a hundred men down in two days.

It was thirty minutes by air from Dau Tieng to Cui Chi, the large sprawling camp that served as Headquarters for the 25th Infantry Division. Ap Cho was about one thousand meters -- maybe thirty-five-hundred feet south of there. The battle halted while the combatants waited for ammunition, supplies, and replacements. Dennis stole a glance at his watch. "We attack an hour from now," Dennis yelled at one of the crew. "Think we'll make it?"

"Oh yeah, you better get some rest, Lieutenant, it'll be a hot afternoon," he replied, waving his book in the air.

Hot afternoon? Hell, I might be dead by lunch.

He refused to think about the pending battle; instead, comforted by the steady whine of the turbines, he lay his head back, shut his eyes, and tried to sleep. Daydreaming, he ticked off the events of the previous summer at Fort Lewis, Washington, where he had met them all. *My gang ... my boys. I wonder where they are, and what they're doing now?*

The hypnotic rhythm of the engines took hold. His head slumped, and Dennis Riley slept fully. His dreams carried him back to a chilly mountain road among the pine forests of Washington, where it all began in the summer of 1967, before the hell called Vietnam.

Chapter Four
Chance Encounter

Like most brand-new, Second Lieutenants of Infantry, Dennis Riley didn't think he frightened very easily. Having mentally and physically prepared for war over the previous six months, he pictured himself a finely-tuned fighting machine. At least that's what his tactical officers and instructors had convinced him he was. A half-year of constant pushups, five-mile runs, and strict discipline had left him superbly conditioned. Quick to react to the slightest sound, movement, or change in lighting conditions, he was always poised for action. He just hadn't expected to find it along this desolate, fog-enshrouded, country road in the middle of Washington State in late June, 1967.

Dennis crawled from beneath the frame of his old car, brushing rusty flakes of muffler from his eyes. Startled by a slight hint of movement, an odd sound, he instinctively reached through the open trunk of his car for a tool, a weapon of any kind. Wrapping his hands tightly around a lug wrench, he cocked it high above his head and planted his feet.

Then the laughter began, and music. The curious sounds were faint at first, like an echo out of the mountains. Someone cleared his throat. *It's a radio ... people laughing.*

Easing the weapon down but not discarding it, Dennis leaned against the body of the car, assuming an indifferent stance, growing more certain that he was about to meet a squad of musical comedians.

"Hey, who the hell are you?"

Their astonished expressions, unaffected laughter, and rumpled khaki uniforms completely calmed him. He lowered the weapon and threw it into the trunk of the car. They were soldiers, too, as much dumbfounded to find him standing there along that desolate stretch of highway as he was to see them coming out of the fog. Jay Cee O'Connor, the big man, spoke first, pocketing his portable transistor radio and extending his hand.

"Nice to meet you," he said, vigorously pumping Dennis' arm. *He's strong*, Dennis observed. *About nineteen or twenty, I guess. Looks like a prize fighter.* Dennis grinned and held Jay Cee's hand for just an instant longer.

"I'm Dennis Riley," he said. "Welcome to the middle of nowhere."

Jay Cee, as if it were his obligation, began introducing his four hiking companions: Wally Gerber, Andy Crammer, Roosevelt Dolan, and Jackie Stoner.

"I'm from Michigan," Jay Cee said, pointing his stubby thumb at his chest. "We just got out of infantry training. We met yesterday at the 'Greyhound' in Denver. We're headed to Fort Lewis."

"You're walking to Fort Lewis?" Dennis said, opening his eyes wide and laughing. "Really, what the hell are you guys doing out here?"

"The bus lost an axle about five miles back," Jay Cee explained. "We decided to take the 'shoe leather express.' Been trying to hitch a ride, but no luck. Our furloughs expire this afternoon."

They're a bunch of hippies, Dennis surmised: *singing, joking, and drinking terrible whiskey from a wide-bottomed bottle, they've come down on me like vagrants stumbling onto a food kitchen. Hell, they're all right, I guess. ...Cool.*

"What's wrong with your ride?" Jackie Stoner asked, twirling an end of his bushy, handlebar mustache. He squatted to look underneath. "Can I help? I'm a damn good mechanic."

"The muffler broke loose and I'm trying to tie it up with a coat hanger," Dennis said, brushing rust and dirt from his coveralls.

"Why does it matter?" Wally Gerber asked, stooping to peer under the car. "It might just wake some of these farmers up. We need a ride."

"I'm never going to get through the gates of Fort Lewis, with the racket this thing makes," Dennis answered. "I'm reporting in just like you guys in a couple of hours. No place to get it fixed way out here."

"You're a GI?" Jackie asked.

"Yeah."

Studying Dennis' face for a moment, then the car, Jackie immediately stripped to the waist and adjusted the scrap of cardboard Dennis had been lying on. Barely squeezing beneath the frame, his huge biceps raised it adequately and he slid out of sight, all the while shouting commands.

"Hand me that duct tape and ball of steel wool I saw in your trunk," he said. "I'll need a stick to push it in, too. Give me a hammer. Hurry up. I'll have this heap fixed right quick."

Dennis smiled inwardly and accepted that his collection of junk, bequeathed to him with the purchase of the used car, was going to end up inside the exhaust pipe. Hurriedly, he gathered the items and passed them to Jackie. Jay Cee and the others stood back, shouting advice and encouragement. Several minutes of loud banging held Dennis spellbound. "I hope he knows what he's doing," he said.

"Ah, not to worry," Jay Cee replied, jabbing at Dennis' shoulder. "I've known him for almost twenty-four hours now. I'd swear by anything he tells you. Besides, he hasn't had a drink from that bottle in fifteen minutes. He'll fix it."

Jackie yelled some unintelligible war cry, followed by a curse as the muffler came flying from beneath the car. They all reflexively jumped as it bounced several times and, finally, landed in the bushes behind them.

"What the hell are you doing under there?" Dennis asked. "I don't have the money to buy another muffler. I was hoping to salvage it."

"Ain't no fixing left in it," Jackie answered. "Guts are blown out. I jammed some steel wool up the exhaust pipe. That'll quiet her for a while. It might even hold 'til we get into the fort. How far is it?"

Dennis squatted to look under the car. *How clever. Now it's "we."* "About ninety to a hundred miles, I guess."

Loud hoots from the others erupted and Dennis laughed, too. *They don't know if they're fifty or five hundred miles from Fort Lewis. I don't think they really give a damn, either.*

"Sounds good," Dennis said, pulling off his coveralls, revealing his own wrinkled uniform.

Jackie wiped the rust and soot from his big hands before putting on his shirt. He stared for a moment at Dennis' khakis, then fixed his gaze on the gold bar pinned to his collar.

"Jesus, I didn't realize you were a Lieutenant," Jackie said. "How come you didn't tell us? I wouldn't have been so pushy, Sir."

"Ten-hut," Wally Gerber commanded, mocking a salute as the others haphazardly snapped to attention.

Dennis casually returned the gesture, then remarked, "I don't mind, guys. Let's hope your patch job gets us into Fort Lewis."

"Let's hit it," Andy Crammer yelled, jerking open the passenger door of Dennis' blue 1957 Chevrolet. "Come on, pile in."

Simultaneously, they slapped hands, hooted, and squeezed inside the car. The battery dead, they held their breath as Dennis let it roll downhill. Popping the clutch, he brought the engine to life; the howling inside the car was deafening. Finally catching high gear, the car roared westward into a dissipating fog.

Chapter Five
Getting Acquainted

The exhaust racket had softened somewhat and Dennis thanked Jackie, praising him for his expert work.

They were packed in tight, the six of them. Jay Cee had taken the front window seat and Rosey got sandwiched in between. Wally, Andy, and Jackie shared the rear.

"She was quite the boat in her day," Dennis said. "I hope it'll get us into the fort and then I'll probably sell her for junk. Too bad. I picked up lots of chicks in this old tub."

"I'm Lieutenant Riley. My friends call me Dennis." Taking one hand off of the wheel, he extended it over the seat to Wallace Gerber.

"Just call me 'Wally,'" Gerber said. "Wallace is an alias my mother gave me." Dennis glanced at him and then shifted his eyes back to the road. The others remained silent.

"I'm reporting in to the overseas replacement detachment and expect to be in Vietnam in about a month," Dennis said. "We should get at least a couple of weeks of training before we go over. I can't wait to get it on and win the war. I want to see what it's like."

"Us, too," Wally said. "We're all going to 'packets.' It's some kind of soldier groups. Then we go on to the 'Nam.' You want to be our Lieutenant, Dennis? That's what we'll call you, 'Dennis the Lieutenant.' We'll get jobs in Saigon, running the officer's club and we'll drink all their whiskey and screw all their women."

"Knock it off," Jay Cee said, stabbing Wally with a commanding look.

Glancing from time to time in the rear view mirror, Dennis studied Wally and the others. Wally's shirt was unbuttoned and Dennis couldn't help but notice how thick he was across the chest. Dennis reached and adjusted the mirror and caught Wally's steel blue eyes staring back at him. They bore into him and Dennis struggled to shift his gaze.

Instinctively leaning toward Dennis, Roosevelt Dolan poked him and spoke excitedly. "Thanks for the ride, Dennis. I'm 'Rosey' Dolan, and this here's Jay Cee. Emphasize the 'Cee,' Lieutenant, the big guy insists. Wally is Wally. 'Cold steel,' we call him. I've been hitchhiking all the way from Atlanta. Spent my travel money on a ring for my girl and I'm flat broke."

"I've heard that before," Dennis said.

Rosey laughed and folded his arms. "Yeah, I was getting desperate. I stumbled onto these guys in Denver. They financed my ride up to where the bus broke down. I'd been praying for something to turn up."

Dennis poked at him. "Dolan ... you've got to be Irish, right?"

"Is the Pope Catholic? Yep, I'm a Mick. Good guess."

"Where you from, Lieutenant?" Jay Cee asked.

"Keystone state. Pennsylvania," Dennis answered. "Moved to Detroit later. Didn't want to work in those coal mines."

"You guys want to get another bottle?" Wally asked, reaching over the seat and grabbing Dennis on the shoulder. "Looks like Jackie's killed that one." No one responded as they were clearly disinterested in drinking any more.

Dennis liked Wally and his rude, nonconformist style. Maybe he was even a little jealous of it. Military officers were denied such friendships and he silently lamented the caste system that prohibited them from becoming friends with enlisted men. *"Don't make friends with those you may have to order into battle,"* my Tactical Officer used to say. *He'd crap if he saw me now.*

"How long have you been in?" Andy Crammer wanted to know as he peppered Dennis with questions about his personal life. "I'm sorry if I seem to be prying. I've just never been up close to a Lieutenant before, or any officer, for that matter." He settled back into a corner of the seat.

"Prying?" Wally blurted out. "Jeeze, you talk like some kinda 'brain' or something."

Dennis shifted in his seat and glanced at the skinny kid. His thick glasses and hawkish nose did give him a scholarly look.

"I joined up in '58, Andy. Went to OCS in '66. The streets put me into the Army. My mother said it would save me from the 'House of Correction.' I've loved this old Army from the first day of boot camp. Guess you could call me a 'lifer.'"

"I'm Infantry all the way," Dennis said in answer to Andy's question about his branch affiliation. "I like the physical challenge. You know, the travel, the romance of it all."

"Yes, you certainly are a 'lifer,'" Andy said as he removed his glasses, folded them carefully, and put them in a leather case.

"How about you, Andy? Why did you join up?" Dennis asked. Andy leaned forward and bumped Dennis as he talked. "Well, Dennis, I received a very untimely draft notice so I volunteered. I chose The Army Band. It took them all of three days to figure out I couldn't play a note. They promptly sent my skinny butt to the Infantry." He leaned back, laughed loudly, and took the last swig from the bottle of whisky.

"How about you, Jackie?" Dennis asked.

"Tennessee," Jackie answered immediately. "Daddy and me couldn't scratch no living out of them rocks. I signed up to get a pair of boots. They fit pretty good. I just didn't know I'd have to go to Vet Nam to pay for them."

Wally laughed. "They tell me that all we have to do is burn shit and walk point when we get there. It won't be so bad."

"Burn what?" Jackie asked.

"Crap, you have to burn it over there I hear. No flush toilets."

"Least I won't be fighting nobody." Jackie sat back, closed his eyes, and appeared to be sleeping.

The other boys refused to quiet down and Dennis felt good talking to them about himself. *I guess they're impressed with me, being a Lieutenant. They want to know all my business.*

"Alaska was my best tour of duty," he said, answering one of Andy's questions. "It wasn't long and two of my officers talked me into going to OCS. I'm glad they pushed me."

Captain Arthur Eaton, his Company Commander, and Major Awbrey Norris, the Battalion Executive Officer, had noticed Dennis' enthusiasm and adaptability to infantry training. Eaton was an OCS graduate himself, and, to Dennis, he was the epitome of a soldier: a caring and efficient leader.

"Captain Eaton was sharp," Dennis said. 'You could tell he was OCS from a mile away. You should have seen those spit-shined boots."

Eaton at first only prodded Dennis to consider attending Officer Candidate School, then finally insisted on it. "You're going to OCS, Riley, and I don't want to hear any 'buts' about it."

Major Norris, Captain Eaton's colleague and golfing buddy, pushed the administrative buttons that allowed Dennis to go. They were both there to see him off in March, 1966, just before they themselves embarked from Alaska for Vietnam. They wrote him several encouraging letters while he underwent some of the most demanding training the Army had to offer. He was stunned and wept privately when Norris wrote that Eaton had "tripped" a mine and had to have his leg amputated just a few months after arriving in Vietnam.

"Major Norris was with him. He helped carry Captain Eaton out of the mine field just like I'd expect him to do," Dennis said, relating the story to his entranced riders.

The miles passed and they chatted back and forth on a hundred themes, telling bawdy stories and jokes, singing every hit tune they knew, thus creating an unconscious solidarity between themselves. Dennis easily surrendered to the merriment of their company.

Rosey Dolan, unreserved in his demeanor, eventually proved to be the talker among them. "I really miss home. My girl, Vanessa, I'm going to marry her when I get back. I might have to," he finished with a childish giggle.

"She's gorgeous -- beautiful," Dennis agreed as he glanced from the road to the snapshots. "I've got a pretty girl waiting on me, too. Beverly Ann Jagoda. Auburn hair ... sexy as hell. I've got a picture --"

"Beverly Ja fucking what?" Wally blurted. "What kind of a name is that?"

"Jagoda, she's Polish. I went to school with her. I couldn't concentrate with her in a room. Guess that's why I quit high school."

"I was the good-looking one in my high school class," Jay Cee laughed. "And I ain't even Polish, Lieutenant."

Reaching out and holding onto the dashboard, Jay Cee turned and spoke directly at Dennis. "Dad wants a lawyer in the family. I'm his last chance. I almost went back to the university this year. Then I met that sweet and sexy Patricia Blackmon." Jay Cee paused and peered out of the front window, as if remembering something. A big smile covered his face.

"Tell us about her," Dennis said

"Damn that girl," Jay Cee said, slapping his leg. "My dad hated her. She loved to race cars."

Would I have been as carefree as them if I hadn't enlisted so young? Dennis thought. Maybe we'll be assigned to the same unit in Vietnam?

"That'll be cool," Wally slurred when Dennis mentioned it. "We'll be the six musketeers. I'd follow you anywhere, Dennis."

Disposing now of any pretense about status, all but Jay Cee comfortably used first names, implying, occasionally, that Dennis could count on their innate regard for rank if they ever met while on duty. "Slim chance of that, guys, but I wouldn't mind if we bump into each other once in a while."

Their talk turned toward the intensifying conflict in Vietnam, and they tried to analyze its impact upon themselves. Dennis was all for it, believing in the need for an American presence there. "To rescue the poor South Vietnamese people from the clutches of Communism," he said, as he mimicked President Johnson.

"I'm not sure it's right," Rosey said. "I'm not so sure."

"It's a fool's expedition," Jay Cee said, arching his eyebrows. "We have no business there. No good will come of it."

They fell silent and Jay Cee quietly turned to watch the magnificent Washington forests slide by. Dennis played with the radio dial; through the static, a raspy-voiced folk singer crooned something about "blowing in the wind."

"That's Dylan; turn that up ... he's good," Andy said.

"Damned anti-war Communist hippie son of a bitch," Wally volunteered without opening his eyes. "They should draft his ass, and send him to Vietnam."

"Listen to the words," Andy insisted, bolting upright. "His songs are like poems -- full of symbolism about the government and war and racism. He's against all that. He's just trying to call people's attention to it."

"I'm a poet, too," Rosey said, pulling a thick notebook wrapped with rubber bands from his pocket. "I write about lots of things. Life mostly." Fondling the small pages carefully, Rosey read several selections aloud.

Either they were stunned into silence by the quality of his writing or they were feigning sleep, but no one commented. Rosey stared at Dennis and waited.

"Good stuff," Dennis finally said. "Heavy on the Jesus angle, but not bad."

Bored, the occupants of the rear seat were soon dozing and, fifteen miles from Fort Lewis, all was quiet inside the car. The muffler, however, was coming back to life. Dennis, lost in his thoughts, didn't notice.

"The Hawk" was on duty at the main gate of Fort Lewis. He was a military policeman whose reputation for law enforcement was legendary across every military post in the United States. In knowledgeable circles, when a soldier remarked that he was headed to Fort Lewis, Washington, the farewell handshake usually concluded with, "Watch out for The Hawk when you get there."

"What fucking luck," Wally said as he rubbed his eyes.

Dennis could see The Hawk's ebony-smooth face and almost felt his penetrating eyes tracking them like radar from a hundred yards out. He started to sweat. The steel wool had exhausted its usefulness ten miles back and the engine now bellowed mightily.

"Get up some speed," Jackie shouted above the noise. "Shut off the engine, push in the clutch. We'll float by him."

Wanting no trouble with the MPs, especially this one, Dennis was willing to try. Killing the engine, he disengaged the transmission and, with their momentum almost spent, they cleared the main gate. The Hawk waved them on with little notice.

Releasing the clutch pedal, the engine re-engaged, bringing the beast back to life. The exhaust thundered uproariously, blotting out all conversation within a hundred yards. Dennis caught sight of The Hawk in the rear view mirror, charging after them on foot, his hands groping for his sidearm while shouting obscenities that only he and the devil understood.

"Jesus, he's pulling his pistol. Step on it!" Wally shrieked, watching through the rear window. "We'll all get shot over a damn muffler."

Losing steam after a while, the policeman stopped abruptly, pointed an accusing forefinger in their direction, and glared. Laughing wildly, they left him in the thunder and smoke of their escape.

Dennis dropped them off at the Enlisted Overseas Replacement Detachment and became embarrassed when their parting took on the same carnival atmosphere that had erupted after making good their flight from the main gate. They were still high on the excitement.

"Cut out all that damn noise," a senior sergeant commanded from the steps of the building. His glare sent Dennis a message that he readily understood.

"I'll see you when I see you," Dennis said. "I've got to go." Jamming the car into gear, he sped away. Lost, he drove around for thirty minutes until he finally found the Bachelor Officer Quarters. After checking in for the night, he lay, exhausted, back on his bunk, closed his eyes and measured the events of the day. *Yeah, they're quite a bunch. Hell of a trip.*

Chapter Six
The Watering Hole

Busy with his own training, Dennis didn't see any of his new friends again until a few days later. All new arrivals were at the Quartermaster, being fitted for jungle fatigues and field gear when Rosey managed to buddy-up to him in the line.

"We saw you in the mess hall, yesterday," Rosey said. "You didn't notice us. You were sitting with a bunch of other big wheels ... officers."

"Oh, yeah, we were getting training schedules and assignments for our Vietnam orientation. We go to the field as soon as everybody gets their gear. The packet is all in now ... two-hundred and fifty men."

"What kind of training? Where at? When?"

Inching forward in the line, they had plenty of time to talk. "Slow down, Rosey," Dennis said. "If you want to train for Vietnam, these thick Washington forests are a good place to do it. I'm told they're very close to what we'll find in Vietnam. We're going on 'maneuvers;' you guys are included."

Rosey shrugged. "See, Dennis, they don't tell us anything. We heard we were going to just do physical fitness and rifle practice. Someone said we'd be getting inoculations, maybe a dozen shots. Ouch, I hate to think of it. I fainted last time."

"Sorry to say, Rosey, we're going to do that, too."

Sharing endless gossip from the enlisted men's barracks, they spent the day getting reacquainted. After collecting a mountain of equipment, and reliving over and over again the saga of how they had outfoxed The Hawk, Rosey laughed, then said, "The MPs are still looking for us, I bet. Have you ditched the car yet?"

"Not yet. I need a hundred bucks for it and can't find any takers. Tell Jay Cee and everybody I said 'Hi,' and I'll buy the beer next time we get together -- that is, if I get rid of the car."

"Can't wait. The guys are always talking about you, Dennis. We brag about having our own Lieutenant." Rosey snapped to attention and saluted smartly as they parted company.

The first week of training passed quickly. Dennis led a platoon of forty men through the well-prepared exercise, honing his map-reading and artillery adjustment skills. He enjoyed it and the play only heightened his eagerness to get into actual combat.

"I can't wait to get a platoon and get on to Vietnam," he said to a senior sergeant who was teaching 'Field Sanitation.' "I don't need this, though. I already know how to wipe my butt."

"I've seen a lot of Second Lieutenants come through here, Sir. They're all eager to go over there and prove something, maybe get a medal. You'll get your chance, but first you've got to learn how to shit in the woods. We don't want to dirty up the Asian countryside. Now, dig that trench about three feet deeper."

The second week of training introduced them to a vast arsenal of new weapons. In a field firing demonstration, they observed the characteristics and capabilities of unique and exotic ordnance: The M-16 rifle, the M-79 grenade launcher, and the Claymore anti-personnel mine, among them.

Dennis was disappointed when Captain Auero, his training supervisor, said, "You guys will be firing the M-14 rifle in practice. This M-16 is just for show. It's for the generals and the politicians, but you'll get one in Vietnam."

The M-16 rifle performed well in demonstrations and Dennis doubted the rumors that were just beginning to surface about its deficiencies. Recent press releases implied that the new rifles were defective and he remembered an evening news report that showed Marines in Vietnam complaining that they jammed frequently. The Pentagon suggested that it was the soldiers' own negligence that caused the rifles to malfunction.

In the beehive of activity at Fort Lewis, Dennis kept meeting members of his Officer Candidate Class and friends he'd served with during his enlisted years. They spent considerable time after training each evening at a local watering hole, renewing friendships and discussing their probable fates, all between guzzles of good, cold draft.

The Beach Club, on the edge of Fort Lewis, was the ultimate rendezvous for young officers. The music was loud, the beer cheap and cold. It was a paradise for lonely and unattached young officers. In "command circles," the place was called: "Gomorrah."

While practicing marksmanship on a weapons range, Dennis spotted Andy Crammer, Jackie Stoner, and Wally Gerber. He instinctively hurried to greet them. All three stood ramrod tall at first and overstated the position of attention. It was genuinely good to see them, his friends, who, just a few days earlier, had helped to make their entrance into Fort Lewis so memorable.

Dennis briefly mentioned the beach club. "That's where I've been hanging out after duty. It's wild, man."

Wally's eyes lit up and he asked, "Say, can you sneak us in there, Lieutenant? I've heard it's the grooviest joint in the state of Washington. We've been restricted to the Enlisted Men's Club …'three point two' beer and no broads. "

Dennis was intrigued by the idea. It would be good to see his new pals again, especially in a social setting. The club was really a dive with few regulations and little regard for the military's caste system.

"To hell with it. Bring all the guys tonight," Dennis said as they broke company and returned to rifle firing.

Dennis and Jay Cee were the first to arrive at the club and they merged quickly into the din and smell of the place. Dennis hoped they could slip in quietly, unnoticed.

"Make a hole and make it wide," Jay Cee said as he pushed through the crowd, creating a path for Dennis. He wore the green fatigue shirt of a Lieutenant Colonel of Infantry, complete with paratrooper jump wings. The uniform fit his broad frame well; with a few wrinkles on his face, one might believe that he was, indeed, an officer of some experience. He studied the crowd for a while and then joined Dennis who had already chosen a table.

Dennis scanned the room. "Look at all the girls, Jay Cee. I wonder if any of them are Polish?"

Jackie arrived a few moments later and he wore a military-style winter parka, in spite of the fact that it was summertime. It completely covered his enlisted uniform and, with the hood drawn over his head, he looked like a living grim reaper. Patrons turned to look at him and, just as quickly, they laughed and turned away.

"Must be part of the entertainment," one officer commented.

Andy wore no rank at all and he came in smiling with a cute brunette on his arm. "Look at that chick. She's about to burst right out of that mini skirt," Dennis said.

"Where's Wally and Rosey?" Jay Cee asked.

Andy frowned. "Wally's out in Dennis' old car, trying to get the pants off 'Fat Betty.' She's the PX manager. He promised to marry her if she'd give him what he wants. Rosey's trying to get him out of the car. I left them. Lord, this was a stupid idea."

"The gang's all here," Jay Cee stood and sang as Wally Gerber strode in with a chubby older woman on his arm. Rosey trailed them. Somehow, amidst the smoke and the noise, they, too, went unnoticed.

The room was at least four parts cigarette smoke to one part air and Dennis could hardly see through the haze. Andy was soon lost in the drunken hilarity of the dance floor.

"First night we've had out since we got here," Jay Cee said.

"Yeah, and it'll probably be our last," Dennis replied. "I'm surprised we haven't been thrown out. Look, even our preacher, Rosey, is having a good time."

Jay Cee looked across the sea of inebriated women, enlisted men, and junior officers. Rosey, demonstrating the latest dance craze, had a drink in one hand and a dazzling redhead on his free arm. Jackie, Andy, and Wally were likewise engaged. They had found female companions and were obviously spending all of their charms in this one place. Their final night, perhaps.

"Look at Rosey -- can you believe it?" Dennis said.

"Oh, hell, Lieutenant, what harm ...? Let 'em have fun."

Chapter Seven
A Soldier's Remorse

The night moved on and, before long, most of "his gang," as Dennis now called them, were all snuggled warmly with other bodies beneath blankets on the moonlit beach. All except Jay Cee. He agreed to stand watch, "to make sure we all get home OK," he said.

Dennis likewise limited his drinking in concern for the others. He was especially worried about Rosey, certain that his lofty morality went right into the toilet that night along with any thoughts of Vanessa.

"He's just a kid," Dennis remarked to Jay Cee. "He'd better learn to keep his feet on the ground if he really wants to marry that girl someday. I know he'll be damn sick in the morning."

It was nearly 4:00 a.m. when they managed to stumble into their quarters. Singing, shouting, and falling down, they awakened the entire barracks. Dennis helped to quiet the disturbance with the Sergeant-In-Charge and assisted his buddies to their bunks. *The poor drunks, they'll get about two hours sleep before the first call.*

Dennis drove slowly back to his own room, happy that the boys had had their final fling. He had learned late that very day that their packet would be shipping out in forty-eight hours. *Two weeks early,* he mused. *I wonder if we're ready?*

At reveille the next morning, a senior sergeant from the enlisted barracks approached Dennis and explained that Privates Dolan, Gerber, Crammer, and Stoner couldn't get out of bed and had missed the morning formation. "Their buddy, Private First Class O'Connor, managed to get the three of them up to the First Sergeant's office for a good, old-fashioned ass-chewing."

"Oh, hell. What happened?" Dennis asked.

"They'll be digging and moving dirt all day, but that boy, Dolan, he's really bad hung over, Sir. He just lays in his bunk staring at the ceiling. Everybody knows you're in tight with these guys. You need to talk to him. Get him moving before he lands in real trouble." The sergeant finished, saluted, and walked briskly away.

Dennis passed Wally, Andy, and Jackie alongside the road as he covered the several hundred yards to their barracks. They leaned on their picks and shovels, waving feebly as he strode by. He could feel their penetrating stares all the way into the barracks. He found Rosey just as the sergeant had described.

Hearing Dennis' voice, Rosey struggled to sit on the edge of the bed, shoulders slumped, his head buried in his hands. "Come on Rosey," Dennis said cheerfully. "Lace up your boots. We'll get some coffee and then go on over to the Orderly Room and talk to Captain Auero."

Rosey didn't move. Leaning closer and touching his shoulder, Dennis detected a faint sobbing. A choking sound echoed from his throat. "What's wrong, Rosey? The other guys are making it, why are you still sitting on this bed?"

Rosey looked up through bloodshot eyes and groaned. Anxious, Dennis insisted that he talk to him. "Say something, Rosey. Are you OK?"

Blowing his nose and wiping his eyes, Rosey began with a heavy sigh. "I've never done anything like this in my life, Dennis. Poor Vanessa, I don't deserve her. I must have been crazy --"

Dennis interrupted, "Hey Rosey, everything will be all right."

Rosey stood, wobbled, and balanced himself against the iron bedpost. "No, it won't," he whimpered.

Dennis grabbed Rosey's arm and shook him. "Rosey, Come on. All you did was get a little drunk and spend some time with a pretty girl."

"Tell me about it."

"Wally, me, and all the others, we set you up, encouraged you. Blame it on us," Dennis said.

Rosey staggered slightly and held onto the bed post with both hands. In a whisper, he began, "You just don't know me, Dennis. I'm supposed to behave better than other people."

He flopped back on the bed and, covering his eyes with his arms, fell silent. After a few minutes, he sat erect, looked Dennis square in the eyes, and stated firmly, "Dennis, I ain't going with you to Vietnam. I couldn't pull the trigger or kill another man. I'll never break another commandment. Do you understand? Doesn't anybody understand?" His foul breath reeked of alcohol, causing Dennis to back away from him.

"Lord, if I light a match we'll blow up," Dennis said. He felt uncomfortable with such emotional prattle, especially from a Private. He knew he was too close now, too connected to Rosey. He began to understand the reasons why officers didn't mingle with their men. He didn't have the heart anymore to reprimand him for failing to report for duty and he felt bad for having been the one to set the stage for all this. *What the hell was I thinking when I invited them all to the beach club?*

"Am I going to jail or to hell?" Rosey asked.

"I have some thoughts on that, Rosey. God hates the sin, but they tell me He loves the sinner. Think about all those bad apples you read about in the Bible. Jesus forgave them. Let's see, there was Mary Magdalene and Saint Peter. Then we have Dennis Riley, Jay Cee O'Connor, Wally Gerber, Andy Crammer, and even Jackie Stoner, just to name a few. Hell, Rosey, you're in fine company, man."

Rosey looked solemnly at Dennis for the longest time, then grinned and asked for his canteen of water. "I need something to put out the fire."

Dennis knew then that the worst was over. Rosey's redemption would be found in an aspirin bottle, some bed rest, and a confessional. "Man, how much did you actually drink last night, Rosey?"

"Gallons, Dennis, zillions of gallons."

Dennis left him and went to run interference with the Commander. Captain Auero was absent but he found the First Sergeant accommodating, knowing that Roosevelt Dolan would be on a plane headed to Vietnam in another thirty-six hours. He was pleased that Dennis had sobered him up.

The incident passed and Dennis gave little thought to Rosey's objections to killing, to war, or to his self-reproach on the matter of faithlessness to Vanessa.

"He's still a little bit drunk," he said to the others as he stopped to talk with them along the road. "Guess he really tied one on and he's feeling guilty, but he'll be all right." Dennis didn't see Rosey or any of them again until their final departure debriefing.

Chapter Eight
First Impressions, Vietnam

The more than two hundred men of "C-packet" completed training in early August and assembled in a large hangar at Seattle's Boeing Field to receive final boarding instructions. Scanning the crowd, Dennis caught Rosey's eye. They simply nodded to each other. The twinkle that had so naturally embellished his smile was markedly absent and Dennis felt a twinge of sadness.

Jackie, Wallace, Andy, and Jay Cee huddled close to Rosey and looked Dennis' way. He smiled and waved.

Inseparable, all five had developed a special bond between each other and it showed. They manipulated their sergeants into putting them all into the same squad during training exercises. They took their breaks together and shared their meals. Seeing them walking along together one afternoon, Dennis felt compelled to comment on their unusual fraternity. "Are you five musketeers going to ride to Nam together?" he asked.

"We're going to win the war," Wally said. "Old Charlie Cong better watch out." The others cheered and slapped "high-fives" all around. Dennis could only grin at their brazenness. *Wally probably will do some great things. He's defiant and bold.*

Their departure time had been moved up by weeks. The senior officers mumbled amongst themselves about "excessively high casualties in the theater of operations." Others testily declared that President Lyndon B. Johnson had finally convinced Congress: another couple of hundred thousand more men could, and would, "Bring the coonskin home and tack it on the wall." With that little bit of Texas wisdom to fortify them, they departed Seattle in a warm drizzling rain on the first leg of their journey to Southeast Asia.

With an overnight delay at Travis Air Force Base, California, they found time to gulp a few beers and gobble their last American-made cheeseburgers. Andy Crammer commented that they were, for some reason, "especially delicious."

Rosey met a Catholic Chaplain outside the officer's club and insisted that all of them were Catholic. Like a good minister, the priest heard everyone's confession right there on the steps of the club. After staring at Wally for a few moments, unsure of what he'd heard, he gave a broad and general absolution, then staggered slightly as he went down the stairs and into a waiting staff car. Rosey was elated. He had been forgiven his terrible indiscretion and the slate was clean again. "I feel good," he said, "really good."

"If the slate's clean now," Wally replied, "then let's go get stinking drunk and then go screw --"

Rosey scowled and slapped him playfully across the shoulder. "Watch your mouth, Wally."

They did get slightly drunk that afternoon; this time it was in the local enlisted men's club and Dennis wore the parka.

The airport terminal at Travis AFB looked like the busiest in the world when they arrived the next morning. They sat close together, in wooden auditorium chairs, watching the flight line through giant plate glass windows, awaiting their boarding call. The "ready-line" was packed with aircraft. Military cargo and troop transports, mixed together with every line of commercial carrier, moved into and out of their berths, back and forth across the airport. They were contracted to ferry troops the ten thousand miles into and out of Vietnam.

Within moments after landing, men returning from Vietnam spewed from the bellies of the big planes. These returnees strutted across the runways with a certain air of supremacy. They had rare and special insights into the war that no one else would ever know. All combat veterans' swashbuckling demeanor boasted the advantage. Those departing for Vietnam for the first time watched them closely, but pretended not to, in awe of these battle-hardened men.

"Those-sharp looking khakis hide the truth of what they've been living the last twelve months," Dennis mentioned to Jay Cee.

Jay Cee grabbed Dennis by the arm. "Yeah," he said, "If you study them -- look at the faces -- you can tell: they've really been to hell and back. I'm getting concerned."

The planes landed quickly, spaced only minutes apart. Refueling, they changed crews and loaded a fresh consignment of troops, all within an hour or two of landing. Jam-packed with baggage and troops, they labored into the sun, back across the Pacific to Vietnam. The pace was hectic and Dennis marveled at the efficiency of it all. Dennis and his friends, along with more than two hundred other nervous and gloomy souls, boarded one of the many planes.

In spite of the crowding, they managed to find seats near each other. Except for some violent tropical weather over the Philippines, the journey was uneventful. The chatter consisted mainly of banter between the very attractive female flight attendants and the few men calm and bold enough to pursue seductive dialogue. Wally led the way, of course. Dennis, Jay Cee, and Rosey stayed silent, watching and smiling at Wally's amorous advances toward the ladies. He got lucky when severe turbulence plopped a gorgeous redhead down in the vacant seat next to him. She buckled in and stayed with him well after the air had turned smooth, holding his hand tightly.

"I've got to try his tactics someday," Jackie said, tugging on his mustache. "He always gets the gal." The aircraft droned on toward Vietnam and soon almost everyone on board was either dozing or deep within his thoughts.

Landing at the giant Bien Hoa air base near Saigon in mid-afternoon, they were met with a heavy blast of hot air seconds after the doors opened; it wrapped around them like a dervish. Dennis had never felt humidity like that. He now believed the captain who had announced a ground temperature of "one hundred and ten degrees." During their hurried debarking period, his new jungle fatigues became drenched with perspiration. Dennis looked around and noticed that everyone else was sweating profusely, too, their fatigues sagging under the weight. "I hope they have air conditioning in the jungle," he joked to another lieutenant.

Dennis brushed past the friendly cabin crew, taking the metal stairs two at a time, anxious to catch up with his friends. They had merged into the sea of uniformed bodies rushing toward the terminal. Stepping into the crowd, Dennis noticed that everyone around him appeared grim-faced. With their jaws set, clutching their baggage tightly, they just followed "someone" up ahead. They stumbled occasionally like untrained school children, bumping into one another, stepping on heels, searching the backs of heads for a buddy they might recognize, a friend perhaps, or just someone to connect with. They were scared, homesick, and sinking into quiet shock.

Only twenty-four hours before hand, these handsome and superbly conditioned young men were enjoying life with all of its pleasures and dreams. Now, the broiling heat of the tarmac melted all thoughts of earthly delights and they sank ever deeper into the truth of their surroundings. Dennis caught up with Wally. Even he was surprisingly quiet and dispirited for once. "Why so glum, Wally? You did get the stewardess' address and phone number didn't you?"

"Naw, she was a Czech or something. She didn't speak a word of English. But I think I'm in a place I don't want to be. Let's get the hell back on the plane."

Dennis didn't answer as he watched khaki-clad mobs of men rushing past them toward the plane they had only moments before emptied. Determined and direct in their movements, they appeared almost frantic as they raced across the asphalt. They would soon be airborne and Dennis was resentful of them. They were going home, their one-year tour of duty completed.

He turned to watch them and then stopped dead in his tracks. An honor guard in full dress uniform was loading coffins onto a conveyor belt leading directly into the belly of the plane. Uttering a quiet prayer as the reality of death settled into his conscience, he turned and continued his journey. *Who am I praying for, them or me? I hope I don't go home in a box.*

Their trip of several hundred yards across the airstrip was covered haphazardly and they had time to be awed by the sight of an Army staging for war. Clusters of departing troops, armed with every model of weapon imaginable, labored under the heavy load of their packs. With dirty, olive-drab towels draped around their necks, they wiped continuously at the perspiration collecting on their foreheads. Graffiti-decorated helmets were pushed back on their heads, revealing pure exhaustion. Marching with a sense of purpose -- rifles at the ready -- their heavy backpacks caused them to stoop. With entrenching tools, gas mask pouches, and canteens bouncing chaotically against their hips, they marched methodically onward, never smiling, chattering, or even glancing toward the new arrivals. Tight-lipped, they were somber and urgent in their step. These green-clad humpbacks came and went in every direction, habitually getting off or onto idling helicopters and revving cargo planes. Truckloads of camouflaged men and equipment raced in all directions.

"That's us in a couple of days, unless we luck out and get a job guarding some colonel's crapper," Wally said, as he bumped against Dennis in the mass of merging bodies.

"Aw, we'll be all right, don't worry. Look at all this stuff. Our boys are kickin' some butt. It could be over by next week."

Dennis marveled at the view unfolding before him: planes, tanks, trucks, men, cannons -- everything for making war -- moving into distant battle zones. "Reminds me of a scene from the D-day invasion, Wally. Awesome."

Giant artillery pieces crossed their front, destined for obscure jungle clearings. Fighters screamed overhead as their afterburners heralded the urgency of their missions. Every conceivable blend of machinery, equipment, and weaponry that could be used to wage war was assembled there and the invasion force stretched beyond the horizon. At first, the breathtaking power of this assemblage, with its deadly mix of men and machine, created a feeling of purpose and excitement in Dennis. He took courage from the sounds and sights. "We are a mighty powerful nation, Wally. How can we lose? Just look at all this. I'm glad I came."

"You are? My grandma was right."

"How's that?"

"I've got shit for brains. I should have stayed in La Crosse."

Dennis laughed. For him, the scene authenticated the reality of the war and the moment matured him. Suddenly, his mood changed from one of light-hearted amazement, of exhilaration, to that of near despair. Assessing it all, he sensed for the first time in his brief commissioned career, the full dimensions of his office. *I'm an Infantry Lieutenant in a war zone. Jesus, Mary and Joseph, what the hell have I done now?*

It was their singularity of purpose, war and destruction and the utterly deadly aspects of the killing equipment, that struck Dennis. An aching sense of gloom crept deeper and deeper inside of him and it lay in his belly like a stone. He searched harder for his friends now. "Hey, Jackie, Andy, Rosey ... over here."

One of the many depot sergeant majors gathered them into a sandbagged corral and began an obviously time-worn welcoming speech. His monotone delivery, hoarse voice, and laissez-faire attitude suggested that he'd given these briefings many times before. He held his clipboard in front of his eyes, avoiding the pitiful glare of new faces.

"Excessive casualties during operation Junction City," he announced, "necessitates that all of the fresh meat arriving today have their destinations changed from duty at the recreation center at Vung Tau, to either the 4th Infantry Division at Pleiku or to the 3rd Brigade of the 25th Infantry Division. The 3rd is at Dau Tieng." No one laughed and no one knew what he was talking about.

"Pleiku, Vung Tau, Dau Tieng ... what's that, Sergeant Major?" a bold voice called out from the crowd.

The Sergeant Major took a quick sip from a flask, wiped his mouth, looked at his clipboard and continued. "Pleiku is the base camp for the 4th Infantry Division. It's also an enemy stronghold and a mortar impact area twenty-four hours a day. The good news is you guys won't be going there." He smiled.

"The last batch of arrivals is on their way now. The bad news is you guys will be going to Dau Tieng, headquarters for the 3rd Brigade of the 25th Infantry Division. It's a mortar impact area all day and all night, too. Tay Ninh Province. It sits along the bottom edge of the Michelin rubber plantation."

He paused, put the clipboard down at his side and remarked, "If you came for a fight, men, you'll damn sure get it there. A battalion of that brigade just fought the biggest battle of the war up there. They killed over six hundred Viet Cong before breakfast. It was during Operation 'Junction City.' 'Soui Tre,' they call it. You'll hear about it."

The Sergeant Major paused and looked over them, then shook his head slightly. "That's why you guys are going there; they need replacements. Feel shit on if you like, boys. Grab your bags and baggage, move in formation over to runway Alpha 222. There's an Air Force C-130 waiting." He stuffed his papers and clipboard under his arm, scurrying toward the next bunker, where another uniformed crowd gathered. "Good luck, you poor bastards," he turned and shouted.

They marched upright, more than two hundred men, four by four, right into the cavernous belly of the sturdy cargo plane. With knees drawn up tight against their chins and pressed shoulder to shoulder, they sat on the floor in rows. They were packed together like sausages, with only thick fiber straps stretched taut across their chests to secure them. The massive rear cargo doors shuddered as whining hydraulics forced them closed, immediately darkening the cargo area. The winged beast took off in seconds, rocking and rolling northward, at treetop level, through the Asian sky. "Makes it harder for 'em to shoot you down," a baby-faced crew chief shouted to the men.

Seated next to a porthole, Dennis pressed his face against the Plexiglas. He was instantly thrilled by the beauty below. In spite of the many water-filled bomb craters that pockmarked the landscape, the scene was unquestionably splendid. Farmers, in their conical hats, appeared as ants, wading knee-deep in the waters of lush and fertile rice paddies. Perfectly squared vegetable and fruit gardens stood in sharp contrast to the thick, green jungle that surrounded them. Water buffalo, oxen, and other beasts tugged on overloaded carts, clogging the dirt roads as they ambled their way to markets. To Dennis, the landscape below appeared as serene and natural as any artist could have painted it. Yet, the intermittent bomb craters gave candid testimony to the lie. *It's beautiful. Too bad. A killing field.*

Chapter Nine
Indoctrination

The aircraft's left wing tip almost kissed the giant rubber trees as they banked and turned one hundred and eighty degrees in the opposite direction, sinking simultaneously onto the tarmac runway at Dau Tieng. With inches to spare, the huge transport rocked and screeched as the pilot reversed his propellers and applied maximum breaking power. Finally stopping at the very edge of a concertina wire fence, the cargo of infantry soldiers dug in their heels and held tightly onto the straps. Most of the baggage, stowed in the rear, came flying through the compartment. The men ducked, dodging left and right to avoid it.

The plane immediately turned, and the pilot revved the engines for takeoff. Only then did the doors open and the crew hurry the men off. As dufflebags and gear were thrown after them, one airman shouted, "Sorry guys, but we don't stay long in the Michelin." In moments, the big plane roared back into the sky. They watched her disappear as an odd silence engulfed them.

A brilliant sun had already begun its downward drift into Cambodia. The approaching darkness gave welcome relief from the heat as they rummaged for their belongings and the leaders tried to restore order. Dragging their bags at the edge of the runway, they huddled in small groups, chattering somberly about their new surroundings.

Soon, Lieutenant Colonel Pullman, a rail-thin man from the Brigade Headquarters, arrived; he organized and, finally, addressed them. His greeting suggested genuine warmth and he tried to shake every man's hand while speaking briefly to all. Calling for the group to assemble in front of him, he shook his head and began, "Yes, men ... the battalions of our brigade have suffered many casualties over the last few months and many more men are at the end of their twelve-month tour of duty. We'd soon be one-third short of our authorized strength if you men had not arrived."

He continued for some time, giving a dismal assessment of the Third Brigade's manpower condition. Glancing at his watch, he finished abruptly, confessing his absolute joy that replacements had finally arrived.

"Thank God you men got here," he said. "The perimeter of this base camp is barely defended. We could come under attack at any time and just might. I'm disappointed that you were not issued rifles, grenades, and fighting equipment before you landed. We'll get you down to your companies as quickly as possible and take care of that. Get squared away tonight."

The colonel huddled closely for a few moments with the more senior officers, then, departing quickly, he left them with a thoughtful remark. "Stay close to your families, boys, close to your buddies. Above all, stay close to your God. Those three will get you through. Good luck to you all." Dennis couldn't see him in the crowd, but he was sure that Rosey approved.

Their new battalion, the 3rd Battalion, 22nd Infantry, consisted of four companies of infantry and one Headquarters and Service company. The leaders assembled the men into five almost equal groups, with a fair share of officers, NCOs, and junior enlisted men being allocated to each company.

"You're assigned to Alpha Company, Lieutenant Riley," an unshaven and tired-looking officer from the headquarters told him. "They're in the field right now fighting 'ole Charlie Cong.' They'll be damn happy to see all you replacements."

By virtue of his rank, Dennis instantly became the leader of a group of some forty men. He looked around and noticed that no one from his gang was among them. They were in the Charlie Company huddle. *I'm alone now -- that's good. I won't have to command these men who are more like brothers to me than subordinates.*

"Let's go men, get your gear. We're moving out," Dennis shouted. Gathering their belongings and following a guide, they silently began a hurried march along the perimeter to the Alpha Company row of tents.

Darkness quickly enveloped them and their first glimpse of war was of perpetually falling artillery flares, brilliantly illuminating the night sky. Swaying beneath their miniature parachutes, the flickering beacons drifted idly between the tall rubber trees, casting an eerie glow and producing strange-looking shadows that quickly faded; this was followed by yet another pop, a bang, and then a burst of dazzling light.

The men were confused by this on-and-off light show. Unable to stabilize their night vision, they became frightened but did not speak of the unnamed fears that lay within them. They trudged silently through the night. Somewhere in the distance, cannons boomed and the sound of heavy artillery fractured the air overhead. It unnerved, yet excited Dennis.

The darkened shapes of Alpha Company's tents loomed into sight and Dennis felt several annoying kicks on his heels as he walked the final few yards. The impulse to wheel and slug the clumsy oaf instantly vanished when Dennis recognized the voice of the culprit. "Hi, Dennis Lieutenant," Wally said. "Remember us?"

Dennis turned to face Wally. There they stood -- his gang -- trying to blend into the crowd. The entire group shuffled restlessly, having finally arrived at Alpha Company. First Sergeant Rudolph Krznarovich, a broad hulk of a man, took charge and began to organize them for the night.

"What the hell are you guys doing?" Dennis whispered to Wally. "You were assigned to Charlie Company."

"We go where you go, Sir," Jay Cee said, putting down his gear. "Did you think we were going to let you go off to some route-step, rinky dink outfit and get yourself killed? By the time we got to Charlie Company's tents, we decided that we'd just keep on moving with the crowd. We didn't like the looks of Charlie Company. What the hell are they going to do now, send us to Vietnam?"

Dennis turned to face them. He folded his arms and shook his head. "Damn you guys, I'm flattered, but you'll never get away with it. Come daylight they'll be counting noses and you'll already be AWOL. You just can't pick and choose where you want to be assigned."

"Well, we're simply following the colonel's instructions," Andy said. "He did say stick close to your buddies, didn't he?"

Dennis threw up his arms. "I'm not your damn buddy," he said. "Jesus, you guys, get your asses back up the road to Charlie Company before they come looking for you. You five are the biggest knuckle-heads in the United States Army."

"Take it easy, Lieutenant," a very calm and authoritative voice spoke behind him. Dennis turned. "I'm Sergeant Hanemaulo. Welcome to Dau Tieng," the dark–skinned Hawaiian said, extending his hand. "They're already looking for these clowns in Charlie Company. They called on the land line before you got here. We'll send them back in the morning. Hold them here for the night."

The Sergeant then turned his attention to the five enlisted men. Pointing a threatening finger, he said, "You dumb jack asses get to the mess hall for some quick chow, then report to me at the Third Platoon Headquarters tent. You'll man the bunker line tonight. We can use the extra help. My advice to you all is to get serious about where you are and what you're doing. We won't send you back to Charlie Company tonight because it's too damn dangerous. Anything moving around here after dark gets shot. Some or all of you might be going back home tomorrow in a body bag. Now, get moving."

"Yes, Sergeant," Jay Cee said turning to the crowd. "Sorry. Come on you guys. Maybe it was a good idea, but I should have stopped it before it went so far." They said good-bye and hurried out of sight.

Sergeant Hanemaulo laughed as he took Dennis by the arm. "It happens all the time, Lieutenant. These boys become friends in training and then, when they get here, they don't want to split up. They sure must think a lot of you, to follow you down here to Alpha Company. It's probably best that you don't see them for a while. Certainly you don't want to be their Platoon Commander."

Reaching for Dennis' bags with one hand and shouldering a rifle with the other, he started walking and beckoned Dennis to follow. "Come with me, Lieutenant. I'll show you where to stow your gear and then get you fed and outfitted."

Traveling in the dark disoriented Dennis, and he struggled to keep up with Sergeant Hanemaulo. Within a few yards, they arrived at a single tent among a row of many. "This is your 'hootch,' Lieutenant. There's three other officers living with you. Let's throw your bags in, then we'll get you some chow and a rifle."

Walking back again toward a tent with a dim light flickering through the flaps, Sergeant Hanemaulo continued. "I'm glad you're here, Sir. You'll take over the Third Platoon. Frankly, Lieutenant, I'm a little weary of doing your job. We haven't had an officer since Soui Tre."

Pausing as if remembering pained him, he stopped abruptly at the door of the mess tent, snapped to attention, and saluted, holding it until Dennis found the presence of mind to return the symbol of respect. He felt uncomfortable returning a salute to the older man, believing that he deserved no such honor.

All I've done was suffer through OCS. But, this Sergeant, he doesn't even know me, yet my rank seems good enough. I think I like this guy.

Sergeant Hanemaulo, the Platoon Sergeant for the Third Platoon of Alpha Company, had been performing as the Platoon Leader, the officer's position, for several weeks. Their last lieutenant, he explained, departed for the states a month before, his tour completed. Dennis learned later that Hanemaulo had served in World War II, Korea, and now, Vietnam. He was no stranger to war or to inexperienced lieutenants. A "book soldier," he followed regulations and required that his men perform likewise, yet his compassion for them showed through at every opportunity. "You take care of them, they'll take care of you," he said during one of Dennis' early briefings.

In the mess tent, Dennis overheard casual talk about his Platoon Sergeant and the Third Platoon. He was impressed to learn that Sergeant Hanemaulo was considered a genuine hero at the battle of Soui Tre. This Battalion, along with the 2nd Battalion, had killed more than six hundred Viet Cong soldiers as they came in human wave attacks against the Americans. Sergeant Hanemaulo and his platoon had held the line in some of the fiercest fighting of the war. For his actions he was awarded the nation's second highest award for valor, The Distinguished Service Cross. From what Dennis could learn, the men believed that he deserved the Medal of Honor. *I'm lucky to be associated with the man,* Dennis thought. *He'll get me through this if I just hang close to him.*

Hurriedly gobbling his late supper of hot dogs and beans, Dennis met Sergeant Hanemaulo outside. Together they walked quickly to a dimly-lit supply tent. A long line of men stood outside, waiting to receive their equipment. They had taken to heart Colonel Pullman's admonition to get prepared immediately. The men were being issued basic webbing and load-bearing equipment: rucksacks, mosquito nets, steel helmets, sleeping bags, ponchos and liners, pistol belts, first aid pouches, two plastic canteens and fifty pounds of associated gear. Sergeant Hanemaulo escorted Dennis to the head of the line, a small privilege he appreciated. He was weary and exhausted, as were all of the new arrivals.

Dennis accepted the mountain of gear without question. He recognized most of it. Some was for comfort, some of it for fighting. Finally, he received his M-16 rifle and five ammunition magazines. He inspected it carefully and fondled it like a mistress. "She'll be my constant companion for the next twelve months and I want to develop a quick romance," he grinned as he conferred with Sergeant Hanemaulo.

"Yep, that weapon will be your lover for the next year," Sergeant Hanemaulo said. "And it might very well be the difference between whether you live or die."

"It does look really neat. Very modern and deadly," Dennis said. "I've never handled one."

Signing a financial responsibility form for the equipment (which Dennis found absurd), he heaved the load onto his shoulders and exited the tent into total darkness, groping and stumbling behind Sergeant Hanemaulo on the way to his quarters. *He's got the eyes of a cat,* Dennis reflected.

The living and sleeping areas were large, general-purpose tents, erected over wooden frames with shipping pallets for floors. Alongside the tents were huge, freshly dug-trenches. *For shelter during mortar attacks,* Dennis presumed.

Rows of what appeared to be sandbagged blockhouses sat about fifty yards beyond the tents. They ringed the entire camp and were the first line of defense. Each bunker was outfitted with fifty caliber machine guns and their barrels poked menacingly through their small port holes. Two or three men manned the bunkers, twenty-four hours a day.

Barbed wire, mines, booby traps, and exploding flame devices comprised just part of the myriad of deadly contraptions that were available to defend the perimeter in case of enemy attack. They were frequently used at Dau Tieng, Dennis learned. The enemy found this base to be an impediment to their supply operations and had many times attempted to annihilate it and the Americans who defended it.

During the next couple of hours Dennis organized his gear, filling the five rifle magazines with ammunition and packing the items he'd been advised to bring to the field.

"You'll be heading out into the rubber trees or the jungles soon and you've got to be ready," Sergeant Hanemaulo advised. "It's better out there, Lieutenant. You can move and shoot like the VC, and you've got your platoon all around you. It's safer than sitting here, waiting for a mortar or ground attack. Sometimes a sniper gets one of us. Can't tell where the little bastards are."

With his help and that of a more experienced lieutenant, Dennis mastered the dynamics of the mosquito net. They briefed him carefully and it came as a surprise when one of them commented that he'd need about twenty magazines for ammunition. "Why did they give me only five?" Dennis asked.

"That's what comes with the weapon in this outfit," the lieutenant said. "You're supposed to get seven, but you need eighteen to twenty. Don't overload them either; the spring isn't strong enough to push the cartridges up into the chamber. Piss-poor rifle and a piss-poor supply system, eh?"

"Where do you get more --"

"Take them off dead bodies or from men who are wounded and evacuated without ever stopping here. You just pick through their stuff, take what you need: boots, socks, cigarettes, whatever. Sometimes you find them on the ground where men panic and drop them during the heat of a firefight. Everything is that way, 'Three Six.'"

It was the first time Dennis had heard the term, "Three Six," and it was quickly explained that it was his radio call sign in the field.

"All commanders are called 'Six,'" Sergeant Hanemaulo clarified. "Platoon leaders use the number of their platoons to identify themselves. The First Platoon Leader is 'One Six,' second platoon is 'Two Six,' and so on. We're Alpha Company, so the CO is 'Alpha Six.' Got it?"

The orientation went on into the night. Sergeant Hanemaulo showed him how to disassemble, to clean, and to reassemble his rifle. Dennis asked him what he thought of the weapon. Sergeant Hanemaulo didn't answer directly, but only said, "Keep it very clean, Lieutenant, always very clean."

Going over maps of the area of operations, they provided Dennis with a compass, marking pencils, and the many special tools that a platoon leader required above the normal issue. They finished at about 2:00 a.m. and Dennis thanked them both for their concern. He felt ready, relaxed, and confident.

Sergeant Hanemaulo, sitting on the edge of a cot, remarked again that he wanted Dennis to be fully prepared when he finally made it to the field and took his position as Platoon Leader. Then he dropped a bombshell: "I'll be leaving for home in a couple of weeks, Lieutenant. This is my last war and it's not a good one. I'll feel good, my conscience will be clear, if I know that the men are in good hands."

"I'll do my best, Sergeant," Dennis answered. "I'm sorry to hear you're leaving. I couldn't talk you into staying, could I?"

"Oh, hell no, Lieutenant. But don't worry, with your enlisted experience, you should be able to lead them real well. Remember, take care of them and they'll take care of you." Sergeant Hanemaulo stood, shook hands, and left the tent. Alone now, Dennis fell back onto his cot and stared at the tiny, pulsating light bulb. It entranced him; exhausted, he fell fast asleep.

Chapter Ten
The First Sergeant's School

It seemed like he'd been sleeping only a few moments. Rudely awakened by loud shouting and cursing, Dennis wiped sleep from his eyes and found himself looking right into the pug-nosed face of a Second Lieutenant's worst nightmare. It was First Sergeant Rudolph Krznarovich, "The Iron Mountain Man," the men had called him. "Big and ugly and loud and nothin' but cussin' for a vocabulary."

"Get the fuck up, Lieutenant. Five mile run starts in three minutes. Be there."

Dennis had no intention of missing his first formation, especially this one. He hurriedly dressed and left the tent. Whistling cheerfully as he approached the forming men, he glanced at his watch: five a.m. *It won't break light for another half hour. Just like OCS. No big deal.*

The new arrivals were gathering into four equal ranks and he recognized most of them from Fort Lewis, the airplane flight, or from the evening before. One young soldier, whom Dennis had met on the plane, was weeping softly as several men tried to console him.

"What's wrong with him?" Dennis asked an older sergeant.

"That's Charlie Martin, Sir. He's scared to death. Guess the reality of where he's at just hit home. Look at him, he's just a kid."

Dennis watched for a moment, measuring the effeminate features of the youth. Moved by compassion, he reached for the soldier's arm. "What's the matter, Martin?"

"I can't take it, Sir. I just want to go home. Please help me," the boy sobbed, wiping his nose with the back of his hand.

Speaking softly, Dennis ushered him to the side of the formation. "Everything will be all right, Martin. Don't worry. We'll take good care of you. I'll try to get you assigned to my platoon. You know me from Fort Lewis. You trust me, don't you?"

The youth's glistening eyes bore in on Dennis and then, finally, he nodded his agreement. A silent pact was made; he would serve Dennis.

"Hold your head up high, get back into the formation now, Charlie. Everything will be all right." The incident appeared to be over; together, they moved back into the larger fold of men.

Looking for his friends, Dennis quickly spotted Jay Cee, Wally, and the others, warming up, running in place, shadow boxing, and sparring playfully with each other.

"Good morning, Sir," Jackie shouted as he dodged a playful jab from Andy. "Have you met the very ugly first sergeant, yet?"

First Sergeant Rudolph Krznarovich was called by many names, but not to his face. "Polack," "Hunky," and "Pissed Off Sergeant 'K,'" were the most mild among a dozen other more obscene titles, none of which were intended to flatter him. The old-timers said he didn't care about what people thought of him. He was tough, crude and rude, and he enjoyed being thought of in that way. Like Hanemaulo, he was also a veteran of the two previous wars and was on his second tour of duty in Vietnam. Relishing his work and position as the "Top" sergeant in the company, it was his mission to get the new arrivals in shape.

The Battalion's policy required that new men would have at least three days of orientation and physical fitness training before they joined their units in the field. First Sergeant Krznarovich was in charge of this indoctrination period and he took extreme pleasure in it. He arrived at the side of the formation and bellowed: "Let's get with it. I love pushing you fucking troops." He threw a stinging look toward the group, then went to work.

"Move out, goddamn it, you sorry sons-of-bitches," he roared, pointing into the darkness just as Dennis took his position at the front of the formation. Automatically they faced right and began running at a shuffle. Krznarovich ran alongside, guiding the way through the dark, shouting cursing encouragement and sometimes physically moving lagging soldiers into position. Coming all the way from the rear to the front of the pack in three or four strides, he fell in alongside Dennis. "Where's your fucking weapon, Lieutenant?" he asked quietly. Dennis was humbled by the question; he'd left it lying on his cot. "I didn't know. I'm sorry."

"You ain't stateside, now, Lieutenant. Take it with you when you shit. Take it with you when you eat. Sleep with it in your hands. Fuck it if you get horny, but keep it with you at all times and you just might not get yourself killed."

He leaned closer to Dennis' face, running backward and never breaking the rhythm of his step. "For a former enlisted man, you don't show much fucking brains. I guess you thought that being an officer was the fast track to a goddamn sports car, eh?" His face was an inch from Dennis' now. "This fucking place is no joke, Lieutenant. Get your shaved head screwed on right or the fucking VC will screw it on for you." He turned and ran back and forth alongside the formation.

Dennis boiled with anger from the verbal thrashing, but considered it wise to hold his tongue. Besides, the pace of the run had left him breathless. They were running now, not jogging. *I'll have his ass court-martialed for disrespect to an officer when I see the Company Commander. I knew someday I'd meet an NCO who hated second lieutenants. This is the guy. How the hell a man of his age can verbally rage like that while we're running at this pace is unreal. I can't believe it. That man is a maniac.*

Dennis turned around and ran backwards for a few steps. It was getting light now and he could see that every man carried a rifle except him. He felt foolish, yet he was grateful that the First Sergeant had spoken quietly and hadn't embarrassed him in front of the men as he was now thunderously doing to a small group in the rear. They simultaneously responded with, "Yes, First Sergeant," to his every admonition. *I don't think my gang has ever heard such language. I'll bet they wished they'd stayed at Charlie Company last night.*

"He's mentally ill. He's crazy," came a voice from behind Dennis. It was Andy Crammer.

"Yeah," Wally gasped. "Christ, he's going to kill us for the Viet Cong."

Physically spent, they finally arrived back in the company area. It was fully daylight now, and the rising sun had already pushed the temperature beyond one hundred degrees.

"Clean up, eat chow, and get your fucking asses back outside by oh-eight-hundred," the First Sergeant said. "Bring your weapons and magazines; we'll be zeroing your rifles today. Fall out!"

Only too happy to oblige, the men broke free of the formation, panting as they raced to the mess hall. Hungry and thirsty, no one bothered to shower or to clean up; it seemed so senseless in the heat.

"Come with me please, Lieutenant Riley," the top soldier said as he stepped quickly to his Orderly Room, a creaky wooden hut used as the Company Headquarters.

Damn right. I'll have my say now.

First Sergeant Krznarovich moved behind a battered old desk and sank hard into a swivel chair. Wiping sweat from his forehead with the back of his hand, he breathed heavily, then stared at Dennis' face for several seconds. Dennis waited, the silence deafening. "Do you think I was rude and disrespectful to you back there, Lieutenant?"

"As a matter of fact --"

"I've heard a lot about you, Lieutenant Riley. The 'Old Man,' wanted to know who the hell he was getting for a replacement, so I contacted some of my old buddies, stateside. Got good reports. Heard you were the leadership graduate out of your OCS class."

The First Sergeant paused, fumbling in his lower desk drawer for something. After a moment, he brought out two paper cups and set them upside down on the desk. "This is a screwed-up war, Lieutenant. The leadership at the top sucks. They can't give you a good reason for being here, but they know why they're here. It's the only war they got and they're killing these kids by the bushel basket, just to make themselves look good. The casualty rate, the dead and wounded, it's more than two hundred a day now."

Searching the desk drawer again, he finally slammed it shut and continued his lecture. "Goddamn it. These boys are barely nineteen years old. Hell, they ain't hardly old enough to buy cigarettes. They jerk off at night in the shit houses because that's the only kind of sex they've ever had, they're so fucking cherry. They're just kids."

"I don't quite agree with your --"

"They have one thing on their minds, and that's getting home in one piece. They're looking for someone they can trust to lead them because they can't rely on the leadership up top. They ain't stupid. They know that the more rank you got, the farther your distance from the fighting." He stood now, leaning forward on the desk with both fists. "Now, what does that say to you, Sir?"

Dennis choked at the diatribe, but more from the unexpected expression of respect. "I guess --"

"Hell, I'll tell you what it says. It says that you are the only thing between their dying, getting their peckers or their legs blown off, or getting on that airplane and going home."

Pointing a massive middle finger at Dennis, he lowered his voice and said, "You're the only officer that they get to look at up close, Lieutenant, and you represent all that is wrong with this crap-ass war. They won't trust you right off -- they don't trust any second lieutenant, but their lives are in your hands and there's nothing they can do about it."

"I see what you mean --"

"I jumped in Sicily, Lieutenant, and we lost half our men in the steeples and power lines. ...a fucking nightmare. In Holland, we lost a division of troops in the parachutes. I remember passing the bloody carcasses of men on the way down."

Dennis stood motionless as the old soldier paused abruptly in his painful reminiscences. Chagrined to look into his eyes he gazed, instead, at a picture of soldiers, storming ashore, hanging on the wall behind him.

"22nd Infantry ... Utah Beach ... D-day," the First Sergeant said, noticing Dennis' abstraction.

Dennis recognized the awesome battle experience of the man he stood before and his desire to share it with his young lieutenant. He relaxed and waited. He sensed that the old soldier wasn't finished quite yet. Dennis didn't know why, but he was beginning to like the First Sergeant. He felt and understood that the man was telling him only what he needed to hear.

Spitting a wad of mucus into a trash can near his desk, the First Sergeant sat down, folded his arms, and continued: "Same crap in every war, Lieutenant. I've been sizing you up and I think maybe we finally got us an officer. I'll warn you though, we don't need no big-headed Prima Donnas who graduated at the top of whatever fucking school they went to. I wouldn't want your responsibility, Lieutenant," he said as an afterthought.

"Now, I've said my piece, Sir. I want you to succeed and I think you will. I'll help you all I can." He paused, reached into another drawer and produced a bottle of whiskey. "Old Granddad. Want a drink, Sir?" he asked.

"Yes, Top, I believe I will. I haven't had breakfast, but I think I need it, thanks."

"Thank you, Lieutenant," Krznarovich said while pouring generous portions of whiskey into the paper cups and lifting his in a toast. "Thanks for listening to me. Good luck, Son. You're going to damn well need it." They swallowed together, looking at each other over the rim of the cups.

Dennis gagged on the whiskey and it hit his empty stomach like a hot poker. Leaving the building, he trotted to the mess tent and drank quickly from a paper cup he snatched from the hand of Jackie Stoner. "God, I never knew that green Kool-Aid could be so good. Thanks, Jackie."

"That's OK, Lieutenant. Where have you been?"

"Getting a history lesson, I think. Maybe it was an ass chewing ... First Sergeant style."

Rosey, Jay Cee, Jackie, Andy, and Wally finished gobbling their food, waved good-bye, and wished Dennis luck. Glad to be out from under First Sergeant Krznarovich's supervision, they were in Charlie Company by 8:00 a.m. Forced to run another five miles by the like-minded First Sergeant of that company, they looked terribly exhausted as they struggled past Alpha's formation, this time carrying full combat packs. It was their first "war story," and they told Dennis about it many times as he met them over the next few weeks.

First Sergeant Krznarovich's orientation passed quickly. He had prepared them for combat as best he could. Dennis felt that he had learned more in these three days than all of the time he'd spent at Fort Lewis. "Keep your rifle clean and your fucking ass down," Krznarovich said as he helped Dennis aboard his first helicopter ride over the jungle.

"I will, Top. I promise that. Thanks."

They lifted in a flight of five helicopters to finally join their unit in the field. The ride was exciting and they flew just above the treetops, south, over the villages of Dau Tieng, Cui Chi, and other tiny clusters of habitation. Looking down, he felt an exhilaration he had never known before.

It's a lot cooler up here with the wind rushing past the open doors. Sure beats the hell out of walking through that jungle. I'll bet we're flying over a lot of enemy. The landscape is so beautiful. I seem to be connecting to this place. I never imagined.... Vietnam -- it's gorgeous. What a shame.

Chapter Eleven
Taking Charge

A thin column of purple smoke drifted up from a small clearing in the jungle. The lead chopper homed in on it and soon they were on the ground, dispersing quickly into the thick brush as they'd been taught to do. A commanding voice shouted, "Get that new Lieutenant over here; I want to meet this 'shave-tail.'"

In a moment, Dennis was at perfect attention, saluting properly his new Company Commander, Captain Bill Wiggins. It seemed like the right thing to do. Immediately impressed with Captain Wiggins, Dennis noticed that he was impeccable in his neatly-tailored jungle fatigues. His boots revealed a modest shine and he was clean-shaven. Dark aviator sunglasses masked his eyes and he chewed casually on what appeared to be an expensive cigar. Dennis wondered how the Captain managed to stay so clean in the stifling heat. He was drenched with sweat, and his boots looked like they had been dragged through a manure pile.

"Thanks, Lieutenant, much appreciated, but don't do that again. We don't salute out here in the field." Captain Wiggins rolled the cigar around in his mouth for a moment. Frowning, he removed it and jabbed at Dennis. "If you're wise, you'll strip yourself of all rank and try to look like anybody else. We have a lot of problems with snipers and you can guess who they want to shoot at the most. Me, and now you."

"Ah, wow, Sir. I can understand that," Dennis replied.

Captain Wiggins surveyed Dennis from toe to head, then continued, "You won't have to worry Lieutenant, you'll have the Third Platoon. Sergeant Hanemaulo. He's the best soldier in the business. If you're good, your boys will take care of you, might even come to respect you. Fuck up and they'll probably put a bullet in the back of your head."

He stuck the cigar back in his mouth, speaking to Dennis through clenched teeth. "We've been in a defensive position here for the last couple of days waiting for you FNGs. I'm glad you finally got here." He extended his hand and nodded as if he was satisfied with what he saw.

Dennis expressed his understanding and said so to the Captain. His comments about not looking conspicuous seemed contradictory considering his flashy trappings; nevertheless, he seemed reasonable, and clearly all business. In spite of himself, Dennis kept thinking, "*PX soldier.*"

Captain Wiggins removed his sunglasses and Dennis saw his dark eyes for the first time. He was a handsome man, well-proportioned, and had a full crop of sandy hair.

"We're in a place called the Ho Bo Woods," Captain Wiggins said. "Get out your map ... see here?" Using his cigar as a pointer, he stabbed at a location on the map. "We're at the base of a jungle area we call the 'Mushroom.' The heavy green area represents triple canopy jungle. It's shaped like an atomic cloud."

"Is that why you call it the 'mushroom?'" Dennis asked.

"Yeah, and there's plenty of VC in there -- a regiment -- maybe two. We'll be sweeping through the area from the bottom to the top tomorrow. You'll run local patrols today and an ambush tonight. That'll keep the bad guys from sneaking up on us."

"Where? How far out do we go?"

"A thousand meters, maybe a little more. You've got to work Charlie all the time to keep 'em off your back. I want you to lead every patrol and every ambush. You'll get to know your men faster that way. Understand?"

"Yes, Sir," Dennis said, looking directly into the eyes of his commander. He didn't want to miss a word.

Puffing and chewing on his wasted cigar, Captain Wiggins continued, "Start by making your men improve their positions. Get acquainted and don't run your mouth too much. Your boys are pretty experienced and they don't want to see Hanemaulo go. Your platoon is that way," he said, pointing again with the cigar. "Any questions?"

"No, Sir. I'm anxious to meet the men and to get to work." Dennis turned and walked toward the positions. It was hard not to salute as he departed the Company Commander.

"Oh, by the way, Riley," Captain Wiggins called after him. "Lieutenant Morris, the Executive Officer, will be in charge tomorrow during the sweep. I'll be back at Dau Tieng. I have a dental appointment."

Dennis fought the urge to think disloyally about his captain, having only met him moments before, but he couldn't help himself. *Dental ap-*

pointment? Now I see how he keeps himself so fresh looking. He is a "PX sol-dier."

Stumbling through the brush, Dennis became tangled in some thorny vines and fell. Sergeant Hanemaulo stood over him, laughed, and extended a helping hand. "We call them 'wait a minute vines,' Lieutenant. They make you slow down real quick."

The Third Platoon occupied a wide section of Alpha Company's sector of responsibility. Sergeant Hanemaulo moved swiftly, taking Dennis to every position. As he introduced the men, two to a foxhole, Dennis was struck by how young they looked. "Average age is about nineteen," Sergeant Hanemaulo said when Dennis commented on it. "About the same in every war. The old guys in Washington start it, the young men have to fight it."

They traveled through the brush out some distance to the observation posts. Sergeant Hanemaulo explained the tactical emplacement of the men and especially his rationale for putting two machine guns together at the right edge of their defensive zone. "Always have fire across your front. Work them in pairs. They're a hell of a lot more effective that way," he said.

"Why are the positions spread so far apart?" Dennis asked, waving his hand across the front. "A herd of elephants could walk between them."

"We only had about eighteen men until you FNGs arrived this morning." He grew solemn and then placed his hands on his hips, surveying the wide front. "Yeah, we're spread thin, we always are. Put lots of booby-traps between your holes. Other stuff, too. You can rearrange the perimeter now that you're up to about thirty men. Remember, you've got ten new men to look after." He patted Dennis on the shoulder and said, "Go for it, Lieutenant; earn your bars." He left Dennis standing there and returned to the command post to attend to supply and other matters.

Alone at last with his platoon, Dennis suddenly felt the full weight of his responsibility and it almost overwhelmed him. *I'm finally here, a Platoon Leader of Infantry, in charge of a group of fighting men at war ... waiting for action. That's really what I wanted to become, what I trained for. Good God, I'm scared.*

He spent the afternoon trooping their defensive line and getting to know the men. They were not too talkative and he understood that they were feeling him out. Some were downright surly and a few of their remarks bordered on insubordination. Captain Wiggins' and Sergeant Hanemaulo's comments on FNGs was a mystery to him.

"What does FNG mean, Corporal?" he asked one of the men, interrupting his digging.

"Fucking new guy," came the curt reply as the soldier shoveled dirt from his foxhole, throwing it in Dennis' direction. The moist black earth landed close to his boots and he recognized the gesture for what it was. *They're disrespectful as hell, testing me.*

Vigorously moving from position to position, issuing instructions for improving them, he removed his shirt and grabbed a machete. Helping them clear fields of fire by cutting the brush low in front of each position, he worked methodically, without taking a break. He supervised the cutting of paths so that they could move easily from position to position at night, then spoke with several men, learning their names and hometowns. Calling for an afternoon meeting with his leaders, he complimented their efforts.

Dennis drank from his canteen, then offered it to the others. No one accepted. "You've done good work, men, but there's much more we must do. Let's put out aiming stakes to the front and mark our sectors of fire. Then we'll add more concertina wire and set up a couple dozen Claymore mines, trip flares, and listening devices. These holes have got to be deeper. Cut some logs for overhead support. Top them with rows of filled sandbags. I'll help."

"What are aiming stakes?" one of the men asked. "Never heard of them."

"Besides digging deep, it's something we should always do," Dennis answered. He removed his helmet, held it against his hip with an arm, and addressed the entire group. "Cut small poles or sticks about two feet tall. Stick them in the ground on the left and right sides of your foxholes, a little bit to the front. They mark the left and right limits of your rifle fire. The foxholes next to you do the same thing. During a night fight, you can see your limits or feel them with your rifle muzzle. That way you aren't just spraying ammo. You take care of your sector, they take care of theirs. Any more questions?"

"No, Sir," several men answered in unison.

Dennis was exhausted as he took time to coordinate his fire plan with the artillery Forward Observer. Finished, he and one of the squad leaders visited the observation posts, relieving the men there so that they could take a break. Late in the afternoon he led a patrol of ten men across the company front as Captain Wiggins had instructed. By dusk, his energy was totally consumed, but he felt confident that their positions were solid. He hadn't had time to measure whether or not he had developed any rapport with his men. In fact, he didn't know how to evaluate such a thing.

Arriving back at Sergeant Hanemaulo's position, he observed that the radio operator, the platoon medic, and Sergeant Hanemaulo had prepared an adequate foxhole for their own protection. There was obviously no room for him.

Damn, I got so busy, I forgot to look after myself. Taking his entrenching tool from its pouch, he began to dig violently, angry at his own forgetfulness. *I've got to work fast; I've got an ambush patrol to lead. We're moving out after dark. I'll need a hole 'til then.*

Taking a few shovels of dirt, he felt a growing presence around him. A hand reached and took the shovel from him. Without a word, four men, one from each squad, began to dig and to prepare his night position. "Take a break, Sir," one of them said, "we'll dig the hole."

"You cool, L.T.," another offered. "You damn cool."

Dennis sat back, opened a can of rations, and watched the men work swiftly as he shoveled food into his mouth. It was perhaps, the greatest moment of his life; they were digging a hole for his protection. To Dennis it was the highest form of flattery. *I'm in, thank God, I'm in!*

Chapter Twelve
First Patrol

Dennis' first nighttime ambush patrol was uneventful and, fortunately, he saw no action. He had taken twelve men from the foxholes and seven of them were new arrivals like himself. Interviewing each man before they left, Dennis realized that the new men were petrified with fear. He spent considerable time and effort calming them. One man bawled openly as they left the perimeter and the others dragged him along against his will.

In the dark, they were extremely clumsy, not having learned yet how to move efficiently in the thick jungle. Unsure of his position most of the time, Dennis worried that he might not be able to call artillery fire if he needed it. He stopped constantly to check his compass and to measure distances, slowing their movement to a crawl. Someone tripped and accidentally fired a shot. Luckily no one was hurt, but it signaled their location. Finally, Dennis decided to settle the platoon into a night fighting position, more for self-preservation than for ambushing any unwary Viet Cong. He had no idea where he was.

In a few minutes, most of the patrol was in varying stages of sleep, and, as hard as he tried to stay awake, he kept drifting off into a nervous slumber. Propped against a huge mahogany tree, he dreamily took measure of their activities. *Improvements are in order if I'm going to do this again. I'm lost, our position's been broadcast to everyone within a mile, and most of the patrol is sleeping. Lord, please make this night pass quickly.*

By 7:00 a.m., they had permission to return to the main perimeter. The Battalion was preparing to move north on its searching mission and he was told by radio to, "Hurry if your platoon wants supplies."

"We've got about a thousand meters to go," Dennis quietly informed the men as they hovered around him. "We can move a little faster now that it's light." Using a machete to clear the path ahead, he led the way. A young Sergeant, Ernie Crawford, stayed close behind him, his shotgun at the ready. Moving to within a few meters of the company sector, they suddenly became the easy targets of sniper fire. Several shots snapped past them in rapid succession and one man fell; he was hit in the fleshy part of his thigh and he cried out in pain.

Dennis slammed himself onto the ground and his stomach fluttered nervously. He knew he had to respond, to give direction, but fear had left him speechless. The platoon medic, "Doc" Johnson, scrambled to his side. "Just a sniper, Sir. The boys will get him," he calmly stated.

Sergeant Crawford and others yelled for a cease-fire, reminding everyone that they were not far from their own perimeter and facing into it.

Dennis recovered quickly. "Good thinking, Sarge, you probably saved us from getting into a shoot-out war with our own people."

They crouched low and waited, scanning the area, searching for the assailant. Captain Wiggins' radio calls became frantic and he insisted that they get back into the main perimeter immediately, but Dennis felt he couldn't move, at least until they had neutralized the sniper. He wasn't sure if fear or good judgment kept him there. His hands shook as he answered a radio call from his commander.

"Supply helicopters are inbound," Captain Wiggins said. "The company is out of their foxholes, ready to move. I'll be outbound on that chopper in a few minutes, get your platoon back in here, now."

It was eerily quiet in the jungle and Dennis hoped the sniper fire was over for the moment. "I think he took a couple of shots and scampered away," he told Sergeant Crawford.

"Don't you believe it, L.T. He's a tricky bastard. He tried to draw us into shooting at our own men. It didn't work, but he's still out there."

Caught between the exhortations of his commander to hustle to the perimeter and the obvious danger in doing so, Dennis reluctantly ordered, "Let's go, guys. Move it out." Stepping cautiously, he took his place up front, scanning all around him and taking courage from the sight of his men. In spite of their own fear, they efficiently obeyed and stepped bravely forward, weapons and grenades at the ready.

The soft hairs at the base of his neck prickled his flesh and he could hear the rhythms of his pounding heart. Silence engulfed them except for the incessant whimpering of the wounded man. Doc Johnson taped his mouth shut, assuring him that he was not badly hurt, and showing him how to use his rifle as a crutch. The wounded man's eyes bulged in fear, but he hobbled forward and the patrol surged ahead. In ten minutes they were at the outer edge of the perimeter. "Be home in a minute," Dennis said.

The sounds of approaching helicopters and the loud "whoop," "whoop" of their blades suggested a special urgency to their mission. "Choppers coming, L.T.," Sergeant Crawford said.

"Yeah, it's our morning resupply. We need to get our wounded man on board, Sarge. Let's go."

A large supply ship began descending into the battalion perimeter and the hidden sniper opened fire, sending several rounds into the fuselage. He was only a few meters from the patrol, slightly to their left. Dennis and his men automatically began firing in that direction and quickly peppered the enemy soldier with bullets, killing him. Sergeant Crawford stood and waved the patrol forward.

"Fucking fool," someone said.

"Just another dead Commie," Sergeant Crawford said, rolling the body over with a long stick. "They most always have grenades underneath them, Lieutenant. You've got to be careful. Turn the body with your hands and it might explode in your face. This guy's clean, but he just had to have that chopper. It cost him his life."

Dennis felt a rush of adrenaline, some strange kind of pleasure at their success. He knelt to examine the body, then bolted upright in dismay. "Christ, he's just a boy. Fourteen, maybe fifteen years old. Jesus, he looks like a piece of Swiss cheese with all these holes in him." Loath to call the kill a victory, he nevertheless radioed the activity to Captain Wiggins.

"Good. You got him; now get your ass back in here," Captain Wiggins demanded.

Suddenly, out of nowhere, two heavily-armed helicopter gunships appeared and began circling outside the main perimeter. They had accompanied the big Chinook. Passing low over them, just a few feet above the trees, they hesitated, turned, and came back toward the American patrol. Mistakenly believing them to be an enemy unit, the gunships stalled in mid-air, hovering; suddenly, their machine guns blazed hot steel upon the helpless figures below.

Dennis and his men hit the dirt, seeking protection in any crevice they could find. He pressed his face into the moist earth and held his breath. "You dumb bastards are shooting my men. You're killing them. Shut it off, goddamn it, shut it off," he screamed into his radio handset.

The gunships made two passes, hosing them down with massive firepower before they stopped. Like vultures they circled several times, then rapidly flew off into a rising sun.

"This is a fucking nightmare, Lieutenant," Sergeant Crawford yelled into Dennis' face. "What the hell happened?"

Dennis, dumbstruck, could not answer. The platoon itself hadn't helped matters as they angrily returned fire on the helicopters after the first pass. It had its effect as the pilots climbed quickly and made their second run from higher in the air where the gunners were less accurate. The beat of their rotors finally vanished in the distance and Dennis regained control.

He stood and brushed off his clothing. Sergeant Crawford, standing beside him, looked him over. "You all right, Lieutenant?"

"Yeah, I'm OK. Check the men."

Dennis, outraged, could hardly contain his anger. His men were dazed, confused, and their eyes begged for an explanation. "I'll see their asses at a court-martial," he yelled to the entire platoon.

"We'll kill the sorry fuckers, if we ever see them again," Sergeant Crawford said. "We got the tail numbers. They best never fly over this platoon, friendly or not. Who screwed up, Lieutenant?"

"I don't know," Dennis answered, anguish evident in his voice. "Let's get our wounded and get the hell back in. What's the situation with the men?"

"Two more wounded," Sergeant Crawford said. "Not real bad."

The patrol collected around Dennis now, angry and bewildered. They wanted answers but he could give them none. Sergeant Crawford made the excuse that the gunships had opened fire without permission and didn't know they were there. Barely accepting that explanation himself, Dennis knew that it didn't satisfy any of them.

"Sergeant Crawford, you've been in Vietnam for a while; you know there's no excuse for firing on your own men. We were lucky. If we hurry, the injured can be on the supply helicopter going out. Let's go."

Furious, Dennis mentally rehearsed the speech he would give Captain Wiggins: "*I want an explanation and an apology. This fiasco was the result of pure stupidity on someone's part. It wasn't an accident. How could gunships be allowed to fire on their own troops?*" He was determined to find the person responsible for this terrible mismanagement.

The men bunched together behind Dennis as they walked. Through the trees he recognized the base perimeter. Walking backwards for a few steps, he shouted to his men, " Don't worry, guys. Heads will roll when we get back in, when I see the Captain."

Holding on to their wounded, they stumbled the last few meters into the perimeter. Dennis' heart jumped when he realized that there was no one there. "The company's gone. They've abandoned us," Dennis shouted.

The main body of Alpha Company had vanished and so had the rest of the battalion. A "stay-behind" force of several riflemen remained to protect the still idling Chinook.

"They've left us, the sons-of-bitches," Sergeant Crawford said, looking dumfounded at Dennis. "What the hell gives?"

Stupefied and in minor shock, Dennis didn't answer. There was no one available for him to rain his fury upon or to ask questions of. *What kind of leadership is this?* he wondered. *What kind of screwed up outfit have I arrived at? Don't they care? Doesn't anybody give a damn?*

Captain Wiggins, waiting deep inside the helicopter, chewed on the stub of his cigar and watched silently as Dennis and his men loaded the wounded men aboard the big bird. The rear doors wrenched shut and Dennis stared upward as it lifted from the clearing. He felt bad that he didn't even know the names of the men who had been hit. "Who were they? Do you have their names?" he asked Sergeant Crawford.

"Privates Art Little, Bob Allchin, and the big guy was Sergeant Leroy Broadnax. Little and Allchin helped you dig your foxhole last night, Lieutenant. Damn shame, ain't it?"

The radio came alive with instructions from Lieutenant Morris. He ordered the platoon to catch up with them. "We're about a thousand meters north of our night position; follow our trail, and hurry," he ordered. "Did the dead gook have any documents on him? A Viet Cong flag, a rifle, maybe? Did he have any grenades?" Lieutenant Morris never asked about the casualties or the condition of the men. Signing off, he congratulated Dennis on the enemy body count.

Running and stumbling, Dennis and his platoon caught up with the company at mid-morning. He made a beeline for Lieutenant Morris and the command group, determined to get some answers. The Executive Officer was barely interested. In fact, he hardly allowed Dennis to speak.

"I've got my own problems," Lieutenant Morris said. He avoided Dennis' eyes, and ran his hands through his thinning hair. He looked very tired. Dennis was reluctant to make matters worse. He listened politely to Lieutenant Morris, deciding that he'd get satisfaction later from Captain Wiggins.

"Shit, Riley, don't go whining about those damn gunships shooting up your patrol. They came out of nowhere with no radio communications. I couldn't help it. They reacted too fast to the sniper fire. You're in Vietnam, Riley. Get used to it." By his tone of voice, Dennis knew that the discussion was ended.

Lieutenant Morris' personal distress was that he'd been left in charge and had to answer for the fact that they had not captured a weapon or any other evidence of the kill. "All I have is your word for it, Riley," he said. "You've got to do better than that. Pick over the body next time, look around for a weapon, documents or something. What the hell did you do, panic?"

"No, Sir, we did search --"

Lieutenant Morris cut him off, waving his hands in disgust. "Those gunships are claiming the hit as their own body count. The Battalion Commander is pissed. He's claiming the body, too. He wants to see you right away."

Dennis wondered how he knew the gunship pilots were claiming a body count, if no one had radio communications with them. Prudence told him it was not the time to ask and he held his tongue. "Yes, Sir," he said, moving out in the direction of the Battalion Command Group. *Maybe I'll get some justice from the colonel.*

A few hundred meters up the trail he found the Battalion Commander and his Operations Group in a grassy clearing, huddled over a large set of maps and fiercely debating the tactics of the current mission. Dennis simply stood and listened. It appeared that Captain Carmen De-Matto, the Operations Officer, was trying to convince the Battalion Commander, Lieutenant Colonel Harry Taylor, that the best method for "Search and Destroy" missions was to allow the companies to operate independently.

"They conduct their hunts by grids, using 'cloverleaf' tactics," Captain DeMatto said. "The men know this routine -- we've had good success using these strategies in the past, Sir."

By a wave of his hand Colonel Taylor indicated that he would have none of it. "I'm telling you, Carmen, your methods will get somebody killed. They'd be isolated into small groups, stepping over the enemy in the spaces they fail to cover. Now, this is my final word on the matter. Get these companies and platoons on line, the whole battalion."

"What --"

"You heard me. Have them stretch out across the base of the mushroom at double arm's interval. Move forward on my signal; I'll be directing them from above in my helicopter. Tell them to stay on line and cover every inch of this area. My chopper's here. I've got to go." Stiff salutes were exchanged and the Colonel was soon airborne. Captain DeMatto was shaking his head in disbelief when he spotted Dennis, standing alone in the brush.

"Hey, soldier, what can I do for you?" he asked, then smiled. "Are you that new 'fuzzy' from Alpha Company that had the sniper action this morning?"

"Yes, Sir, I'm Lieutenant Riley."

His friendliness disarmed Dennis and he felt no ill will toward the Captain. He appeared to be an experienced officer, older than most captains. He had a nasty scar across his cheek and had developed a middle-aged paunch.

"I was told to report to the Battalion CO, but I see that he's gone already."

"Yes, Lieutenant, he did want to talk to you about that Cong you nailed this morning. Good job, you and your men did.

"Thanks, Sir."

"The Colonel's been trying to authenticate your kill to Brigade, but the aviators need a trophy to report. Too bad you didn't collect any booty. Next time carry some old documents or a Chinese hand grenade or something. The cops back home call it a throw-down weapon."

Folding his arms, Captain DeMatto looked at Dennis for a moment, shrugged, and said, "Go on back to your unit, Lieutenant. They'll be getting on line about now. By the way, I am sorry about those gunships and your men. Tell them how very sorry the Battalion Commander and we all are. If they blame you, tell them it was all my fault."

"Yes, Sir," Dennis said, trying not to show his disgust. His parting salute caught Captain DeMatto by surprise.

"It's a strange war, Lieutenant. We only salute the Colonel, but thanks anyway. Now, get back to your platoon."

Returning, Dennis found his men had little time for further complaint about the incident. They were preoccupied and completely bewildered by what they were now supposed to do. The commanders were trying to stretch more than six hundred men, side by side, about three feet apart, across the bottom edge of the mushroom. Alpha Company, in the center, was the anchor and Dennis' platoon, in the middle, became the base for the entire battalion.

Eager to please their new Platoon Leader, the men tried to follow his instructions, but it proved to be an impossible task. They thrashed about, trying to get "on-line," but the tropical growth was so dense they could barely see the man next to them. Thick bamboo stalks and massive ant hills formed impassable obstacles. In other places small clearings caused groups of men to cluster there. The Colonel, flying high above, was livid at the confusion. "I want a straight line," he demanded.

The leaders began shouting and calling out to one another, trying to keep their units intact and to move them into the correct position. The enlisted men, hidden in the thick undergrowth, shouted foul curses back and forth at their leaders. The level of vituperation directed at the Colonel shocked Dennis and he could see that unit integrity and cohesion were slipping away. He was powerless to stop it as each man was really alone.

Likewise, he could see nothing in front or on the sides of him as he struggled against the jungle. Finally, after much thrashing about, Colonel Taylor either gave up or was satisfied enough with his line that he ordered the mass of men to move forward, straight into the jungle wall. Progress was almost impossible as each man hacked and chopped his way forward, a few inches at a time. The men called out to one another, searching for human contact. Within minutes they automatically formed back into columns, one behind the other, with a "cutter" as point man, and a shotgun at the front. "Fuck that goddamn Colonel," someone shouted.

"Got that right," Dennis replied angrily.

Each point man hacked with his machete for ten or fifteen minutes or until he was exhausted, then he was replaced by another man. It was the only tactic possible in the thick jungle. Colonel Taylor said nothing, his radio strangely silent now.

"Maybe he's finally realized we ain't on the plains of West Point," Sergeant Hanemaulo remarked in a rare moment of open displeasure with his commander.

Mastering the column technique, the units moved more quickly now, using traditional and proven tactics. The entire incident, from patrol to searching the jungle, proved to Dennis that he was in the company of many fools. He had lost faith in his leaders already. From that day forward he was determined to look out for himself and his men, vowing that he would not allow his superiors to kill him or them, just to advance their own careers by accumulating body count.

What do they think this is, a basketball game where bodies are the score? I'll control the tactics from here on in. I'll do what makes sense and what's right. "Take care of your men." Hanemaulo's words echoed in his mind.

Dennis had plenty of time to consider his growing disillusionment with his leaders. They searched the mushroom for three days, taking eleven casualties in the process, never seeing the enemy. He was too elusive, popping up from "spider holes," taking a well-aimed shot, and then diving back down again. Frequently, they encountered booby traps or 'punji' pits. Several of them were brimming with poisonous snakes. Often they took sniper fire from behind the broad leaves of tropical trees. They were no match for the Viet Cong.

Returning to the Dau Tieng base camp, Dennis learned from intelligence reports that they'd been tramping over the operational area of an entire Viet Cong Regiment. They were hidden, living underground in a labyrinth of catacombs, just as they had done for decades. They had been there since the French Indo-China war and they owned the Ho Bo Woods.

Dennis handed the reports to Sergeant Hanemaulo, as they sat on a cot, discussing their input to an after-action report. "We're a bunch of damn fools, huh, Sarge?"

"Don't let it get to you, Lieutenant. There's some good men up top, somewhere. You'll see, they always show up when you need them. It takes just one good leader."

"Seriously, Sergeant Hanemaulo, I'm beginning to doubt my reasons for being here. I was a real patriot when I left the states. After the Hobos, I just don't know. Something ain't right."

The old soldier sat silently for a moment, then stood, facing him. He reached for Dennis' shoulders with both hands, shook him slightly, and said, "If you're in doubt, Son ... if you don't know why you're here, why you should be here, then how the hell do you think these men feel?"

"I guess I was just feeling sorry for myself."

"You're all they got, Lieutenant. If you ever show, even for a second, that you're disillusioned, well, by God, then you'll have chaos in your ranks. You owe them more than that." He released Dennis, waiting for a response that was not forthcoming. Dennis, his mouth wide open, simply stared at his teacher. Hanemaulo slapped him on the shoulder and laughed. "Enough preaching, eh, L.T.? Come on, let's go get a beer."

Chapter Thirteen
A Routine War

Alpha Company stayed within the confines of the base camp during September and busied themselves with local search and destroy operations. Daylight patrols resulted in periodic firefights with one or two fleeting enemy, none of which involved Dennis or his platoon. Night ambushes became routine and he began to get a feel for the jungle, always marveling at the exotic plants and strange-sounding animal life.

Frequently, all companies operated side by side. Often, it was Alpha and Bravo together or the mix might include Charlie and Delta Companies. During the preparation of a night defensive perimeter, Dennis had the occasion to meet with the elements of Charlie Company. They were linked together in a mutual fortification effort. It was Dennis' responsibility to verify that the tie-in had actually occurred. He checked his own men as he moved quickly toward the Charlie Company sector.

Wally Gerber was the first man he met. Without any regard for security, Wally began shouting for the others to, "Come-a-running, guys. Dennis the Lieutenant is here." They came, leaving their positions and gathering around Dennis, humbling and embarrassing him with their adulation.

The spontaneous visit was brief, but enjoyable for all of them. Jay Cee had been made a Fire-Team leader and Wally carried the Number One gun in the weapons squad of his platoon. "A mighty damned important position, Wally," Dennis said.

"Jackie and Andy are assigned to the machine gun squad too, and they've been kicking ass," Wally bragged. "They're already heroes. They bagged a gook from their listening post just last night."

"Slit his throat, just like a pig," Jackie sneered, trying to imitate Wally. "Our CO says we're going to get a medal. It was wild, man, you should have seen it." Jackie's voice lowered and he admitted that he was exaggerating; the execution had made them both feel awful. "Andy threw up right after that. I got sick about it, too."

Rosey remained silent for a while, smacking his lips in disgust at their vivid description of killing. "God will get you for that, Jackie," he said solemnly. "My word, slitting his throat, and stop calling them gooks."

Dennis was delighted that they had all settled in at Charlie Company. He told them of his own exploits. In particular, he described his anger over the gunship incident. With empathy, they clamored their own rage at such foolishness.

Dennis bid them a quick farewell, saying that he'd see them back at Dau Tieng where they'd all drink a beer or two, then moved quickly back to his own platoon.

Operating out of the base camp at Dau Tieng became routine. The units patrolled and searched within several thousand meters of their perimeter during the day, returning to their tents at night. Rested troops then took their turn on ambush. The days became weeks. Although they were bored, they became better soldiers.

Colonel Taylor seemed an illusory commander. Like Captain Wiggins, he was seldom heard or seen. Over time, Alpha Company engaged in several small unit actions, a few of them successful, but injuries increased from sniper fire, booby traps, and unseen land mines. A cloud of inefficiency hung over the battalion and everybody sensed it. Body count was the only measure of success and every commander thirsted for it, especially Colonel Taylor. By late October, 1967, they had plenty of American casualties to report, but very little enemy body count to justify them.

"The Colonel has a need to produce better results," Captain Wiggins confided to Dennis on one occasion when they were both in camp. "Brigade and Division are on his ass. That's why we're always out there in the brush looking for a kill."

"I'm getting used to the routine," Dennis said. "Three days out, three back in camp. It's not so bad."

Captain Wiggins adjusted his gold watchband, then his sunglasses. He patted Dennis on the back and said, "OK, Hero. You're so cherry you probably will survive. Myself, I'm staying right here in this base. My tour is about up and I just want to keep that man from killing me."

Dennis acknowledged that, to him, it seemed that their constantly shifting and limited missions were a big part of the problem. "We're told that we'll be going to spearhead an attack into known enemy locations and then the action fizzles into local search operations around Dau Tieng, or north into the Michelin rubber trees. Can't our leaders settle on a plan or are they pulling it out of their asses?"

Captain Wiggins unfolded a lawn chair and sat down, crossing his legs. Lighting a fresh cigar, he studied its ash for a moment and finally offered, "Hell, you're psychic, Three-Six. That's exactly where you'll be going for the next week or so -- into the Michelin rubber plantation. Watch your step in there, Riley. It's a deadly son of a bitch."

"How so? What's the difference if we chase Charlie through the jungle or the 'rubber?'"

"A lot of difference. You should know by now that Colonel Taylor doesn't understand this kind of war and he knows less about the rubber. He sees these operations as something of a sport, like hunting. The rubber plantation is a better place to hunt. You can see in there." Captain Wiggins flicked the ash of his cigar, and stared at it, thoughtfully.

"You'll go out for a week or more," he continued. "You'll thrash around in the brush and, if you bag a gook or two, he becomes a great success. Larger operations scare him, the jungle scares him. Casualties won't balance out. In fact, I think the whole top command is that way. They're paralyzed by the big fight. Afraid the folks back home won't buy it."

Dennis became uneasy with Captain Wiggins' evaluations. He sensed inherent disloyalty in his commander and he wanted no part of it. He politely excused himself and sought counsel from his Platoon Sergeant, Hanemaulo. Going directly to his tent, he found him sitting on a footlocker, cleaning his pistol. Dennis sat next to him on a canvass cot.

"Hi, Top. Tell me about the rubber," Dennis said.

"I guess I should," Hanemaulo replied, laying down his rags and oil can. He methodically reassembled the weapon as he talked. "Patrolling through that plantation is very dangerous, Lieutenant. The men hate it. Those trees can grow to fifty feet tall ... taller sometimes. The trunks are thicker than a fat lady's ass and the wide leaves block the sun. They have more limbs than an octopus. It's damn near dark all the time, and they can't even see you from a chopper." Hanemaulo worked the slide of his pistol, seemingly preoccupied with its function.

"Come on, Top. How do I operate?" Dennis asked.

"Movement is easy. It's quick -- maybe too quick -- not like the jungle. Keep the men wide apart, watch for mortar fire, mines, booby traps. A man feels real alone in there," he concluded solemnly.

"I'm just getting good in the jungle and they send me into a rubber plantation," Dennis said, lighting a cigarette. "I guess we better get our boys ready. We head in there in the morning. Any luck and we'll get the Colonel some body count."

Sergeant Hanemaulo laid his pistol down and stood, looking squarely at Dennis.

"Sorry, Lieutenant. Not 'we.' I won't be coming with you into the rubber. I'm leaving tomorrow. Use one of the squad leaders as a Platoon Sergeant until a replacement comes in. It's all on you now, but don't worry, the men trust you. They'll do almost anything you say."

Sergeant Hanemaulo gestured with his hand, shaking his finger at Dennis. "That's an awesome amount of power and responsibility, Lieutenant. I'm counting on you to use it right. Good luck, Son. I was proud to serve under you. You've turned into a hell of a good officer."

He smiled, saluted, then shook Dennis' hand. He left the tent and walked briskly toward the Third Platoon living quarters. Dennis never saw him again.

Chapter Fourteen
Death in the Michelin

Spread wide as Hanemaulo had instructed, they entered the rubber the following morning. Passing small groups of civilian workers and little children, Dennis felt comfortable in his surroundings. "No fighting going on with all these civilians around," Dennis said to Sergeant Crawford, now acting as the Platoon Sergeant. "I kind of like it. We can at least move without chopping every inch of the way."

Sergeant Crawford stopped. "Hold it up, L.T. We've got to talk."

Dennis stopped in his tracks. "What?"

"You're too damn easy to please, Sir. I see I've got to 'school' you a little bit. Listen to me. In the jungle, everything is hostile and you can shoot when the hell you feel like it. Here, you have to watch for the rubber workers."

Dennis motioned for Sergeant Crawford to sit on the moist earth beside him. They leaned against one of the tall trees.

"How do you know who is who?" Dennis asked

"I thought you knew. Charlie wears black pajamas, the good guys wear white." Sergeant Crawford snickered, then became serious. "We've got different rules in here, L.T. We ain't in the Hobos."

"What rules?"

"You can only fire when you get fired at. They snipe at us from five hundred yards sometimes, but watch the rubber workers -- how they act. They'll tip you off, every time."

"Tip us off?"

"Yeah. First you see them, then you don't. They disappear all of a sudden; then you know you're about to get your ass waxed. Hell, they're all VC as far as I'm concerned, but you can't kill them 'til they kill you. It's fucking crazy, eh?"

"I'm beginning to think that everything about this war is crazy. Let's move out."

Moving carefully, watching every step for booby traps and mines, each tree for snipers, Dennis stayed busy admonishing his men to stay wide apart. They were nervous with such isolation and naturally drifted toward each other. After several thousand meters of movement, he felt confident that his platoon had adapted to its new surroundings. "They're a well-oiled fighting machine," he boasted to Eddie Runge, his new radio operator. "Hanemaulo would be proud."

Specialist Fourth Class Eddie Runge had recently joined Dennis' command group. He was a stout youth, with curly red hair and a smile that could melt an iceberg. He was about Dennis' height and was friendly and full of wit. Dennis had noticed him during the action in the Hobos. He had been the first to return gunfire, killing the enemy sniper. Eddie hailed from California and talked incessantly about the pretty girls there. "I've got a lot of pretty women waiting on me, Lieutenant. I have to get home in one piece."

"You will, Eddie, I promise. Damn, it's spooky as hell in here."

"This is my third time in the rubber, Three Six. This place will get somebody. Hope it ain't me."

Deep into the rubber they stopped to watch Vietnamese peasants harvesting the dripping sap from the trees. With large knives, they cut diagonal slashes across the bark; this allowed the dark juice to flow into a small bowl that was suspended on a wire girdle.

"They let it drip for a couple of days," Eddie explained. "Then the workers collect the gum. They'll store it and wait for the French plantation owners to come in. It's business as usual for the almighty dollar."

Dennis learned early that the wide trails within the orchards were regularly booby-trapped. The point men frequently halted to show Dennis where the Viet Cong had placed grenades or other explosives in their path.

They stooped to examine one. "They use discarded soft drink cans and attach them to the base of the trees," Sergeant Crawford explained. "Then they tie a thin wire to the grenade, stretch it across the trail, and tack it to a tree, about ankle-high. One of our boys pulls a grenade out of the can as he steps and kaboom, the shit hits the fan."

"How do the workers get around in here?" Dennis asked.

Sergeant Crawford shook his head. "They know where the booby traps are; we don't. I wish I did."

Late on the second day they suffered two serious casualties from such devices. Helping to tend to the wounded, Dennis looked carefully at every tree. Suddenly he realized that the sap collection bowls were turned upside down. "That's it," he shouted. "The booby traps are at the base of the trees where the bowls are turned over. Watch your step."

The patrol moved deeper into the canopied forest and the enterprising men of the Third Platoon, upon finding a booby trap, would upright the adjacent bowl as they passed the device. "This will mess up Charlie Cong real good," Sergeant Crawford said. "He can step on his own damn booby traps now."

Dennis thought it was a good idea, too, and he allowed the men to reverse the bowls, marking the locations on his map to ensure that they would not travel those areas again. Darkness approached, and the platoon vigorously began its defensive preparations, digging foxholes and cutting stout, young, rubber trees for overhead cover. Laid on top of their holes, the trees provided solid protection from incoming mortar rounds. Several layers of sandbags, stacked on top of them, strengthened the fighting emplacements even further. Dennis and Sergeant Crawford stepped back, admiring the work. "Damn good positions. You'd think Hanemaulo was still with us," Sergeant Crawford said.

"In some ways, he still is," Dennis replied.

Colonel Taylor called and announced that he, the Battalion Sergeant Major, and others of his staff would be checking positions within the hour. He requested a guide from the Third Platoon. Dennis obliged by meeting the party himself. Leading them into his platoon area, he was quite satisfied that the men had built excellent fighting positions in the short time they had before darkness completely swallowed them.

In the dim light, Colonel Taylor and his group stepped gingerly from position to position, commenting on the work and rendering advice. Walking alongside of him, Dennis had his first opportunity to see the man up close. He was well over six feet tall, lean and wiry, physically fit. He had removed his helmet for a moment and Dennis noticed his short-cropped silver hair, and deeply set age lines. He waved his arms incessantly as he spoke, and seldom looked at anyone directly. There seemed to be a permanent raspiness in his voice, an irritable grating that bothered Dennis.

Midway through his inspection, he stopped abruptly and exclaimed, "Good God, Lieutenant Riley, have your people been cutting the rubber trees for overhead cover?"

Dennis answered that they were. "I felt that these sturdy trees were the best building materials available, Sir. I didn't see anything wrong with that."

"You idiot, Lieutenant Riley. You'll pay for every one of these trees. Don't you know how valuable they are to the local people? We'll have to make reparations to the owners."

"I'm sorry. I didn't realize, Sir --"

"That's no excuse, Lieutenant. I'll have a statement of charges placed in your records and take the money from your pay. Don't you appreciate the fact that we are guests in this country?"

Colonel Taylor's severe admonition of Dennis continued for a few moments when, suddenly, mortar rounds began exploding all around them. The Colonel and his group dove for cover, squeezing into the holes with the men. Several rounds hit directly in front of the platoon, splintering rubber trees and showering hot shrapnel in every direction. In a few minutes the attack ended; Colonel Taylor emerged from the bunker visibly shaken. Dusting himself off, he nervously asked for a guide to take them to the next unit. "Check for casualties," he mumbled as he and his group hurried away. Dennis did, and found that the trees had done their job. No one had been hurt.

"It was worth the cost, eh, Lieutenant?" Eddie said. "I guess at about a hundred dollars per tree, you ought to have it paid off by the time you make general." They laughed and Eddie produced two cans of warm beer from his pack which they drank in celebration of the event.

Dennis slept well that night, confident that his men were alert and protecting the inner circle. At daylight he was summoned to the Battalion Command Post. A large gathering of officers stood in a semi-circle, watching and listening to Colonel Taylor. Dennis had never seen some of them and he was puzzled. He remembered Sergeant Hanemaulo growing angry when his own men had clustered in groups. "One mortar round will get you all," he had barked.

"Lieutenant Riley, meet your new Company Commander," Colonel Taylor said as Dennis threw him a crisp salute. "This is Captain Herbert Chancey. He's on his second tour of duty; maybe you can learn something from him."

The stocky Captain smiled easily and extended his hand, which Dennis found to be firm and steady. "Heard a lot about you, Lieutenant

Riley," he said. "They say you build a heck of a bunker. We'll do great things together."

Dennis grinned at his inference to the previous evening's events and decided he liked Captain Chancey. *A sense of humor never hurt and at least he doesn't have a big cigar in his mouth.* Dennis instinctively evaluated him: *He looks like a soldier, and he's built like a football player. Guess that's how he got all those bad scars on his wrist and neck.*

"Glad to have you in Alpha Company, Sir. I'll show you around when we get back to the positions."

"You won't be sitting on your duffs today, Riley," Colonel Taylor said. "All units will be sweeping back over the terrain you covered yesterday. Those mortars didn't fall out of the sky; the enemy are in here somewhere and we're going to find them. I'm not very happy with the way my companies have been operating. Maybe Captain Chancey can put some life in Alpha."

Motioning for everyone to squat or to kneel, Colonel Taylor spread his maps. He described a complex scheme, instructing them to search in areas he'd outlined in red. Dennis shuddered when he saw that Alpha Company drew the same area where he'd discovered the booby traps and had taken the casualties. "Never walk back over the same area, at least not from the same direction," Dennis remembered Hanemaulo saying. "The first time through, you kick up the Viet Cong. The second time, he's waiting on you."

Colonel Taylor stood, folding his maps. The others did likewise, preparing to depart to their units. "Not so fast," Colonel Taylor said, "I have more to say. I'm not pleased with the way things went yesterday. We had casualties and nothing to show for it. I'm not very pleased with my staff officers, either. You commanders have been complaining about the poor supply and services you receive. I've got a little something in mind that'll help these officers realize how lucky they are to be on my staff." Gesturing to the covey of silent men behind him, he introduced some of them.

Dennis recognized the Adjutant, the Intelligence and Operations Officers, but hadn't met the Supply Officer before. They stared at their boots as Colonel Taylor continued, "They'll be assigned to the companies today. They'll go with you on operations. Maybe when they get a little taste of what the men have to put up with, they'll become more efficient."

Dennis was appalled. "That's Doctor Ira Mersack back there, our Battalion Surgeon," he whispered to Captain Chancey. "He's a heck of a good man. These guys have no business out here, especially Doc."

"Doctor Mersack and Captain Sommers, our new Supply Officer will go with Alpha Company," Colonel Taylor said. "I'm sure Lieutenant Riley can find something exciting for them to do. Move out in thirty minutes, Chancey. That's all."

Stiff salutes were exchanged. Together the four men walked back to Alpha's positions. "All right, Lieutenant Riley, we're away from the boss now; what's on your mind? Clue me in ... quick," Captain Chancey said.

"Sir, this is Doctor Ira Mersack. Best sawbones that ever pulled shrapnel out of a man's ass. Captain Sommers, I gather you're the Supply Officer? I don't know you, Sir. Did you just arrive?"

"Yesterday," Captain Sommers said somberly. "I'm not an infantrymen, you know. My specialty is motor maintenance. I'm a little concerned --"

"We'll take good care of you, Sir," Dennis said, smiling. "Don't worry."

"What about me? Riley," Doctor Mersack asked, "don't I get protection from the famous bunker builder, too?" He laughed as he shifted his heavy medical kit from one shoulder to the other and adjusted his glasses. He was a thin man, scholarly, and not physically suited to this kind of activity. Dennis noticed that, in spite of his discomfort, he showed a positive attitude.

"Maybe I can do some bunions and warts today," Doctor Mersack said, chuckling. "I was on balls and butts all last week."

"This is my first time out with this outfit, but I'm glad to have you both along," Captain Chancey said. "I think the best thing we can do is listen to Dennis here. He's been over the trail we're going to search today; let's follow his lead."

"Thanks for the vote of confidence, Sir. Yes, I have been over that ground and I'm going to tell you right off, it ain't smart to go back over it again. Charlie's in there with booby traps and mortars. Stay spread out. Doctor, Captain Sommers, stick with me. The Third Platoon will lead the way."

Stepping carefully over the previous day's route, Dennis explained his tactics to each staff officer, hoping it would make them more comfortable. He pointed out possible danger signs and advised them to kneel at each halt in the movement. "Keep a low profile," he said. "Always stay low."

Captain Sommers looked pale and he could barely respond to Dennis' comments. *He's scared to death,* Dennis thought, *but I can't blame him. I'm kind of shaky myself. It smells like wood smoke up ahead.*

Dennis motioned for the column to halt and get down. "Sergeant Crawford, get a team up front and check it out," he ordered. They crouched and waited.

"Three Six, there were Beau Coups VC up here," Sergeant Crawford called over the radio. "They were cooking rice balls and that stinky fish sauce. I can see where they broke brush running ahead of us. We're trailing them, now. Stand by."

Dennis knelt and faced his allies. "We've got company up front, Doc ... Captain Sommers. Both of you stay down. Don't worry, Sergeant Crawford has it in hand."

Dennis reported his activity by radio to Captain Chancey who trailed him with the other platoons. He, in turn, relayed the information to Colonel Taylor. Within minutes, Captain Chancey insisted that they move forward.

"Just like I figured, Eddie," Dennis said, handing his radio operator the receiver. "The Colonel smells a body count. Doesn't matter that we have two noncombatants with us. It just complicates things."

Men began moving at the front of the column and Dennis beckoned to those around him. "OK, we're moving forward, guys. Take one step at a time and keep your eyes open. Here Doc, take my pistol."

"I can't do that, Dennis, but thanks, anyway."

"Three Six, we're hot on their trail," Sergeant Crawford reported. "You behind me?"

"We got you covered."

"Let's go," Dennis said, and, at his signal, the entire platoon stood to advance. Moving only ten or fifteen meters, Dennis spotted the rear guard of Sergeant Crawford's small team and signaled a halt. "We've caught up; hold it here."

He and Eddie knelt automatically, and Doctor Mersack followed their lead. Slow to react, Captain Sommers remained standing. The Company Artillery Forward Observer, a newly-assigned Lieutenant, came alongside of him and they spoke briefly.

In the middle of their handshake, a large Claymore mine, hidden in the underbrush, exploded within a few feet of Dennis. The Artilleryman fell, his body torn by bits of white-hot metal. Doctor Mersack was beside him in a stride. The top of Captain Summers' head bled profusely and he fell backward, screaming in pain. A medic was beside him in seconds, frantically pulling bandages from his bag. "He'll be OK," Doc Johnson yelled. "Doctor Mersack, I need you as soon as you get a chance."

Doc Mersack ran to the side of Captain Sommers, felt his pulse and issued brief instructions to the medic. In four steps he was again kneeling beside the wounded artillery lieutenant. "He's still breathing. He needs plasma," the doctor said in a steady voice. Inserting a needle and tubes into his veins, Doc Mersack worked frantically, pulling medical devices from his bag and injecting fluids. The boy's face turned pale and he began to gasp for air. "We're going to lose him. We need to get him to a hospital."

"They've called for a chopper. Looks bad, eh, Doc?" Dennis asked, kneeling beside him.

Not answering, the doctor felt the wounded man's carotid artery and then started pounding rhythmically on his chest. "Good God, no," he yelled. "His heart has stopped. He's going into shock, Dennis. We'll lose him if we don't get him out."

Kicking and screaming, the young lieutenant's life ebbed from him. Dennis looked at his watch; the boy had lived about five agonizing minutes from the time he had been hit. Doctor Mersack methodically gathered his medical apparatus and carefully placed all of it back into his bag.

"Do you know his name, Dennis?" he asked.

"No. Sorry, Doc."

"Find out for me, OK? I'd like to write his parents."

Dennis knelt beside the body and snatched the dead man's dog tag chain from around his neck. He read one of the metal plates: "Muse, it looks like. Baptist. First name, Jerry. Damn, he never knew what hit him." Inserting one tag between the teeth of the corpse and pressing his jaw shut, Dennis asked aloud, "Damn, why the hell didn't you get down, Jerry?"

Doctor Mersack closed the dead man's eyes, then moved quickly to kneel beside Captain Sommers. His eyes were closed and he appeared to be sleeping. The Doctor checked his pulse and said, "Strong. You did a good job, Johnson. I think he'll make it. Where the hell is that dustoff?"

Doctor Mersack returned to the dead man. Checking his pulse, a useless gesture, he nodded at Dennis as if to confirm again that Lieutenant Muse was officially dead. Dennis noticed moisture in the doctor's eyes and said, "It's all right, Doc, you did your best. You did what you could."

A violent burst of machine gun fire erupted about fifty meters to their front and Dennis recognized it as an American M-60. Leaping to his feet, he screamed to the platoon, "Let's go, you guys. Crow's got contact."

Another platoon, The Fourth, led by Lieutenant John Erby, joined Dennis as they raced forward. John was stripped to the waist and held a heavy machine gun against his hip. "I got the sons of bitches, Dennis. You take care of your wounded. I got these sons of bitches." Crashing through the brush like a wild bull, Lieutenant Erby and his men left Dennis trailing a few meters behind.

Several more bursts of machine gun fire exploded ahead of them. In seconds, Dennis and his men were at Lieutenant Erby's side. Sergeant Crawford looked on. Erby used the muzzle of his machine gun to roll the bodies of two dead Viet Cong, then blew smoke across the top of the barrel.

"Got 'em," he said. "Got 'em goddamn good. How's the Doc and that supply guy -- your other boys?"

"Doc's OK. Captain Sommers might make it," Dennis answered. "Lieutenant Muse is dead. Neither one of them made it a whole day in the field. It's a crying shame. Good work, John. You too, Crow; you made them pay."

"Crow? OK, Lieutenant. Real cool, just call me 'Crow,' from now on."

Dennis' platoon screened the area for more enemy activity, but it appeared that most of the Viet Cong had fled, blowing the Claymore mine as their last act before they departed down familiar trails. The two dead enemy were unlucky "stay-behinds," John Erby observed.

Captain Chancey, stunned at their own losses, worked tirelessly with the men to clear a landing zone. "Bringing those staff officers out here was stupid, just plain stupid. I wonder how the Colonel feels now?" he said bitterly.

"He doesn't feel," Dennis said as he helped to bag Lieutenant Muse's body.

They returned to their bivouac late in the afternoon. Resting against some trees, Captain Chancey told Dennis how, on his previous tour of duty as an American Advisor, his South Vietnamese Army platoon had abandoned him in the jungle. "The Viet Cong ambushed us just before dark. The South Vietnamese ran like hell and never fought back. They left me out there. I took a bullet in my wrist. See here?" He waved his arm and showed Dennis the depth of his ugly scars.

"I played dead while an enemy soldier looted me. He took my wallet and watch, then stuck a bayonet in my neck. Lucky for me, it missed my jugular."

Dennis looked at him, incredulous. "Really, Sir? What happened then?"

"I crawled out after they left me for dead. I swore I'd never get mixed up with another bunch of assholes like that. When I healed, I asked to go back to an American unit. Guess we have idiots on both sides."

"It won't happen this time, Cap'n," Dennis said as they arrived back in their defensive positions. "We hang tough in Alpha Company."

They settled in at Dennis' foxhole, dropping their heavy rucksacks. Opening cans of rations and spooning in the pasty contents of ham and lima beans, they spent the evening getting acquainted.

"Let's keep our powder dry and get these boys home safely," Captain Chancey said while preparing a sleeping position behind a bunker. "It's the least we can do." He immediately fell asleep.

Dennis spent the night in prayer for himself and for his fallen comrades. He had never seen anyone die before and the memory of the young lieutenant's writhing pain had sobered him. In the morning he took out paper and began a letter home. *Dear Mom, today, for the first time, I watched an American soldier die.*

Several more days of patrolling within the rubber produced few results. Another Claymore mine exploded and PFC Jimmy Erickson, a platoon favorite, lost his eyes forever in the blast. A hovering helicopter, nimbly defying the winds, winched him a hundred feet into its cargo bay. As a gesture of character, Jimmy saluted all the way up. His head was swathed in bandages, but his youthful grin poked through. "What a great kid," Dennis said.

"He just turned eighteen today," Eddie Runge replied. "How's that for a lousy fucking birthday present?"

Chapter Fifteen
Nui Ba Den

Word had come that they would be moving soon to Tay Ninh Province where large concentrations of enemy troops were reported to be operating. In late November, the battalion moved back into its base camp, resting and preparing for further operations. Dennis occasionally saw his gang there. They never lost touch and Dennis was very proud of how they had developed as soldiers.

"I've already made Specialist Fourth Class," Wally Gerber boasted to him at a chance meeting one day. "I'm the top gunner in the Company, now, and Jay Cee is an assistant Squad Leader. He's up for promotion, too."

"Great," Dennis said. "I knew you guys would make a name for yourselves."

Wally's voice lowered. "We've seen our share of action, Dennis. Jackie's been wounded. He's OK, though. No sweat."

Dennis cringed at the news, grateful that he was not assigned to Charlie Company or connected to his boys in any official way. He had made it a point not to develop any personal relationships in Alpha Company. At that he had been successful, except for a very worrisome association with Private First Class Charlie Martin.

Captain Wiggins departed without ceremony, wishing Dennis luck. "I'll be home for Christmas. Take care of yourself, Riley," he said, offering a weak handshake as he boarded a jeep to transport him to the airfield.

"You, too, Sir," Dennis replied hoping his excitement didn't show. He was relieved that Captain Wiggins was gone. Captain Herb Chancey had taken full charge of the company. He appeared to Dennis to be a tough leader -- savvy and experienced. He was very familiar with Tay Ninh Province from the time of his first tour of duty. He considered night patrolling to be the key to success there. "There are too many civilians around to conduct daylight operations," he observed. "You've got to get 'em at night, Lieutenant Riley. We move to Tay Ninh tomorrow."

"Right on," Dennis replied.

Nui Ba Den or "The Black Virgin," as she was known in local folklore, was a funnel-shaped mountain, towering some three thousand feet above the lush, fertile valleys of Tay Ninh province. From a distance, it appeared to be an ebony-colored volcano.

"She looks ready to explode," Eddie Runge said during the company's early afternoon approach.

"I've heard a lot about it," Dennis said. "They say the Viet Cong hold the sides of it and we hold the bottom and the top. We're supposed to stay here through Christmas and secure all of the mountain by then. We've lost a lot of good men on those slopes, I've heard."

The column of infantrymen slowed, then halted. "It looks like we're going to set up camp here at the base, Eddie. Captain's waving like mad. Call the Squad Leaders and get them up here. I'm going ahead to see the "Old Man.""

It was already late afternoon when Captain Chancey told Alpha Company that someone would be climbing the slopes of the mountain that night. They had taken bets on who would get the ambush. The Third Platoon won.

Captain Chancey's patrol order was simple and routine: "Skim the upper slopes of Nui Ba Den, establish an ambush and kill anything that moves," he said. "Destroy any captured booty, and bring us a prisoner, if you can. We need up-to-date information about this mountain. Understood?"

Dennis had been mentally planning the patrol and he elected to travel light, with only one day's ration of food, water, and ammunition.

"Your radio communications will remain silent until you have positive contact with the enemy, Riley," Captain Chancey instructed. "Depart just before dark and return no later than first light in the morning. Your mission is to strike at any sign of movement along the numerous trails that randomly crisscross this area."

"Yes Sir, Third platoon can do," Dennis replied, confident in his own abilities and in those of his men. They were the best in Alpha Company and he felt sure that Captain Chancey recognized it.

Hell, this job is simple enough, Dennis thought. *Find the enemy and kill him. It's the kind of mission that leaves no doubt. Too many times before I've had confusing orders. Sometimes it's impossible to explain to the men.*

"Free fire zones," versus restricted territory. Times when you can shoot and times when you can't, as if the war is run on a time clock.

Although he was eager to strike, there remained ample daylight for preparation and Dennis opted not to waste a moment of it. He selected the ablest non-commissioned officers and the most experienced men in the platoon. Master Sergeant Charles Allred, their new Platoon Sergeant, was every bit as good as Hanemaulo. He was a Korean War veteran and his skill and concern for the men were everything Dennis had hoped for in a Platoon Sergeant. They sat on boxes of ammunition and Dennis studied Allred's leathery face as they made plans. He was of average height, gray-headed, and slightly balding. His dark brown eyes were set deep in his head and, looking at the lines on his tanned face, Dennis estimated he was over forty years old.

"Staff Sergeant Crawford comes along," he told Allred. "He's aggressive and skilled in small-unit tactics. Just call him Crow. He insists ... says he doesn't like that "Sergeant" crap. He can be a pain in the ass sometimes, but he's good at what he does."

"We can't go without Specialist Eddie Runge, our communications expert. I want him close to me at all times," Dennis continued.

Sergeant Allred, sitting on a crate of ammunition, wrote into his notebook as Dennis spoke. He chewed his tobacco slowly, then asked: "How many do you want to take out tonight, Sir?"

"We'll need about twenty men -- all tigers. The best-trained, most physically fit, and the most ruthless. We've got plenty of them. Too bad. They were probably nice kids back home."

Sergeant Allred removed his helmet, laid his rifle across his lap, and nodded that he understood. "I'm new here, Lieutenant and Captain Chancey tried to explain the 'rules of engagement' to me. He says shooting before 7:00 p.m. is prohibited. Why is that?"

"I'm not sure," Dennis replied. "It seems to me that South Vietnamese politicians established this protocol in cooperation with, shall I say, American political cronies? It's all gimmicks by the South Vietnamese. Anyway, you can't shoot them before the designated time."

"OK, Lieutenant," Sergeant Allred said. "This is different. In Korea we pulled the trigger anytime we damn well pleased."

Captain Chancey approached them, sat down on a case of ammo, and listened to Dennis explain his plans.

"About the curfew," Captain Chancey said, "I know it's silly, but don't let these restrictions impact negatively on your operation, men. We'd catch hell for it."

Dennis was reminded of Captain DeMatto's suggested throw down weapon. "Yes, Sir," Dennis said, "What time do we use, Eastern Standard? Pacific?"

"My time, Lieutenant," Captain Chancey laughed. "Just don't shoot any 'friendlies,' until after dark." Although they didn't speak of it, everyone knew that, on the slopes of the Nui Ba Den, there were no 'friendlies.'

Sergeant Allred and Dennis checked each man carefully: dog tags, camouflaged faces, ammunition, water, and rations were just a few of the hundreds of things that would determine the success or failure of their patrol. Examining each man from top to bottom, Doc Johnson evaluated their physical condition with a quick medical checkup. He reported a few stiff muscles, some abrasions, boils, and one bad cold.

They rehearsed the plan for movement and the tactical configurations of their ambush. Sergeant Allred forbade the wearing of rings or the carrying of any documents or letters that "might identify us or our unit." He told them to remove all cosmetic scents like shaving lotion or deodorants by thoroughly rinsing before they put on camouflage paint. By 6:30 p.m., he reported to Dennis that he felt they were ready to go. "The whole platoon's looking good, Lieutenant. Everybody's ready. Take your pick."

Together they sat on the trunk of a fallen tree, consuming their evening rations from tins. "We're fat with manpower now, Lieutenant. We've got thirty-five men in the platoon."

Together they selected twenty men for the mission. Dennis orchestrated carefully the mix of soldiers and weapons they would need, leaving those of lesser experience or poor physical condition behind.

"You 'stay-behinds,' come running if we get into trouble," Sergeant Allred directed during their final rehearsal.

Curiosity flashed across PFC Charlie Martin's gentle features when he was told that he would be a part of the reaction force. "Hey, Lieutenant, why are you leaving me back?" he said. "I go where you guys go."

"Not this time, Martin. It's Doc's orders," Dennis answered. "I'm taking only those men who are in good health. Doc says you've got a bad cold. You don't come with us."

By his stern denial, Dennis was really attempting to conceal from the rest of the platoon Martin's recent revelation to him that he was homosexual and had asked to be classified as a Conscientious Objector. It was a lie and Dennis knew it, but he decided to go along with the ploy. *His demeanor suggests that he's gay, and most of the men think he is gay. It's best to let him play this game and get him the hell out of here.*

As an afterthought, Dennis added, jokingly, "Besides, you smell like after-shave, Martin. All the water buffalo in Vietnam will start trailing us." He immediately regretted the tasteless attempt at humor, but Charlie shrugged it off.

"OK, Lieutenant, but it ain't me the buffalo like to follow," he said. "I seen you kissing one once."

The men laughed at Charlie's joke, but Dennis recognized that he was really trying to curry favor with his peers. He hoped they wouldn't question the real reason for Charlie Martin's absence from the patrol.

Dennis was grateful that Captain Chancey had suggested the qualifying rules, advising that a small patrol, comprised of the most experienced and healthy men, would stand the best chance of success. Dennis had been sheltering Charlie even before his request for conscientious objector status. Sergeant Allred had pointed it out to him earlier.

"You're playing favorites, Lieutenant. You can't get close to these boys and still command them," he said. "I noticed how you treat that boy, Martin. Just want to warn you, Sir, it won't work. You'll pay the price later."

Initially, Dennis felt that Sergeant Allred had unfairly judged their relationship, but he knew that his insightful platoon sergeant was right. He had been favoring Charlie, never chastising him for rule violations or putting him in any danger. *Nevertheless, he'll have to stay back on this one,* Dennis concluded.

Hoping that he had adequately covered for Charlie, Dennis turned his attentions to other matters. "I got the point, Lieutenant. Me and First Squad are itching to get moving," Sergeant Crawford boasted.

Crow was on his second tour of duty in Vietnam. He admitted to a subconscious craving for violence and he relished going on dangerous missions. Completely obedient and cooperative when action was imminent, he was equally impossible to deal with during idle times. In garrison, he drank too much, gambled heavily, and sparred or wrestled with anybody he thought might give him a good fight. Win or lose, he always enjoyed it.

His squad loved him, but his superiors described him with caution. "A good soldier," Sergeant Hanemaulo had said of him before he left. "But you'll have to make exceptions for that rascal."

"We'll screen forward of the main body about fifty to one hundred yards," Crow continued. "How fast we move will depend on the vegetation and terrain." Crow knew that his squad would be the first to suffer the full brunt of an enemy ambush should they have the misfortune to be discovered prematurely. True to his character, he eagerly sought that risk.

"Do your men know that you volunteered, Crow?" Sergeant Allred asked.

"Damn right, Sarge. They wouldn't have it any other way."

They assembled into their departure formation. Dennis, checking their gear, felt the anticipation of each man, recognizing the wariness etched upon their faces. Rivulets of sweat poured through their camouflage paint, streaking and smearing it as they constantly mopped their brows. Perspiration glued their jungle fatigues to their skin and they were miserable with the added weight. "We might have heat casualties before we even start out, Sarge," Dennis said. "God, it's hot."

With darkness less than an hour away, they exited the perimeter one by one: grim-faced, tense, Crow's squad in the lead. Eddie Runge, Sergeant Allred, and Dennis watched silently as each man stepped nimbly through the safety paths of the concertina wire and defensive mines.

Staff Sergeant Carl Bankston followed with the second squad, leading the left file and providing flank security. An excellent man for the job, he exuded a calm aura of leadership. His poise in all matters was the source of his men's obvious loyalty toward him. Carl had arrived in Vietnam with Dennis. They trusted each other. "He's cool," the men often said of him, and Dennis agreed.

Sergeant Willie Brown and his Third Squad brought up the rear. This diminutive warrior was the undisputed leader of the Black and other minority soldiers. When introduced to Dennis some months earlier, he described himself as "one-hundred-and-fifty-pounds of rompin', stompin', mean-ass infantry." His choice of words was not at all offensive to Dennis. It was the common vernacular of a foxhole soldier and Dennis had learned to enjoy it.

Sergeant Brown had boundless energy, high self-esteem, and a personality to match. Often hilariously funny, he could turn serious in an instant. "I'm glad we got him," Dennis said to Allred as Willie Brown passed them. "They'd follow him anywhere."

Platoon Sergeant Allred led the rear guard with a machine gun team. Gesturing with a "thumbs up" sign, he left his lieutenant's side, oozing confidence as he slid toward the left file. Allred had been with them only a few weeks but had quickly become the rock of the platoon. The men respected his unique brand of common sense and were in awe of him. Years earlier, he had been awarded the Distinguished Service Cross for heroism in the Korean War.

"The man says he killed thirteen Chinese Communists with an entrenching tool when he ran out of ammo," Crow bragged.

"It was three when he told the story to me, Crow, but if you guys want to believe thirteen, then all the better for him."

Accepting Dennis, a young and unseasoned officer, as his platoon leader without a hint of jealousy, Master Sergeant Allred was completely obedient to Dennis' decisions and offered quiet counsel only when it seemed necessary.

Using prearranged arm and hand signals, Dennis slowed the column long enough to catch up and take his place in front. He joined Crow's point element, but remained far enough back so as not to interfere. With the patrol fully stretched out, they began their difficult climb. Dennis was surprised at the speed of their ascent up the rugged slopes of Nui Ba Den. Unconcerned, he did nothing to slow the movement as he wanted to fix their night ambush position as soon as possible. "We're flying. We'll be there in no time," he quietly remarked to Eddie Runge and Doc Johnson.

With little daylight remaining, Dennis called for a halt. Raising his field glasses, he methodically surveyed the valley below. At a scant distance, still visible through the descending darkness, the tiny village of Sui Da emitted thin whispers of smoke from several cooking fires. Amid the still and humid air, they collected methodically above the valley like a protective shroud.

The area below was a Viet Cong sanctuary and their support elements were the object of this nighttime probe. Ammunition, rice, and cooking oils were regularly backpacked or brought down the mountain by oxen. Small carts were then used to distribute the supplies to the enemy forces hidden there. American units patrolled the mountain incessantly in an effort to stop them.

Tay Ninh province snuggled up against the Cambodian border at the southern end of the Ho Chi Minh trail. Dennis was looking down onto their main supply route, but could see little because of the haze. The patrol had halted, about a third of the way up, to rest and to allow this hasty surveillance. Breathless and always weary, the men were grateful for the short respite.

"There's no hurry. We'll wait until it's almost dark. We need the concealment. Then we'll move out," Dennis said quietly to his small group.

Lingering as long as possible, Dennis watched intently. Soon, mild breezes stirred the smoky clouds below, allowing just a glimpse of an on-going exodus of oxen, wagons, and rice farmers from the fields. They raced against the setting sun, seeking sanctuary anywhere they could find it.

"Nui Ba Den is about to explode and the villagers know it," Dennis said to Eddie. "They expect fighting or shelling soon and they're running like hell to escape it."

"There's only a quarter moon tonight; it'll be up in about thirty minutes," Sergeant Allred said, emerging from a thick stand of tropical plants. "The boys have had a good rest. Let's get going."

The patrol waited patiently for a few more minutes until they were almost completely enveloped by darkness. Then they quietly stood, adjusted their equipment, and stepped into the unknown.

"They know we're here," Dennis whispered. "Pass the word. Tell the point to get their asses moving without us. I want to watch the valley for a few more minutes. We'll catch up." They did as he required. Later, he had trouble overtaking his small group.

Together finally, the patrol surged higher, delighted when movement eased with an unexpected broadening of the path. Danger notwithstanding, Dennis' thoughts strayed chaotically as they climbed. Distracted from the matters at hand, he thought about PFC Charlie Martin. *He's an admitted homosexual and it's not true. He's just trying to get out of combat. Charlie's story about his sexual orientation doesn't bother me as much as his request for Conscientious Objector status. It'll stigmatize him for life if headquarters approves.*

"He's been kind of insubordinate lately," Sergeant Allred explained when Dennis pressed him for advice on the matter. "He fusses about work details, and even fell asleep on guard duty the other night. You're going to have to take some disciplinary measures, Lieutenant."

"How can I, Top? Vietnam is punishment enough. I should have seen it coming that first morning at Dau Tieng. I'll get him transferred out to a garrison unit real soon."

It was totally dark now and Dennis attempted to ease the tension in his small group. He occasionally whispered comments about some minor tactical detail or developing aspect of their plan. He asked Eddie Runge why the riflemen had fastened the looped parts of machine gun ammunition links to the muzzles of their rifles. Into this expedient they had attached their rifle-cleaning rods in much the same manner as pioneer sharpshooters had carried their ramrods. "Is this something I should know about?" he asked.

"Sir, I'll tell you straight up. We've got no faith in this fucking M-16 rifle. Most of them jam after a few shots. You've got to run a ramrod down the barrel to get the old cartridge out.

"I thought so."

"Sergeant Bankston came up with the idea that, if we attached the cleaning rod to the barrel, we'd have it ready when we needed it."

"Good idea." Dennis kept silent on his real feelings about this peculiar invention and the need for it. Infantry soldiers were notoriously creative in arranging special contraptions and remedies. Dennis had once eaten "field-ration-pizza," made from a variety of C-ration entrees and spiced with delicious condiments mailed from home. Each morning he brewed coffee in a tin can, just as America's hoboes had done years before. His heating fuel now was a small ball of composition C-4, a highly explosive plastique. These inventions were commonplace and Dennis marveled at the ingenuity of foot soldiers in the field. He could not, however, concede to the need for fighting men to attach ramming rods to the barrels of their weapons.

"That's why we lost Bunker Hill, Eddie. We had a bad rifle."

"Hell, I thought we won that one."

Taking another break along the trail, Dennis rested against a tree and chatted quietly with Eddie and Doc Johnson. "Back in the early 60s," Dennis explained, "the Army started arming everybody with the M-14 rifle. It's a hell of a good weapon. I couldn't wait until we got it, but they forgot us at the 'top of the world.'"

"Did you ever get it?" Eddie asked, stretching out and resting his head on his rucksack. The gesture relaxed Dennis and he did the same.

"Yeah, in '64. I loved it -- everybody did. It never jams."

"Then why did the Army buy this damn M-16?" Doc Johnson asked. "Not that I am ever going to shoot anyone."

"They said at first it was for Airborne and Ranger units," Dennis answered.

"It's a piece of shit," Eddie grumbled.

Dennis sat up and displayed his own weapon, a twelve-gauge pump shotgun. "Sergeant Hanemaulo told me we're out-gunned in this war."

"Got that right," Eddie said, and they fell silent in their thoughts.

"It's plenty dark enough, L.T.," Eddie whispered. "We'd better get moving."

"Yeah, let's go."

In the blackness, they could scarcely see the man in front of them, yet they moved forward boldly. Suddenly, Dennis sensed hot breath on the side of his face and felt a nudge from Sergeant Allred. "Crow's got movement up front," Allred whispered in Dennis' ear. "Let the point feel it out."

How Sergeant Allred could cipher these things in the dark from his position in the rear of the column mystified Dennis. After a while, he, too, could distinguish several figures crawling forward and to his right. He just assumed that Crow led the way and that he knew the importance of their movement remaining a secret. Dennis held his breath, waiting for some development.

The unnerving silence was broken by a short, muffled gasp, and Dennis knew instinctively that it was the sound of a man dying just a few yards from him. After several minutes, Crow and two other men effort- lessly dragged the garroted corpse before him, where they slammed the body onto the ground. "Been looking all over Southeast Asia for a son-of- a-bitch," Crow said, "and I found him right here on Nui Ba Den." He was high on an adrenaline flow and breathing rapidly.

"Tell me about it, Crow," Dennis said, kneeling beside the body and checking for a pulse. "He's dead."

"He was moving real slow across our front. We walked right up and scared the be-Jesus out of him. He started running. He was carrying what looked like a rifle, but Martin said it was a hoe. I couldn't tell, but after we nailed him, it did turn out to be a hoe. Can you beat that? The damn

VC are night farmers now. Well, this one won't be choppin' no more cotton."

That they might have killed an innocent farmer, racing against the curfew, didn't seem to bother Crow or the others, but it distressed Dennis terribly. It was a criminal offense. He found himself praying that a search of the dead man would reveal his culpability.

Sweating profusely, Dennis dug through the deceased's pockets, looking for evidence of his "crime." Suddenly, Crow's words came back to him and struck like a boxer's uppercut: "But Martin said it was a hoe."

Just a slip of the tongue in all the excitement, I guess. Martin isn't out here. I'd have seen him. Still, I could have missed him in the dark and Crow usually says what he means. Better check just as soon as I finish searching this stiff.

Dennis' frisking of the corpse was almost complete when he discovered a very common-looking notebook beneath the man's shirt. Pulling a poncho over his head to hide the glow, Dennis flicked a lighter. The notebook revealed that the dead man was, indeed, a Viet Cong guerrilla. The crude sketches were obviously maps denoting the many trails that ran the length and breadth of their area of operations. Unit identifications and even the names of local guerrilla leaders were conspicuously cataloged.

"This guy's quite a catch," Dennis informed the group when he came up for air. "He was definitely VC and headed somewhere special when you bagged him. Good work, Crow. Let's hope none of his buddies got away."

Even in the dim light, Dennis could see the relief spread across Crow's face, confirming his suspicion that his bloodthirsty attitude was just a show. He, too, was thankful that the assassination had been within the rules. The notebook had given a hint of the major trails running through the area. If they could recognize them in the dark, the problem of ambush site selection would be relatively simple. Instructing that the body be hidden in the heavy underbrush, Dennis passed the word to move out again.

Crow watched silently as Dennis glided swiftly past each man on his way to the point. The speed and directness of his leader's movement unsettled him. Crow knew where he was headed, and why.

"Halt," Dennis demanded, whispering hotly into the neck of the point man. Charlie Martin froze in the middle of his step and dropped to one knee.

"Good reaction, Martin," he said. "What the hell are you doing out here?"

PFC Martin turned slowly toward Dennis who also knelt. Barely able to see each other, they felt only the humidity of their bodies and, for several seconds they shared a strained silence. Searching for the words that would ease the tension, Dennis finally spoke. "I asked you, Martin, why? What are you doing on this patrol? I told you to stay back with the reaction force. You're complicating the hell out of things. Don't you see how this contradicts your conscientious objector statements?"

"Aw, heck, Sir. I just wanted to help out. Please don't be mad at me."

Dennis' rising anger momentarily left him speechless. Recovering quickly, he bombarded Charlie with questions. "Why did you violate my orders? Does your squad leader know that you are out here? How did you sneak into this patrol?" Dennis was cross-examining him more from his own fury than from genuine concern for Charlie's welfare. Feeling a nudge against his elbow, Dennis reeled and peered into Sergeant Crawford's dark and serious face.

"Don't blame him, Lieutenant," Crow said, clearing his throat. "I told him to come along. I squared it with his squad leader and he didn't seem to mind."

"I don't get it, Crow," Dennis raged. "Why would you violate my instructions? I had good reason to leave him back -- things you don't even know about. I don't need anybody second-guessing me."

Crow paused for a moment, and looked around, scanning the darkness. Feeling no danger at the moment, he spoke openly. "The kid's been catching hell from the other men, Lieutenant. They know he's kind of delicate and they just like to screw with him. Somebody said he's got brown stuff on his nose from having it up your ass. Charlie tried to punch him, but we stopped it. I told him to get his gear and come with us. You know, get him away from the other men."

Dennis moved his face within inches of his favorite squad leader. "I can't accept that, Sergeant. You have no idea why I made him stay behind. You can bet your sweet ass I'll deal with you and him when this patrol is over."

It was a good performance -- an act -- as Dennis found it difficult to scold a man he considered to be one of the best young leaders he had ever met. Out of respect for Crow and his unique fighting abilities, Dennis decided to let the incident pass and to allow his temper to cool.

Turning away, he addressed Martin. "Charlie, you're attached to Sergeant Crawford's squad. Move out and be careful." Talking carelessly about administrative matters, Dennis had almost forgotten that they were in the middle of enemy territory.

They had already wasted too much time, but the operation ran more smoothly for the next half-hour. Dennis grew more preoccupied with Charlie Martin as he pushed through the foliage. *Have I really been patronizing him? Do the others see it? Are they resentful? I guess I have shown him too much favoritism.*

Dennis had to admit he had been coddling Charlie all along, even before his decision to explain his gay inclinations, excusing them because of a letter he'd received from Charlie's mother weeks earlier. In it, she explained his plan to use homosexuality as a means for being removed from combat. She apologized for the deception, but said she loved him, nonetheless, and asked that Dennis help.

"He could never hurt another person," she wrote. "He is too loving a human being." Charlie was unaware of the letter and he continued to pursue his scheme exactly as he'd conceived it. Dennis had burned the letter and mentioned it only to Sergeant Allred. Mulling it over in his mind, he hardly noticed when the patrol started moving again. He flowed along with them, more thoughtful of Mrs. Martin's carefully-written words than he was of his immediate surroundings.

Chapter Sixteen
An Inappropriate Soldier

Mrs. Charlotte Martin
90417 Congressional Dr.
Minneapolis, MN 55431
November 15, 1967

LT. Dennis J. Riley
Co A, 3/22 Infantry
APO San Francisco 96268

Dear Lieutenant Riley,

   I hope that I don't offend you by writing, but I must try to explain my son's peculiar behavior. Charlie has written to me that many of the men in his unit find him lacking in combative skills and somewhat boyish and fragile. Frankly, they say that he is a homosexual. Nothing could be farther from the truth.

   Months ago he wrote to me that, since others believed him to be of such persuasions, he would use it as a means for getting himself discharged from the Army. I am torn between this lie and having my son home. When he received his draft notice, I urged him to seek a deferment on religious grounds. He refused, saying that he would do his duty like the rest of the boys in his high school class, most of whom are now in service. He shipped off to Fort Lewis last summer, where he met you. He told me how you comforted him on his first day in Vietnam.

   I am asking that you report his supposed "deviance" to the proper authorities and thereby have him dismissed from the Army. I was certain that he'd be home by now, anyway. Charlie is not very well suited to what you are doing there in Vietnam, and I don't agree with the war, either. Please help me in this, Lieutenant. I don't know where to turn.

   I don't expect an answer right away because I know how busy you are. I wish only to establish some kinship, as you are so closely connected to Charlie and me. He will do as you say. Please do not tell him of my interference; he would not understand and might just rebel against an early release for him. Thank you for helping my son. Charlie could not hurt another person. He is too loving a human being. Please be careful and take care of each other. May God bless you.

                                        Very Sincerely,

Mrs. Charlotte Martin

Dennis personally didn't care about Charlie's decision. He wasn't the only soldier to have ever used the tag "homosexual" as a way to escape Vietnam or any other war. "I like him as a person, but I'm disappointed that he and his mother have put me in such a compromising position," Dennis explained to Sergeant Allred the evening before. "I need your advice, Sarge."

"He'd make a good 'Duty Soldier': somebody's KP," Sergeant Allred had said. "Get him out of here before someone hurts him. It's his decision; he'll have to live with it later. Let him go."

A firm voice from behind served to snap Dennis out of his preoccupation. It was Sergeant Willie Brown.

"Get down," he said. Dennis automatically followed his lead. "There's a slight rise off to the left. It has kind of a furrow alongside it. It'll make for a good ambush site." Sergeant Brown rolled onto his side and calmly stuffed a huge wad of snuff into his swollen lower lip. He spit dark tobacco juices through his teeth onto the foliage and Dennis grinned at this uncouth symbol of audacity. The moment brought Dennis back to reality. *At least someone is paying attention to the mission; it certainly isn't me.*

Dennis signaled the men into position as the location was truly ideal. The furrow, a deep cut, ran alongside an embankment about two feet high. It offered excellent protection against any incoming small arms. Parallel to the trail, the cut ran alongside of it, then turned sharply left. It would enable them to employ the classic "L"-shaped ambush, if they could only get into position quickly enough. They all smelled and felt the presence of the enemy. "In a minute," Eddie said, "he's going to get a damn good whiff of us."

With Sergeant Allred's help, they placed the riflemen against the staff or the long section of the L, with a pair of machine guns across the base. The gunners understood that they were to fire across the front of the riflemen. Quickly settling in with his command group at the corner of the L, they waited; their own shallow breathing overpowered all other sounds in the jungle.

Barely into position, Dennis watched. Through the shadows, the lead element of a Viet Cong patrol came into view. Dennis guessed that they were the point security for the supply wagons that would certainly follow. The top part of the mountain was more of a plateau and had slopes gentle enough to accommodate the enemy's narrow wagons. They could make it almost to the bottom using their well-hidden trails.

"On my signal," Dennis whispered to Sergeant Allred. "Pass it on."

Whoever they were or whatever their mission, they were poorly disciplined. The lead man carried a lantern, and they chatted loudly amongst themselves. Occasional laughter interrupted the night and the unmistakable aroma of nuoc mam, their disgustingly putrid fish sauce, permeated the air. "Jesus. You really can smell them," Eddie whispered.

Unwittingly, the Viet Cong entered the killing zone. There were about fifteen men in all. Not a muscle moved among the men lying in wait; not a breath was taken.

"In a moment, they'll be completely inside the L. Then we'll open up," Dennis said softly. "We're going to slaughter them."

Suddenly, someone coughed, loudly, and with enough volume to alert and disperse the prey. The cough seemed intentional, like a signal of some sort, and Dennis was furious. Surely, no one would alert the enemy at such a critical point -- it would be suicide. "I've heard that cough before," Eddie said.

Dennis seethed. "Damn it, Martin gave us away. I'll shoot the son-of-a-bitch myself," he yelled out. "What a sorry fix he's got us in."

Trip flares illuminated the night. Gloomily, the Americans watched as the enemy, effectively warned, scattered like bowling pins. Some dived for immediate cover, others slithered into the underbrush, and a few escaped, full-tilt, back up the trail.

The premature disclosure of the ambush ruined any chance for success. Nevertheless, they raked the area with a devastating barrage of fire. Typically, the M-16s malfunctioned and they fell silent, one by one, as the men rammed the barrels. The sturdy and always dependable M-60 machine guns, however, blasted their targets effectively with horrendous bursts of firepower, the gunners creating something respectable out of the fiasco.

Dennis' sense of time merged with the chaos. It stood still for him. The action seemed to take only seconds, yet the engagement lasted for the better part of an hour. "Time is like that in a life-and-death struggle," he remembered Billy Potter saying. "For some it is eternity. For others, it's just an instant." In Dennis' mind, time in battle always stood still and motionless.

Chapter Seventeen
First Casualty

The Viet Cong had escaped while returning just a few scattered and ineffective shots. The action appeared to be over. The enemy, spooked by Charlie Martin's untimely cough, fled in a confused blur and the ambush lost its quarry. Dennis, about to break radio silence and report the action, waited for Sergeant Allred. He was on his belly, crawling toward him with an ammunition and casualty report. "We took no hits, L.T., but we've shot up about a third of our ammo. Looks like we wounded someone, too. Crow crept forward and found some fresh blood on the leaves."

Dennis admired Sergeant Allred's presence of mind, given the disorder that now surrounded them. "Lieutenant, an ambush moves to a more secure location as soon as they're discovered," Sergeant Allred said. "Pull back a couple of hundred yards. The bastards might counterattack."

Dennis considered issuing instructions for withdrawal. This night, however, Colonel Taylor interfered with his plans. By radio, he overrode this common-sense rule, interrupting the conversation between Dennis and Captain Chancey. He insisted that the patrol remain in place and search the area for Viet Cong dead or wounded, even if it meant remaining until daylight. Again, the bizarre need to count bodies as a measure of achievement directed the action. Sensible tactical considerations became insignificant nonsense to leaders secure in their base camps.

"We're stuck here," Dennis told Sergeant Allred, "at least until we can produce a cadaver, real or imagined. Body count is the name of the game. It's the only thing he'll accept."

"The Colonel needs one real bad, huh?"

Dennis could find no sympathy in his heart for Colonel Taylor although everyone knew that his back was against the wall at Headquarters. It had become clear to him that the Division pecking order had been established solely by how many enemy carcasses a commander reported.

Perhaps it wasn't intentional. Maybe it just happened that way, but at Commanders' meetings, those officers with a high number of kills sat conspicuously near the front, wise-cracking with the Division Commander and his deputies. The low achievers, Colonel Taylor among them, sat in the rear and kept their mouths shut.

Dennis, on a recent liaison visit to Division Headquarters, had witnessed a heated disagreement between two senior officers regarding the authenticity of a reported body count. It seemed that some ambitious battalion commander had instructed his men to dig up a Vietnamese graveyard they'd stumbled upon. He then proceeded to declare the contents of the graves as "enemy killed in action." That radio communication, overheard at Headquarters, was too much for even the Division brass hats. It was subsequently ordered that, henceforth, all enemy bodies would be fresh. It was Dennis and members of his platoon who had exhumed the graves, instructed to do so by the insensible Colonel Taylor.

Allred was livid when he heard the Colonel's order. From their prone position behind the berm, he turned to Dennis and fumed. "Jesus Christ, Lieutenant, we just can't sit here. They'll be all around us in a few minutes. Pull back at least a hundred yards."

Through clenched teeth, he pleaded with Dennis to consider his advice and to weigh the danger they faced. Although Dennis agreed with him and knew that the suggestion made good sense, he could not violate his oath of office. To disobey an order was unthinkable to Dennis. "No, Sarge, we'll stay here and do like the bastard says. Sorry."

Sergeant Allred cursed, spat, then nodded that he understood. Dennis watched as he silently wormed his way back to the men. It didn't matter anyway; the enemy began probing the ambush site with small-arms fire just as he and Sergeant Allred finished speaking.

"They're counter-attacking," Eddie Runge shouted, taking aim with his rifle. The patrol was now engulfed with bullets, grenades, and automatic weapons fire from behind and in front of them. High, scattered, and ineffective at first, it soon began to find its mark. Instinctively, the men circled for protection and blindly returned fire into the shadows.

Superior firepower belching from the machine guns managed to limit the penetration. It caused the Viet Cong to abandon the attack as suddenly as it had begun. The patrol suffered two minor flesh wounds in the fracas.

An acrid smell of cordite drifted through the damp jungle air, settling over them as Dennis reported his circumstances to the Battalion Headquarters. Captain Chancey, the usual and proper link between the patrol and battalion, was completely cut out of the communication.

Guardedly reporting the silence that now engulfed them, Dennis waited impatiently for instructions. Colonel Taylor, assuming that the enemy had withdrawn, demanded that a team go forward to search for bodies.

"Get your men at double arms interval, spread out and find those bastards before they cart off their dead," he shouted across the radio. "You bring me a dead VC, Lieutenant. I want a body count, tonight."

Eddie Runge, privy to the ridiculous instructions, mumbled something about having "a real asshole for a boss. The idiot is nuts, L.T. Tell him to get his own body count."

Reluctant to select any one squad for this perilous chore, Dennis ruefully picked Crow and his men. Their position placed them farther forward than any of the others and they could get in there and back quickly. "You go, Crow. Dennis ordered."

"No sweat, Three Six."

Dennis knew full well that Charlie Martin was a member of Crow's squad now, but he didn't feel sorry for him. *It was his choice. It's no accident that he's on this mission. Serves him right.*

Quietly, Crow and his men crept forward into the darkness. Crouching, with weapons at the ready, they resembled a prowling line of humpbacks. Dennis sweated and his stomach convulsed as he waited and watched, haunted by the knowledge that any one of them might not return. He hadn't had a man killed yet in his platoon and he dreaded the moment it might happen.

Crow's squad advanced only a few meters when the ghostly calm was shattered by the unmistakable blast of a concussion weapon. "It's a Claymore mine," Eddie shouted. "Stay down." He was correct. It was, indeed, a large mine, set by the enemy as they made good their escape.

Dennis and the others had learned in the Michelin that these mines were usually fashioned out of discarded basins or kettles, filled with a mixture of plastic explosive, nail fragments, barbed wire, and other bits of ragged metal. They were sometimes triggered by the spring and stylus of a ball point pen or could be detonated remotely by using a trip wire. Regardless of how they were employed, these primitive expedients were as volatile as any commercially-made bombs. They were highly effective instruments of destruction; this one sounded very powerful.

Momentarily stunned by the blast, no one moved. Even the never-ending ruckus of thousands of jungle creatures stopped dead, creating an unrealistic and eerie calm. Too frightened to draw a breath or to move a muscle, the patrol imitated their wise example in anticipation of what would come next. The air finally split with the distinct cry of an injured man. Dennis' flesh shuddered as he anxiously awaited some report. It came, crying through the night in the shrill cries of, "Medic! Medic!" Doc Johnson rushed forward to aid the screaming victim. Meanwhile, Crow arrived at Dennis' side, gasping for breath. "Don't go forward, Sir," he begged with rare emotion. "Please, you don't want to see him."

Dennis knew immediately that he was referring to Charlie Martin. Like a wild animal, Dennis exploded recklessly through the underbrush, focusing exclusively on getting to the wounded man's side. "He'll be OK. Please, God, let him be all right," Dennis wailed.

Chapter Eighteen
Dreadful Journey Home

He could not explain it, but, for a few moments while holding Charlie's lifeless body, he pretended that he never knew him -- that he was just another nameless casualty. Very slowly, he came to accept that Charlie Martin, an innocent and troubled youth, but still his friend, was dead.

"Why him, God?" Dennis asked through tearing eyes. "Why him? Why do you snatch the weakest, the most fragile amongst us for yourself?" Surprising even himself, he openly questioned the Deity with unexpected bitterness. For a moment he hated God, but, succumbing to his religious teachings, anger soon gave way to a sense of shame and then awe: *Who am I to even dare question His great plan? A power greater than mine directs this theater of horror, and I don't have the nerve to provoke Him further.*

Cradling Charlie in his arms, he sat for awhile, rocking him back and forth. It seemed like an infantile and foolish thing to do for an officer -- a commander. *It doesn't matter; the men understand. Somebody's got to love him and show it. Hell, Hanemaulo would have done it.*

The others stood, encircling them while mumbling soft sympathies. "He wasn't no coward, he was a damn good soldier," Sergeant Brown reminded them.

"Yeah, he was OK," Dennis heard another say.

"I'm real sorry, Lieutenant," someone else said.

"We'll take him now," Sergeant Bankston offered, stooping to take the body. "The guys just want to help; they feel like hell. They know he wasn't a faggot."

"Yeah, thanks, Sarge. Glad you see it that way."

"No time to cry for him, Lieutenant," Sergeant Allred said. "We've got work to do; we're surrounded by that enemy patrol we hit and they're hell-bent on revenge. Bury your emotions and let's get with it."

Daylight beckoned. Sergeants Bankston, Brown, Crow, and several other men prepared an improvised gurney, then gently prepared the body for evacuation. Dennis could feel Charlie's eyes watching him as Sergeant

Allred counseled: "The first one's hard, Lieutenant; from there it gets worse. I know, I've carried lots of them off the battlefield. Come on, Son." He lightly jabbed his lieutenant in the ribs as he spoke. "Piss on that Colonel, let's get the hell out of here."

They removed Charlie's clothing to use as canvas for the litter. The men slid stout poles through the legs and arms of the bloody garments, while buttoning and belting them for added strength. In morbid silence, they lifted him from the bug-infested earth and gently placed him upon the bier. A pool of thickening blood, filling with ants and other insects, hummed loudly as they feasted. They would remain for a while as the only mark of Charlie Martin having ever been there. Sergeant Allred beckoned with his rifle and, starting out slowly, the macabre procession moved east through the brush, toward a safer haven.

It was fully dawn now, and they increased their stride, confident that Crow's watchful eyes would guarantee no interruption from the enemy. Establishing a direction for hasty withdrawal, Dennis notified each man to employ escape and evasion tactics -- every man for himself -- if they got hit by a superior force. Crow took no instructions in moving to the point. Assuming he was the best man for the job, he automatically found himself up front, his squad following.

"There's no one better at setting the pace and direction. Crow is an expert," Sergeant Allred remarked as the cortege passed by.

Four men were required to usher the body: Sergeant Bankston, two others, and, from time to time, Dennis and Sergeant Allred. Stumbling and falling under the heavy weight, they sped directly downward from the mountain. Unable to return by the previous route as it had surely been compromised, Dennis decided to "dogleg" into the safety of the company laager, hoping to avoid any further clash with the Viet Cong. "Go due east for about three thousand meters, Crow," Dennis said, "then turn south for the final leg. It might be a mile."

"You got it, Lieutenant."

Their mutual purpose was to get Charlie speedily home; the mission no longer mattered. Racing pell-mell, as if delivering the dead man had been their purpose to begin with, the ambush and its imbecile consequences were evident to all. They were silent, incapable of discussing it. Setting their jaws in collective composure, they raced toward sanctuary, hoping that fatigue or another meeting with the enemy would not slow their pace.

All went well for the first hour and several men insisted on the honor of carrying their dead comrade. Others filed by the litter from time to time to touch him. His body had already begun to turn yellow from the intense midmorning heat and it quickly bloated almost to the point of bursting. Dennis urged the patrol to move even faster, trading caution for speed. "I don't want Charlie's mother to see him like this, Eddie. Once he starts rotting, you can't stop it."

A burst of automatic weapon fire caught Crow full in the face at about ten a.m. and they dumped Charlie's abused body onto the ground, frantically scrambling for cover. Managing to locate Crow's position during a lull in the firing, Dennis was relieved to see him propped against a tree holding his shattered jaw in place. Sergeant Bankston hovered over him, frantically preparing bandages. Sergeant Allred found them and grimly reported that Doc Johnson, who had been walking right alongside of him, had been killed instantly with a bullet through the heart. "I'll miss him," he sighed.

Crow's face was scarlet with rage. Snatching a pen from the pocket of Dennis' fatigue shirt, he began to sketch on his pant leg while holding his bloody jaw in place. In spite of his injury, he took the time to draw the distance to, and the direction of the enemy gun emplacement. With fire in his eyes and vigorous finger jabbing, he urged Dennis and the men forward into the brush. Within moments, Sergeants Carl Bankston and Willie Brown, along with several other men, silenced the gun. They returned with an AK-47 assault rifle and a Viet Cong flag, leaving two enemy dead for the elements.

"Got 'em for you, Crow. Here, want a souvenir?" Sergeant Brown handed him the blue and gold trophy. Crow snatched the enemy flag while holding his jaw tight through the flimsy bandages, his eyes expressing gratitude.

Collecting themselves, their bodies, and their courage, they marched southward once again. Dennis had forgotten Charlie in the confusion of the skirmish and his concern for Crow. He looked behind him, searching to verify that his dead friend and now Doc Johnson were still with them. Dennis was aghast at what he saw: their nearly naked bodies were draped beneath single poles, tied at the wrists and ankles, each of them slung much in the fashion that hunters carry large prey. It disgusted him and he halted the column, inquiring as to why their bodies were being so cruelly treated.

"The litter tore up when we dumped Charlie," Eddie Runge said. "The clothing shredded and his dead weight was ripping the cloth. We've got no choice. Nobody likes it, L.T."

Charlie's filthy buttocks brushed and bumped against the ground as the bearers staggered under the swaying load. The flesh at his wrists and ankles shredded and his weight tested the thongs that tied them, cutting through to exposed bone. His head flopped up and down, back and forth, bouncing grotesquely in rhythm with the stride. Protruding almost out of their sockets, his bulbous eyes proclaimed the agony and fear he felt at the moment of his death. A pinkish sticky saliva oozed from his mouth and dripped across his cheek onto the ground, marking the path with the gooey substance. Dennis stopped, bowing low as the gruesome procession passed by. Despair enveloped all the men as they trudged methodically onward.

Finally breaking clear of the thick foliage, they moved swiftly across rice paddies and farmland, their tormented journey interrupted suddenly by the faint, whooping sounds of an approaching helicopter. "A Huey, a gunship, is moving across our front," Dennis shouted. "Hold it up while I try to call him." He immediately radioed Battalion and asked for her identifying call sign.

"She's a gunship sent out to fly protective cover for us," Dennis announced to the waiting platoon. "Battalion says they can't set down to help us; it against the rules, damn it."

"To hell with the rules, Lieutenant," Sergeant Allred said, glaring at Dennis. "We've got to get Sergeant Crow out of here before he bleeds to death. The platoon is falling apart. They can't take much more. Do something, goddamn it."

It was one of the few times Dennis heard Sergeant Allred raise his voice or curse so vehemently and it did something to him inside. Having obtained the chopper's call sign, Dennis burst into the pilot's headset with a begging message, imploring him to land and retrieve his dead. Moved by their plight, the aviator reluctantly agreed to assess their condition, the landing zone, and the possibility of retrieval.

"Alpha Three Six, this is Stinger Nine Six. We'll try to help you. We've got some water and ammunition that we can kick out to you, but these birds are too heavy to land. We might not make it back out. I've got a crew to think of. We'll take a look."

Relieved, Dennis knew also that landing the chopper would disclose their location and place the aircraft and its crew in jeopardy. With his thoughts only on the dead and wounded, he begged, "Stinger ... please, please try, and thanks anyway if you can't." He looked at Sergeant Allred, shrugged, then both returned to the nursing of their men.

Sergeant Bankston ignited a yellow smoke grenade marking their exact location. Crow, weak from the loss of blood, holding his bloody and bandaged jaw against the unraveling gauze, used his men to encircle and secure the rice paddy as a possible landing site. The pilot artfully descended, hovering a few feet above the ground while his crew dispatched the water and ammunition.

Through the Plexiglas nose of the aircraft, Dennis watched the shock on the pilot's face as he measured their pitiful condition. He saw him close his eyes briefly. Then gently, feeling the surface of an earth beneath him, he landed.

Charlie and Doc Johnson were now being dragged across a stagnant marsh by a covey of extremely exhausted men. Crow, still walking, still leading, reached in frustration with both hands to help them as they neared the bird. His entire lower jaw disappeared forever into the muck. He fell to his knees while others probed desperately for his jaw. Unsuccessful, they gently lifted him from the mud.

The door gunners, realizing the nature of the cargo, waved their arms in protest, yelling above the roar of the rotor blades that the extra weight precluded transporting any casualties. Crow's mangled face with its jaw ripped from it poured blood and he stared helplessly at them. Overwhelmed by his agony, they picked him up and agreed: they would carry Crow, no other wounded, and certainly not the dead.

"We can't do it. We ain't taking your dead," one of them shouted. They promised to speed Crow to a field hospital. "He's dying, I know," a crewman said.

Dennis was frantic and despondent. He could not believe the callousness of such rules. Growing angry at first, then imploring, he insisted that they help his platoon by lightening their burden.

Disconnecting his communications cord, the young aviator leaped out of the aircraft, knee deep into the slime, while his assistant steadied the bird.

"I'm Mike Adkinson," the pilot said, extending his hand. "I know you've been catching hell all day, Lieutenant." He smiled then, and put his hand on Dennis' shoulder. "I feel for you, but, the only way we can fly this bird with your dead and wounded is to kick out everything we have. The door guns, ammo trays, ammunition, everything. Even then we might not make it. These birds are so heavy we sometimes have to bounce them off the runway to get them in the air."

"I didn't know," Dennis said, looking the pilot square in his eyes. "I thought you guys were just being overprotective of your machines. Thanks for taking Crow. Maybe he's got a chance."

The aviator threw up his arms in frustration. "Aw shit, Lieutenant, let me ask the crew."

Only visual words passed between them, yet some understanding occurred. The pilot motioned to the crew and they began discarding ammo trays, metal cans, boxes, and other equipment. Loading Charlie and Doc Johnson, poles and all, they reached for Crow. Waving them off, he crawled on the aircraft, unassisted.

Dennis backed away, catching a glimpse of Sergeant Allred waving the captured AK-47 and Viet Cong flag at the pilot. Yelling his thanks, the aviator snatched them through a side window. In seconds they were away, struggling to gain altitude. Circling and banking, again and again, they increased speed and lift. Dennis chilled, watching the heavily-bandaged Crow attempt a weak salute to the men below as he leaned out of the door of the departing aircraft. They had made it. The mercy flight was gone and he felt alone, as they all did.

"They're some damned fine aviators," Sergeant Brown remarked.

"The crew offered to stay on the ground, and to walk back with us; you can't beat that," Eddie Runge said.

"I only knew gunships from down in the mushroom," Dennis said to several men still milling around. "Stinger Nine-Six, he called himself. He's a hell of a man ... a hell of a crew."

Chapter Nineteen
The Death Tent

Twilight approached and they moved again in a single file: swift but dangerous tactics. Suddenly, Sergeant Bankston and his point man abruptly knelt on one knee and the column froze. "Not again," Dennis moaned, preparing for yet another battle. "Please. Not again." He lost sight of the point for just a moment, then, rejoicing, recognized the men of their reserve forces as they merged with his shattered platoon. "It's O.K., they're our guys. We're home."

After a brief moment of glad-handing all around, they were off again. Dennis estimated that they were only several hundred meters from the safety of the company perimeter. In less than thirty minutes they were all inside the wire, recounting their ugly tale to the gaggle of men that embraced them within their circle.

"Report to Colonel Taylor, Lieutenant," Sergeant Allred said. "He's at the CO's position and he's chomping at the bit. Try to come back with all of your ass."

Hastening across the hundred yards of the perimeter, Dennis arrived at the company command post just in time to hear the terse admonitions of Colonel Taylor as he berated Captain Chancey for his inability to influence the ambush. Dennis saluted, reporting in strict military fashion, attempting to interrupt their heated dialogue. Colonel Taylor did not return the salute; instead, he ceased his harangue of Captain Chancey and turned his wrath on Dennis.

"What the hell do you have to show for yourself, Riley?" he sarcastically asked while jamming his fists onto his hips. "You've lost three men … a dozen wounded, and you have a body count of only three VC. Even scores don't win wars, Lieutenant."

"Three?" Dennis tried to ask.

Colonel Taylor would not allow it. He continued his lecture by explaining the deficiencies of Dennis' tactics and yelled that they would never win the "ball game" the way he had competed. He questioned

Dennis' courage, the breadth of his experience, and the source of his commission, all in one sentence.

Dennis let it pass, however, as he was no longer listening to what Colonel Taylor had to say. In the darkening scene behind him, his nightmare reappeared. Three very stiff bodies were being loaded onto the bed of a canvas-covered cargo truck.

They gently placed the hardened cadavers between boxes of rations and ammunition and Dennis trembled that they would be treated as common commodities. Embittered by the madness of the past twenty-four hours, he could not accept Colonel Taylor's evaluation of their efforts, nor his unjustified lecture on efficiency. In mid-sentence he turned and walked away. In the approaching darkness, Colonel Taylor paid little notice; he simply turned on Captain Chancey anew.

Returning to the platoon, Sergeant Allred told Dennis that Colonel Taylor had ordered the pilot to set the bodies off at the battalion perimeter. "Crow died en route; he bled to death, I'm told," he lamented sadly. "The platoon is beside themselves with grief." He further explained that the captured AK-47 rifle now belonged to Colonel Taylor. "He confiscated it from the pilot by threatening him for violating regulations."

"He'll move up two rows at the next commander's meeting," Willie Brown said, spitting brown juices to emphasize his disgust.

Dennis hadn't accompanied any casualties to the rear before, but he decided to jump aboard the truck and ride the last journey with Charlie, Crow, and Doc. A small group of men waved an understanding farewell as the truck lurched forward.

This is the way Charlie and I began just a few months ago. We were riding along together in that C-130. I never thought it would come to this.

They arrived at Graves Registration near the Brigade Headquarters at about midnight. Charlie had been dead less than twenty-four hours, yet this mangled, bloated corpse looked nothing like Charlie Martin. Rigor mortis had cemented his outstretched arms and legs in Kafkaesque repose, reminding Dennis of a dead cockroach, lying on its back. He shook off the offending thought as the mortuary personnel empathized, assuring him that, after skillful preparation, they would all look quite normal. Refreshing himself with coffee in a nearby mess tent, Dennis tried to consolidate his feelings.

He had not been prepared for the reality of death, especially the deaths of special men, men that he wasn't supposed to love, but did love, whose lives were snuffed out so quickly and unnecessarily.

What is the purpose of it all? Can any man here be my friend? Must I remain in this sickening theater of horrors without ever again knowing the companionship of other human beings? Can I ever again acknowledge and admire the unabashed spirit of men like Charlie and Crow and Doc? Never again. Never, ever again will I allow myself to be ensnared by the baffling sentiments of brotherhood. The consequences of such relationships are disastrous -- the pain too great.

Dennis' eyes filled with tears as he lay his head in his arms and drifted off to sleep. Somewhere in his nightmare he was awakened by a strong but charitable shaking. Lifting his head from the table, he heard the mortician announce, "They're about ready now, Sir."

Each body lay naked, cold and impersonal against the roughness of the concrete floor. Face up, arms tucked neatly against their sides, legs tightly closed: Dennis observed the stiffness of their flesh. He imagined them breaking Charlie's arms and legs to get them straight, but he could see no evidence of it.

Pressed against one another, shoulders and hips touching, their eyes remained opened and he felt them gawking at him. With scrotums shriveled like a child's, their penises were almost nonexistent from the blasts of cold water that had hosed away the waste. Bits of flesh and hair swirled, mixing with pinkish water as the drain devoured its ghoulish meal of blood, bile, tissue, and intestine.

Twisting the nozzle shut, the hose man completed his task. Wiping his hands on his apron, he handed Dennis three large shipping tags and the stub of a pencil, instructing him to print identifications for the dead and to affix the tags to a large toe on each cadaver. An odor of death permeated the humid air inside the tent and he gasped as he knelt at their feet. Only the detached coolness of the hose man enabled him to attend to his ministrations. As he penciled Charlie's name, Dennis examined his friend for the last time.

His peaceful look contradicted the nature of the gaping hole in his upper torso. Looking into it easily confirmed the power of the blast that killed him; minuscule droplets of blood still oozed from the wound. His wrists and ankles were wrapped with gauze, masking the torture of his evacuation. His nostrils were plugged with tiny droplets of water resembling little reservoirs of final tears.

Dennis completed the tags as best he could: Last Name, First Name, Middle Initial. He omitted information that he could not recall: Service Number, Home Address. Finally, the tag asked for the signature of the person making the identification and the cause of death. "Madness. Dennis Riley," he scribbled.

Finished, the hose man frowned as he examined the tags and helped attached them. "I understand, Lieutenant. It's damn tough to see them alive one minute and dead the next. I'll finish the tags and take good care of them."

Saying "Good night," Dennis thanked him for his caring preparations. He backed his way through the tent flap and, sucking in the steamy night air, he stood in silence for a moment, staring into the heavens.

Dennis shouldered his rifle and began a brisk walk back to the tents of Alpha Company. He searched his soul for a prayer that would release him from his grief. His thoughts drifted to his boyhood catechism and the story of Job. Slowly, he accepted that he could never understand what God planned for him. Only an unquestioning, child-like faith in a Supreme Father would allow him to function now.

"That's all I got left," he whispered.

Chapter Twenty
An Intoxicating Night

"Want a beer, Lieutenant?" came a throaty voice from alongside the road. "Might do you some good." The tall figure stepped out of the dark and onto the middle of the roadway, abruptly stopping Dennis' advance. Reaching out, he pressed a cold can of beer against his chest.

Dennis grabbed it. "Thanks, Father Tobin. What are you doing out here in the middle of the night?"

"They tell me the stagecoach of death came riding through your platoon last night, Dennis. Sorry to hear it. We Irish like to wash the dust out of our throats after he passes." Placing his arm around Dennis' shoulder, he turned; together they walked through the night, the priest asking questions about the action and murmuring personal encouragement, blended with his impulsive Irish wit. Dennis inhaled the beer; immediately the Reverend James Tobin produced another from his baggy side pocket.

"Damn, it's cold, Father. Where did you get cold beer?"

"Oh, I pilfered it from the Brigade Officer's Club, Dennis. It's just up the road a bit. Come on with me and we'll drink a toast to your boys."

"OK, Father Jim, but first I've got to admit, I didn't know the Brigade Officers had a club. Is that why we're so screwed up, our leaders are planning strategy over a bottle of rum?"

Father Tobin and Dennis walked down the middle of the dusty road. The priest spoke first. "I was listening to your radio communications today and I know you're feeling bad. I'm so sorry."

"Everything we do is a failure," Dennis replied. "Hell, I do feel like a drink, a lot of them."

"When do you rejoin your platoon, Dennis?"

"The battalion moved up to a fire support base called 'Burt' late this afternoon. Its north of Nui Ba Den. I'm supposed to go out on the first supply chopper tomorrow morning."

"I know you'd like to be with your platoon right now, but tell me about these boys: Martin, Crawford, and Doc Johnson. I anointed them all before you came in. I'd like to write their families."

Dennis respected Father Tobin. He was a tall man, handsome, about thirty-five years old. He had grown dissatisfied with parish life, he told Dennis. "Delivering communion to little old ladies, 'shut-ins,' and then seeing them at bingo on Wednesday nights really pissed me off," he said. "I decided there might be a little more action, maybe a little more honor in the Army."

Dennis found some relief in the priest's company and he felt better talking about Charlie and Doc. He couldn't bear to even think about Sergeant Crawford. He simply avoided it, hoping that Crow's torn face would soon vanish from his thoughts.

In a few minutes, they entered the courtyard of a beautiful French Colonial-style mansion. Dennis had noticed it before, but had never ventured into it.

"So this is where the brass hangs out, eh? Hell, I'd have never guessed it, the sons-of-bitches," Dennis said. "Oops, sorry, Father, but they are."

"Ssshh, Dennis. Now I know you're bitter and would rather be back in the field with your men, but let's put on a happy face in here. Enjoy your night off, don't worry about the men; you'll be back with them before you know it."

Finally releasing his hug on Dennis, the priest nudged him through the Venetian doors; they strode through the haze of cigarette smoke to the bar. It was crowded with many officers, young and old. Dennis noted an American woman sitting in the company of several higher-ranking men. She was a commanding presence, older, but still stunningly beautiful. Holding her cigarette high, she laughed with abandonment at something someone said.

"Must be a Red Cross worker judging from her uniform," Dennis commented to Father Tobin.

"No, Dennis, that's the Brigade Commander's wife. He dresses her in those uniforms to make it appear that she's in some official capacity. I'm surprised to see her tonight. Colonel Davison parks her here when he's involved."

"No kidding?"

Several warrant officers and young lieutenants sat at other tables, sporting aviator wings on their flight suits. They drank from bottles of what appeared to be fine Scotch whiskey and they were loud and boisterous. Every word spoken created instant hilarity and Dennis ached inside. He couldn't comprehend how any man could sit in here and booze it up, having fun, while good men lay cold and stiff just a few hundred yards away.

"They're pilots from the aviation units, Dennis," Father Tobin said, twirling around on his stool to look at them. "They come in here often to play and party. They live in constant danger, just like you and your men. They deserve to blow off some steam once in a while."

"What you gentlemen having?" came a soft feminine voice from behind the bar. "Hi, Father Jim. See you got another soldier-boy friend tonight. He go for fly ride, too?"

Dennis turned toward the bar. His mouth fell open when he saw her. He hadn't seen a woman that close up in months and this girl was striking in her beauty. She was obviously descended of French Vietnamese parents. *About nineteen or twenty years old. She's beautiful. Damn, what I wouldn't give...*

"Oh, Miss Chi, meet Lieutenant Riley," Father Tobin said. "Yes, he's my good friend and he's had a hard day. He needs a drink. What will you have, Dennis: Bourbon, Scotch?"

"I'll have a Miss Chi. She Polish by any chance? Aw, hell, Padre. I'll have a bourbon and water. A weak one, please. I'm already buzzing from the beer."

"Oh, goodness, Dennis, one will never do. You look like you could use several dozen." The priest laughed, throwing back his head. "Anyway, they close this bar in twenty minutes, but they won't toss you out as long as you still have a drink. We'll have thirty stiff bourbon and waters, Miss Chi. Put it on the Bishop's tab."

"Thirty bourbon and waters; who the hell is going to drink thirty?"

"We are, my friend, and some of our other friends, too. I didn't take a vow of sobriety, Dennis, just chastity, and looking at Miss Chi, I'm wondering if I did the right thing."

"You sure you're a priest?"

"Drink up, Dennis, and then tell me more about your fight on the mountain. I know your boys would like to have a drink about now, but they're stuck out there without you so you have a drink for each of them. How's that sound?"

"Great Padre, just fucking great." Dennis reached for his first drink from the dozen or more that Miss Chi quickly prepared. She delivered them with a knowing smile behind her black eyes. Tapping his glass against Father Tobin's, Dennis exclaimed, "Here's to Charlie Martin." He swallowed the drink in one gulp, coughed, and reached for another. He didn't notice that Father Tobin, although he had raised his glass, declined to imbibe.

"Here's to Doc Johnson, a fine medic," the priest answered as he raised another glass in a toast. Again, he pretended to drink; instead, he placed the glass in front of Dennis.

"To Doc," came the booming chorus of many voices. Startled, Dennis noticed that many of the pilots had joined in. Several elbowed their way forward to the bar. An assembling crowd now surrounded him.

"To the Stingers, the Hornets, the Black Widows, and all the pilots in the sky," someone yelled. "Here's to them that are sticking in the fucking ground," shouted a pudgy warrant officer.

"Hot Steel," bellowed the priest

"To Crow and the Third Platoon," Dennis replied.

"To Crow and the Third Platoon," echoed the chorus of drinkers. They raised their glasses and drank. Father Tobin chuckled.

Dennis' eyes began to mist and he swallowed hard. His head began to spin. Waves of emotion swept over him as Father Tobin led the toasts and the crowd moved closer, embracing him in their circle. Even Miss Chi and the Brigade Commander's wife with her entourage joined in. Dennis felt something pass from deep within him.

"Thank you all, thank you," he sobbed, tears running freely down his cheeks. He laid his head on the bar.

"You belong back with your platoon, Dennis," Father Tobin whispered close to his ear. "They need you tonight, not when some supply chopper goes in. We can get you out there. Are you man enough to go?"

Dennis' mind was in a fog and spinning faster and faster. He was thoroughly inebriated from the drinks and fatigued from the release of emotion. Dennis snapped his head upright, smiling. "Yeah, I'll go. Damn right. How's we gonna do it, Padre?"

"These pilots are good friends of mine; they'll take you back out to-night. You're sure?"

"You mean right free-kun now?"

"Yes, right free-kun now."

"All rye, damn it," Dennis slurred. "Lemme pour a couple of them bourbons in a tall gla-a-ass and let's gee the hell out of here." Turning to face the crowd, he bellowed loudly, "Who's got the balls to take me out to the Black Virgin to-nigh?"

"Any of us will, Lieutenant, if you can tell us where your unit is located," the stocky aviator said, putting his arm around Dennis. He laughed as he spoke: "Padre here buys the drinks and we fly his cargo. You'll be the third man he's sent out this month. He's a clever devil, our Father Jim. He gets 'em drunk and sends them back to their Companies -- not always at night, though."

"I ain't drunk," Dennis said, gripping his drink tighter and holding it against his chest. "You boys know where Fire Support Base Burt are ... is? Cambodian border ... don't know where zactly. Anyway, with Padre Tobin along, we'll fly like angels." Dennis waved his arms. "Ain't no fuckin problem, eh?" He gulped more of his drink, refilled it, and held on tight.

"OK, Grunt, let's go," the pudgy aviator shouted as he and another man steered him toward the door. Father Tobin led the way and the crowd clapped and cheered their approval as the gaggle danced through the narrow doorway into the black night.

The men helped him into the back seat of a jeep and, very noisily, Dennis, Father Tobin, and the two pilots drove without lights toward the airfield about a half-mile away. Dennis closed his eyes. His head spun faster while he tried to think of making love to Miss Chi. He felt like vomiting, but his pride and the cool wind prevented him from doing so. In minutes, they were alongside rows of parked helicopters.

"Be quiet," whispered one of the pilots. "We don't want the guards to see us."

"What the hell they gonna do, send us to Vietnam?" Dennis giggled.

The pilots crept stealthily among the aircraft. Dennis stumbled and fell several times, but somehow managed to keep up. They stopped at a helicopter with a huge spider painted on the front. "We're the Black Widows," explained one of the aviators. "We make widows out of the VCs' old ladies. Jump in," he chuckled, grabbing Dennis' shirt as he slid open the side door.

Dennis complied as nimbly as he could, careful not to spill any of his drink. Settling into a passenger seat, he fastened his safety belt as the big rotors began to turn. The aircraft rocked rhythmically as they gained momentum and orange lights illuminated the dashboard, casting an eerie glow throughout the cabin. The enormity of what they were about to do suddenly overwhelmed Dennis and he began to return to his senses.

Christ, what have I done now? These guys aren't authorized to take this bird up in the middle of the night. They're as drunk as I am, if not worse. I've got to call a halt to this foolishness. Unbuckling his seatbelt and yelling at the pilots to shut it down, he stopped when Father Tobin stuck his head and shoulders in the door and bellowed, "Good luck, Dennis. Your boys will be glad to see you. Don't worry, I've blessed this ship and the crew and you won't have any trouble. Take her up and away, boys."

The pilots waved, grasped their control sticks and powered the bird almost straight up. Dennis gasped and shouted, "Hey, the son of a bitch ain't coming with us?"

"He never does," came the laughing answer.

Climbing to several thousand feet, the chopper raced at maximum speed toward the dense jungles northwest of Dau Tieng. Dennis hung his head out of the door, allowing the stiff winds to sober him. In the moonlight he surveyed the land below. Lights were flashing at distant points and he assumed they were artillery splashes. Parachuting flares confused him and red tracer bullets ricocheted in many directions, bringing home the shear folly of his act.

Dennis realized that he was flying with two slightly inebriated aviators, a couple of thousand feet above the most treacherous territory in the world. None of them had any idea where they were going or how to get there. The aircraft would probably be registered as stolen, but it was too late to do anything about it. "Damn you, Father Tobin," he shouted into the wind.

"Put on the headset," one of the pilots yelled and motioned to him to hook up his communications cord. Complying, Dennis heard him say, "We think we're right over your Battalion. We're catching hell from the tower at Dau Tieng. You still want to go in? What do you say, Riley?"

"Put me down, guys. I'll take my chances with the Viet Cong."

"OK. Bub, we'll hover for a few seconds as low as we can. Jump when I say, 'Go.'"

Instantly, the aircraft sped earthward. Dennis shouldered his ruck-sack, grasped his rifle and other gear, then stood in the door, waiting for an opportunity to jump. At about thirty-feet and descending, he could detect tall grasses and reeds bending in the wind. Without hesitation he jumped, falling rapidly into a warm, grassy swamp. Landing unhurt, he began the task of extracting himself from the muck and water, inching slowly forward while he regained his night vision.

The noise and prop wash from the chopper soon faded. They circled once as they climbed and raced back to Dau Tieng. An awesome silence engulfed Dennis and he paused to catch his breath: *I'm in the middle of nowhere -- outside the perimeter -- still half drunk. I'll probably get shot by my own men. Maybe a snake will get me.* "Aw, fuck it."

It was then he realized that he still had the glass of bourbon in his right hand. He had spilled only a small amount in the jump. He threw the glass into the weeds, took a westward bearing, and began moving swiftly as he shouted, "Hey anybody, can you hear me? It's me, Dennis-the lieu-tenant-Riley."

An uncanny silence echoed from the woodline before him. Dennis tried again.

"Joe Dimaggio. New York Yankees." *I saw it in a movie, once. Hope it works for me.* "Hey everybody, this is Joe Dimaggio, Willie Mays, Al Ka-line," he bellowed into the night.

"Shut the hell up, GI," came a angry voice from the darkness. "You'll tell every Zipperhead in Vietnam where we are. Are you that crazy Lieu-tenant? The whole Battalion is looking for you."

"Yeah, that's me. L-e-u-t-i-n-i-n-t fucking Riley. And who the hell are you?"

"We're the listening post from Charlie Company. Come closer. Real slow-like, man ... so's we can make you out."

Dennis complied, moving cautiously toward the voices, his rifle at the ready. Still drunk, but sobering fast, he knew that these men had their fingers on triggers, too. Staggering and stumbling, he tripped over a root and fell headlong into their position. His faced caked with mud, he rolled over and grinned. "Damn, if it ain't Jackie Stoner and Andy Crammer. I'm died and gone to heaven. God, am I glad to see you guys."

"Lieutenant Riley. We knew it had to be you, you crazy nut," Jackie said. "The Battalion Commander has patrols all over the place trying to pick you up. That chopper woke a whole Viet Cong regiment. They just had a firefight over in Bravo Company."

"Oh, hell. Sorry 'bout that."

Andy helped Dennis up. "Word is that anyone who finds you is supposed to cut off your head and deliver it to the Colonel. Wait 'til the guys hear. Oh, sorry, should've asked first. You OK? Dennis?"

"Yeah, I'm OK," he said, finally standing. "I got smashed. So the Old Man is pissed, eh?"

Andy held his arm and steadied him. "He said to bring you into Alpha's position and he'd see you in the morning. We'd better get moving. You know you're so drunk you can't even spell Lieutenant?" Andy laughed and handed him over to Jackie.

"Let's go," Dennis said, "and fuck the facing music."

They helped him arrange his gear and led the way over freshly-cut paths back into Alpha Company's positions. They cleared passwords along the way and many men spoke cheerfully to Dennis as he passed their positions in the dark. Apparently, there had been a full alert. "Everyone's looking for me? I'm honored," Dennis said.

"Way to go, Lieutenant," someone called out.

"Thankee much, man. I'm really glad to be here."

"Good luck," said another as he stretched to pat him on the shoulder.

Dennis stopped abruptly. "I've screwed up guys, but I feel good. Thanks for finding me."

"Fuck it; it don't mean nothin'," a familiar voice called out.

Within minutes Dennis was reunited with his Platoon Sergeant and radio operator. Sergeant Allred frowned, but quietly welcomed him. "Thanks for coming back so quickly," he said, handing him a steaming hot tin of coffee. "The men appreciate it. They know why you came back the way you did, Lieutenant."

"I screwed up, Top."

"Yeah, and you know your ass is in a sling at Battalion Headquarters. Colonel Taylor is a stark raving maniac. Heard you stole a helicopter at gunpoint, forced two pilots to fly you in here. Is that true, Lieutenant Riley?"

Dennis laughed. "Aw, hell no. They're as drunk as me. Father Tobin cooked it up. They're trying to save their own skins. What the hell, it was a great ride."

Dennis stumbled and fell on his face in the dirt. Sergeant Allred turned him over and placed a log beneath his head. He squatted beside him and watched over his Lieutenant throughout the night, awakening him at first light. Dennis' head banged and his thirst was unquenchable. "I'll have two aspirin and a Bloody Mary," Dennis groaned when Allred asked if he could get him anything.

"Time to head over to Battalion, L.T.," Sergeant Allred said, chuckling. "Here, have some coffee. Wake up, now. Throw some water on your face. Lord, you look like hell.

"Feel like hell, too."

"Good luck with the Old Man. By the way, don't be too disrespectful with him. I don't think the Colonel is that mad at you. I've heard rumors during the night."

"Yeah. Damn, whatever possessed me to drink all that whiskey?" Dennis shook his head, grabbed his rifle, and started walking.

Chapter Twenty-One
Fire Support Base Burt

Dennis brushed the dirt from his clothes and tried to straighten his uniform as he ambled slowly toward the Battalion Command Post. He found Colonel Taylor and his staff sitting around an early morning cooking fire, preparing coffee in tins.

"Lieutenant Riley reports, Sir," he said, throwing a crisp salute from the position of attention. "You wanted to see me?" The staff officers and other commanders assembled there could hardly choke back their excitement as they waited for the Colonel's rebuke. They stood in unison as Dennis arrived. He was, obviously, the entertainment for the day.

Colonel Taylor's back was to him. He ate from a can of rations and questioned Dennis between mouthfuls. "Stand easy, Lieutenant Riley," Colonel Taylor began. "First question: did you pirate that helicopter at gunpoint? Yes or no? I want straight answers."

"No, Sir."

"Did Father Tobin have anything to do with your damn stupid introduction into this perimeter last night?"

"Well, ah ... yes, as a matter of fact I believe the good Father did come up with the idea. We had a couple of --"

The Colonel threw down his tin, wiped his hands on a cloth, and turned to face Dennis. He jabbed his finger at him and said, "I said I wanted straight answers, Lieutenant. I don't want to listen to your bull. You realize that you compromised the safety of every man in this battalion by bringing that chopper in here?"

"Yes, Sir."

"Hell, we had an action in Bravo Company sector just minutes after you arrived. The Viet Cong are all around us here. As for Tobin, that rascal. He has very little understanding about how we run things in the Army. He'll ruin your career, Riley."

"I figured I didn't have much of a career left," Dennis answered with uncommon bravado.

"Well, Lieutenant," Colonel Taylor said, putting his hands on his hips. "Actually, what you did was a case of real bad judgment, real bad. Yet, I can't fault your initiative. I like your spunk. I hear your men are glad to have you back. You're damn lucky you didn't get shot by one of them."

"Thank you, Sir. I won't do it again."

"Damn right you won't. I'm not disposed to thrash you as harshly as you deserve, though. Captain DeMatto here seems to be an admirer of yours. Says you lend a little interest to an otherwise dull evening. Yes, I like that in my officers."

"Yes, Sir."

"Nevertheless, young man, you'll have to pay the price for your indiscretions. I intend to punish you by --"

A massive explosion erupting from high in the trees behind them silenced Colonel Taylor. The group scattered like cattle under a bolt of lightning. Thick black smoke rolled across the perimeter and, standing alone, Dennis watched the throng of officers dive for cover. Colonel Taylor was buried beneath the cowering torsos of half a dozen men. Leaves, tree limbs, dirt, and debris covered the writhing mass. Several bullets ricocheted ineffectively above and around them, none finding a mark.

"Get a unit out there," Captain DeMatto shouted, looking fearfully at Dennis from a low spot in the earth.

Dennis grinned as he raced to comply. He knew that the Viet Cong who had blown the mine was far away, giving him an unexpected chance to be dismissed. *Fools don't know much about Claymore mines. It scared the crap out of them. I wonder what the Colonel had in mind for me?*

Captain Chancey had half of Alpha Company behind him as he passed Dennis, running toward the Battalion Command Post. "What the hell was that?" he asked.

"Just a Claymore. It didn't look like anybody got hurt."

"We'll check it out. Three Six, go back to your platoon. Wait for me there."

Dennis rested most of the day. Captain Chancey gathered his leaders in the early afternoon and presented a detailed analysis of their activities. Dennis was dismayed at the scenario he drew. "Listen to me good, boys," Captain Chancey began. "We're in the middle of a cease-fire with the

North Vietnamese. They're calling it a 'New Year's truce.' We've had it easy lately, except for that mess Riley got into on the mountain."

"A truce?" Lieutenant Erby said. "What the hell for?"

Captain Chancey motioned for them to sit. He looked grim as he spoke. "1968 is upon us, boys. There are going to be more 'cease-fires.' In February, we'll have 'Tet.' It's the Vietnamese New Year. A big holiday. Washington seems to think that, if we stop the bombing of the North and pull back in, they'll negotiate an end to this war. Maybe this year will bring peace. I don't know."

"Hope it works," Dennis commented.

Captain Chancey frowned. "I don't know about politics, men, but I do know this: we're about ten to twelve kilometers from the Cambodian border, a bad place to be."

"How's that, Sir?" Erby asked

"I've been here before."

"Why are we here now?" Sergeant Allred said.

"We've got a very serious mission," Captain Chancey said. "We'll use the lull in the action to build an artillery fire support base here alongside this road. Two other bases are being built to our west and north. That's all we can do, according to the rules of the cease-fire. Defensive ambush patrols will operate at night, but we can't initiate any offensive action."

Captain Chancey removed his steel helmet and ran his fingers through his hair. Startled by the roaring sounds of armored vehicles approaching, he said, "Sounds like armored personnel carriers. They're from the 2nd Battalion, 'Fullback.'"

"All right, now," John Erby exclaimed. "Armor ... fifty calibers."

"Be glad they're finally arriving," Captain Chancey said. "It won't be long and you'll be hearing artillery pieces and other heavy shooters rolling in." He rose from his perch and knelt. Using a twig, he began to trace in the dirt. The men either squatted or knelt, facing him.

"Look here, I want to show y'all something," Captain Chancey began. "This dirt road we're sitting along runs north and south. It's main road number 244. It's only ten clicks to Cambodia. This might look like any old dirt road in the middle of nowhere, but don't be fooled. It's the main supply route into War Zone C. Take a look."

Captain Chancey waved an arm and beckoned them to look at the road. "Look at it real good. It's beaten down. Right here in the middle of a jungle. How do you think it got that way?"

No one answered in deference to Captain Chancey's mood. He made the moment even more solemn as he continued. "We'll be arranged in an oval in this clearing; get ready for a good fight." He then drew a large, egg-shaped diagram with his stick, poking at it as he issued his orders.

"We'll take the right side. Set up positions east of the road. The boys from the mechanized unit will be on the west side of it. A Battery from the 3rd Battalion, 13th Artillery will set up here. They're self-propelled ... on tracks. To the south, but still inside the perimeter, we have A and C Batteries of the 2nd Battalion, 77th Field Artillery. They have about a dozen 105 MM Howitzers. Even the Brigade Commander's going to be with us for once."

"Oh, he's sent his old lady back to Saigon?" Lieutenant Erby asked. Laughter erupted and Dennis realized that he wasn't the only one privy to Colonel Davison's special lifestyle. Captain Chancey waved his stick and frowned, immediately halting their petty behavior.

"Get serious, men. I don't have any special knowledge about where the enemy is or what he's up to, but let me tell you this: about one year ago, at almost exactly this same spot, my South Vietnamese Ranger platoon was wiped out. I was shot up pretty bad and barely managed to escape. We might just step on some of their bones walking around here." Captain Chancey paused, sketched methodically with his stick; the junior leaders, recognizing his moody temperament, waited.

"So this is where it happened, Sir?" Dennis stated.

"Yeah. The North Vietnamese 9th Division flat out owns this place. It has for years, and I respect those bastards -- you will too. I can't say why, but I feel ... I just know that something big is cooking."

"Same-o, same-o," Sergeant Allred agreed. "I feel it in my bones."

"This is the stompin' ground of the 271st and 272nd NVA Regiments from the 9th," Captain Chancey said. "They ain't gonna let us take their road without a fight."

The sound of a distant explosion filled the air and they stood simultaneously, making ready. "It came from the south, along the road," Sergeant Allred said. "That's 'Fullback;' he probably hit a mine. Those damned tin cans ain't nothin' but coffins."

Captain Chancey's radio squawked and he grasped the handset, listening for a few seconds. "It's started. They just lost an armored personnel carrier and a couple of men. One KIA."

"Jesus, I've got friends in that outfit," Erby said.

"Enough talk," Captain Chancey said, waving his hand for silence. "We'll hold the northeast piece of the pie. Dennis, your Third Platoon will have the left flank and I want you looking north and east. Make physical contact with those APCs from Fullback. Bravo Company has the middle, but they'll send a platoon to the top and plug any gaps between us and the mechanized infantry. Link up with them, too. Charlie Company is facing east and south. They'll tie-in with a mechanized platoon, too. Now let me show you where the artillery will be spotted."

Spending a few minutes describing and marking the locations of artillery and other armaments, Captain Chancey's drawing took on the essence of a master battle plan. Dennis was awed by his mastery of tactics, but more by his keen insights. "He ought to be at the Pentagon," Dennis whispered to Lieutenant Erby. "We'd be out of this war in a couple of weeks if he were in charge."

Captain Chancey erased his artwork with a few strokes of his boot. "One last thing. There's been too much talk about this truce. Cease-fire my ass; don't you believe it. Get your men in the mood for a fight. Have them dig deep, build solid positions, double the ammo and trip flares and booby traps ... everything. Each platoon will send out ambushes. Dennis, Third Platoon goes out at 1830 hours."

Captain Chancey assigned daylight and nighttime patrols to each platoon and issued further instructions. He stretched his wrist as if to ease the pain in his old wound, then asked: "Questions? None? OK, gents, it's the first day of January. Happy fucking New Year. Now let's break up this mob and get to work."

"I'll take the patrol, Lieutenant," Sergeant Allred said, grabbing Dennis by the arm as they walked. "You better stay with the men tonight."

"Why do you want to do that, Top?"

"Ah, I just have a feeling about this place. I think you need to be inside the perimeter, supervising the preparations. I think maybe they're going to need you tonight."

"Whatever you want, Top."

Dennis and Sergeant Allred trooped their line and were astonished at the pace of activity. Men were shoveling dirt high into the air out of deep foxholes while others stacked logs across them. Sandbags were being filled, and communication paths had already been cut. The men were placing many times the usual number of Claymore mines, trip flares, and booby traps to their front. "You don't have to tell these boys much, Lieutenant; they know something big is up," Sergeant Allred observed.

Dennis ambled across the road and met the platoon leader of the mechanized unit. They discussed positions and tactics, but were soon interrupted by the snapping of limbs and the rustle of brush. "Don't get excited," the Lieutenant said. "That's just our Colonel, 'Fullback Six.' He always comes-a-callin'; he likes to check each position himself. He's a hell of a good guy, but he don't know much about being quiet."

"Hell of a good guy?" Dennis replied. "I've never heard anyone talk about a colonel that way, considering my boss. I'm getting the hell out of here. See you later." Dennis waved, turned, and started to walk away.

"Hold it up, Lieutenant Riley," a strong but kindly voice demanded. Dennis froze in his tracks.

Obediently turning around, he stood reverently as a tall, lanky Lieutenant Colonel of Infantry approached him. The bevy of men accompanying him stopped and let him continue on alone. Dennis extended his hand. The Colonel reached and drew Dennis to him in a mighty bear hug and held him for a few moments. "Good to see you, Riley," Colonel Norris said. "Still chasing those Polish girls?"

"Good to see you too, Sir. My God, I never thought I'd see Major Norris out here in this jungle. You remember my passion for Polish women, huh? Jeez, what in the world are you doing out here?"

"It's Lieutenant Colonel now, Riley. I'm on my second tour of duty. I got lucky and got a command, the 2nd of the 22nd Mechanized Infantry. They're a great group of men."

Holding onto Dennis by the arm, Colonel Norris turned him toward the others. "Let me introduce my Charlie Company Commander and his Lieutenant. Boys, meet Sergeant ... Oops, I mean Lieutenant Riley. Sent him to OCS."

Colonel Norris grinned widely as he released Dennis' arm. "I've been hearing great things about you, Riley. I'm mighty proud."

Dennis was too stunned to talk intelligibly. "Aw, shoot, Sir, my boss doesn't think I'm so hot. Imagine, seeing you way out here?"

"It's not so strange. All good infantrymen eventually go to the 22nd Infantry Regiment," Colonel Norris beamed. "Let me introduce my boys: this is Captain Bill Allison, 'Wild Bill,' we call him." The colonel pointed at a physically fit, very composed captain of infantry. He stared at Dennis for a moment, then grinned and waved.

"And this is Gordon Kelly, one of his Platoon Leaders." Lieutenant Kelly offered his hand. "It's nice to meet you, Riley. Welcome to Vietnam."

"I've been lucky, Riley," Colonel Norris bragged as Dennis smiled and shook hands with everyone. "I've got the best damn men in Vietnam working for me." He looked kindly at his subordinates, then draped a long arm across Dennis' shoulder.

Dennis beamed.

"You say Harry doesn't think you're so hot?" Colonel Norris asked. "Oh, yes, he does, Riley. I know Harry from way back. He tells me good things about you." He faced Dennis. "But, if you're unhappy here, Son, how'd you like to join my outfit?"

"Watch out, Riley," Captain Allison said. "Grandpa will sucker you into the Second Battalion in a heartbeat."

The three of them laughed heartily and Dennis watched the mutual affection pass between them. *Hell, they're a club. They love the man. I wish Colonel Taylor had some of his charm.*

"Let's go troop your line, Riley," Colonel Norris said. "We'll see what you got. Then you come over to my Battalion; it'll be good to have the big picture."

Dennis readily agreed, happy to be in the company of such gracious men. "I was getting down in the dumps, Sir. You guys kind of perked me up. Thanks."

They spent the next hour walking Alpha Company's positions, stopping at each foxhole to make introductions and to render encouragement. Midway through their tour, Colonel Taylor came out to meet them. Dennis was proud to stand beside Colonel Norris, his friend and mentor.

Colonel Norris was entirely complimentary of all that he'd observed. "Good troops, you got here, Harry. I'm trying to convince Riley to come over to my outfit."

Colonel Taylor smiled weakly and folded his arms. "No, Awbrey, he's a bit of a screw-up, but I think we'll keep him."

The banter improved Dennis' mood and they walked south across the Bravo and Charlie Company positions. Finally arriving at the southern end of the oval where the road cut through, Colonel Norris paused and grew serious as he spoke. "Lieutenant Kelly ties in here with your Charlie Company. I put my best fighting men looking south tonight." He paused and began cleaning his glasses with a thin tissue. Adjusting them on his nose, he asked, "Can you guess why, Dennis? Bill ... any of you?"

Dennis didn't understand his reasoning and remained quiet as he struggled for an answer. They were looking north into Cambodia, the obvious direction an attack would come from. *He just rolled up from the south, yet he puts his strength there, looking back to the south. Why?*

"That a battle will occur seems evident," Captain Allison said, "even to the men in the foxholes." He removed his helmet, held it by the lip, and began gesturing angrily. "We know we're going to get hit, the men know it, yet there is an appalling lack of intelligence or any other information from Headquarters. It exasperates me to no end, Sir, if you'll excuse my lack of humor."

Colonel Norris laughed. "That's all right, Bill."

"You must know something, Sir?" Lieutenant Kelly asked, gesturing toward the south. "Why do you have us looking back down the road we just came up?" His tone implied great admiration for Colonel Norris and temerity was not an issue here.

Colonel Norris placed a hand on Gordon's shoulder. "Gordon, have you, or have any of you ever read *Clausewitz on War*, or Sun Yat-sen? Better yet, do you understand, 'Hit em where they ain't'?" He paused and waited for an answer, but none was forthcoming.

"Any of them Polish?" Dennis asked.

"German," Captain Allison answered. "The other guy was Chinese."

Colonel Norris grew somber. "The enemy reads books too, men. We make the mistake of thinking we're fighting a primitive, uneducated Army. Their General Giap has proven he's one of the world's greatest tacticians. If they are going to hit us and try to keep these supply lines for themselves, they'll hit us from the south."

"I couldn't agree more," Captain Allison said.

Colonel Norris paused and lit the end of a ragged cigar stub. Taking the time to blow out a huge puff of smoke, he continued. "Gordon, Bill, double up on everything. A 100 percent alert tonight. Dennis, if you have any rapport with your Charlie Company Commander, mention what I've said."

Colonel Norris paused again and stared out into the jungle for several moments, then, turning toward Dennis and the group, he said, "I think we're in for a hell of a night, boys. Don't be timid when Charlie gets here. Kick his ass all the way back to North Vietnam. It's getting late; let's get back to our positions."

Dennis snapped to attention and moved to salute, but the big Colonel would have none of it. He reached to embrace him. "Good luck, Riley. It's been mighty good to see you. Let's have coffee in the morning."

Elated from his chance encounter with Colonel Norris, Dennis walked directly up the road dividing their sectors. Pausing to watch the artillerymen prepare their big cannons, he grew inquisitive. "What's that weird-looking thing?" he asked a worker. The man was stripped to the waist. His large muscles rippled and his ebony body glistened with sweat as he unloaded big shells from a truck.

"Which one? Oh, that piece. Them's "quad-fiftys," brother. Four, fifty-caliber guns, all in synch, and mounted on tracks. It's an old-time artillery weapon. Want to take a look?"

"Yeah, but don't let me stop you --"

"Glad to take a break, man. You with that leg outfit?"

"Yes."

The worker stopped and smiled. "Hell, man, let me show you 'round. This here is beehive rounds we been unloadin' for the big guns. Has a million little arrows tucked inside." He patted a case of the wooden ammunition crate, stacked high beside one of the larger guns. "When this shit go off, it blow the hell outta them little fuckers." He took off a glove and extended his hand. "I'm Sergeant Williams. Greenville, South Carolina. And who you be? Where you from? You a Lieutenant?"

"Yes ... Detroit."

"Dee-troit. Now that's all right. Dee-troit Lions. They ain't won a fuckin' ball game since '57. You like the Dee-troit Lions?"

"I did in 1957. I don't much care about them right now."

"I was just jivin' you, L.T. I checks an officer out before I mess with 'em. So you from Dee-troit? Well, that makes you OK. Let me show you our stuff. Jump on up here on this big gun tube. Yeah, up here where you can see sumpin'." Dennis grinned and searched for handholds. Sergeant Williams mounted a large howitzer in two steps and extended his hand.

"Easy does it," he laughed as his strong arm pulled Dennis from the ground and onto the artillery piece. "See them pieces down there to the south?" he said pointing. "That's Alpha and Charlie of the 2nd of the 77th. My outfit. We got ten guns pointed north, south, east and west. Five more from 3rd of the 13th up there, pointing north. You legs gonna hafta keep your asses down when we start shootin' tonight."

"How do you know you're going to shoot tonight, Sarge?"

"The man don't bring no big pieces like this here to one spot 'less he 'tends to shoot somebody. See, Dr. King got 'em all tied up back home. The Man can't fuck with the brothers no more, so now Whitey come to Vet-nam. He wanna kill them Commies, them yellows. See, it's all about color."

Dennis' dismay showed upon his face. "What?"

Sergeant Williams laughed. "Aw, don't look so sorry, Lieutenant Dee-troit. You can't help it, it's in yo' blood. Yo' momma and yo' daddy give it to you."

Dennis grinned and shook his head. "Why are you here then, Greenville? What are you fighting for?"

Sergeant Williams stared at Dennis, placed his hands on his hips, and feigned shock. "Now that's a dumb question. I'm a fighting for America, my brother. The same as you ... for my country. It's gonna be a better place someday, you hear? We ... you and me, all us Vietnam vets, we gonna make it that way."

Helping Dennis to crawl down from the big artillery piece, Sergeant Williams held his hand for an instant, then shook it firmly. "Thanks, Sarge," Dennis said. "Keep your powder dry. See you tomorrow." Dennis walked swiftly back to his platoon positions, pondering men like Sergeant Williams.

"Where the hell have you been, Riley?" Captain Chancey asked as Dennis passed him. "Your patrol is due to move out in five minutes."

"Getting an education, Sir, just getting an education."

Chapter Twenty-Two
Ground Attack

Sergeant Allred was waiting for him at the edge of the perimeter. "Hey, L.T., I'm glad you're back." He bit off the end of a plug of dark tobacco and stuffed it in his mouth. He chewed slowly for a moment, then spit and said, "I'm taking ten men, Lieutenant. We'll go straight out to the northeast about fifteen hundred meters. Bravo Company has a patrol up north, by the road junction. We don't want to get tangled up with them."

"Who are you taking, Sarge? What squad?"

"I picked them from all over: a couple here, a few there. I didn't want to weaken the sector in any one spot. I've got Jimmy McClendon; he's damn good. I'm taking Ed Crowley and Saponchech, too. 'Check's' tough on that machine gun; I've got to have him."

"Captain's having a fit, Top. I was gone too long. It gets dark soon; you'd better go."

Sergeant Allred nodded, spun on his heels, and left Dennis standing there.

"Good luck, Top," Dennis shouted after him. "Send me a situation report every thirty minutes. You get in trouble, you call... haul your ass back in here."

The ten, grim-faced men silently fell in behind their platoon sergeant. Jimmy McClendon smiled and waved at Dennis as he stepped through the wire. He took his place on the point. Within a few feet, he was forced to raise his machete; he began chopping a path through the thick forest. Dennis watched until they were out of sight. *Brave men. Boy, if I were in their shoes...*

Jimmy McClendon chopped vigorously at the jungle wall. He was pleased that Sergeant Allred, his platoon sergeant, stood behind him, his rifle at the ready. Jimmy's best friend, Ed Crowley, was also nearby. PFC Saponchech looked menacing, with a dirty olive drab bandanna tied around his forehead. He fingered a long belt of bullets dangling from his machine gun.

"How far are we going, Sarge?" Jimmy McClendon asked.

"We're supposed to go fifteen hundred... don't think we'll have to go that far," Sergeant Allred said. "Be real quiet, Son. Walk softly, keep your eyes peeled."

Jimmy nodded and continued cutting a path. The foliage was extremely thick and he sweated profusely from the toilsome work. Dusk had descended early in this jungle and it was becoming difficult to see. From time to time, red ants and other insects bit at Jimmy's salty flesh. He cursed, brushed them off, and continued to swing his machete in constant rhythm to a tune he hummed in his head. He knew that Sergeant Allred would relieve him in a few minutes, assigning a fresh worker to the task of cutting. He always did.

"Hold it up, McClendon. Take a break," Sergeant Allred whispered. "We'll get someone else on the point." Sergeant Allred turned to face the patrol. "Any volunteers?" he asked.

"I'm the man," Ed Crowley said. "Give me the big knife." He stepped beside Jimmy and stretched to take the machete. At that instant, a dozen bullets from AK-47 rifles and Chinese Communist pistols passed completely through the bodies of both men. Jimmy died instantly, Ed Crowley within a few minutes. The patrol had unknowingly halted less than twenty feet from a North Vietnamese forward observation party.

Emil Saponchech pulled back steadily on the trigger of his M-60 machine gun, spraying bullets far and wide. He lunged forward into the brush shouting, "I'll get the fuckers, Jimmy. I'll kill them all! Kill! ... kill! ... kill!

Emil stood straight up, firing from the hip. To his left, he spotted movement. A continuous stream of hot bullets spewed from his gun, promptly killing four NVA who cowered behind a clump of shrubs. They screamed hideously as Emil pumped spray after spray of bullets into their bodies. Satisfied that they were dead, Emil turned to his right, searching for more targets. Pressing again on the trigger, he killed three more enemy soldiers who were attempting to raise their pistols and defend themselves. "I got 'em... I got all them fuckers, Jimmy. I got 'em all!" Emil screamed.

Although no more enemy were visible, Emil continued to squeeze the trigger of his gun, showering fiery lead into the jungle. He swung the barrel left and right, eventually turning back toward his own patrol. "I'll kill all you bastards," he shrieked.

Sergeant Allred ran forward, tackling Emil at the knees. Other men rushed to help; together, they wrestled the smoking weapon from the crazed gunner. In the melee, someone slammed Emil across his head, knocking him unconscious.

"Good God!" Sergeant Allred shouted. "I though he was going to kill us. Somebody check those NVA bodies. Pick over them. Quick... then we're getting the hell out of here."

Sergeant Allred visited the still bodies of Jimmy McClendon and Ed Crowley. He checked for signs of life, but found no pulse; no breath was left in either of them. "They're dead. Jesus, damn... they were some mighty fine boys." He turned and asked the men who had finished frisking the dead North Vietnamese Army soldiers, "What did you guys find?"

"They were all officers," one of the men reported. He shook uncontrollably, and his voice trembled with fear. "They were carrying pistols and mortar firing tables. Let's go, Top... let's get the hell gone. We're going back in, right?"

Sergeant Allred studied the young men of his patrol. He reached for his canteen and gulped water for a moment, then methodically returned it to his hip pouch. "OK, boys, now calm down," he said. "I know what you're thinking. Yeah, we're isolated from the main unit, and we're probably surrounded. Don't sweat the small stuff. I know you're scared, anxious... might feel like running. Don't do it, we've got to hang tight."

One young soldier knelt and sobbed loudly over Jimmy McClendon's body, interfering with the litter team. Sergeant Allred grasped him by the shoulder and gently tugged him away from the body. The old soldier stood and motioned for all of them to gather around him and kneel.

"I've got something to say, boys," he said, then neatly spat tobacco juice between his feet. "We've been hit bad... losing Jimmy and Ed. You guys are right, these were NVA were officers. They were fixin' to call mortars on the whole battalion. I reckon we're in for a pretty good-sized attack. We've got to warn the perimeter and then get our KIAs back in. Don't be afraid... hang together and we'll all get back in." He picked up his radio handset. "I'll tell the Lieutenant, and see what he wants us to do."

Panicky, but believing in their savvy leader, each man nodded his agreement. Darkness had now completely enveloped the patrol. Sergeant Allred, through touch and feel, positioned each man in a wider circle for protection.

Sitting on top of their bunker, talking to Eddie Runge, Dennis was mid-way through opening a can of rations when he recognized the rattle of machine gun fire and exploding grenades. It echoed from the jungle that the patrol had entered only minutes beforehand. Simultaneously, his radio crackled with Sergeant Allred's steady voice.

"I'm in contact, Three Six; no time for palaver. We're about four hundred meters out. We ran into an NVA patrol. They were waiting on us. We've got two KIAs. McClendon and Crowley. They're both dead. I've got one wounded man."

"I hear your fire, Top. Can you hold them off?"

"Roger that. We'll hold, but you can hear them all around us. Saponchech went crazy with the machine gun. He made a lot of noise,.. put four NVA in one pile, three in another. We're in control, but not for long. Advise."

Dennis looked at his watch as he squeezed the radio handset. He mentally marked the time: *6:44 p.m. The battle for Fire Support Base Burt has started a lot quicker than I expected.* "This is Three Six; stand by, Top. I'll get you some help."

Dennis paused in thought for a moment, then automatically issued his instructions.

"Sarge, pull back one hundred meters and fire a burst of six from an M-16, every thirty seconds. Keep it pointed east. John Erby, Four Six, is out there checking his listening posts. He'll gather you all up and help you to get back in. Do you hear me? Do you understand?"

"Good copy --"

The calm voice of John Erby interrupted their conversation. "Three Six, this is Four Six. We'll find them and help get them in. No sweat. Over."

Dennis thanked the fourth platoon leader. He could hear sporadic firing and it wasn't far off. *Damn, I should have been with them. Jimmy McClendon, Ed Crowley: I just saw them. I've got to do something.*

Dennis impulsively shouted. "Tell Sergeant Bankston to saddle up his squad; we're going out there, Eddie."

"Good goddamn. You're shittin' me! Aw, hell, Lieutenant. OK. Give me a minute."

Staff Sergeant Carl Bankston and eight men appeared at Dennis' side in a matter of moments. They were nervous and excited, but equipped and ready to go. "Where to, Lieutenant?" Carl asked.

"Straight ahead toward that firing," Dennis said, pointing. "Allred's out there with two dead and one wounded. There's NVA all around him. Lieutenant Erby's trying to find him. Let's go."

Racing directly toward the periodic weapon fire, Dennis and his men scrambled over logs, becoming entangled in thorny vines, and stirring up hordes of flesh-eating red ants. With little regard for stealth, they overcame the vicious obstacles. Spearheading right into Sergeant Allred's position, Dennis called out, "Top, Sergeant Allred, is that you?"

"Yeah, over here L.T., over here. Help us with the bodies." Sergeant Allred was barely visible in the dark, but Dennis could see that he was struggling to hoist a limp figure onto his shoulders. Two more men lay on the ground beside him.

"Got three? I thought you said there were two KIAs. Who's that you're carrying? Is that the wounded man?" Dennis asked.

"PFC Catena's wounded, but he can walk. I'm toting Saponchech. He went kinda crazy. He couldn't get enough. He kept firing at anything that moved. The medic knocked him out with a shot of something. Christ, this big Hunky's heavy; I think we'll have to put him on half rations."

Lieutenant Erby and several more men arrived. Together they helped shoulder the dead. Both patrols safely made their way back to the perimeter. "I appreciate your help, John," Dennis said.

"No sweat, Dennis. I've got to get back to my own platoon. I left a trailer load of mortar ammo out in the open. We need to put it into holes. It'll take all night. If the pay wasn't so good, I'd quit this damn job."

They slapped hands as John returned to his position. Dennis followed the disappearing figure into the dark and thought about him. *John doesn't have to be here. He's a high school "All American." U.S.C. in 1967. He could have been a pro.*

Jimmy McClendon and Edward Crowley were tagged, wrapped in ponchos, and delivered to a helicopter pad in the center of the perimeter. Dennis and Sergeant Allred checked their platoon's fighting positions, speaking encouragement to every man. They appeared nervous and fearful; one man cried openly, shaking with uncontrollable fear.

"That's Private Farmer. 'Old Shakey,' the men call him," Sergeant Allred said. "Shoot him up with something, Doc. Put him in the hole with Saponchech. They'll sleep this one through."

At one minute before 9:00 p.m., enemy mortars began to pound the perimeter. Dennis heard screams from the fourth platoon positions. Buried deep in a hole with Eddie, Sergeant Allred, and Doc Friedman, a newly assigned medic, Dennis remarked, "I wonder how John is handling things. We've been mortared before, boys, but this is something else. Sounds like an automatic mortar gun of some kind. My God, listen to them hit."

A continuous stream of exploding shells blasted the perimeter for several minutes. Dennis and his group huddled in their foxhole.

"Like sheep shit on a mountainside," Eddie said. "Looks like they've hit a track or two down in Charlie Company of the mechanized infantry. Big fires are burning... Beau Coups explosions."

"They'll be coming right behind the mortars," Sergeant Allred advised. "Get ready." He peeped through the portholes of their bunker and shook his head. "It's always the same," he said, "always the same."

"Listen to the radio," Eddie said, handing the receiver to Dennis. "Charlie Company has a patrol stuck out there along that road to the south. That's Lieutenant Mike Balser, Second Platoon. The poor bastards."

Dennis pressed the handset to his ear. "Balser's taking some heavy casualties. He says hundreds of VC are passing by his position. They're coming right up the road -- south to north."

"Who... who are the poor bastards?" Doc Friedman quizzed.

"The goddamn Viet Cong," Eddie replied. "If you knew Mike Balser, you wouldn't ask. They call him 'The MD.'"

"He's a Doctor?" Dennis asked.

"Aw, hell no," Eddie answered. "The men tagged him 'Mad Dog,' the day he got here. If he makes it tonight, you'll see what I mean."

Dennis grinned at the chutzpah, but grew concerned. *Damn, Colonel Norris and Captain Allison were right. The main thrust of the attack is coming from the south. Mike Balser is smack in the middle it.*

Chapter Twenty-Three
The Lost Patrol

Sixteen men from the Second Platoon of Charlie Company left the perimeter of Fire Support Base Burt at dusk. Second Lieutenant Michael Balser, in Vietnam for all of ten days, walked the point. Stepping carefully through the jungle foliage, they guided along the road, heading south, away from the main perimeter. They passed Lieutenant Gordon Kelly's position and he threw them a friendly salute. Mike smiled and returned the gesture.

Gordon slid down the front slope of his armored personnel carrier and nudged his platoon sergeant. He pointed after Mike Balser and his patrol. "Ambush patrol from Charlie, 3rd of the 22nd... we don't want to shoot in that direction tonight."

"Yes, Sir. They're a good-looking bunch. Quiet and loaded for bear. I'll spread the word."

Lieutenant Balser, leading his first combat patrol into enemy territory, was filled with misgivings. He didn't need the counsel of his capable platoon sergeant to know that they were probably walking directly into massing formations of North Vietnamese Regulars. He had heard the battle reports from Alpha Company.

"You see Fullback's guns, Sarge?" Mike asked Sergeant Voltz, who walked alongside of him. "Why do you think they're pointing south?"

Sergeant Voltz paused and turned to watch the trailing members of the patrol. He touched Mike Balser on the arm. "They're pointing south because they know something. I think there's a lot of VC out there, L.T. You can smell them. Everybody knows... the men are agitated, but ain't none of them afraid."

"Yeah, the Captain said we'd be 'early warning,' but I think we're just bait. Fuck it. Let's go find a spot... dig some holes and see what happens."

Mike found his position easily and called to his men. "There's a shallow depression running alongside the road. We'll set up in three groups and use the cavity for protection. The command post will be

Scotty Watson, with the radio; Doc Marcum, and myself. Sarge, set up the other positions. We'll sit back about five meters. Move out... be quiet."

A shroud of pitch-black darkness enveloped the patrol as they settled in, waiting. Mike, Scotty Watson, and the medic, Jimmy Marcum, lay on their bellies, side by side. They passed the time whispering about possible courses of action to take, should they be discovered. As the evening wore on, they sensed increasing danger and Mike insisted they focus on the brush in front of them. "Try to gain some night vision," Mike ordered. "I don't like surprises."

After a time, the snapping of limbs and the rustle of brush alerted Mike to movement forward of him. He grabbed his rifle and began crawling toward his three forward positions. A pistol shot cracked behind him and he turned, slithering back to his small command post. "What the hell was that?" he whispered.

"I just shot an NVA," Jimmie Marcum announced. "He walked right up on us. There's lots of them out there."

Mike crawled a few feet forward and bumped his nose against rubber sandals. They were pointing skyward. "I'm convinced, Doc," he said. "They're here... all around us." The enemy were scattered throughout the thick woods and Mike's patrol had unknowingly settled in amongst them.

Without hesitation, Mike pulled the pin from a grenade and lobbed it forward. The screams of enemy wounded and dying echoed throughout the jungle. This unexpected explosion set off a stampede, and hundreds of North Vietnamese Communists rose from their positions. As if it were a signal from their own, the mass of enemy soldiers began a run toward Fire Support Base Burt, trampling Mike and his patrol as they surged forward.

Meeting the enemy head-on, the small group of defenders poured rifle and pistol fire into the flanks of the attackers. Grenades exploded and bodies fell. The screaming swarm of enemy paid little attention and continued their self-destructive race, straight into the guns of the waiting Americans at Burt.

In less than five minutes, the column was gone. Eight enemy bodies lay scattered around the patrol's position. Mike radioed his company commander, learning that the entire fire support base was under heavy attack. Radio operator Scotty Watson had forewarned them.

Fearing a second wave of attackers, Mike called for artillery support. "I've got wounded and dying. Fire my final protective fires!" he screamed. "Give me all you got."

"We're under heavy attack... all guns committed," a frantic voice replied. "I'll forward your request, but I can't promise you anything."

The ballistic crack of heavy artillery rounds ripping overhead, coupled with unexpected illumination, forced the patrol into action. The able-bodied dragged the wounded farther into the jungle, where they circled for protection. A large artillery shell exploded nearby. It lifted men into the air, then slammed them back onto the ground. Mike Balser, dazed by the blast, shook his head, then rushed into a mass of flying tree limbs and debris. He stumbled across the body of Scotty Watson and fell forward onto his face. Mike rolled over and looked up to see the medic, Jimmie Marcum, fumbling with bandages.

"What the hell... who's that?" Mike asked.

"Scotty's dead," Jimmie said, kneeling beside the unmoving radio operator. "Something hit us... artillery shell, I guess. I've got a bad wound to my shoulder, but I'll make it. What are we going to do, Sir?"

Mike knelt to help Jimmie with his bandages. The patrol members still able to function assembled around their leader, seeking direction. "Redistribute the ammo, lay low, keep quiet," Mike ordered. "Real quiet."

They did not nod their agreement or show any other signs of understanding. Gestures and whispers could not express the fear they felt. They trembled in anticipation of what would come next. They didn't have long to wait. American artillery shells began exploding all around them in an attempt to break up the advancing columns of enemy. Scotty Watson's radio warning had launched the barrage. The pungent smell of cordite filled the nostrils of each man. Bursting shells showered tree limbs, whole trees, and nests of flesh-eating ants down upon them. The ants were instantly attracted to the blood of the wounded, yet the men stayed absolutely silent and did not move.

Red and green tracer bullets crisscrossed at ground level and through Mike's ranks. The rattle of rockets, and mini-guns from helicopter gunships, created a red-hot river of death as they showered the enemy from above. Fighter-bombers screamed overhead, throwing their huge bombs directly into the concentration of attacking Communists. Balls of fiery napalm fell so close to the patrol that they felt the heat of liquid death wash over them. Exploding cluster bombs dropped indiscriminately amongst the Americans and North Vietnamese. Twenty-millimeter shells spewed from the automatic cannons of supersonic aircraft, creating an eerie combination of disproportionate sound.

Unable to do anything but hug the earth, Mike sensed the horrifying destruction developing all around him. He was powerless to do anything about it, and he waited, lost in thought. *This sanguine aerial battle -- artillery, gunships, fighter bombers -- alternating their delivery of deadly steel, leaving us with more dead -- more wounded... God, please make it end.*

Chapter Twenty-Four
The Battle Rages

Lieutenant Dennis Riley, secure in his foxhole at Burt, listened intently to the dozens of battlefield radio reports. He grew impatient to do something, to perform. Laying down the radio handset, he turned to his companions and exclaimed, "There's hundreds, maybe thousands of them. Wild Bill Allison and Gordon Kelly are probably in the thick of it right now. We've got to do something to help, but what?"

"Stay in this goddamn hole, guys. That's what," Eddie said. By 11:30 p.m., all sides of the perimeter were under a heavy and sustained attack. The enemy's green tracers mixed with the American's red-tipped bullets, and, at one point, became superior to American firepower. Mortars dropped persistently into the perimeter and rifle-propelled grenades whooshed across the clearing toward the armored carriers of Fullback.

"They're concentrating on the mechanized infantry. They don't like those fifty-calibers chewing them up," Allred said.

"Not much we can do," Dennis replied.

"Look, Lieutenant, if we can get a few men out of their holes and moving, we can intercept some of those VC gunners coming across the clearing. Keep them off of Fullback."

"Ah... All right, Sarge. Let's go."

Dennis and Allred gathered a few men. Together they crawled to within several feet of an enemy anti-tank team that had made it inside the circle. With their own light anti-tank weapons, grenades, and rifle fire, they blew them away in an instant. Another enemy team appeared and they quickly met the same fate. All together, the small patrol stopped six anti-tank squads from placing fire on Fullback's tracks. Without clear targets, Dennis ordered his men back to their defensive positions.

By midnight, the oval was a ring of red-hot flame. The enemy poured across Dennis' positions straight into the deadly return fire of the mechanized unit's fifty-caliber machine guns. Helicopter gunships strafed the outer circle, and napalm bombs fell from the air, splashing a huge wall of flame that seared the flesh of the attackers. Shell after shell, the artillery inside the perimeter fired their mighty guns, flat out across the perimeter.

Dennis, seeking protection, hunkered down in his hole alongside Allred, Runge, and Friedman. He peeped out occasionally to assess the battle's progress. Through the combined battle fires of American artillery, bombs, riflemen, and machine gunners, the attackers were, step-by-step, repulsed. At about 1:00 a.m., the enemy's volume of fire weakened. Men and machine were being systematically chewed up by the massive American firepower.

"It's nearly one o'clock in the morning," Dennis said. "The attack has weakened. How about we get the hell out of this hole? Everybody move out and check the men. See if anybody's hurt."

Sergeant Allred and Dennis went left and right in different directions to check the squads. Tumbling and falling across bodies, some quiet and others squirming, Dennis shot those he could identify as North Vietnamese. The trail of dead and dying led east, away from his positions. Stimulated by adrenaline, Dennis became excited and enraged. He stalked the retreating enemy and soon discovered himself outside the protection of his own perimeter. Strange voices shouting in Vietnamese flowed out from the brush. *I've walked right into them. Jesus, they're ten feet away and all around me. I've got to lay low.*

Dennis fell immediately to the earth, feigning death. The enemy trampled him as they surged forward in another attack.

Fresh troops, making another run at it. I've got to stop shaking. I've got to stop it. I can't let them see me. Holy Mary, Mother of God, pray for us sinners, now and at the hour of our death...

This boyhood prayer was all that Dennis could think of. He frantically repeated the supplication over and over again; finally, an enemy machine gun crew placed the front bipod legs of their weapon against his body. He stopped praying, the vibration and noise of the firing gun demanding absolute concentration. He clamped his teeth, froze his body, and waited.

In a few moments, the enemy picked up their gun and were gone. Dennis lay still while hordes of NVA passed over and around him. Suddenly, he regained his composure and stood. Running blindly, he joined the enemy's ranks. Although an impulsive move, he realized that it was the only way he'd ever get back in. If he remained where he was, the

American napalm and artillery would surely kill him. It took less than two minutes for Dennis to land, rolling, back inside his bunker.

"Where the hell you been, Lieutenant?" Sergeant Allred asked. "I've been looking all over creation --"

"You won't believe it, Top, you just won't believe it. I've been out there with them." Dennis gasped for air and Doc Friedman asked him if he wanted anything for his terrible trembling. "No thanks, Doc. Let me catch my breath. What's been happening?"

"Bad as they are, the attacks in our areas are just a diversion," Sergeant Allred informed him. "What we had earlier was only the first charge. Charlie Company and Fullback are catching the full brunt of the main attack right now. It's coming up from the south." Alpha and Bravo are holding their own. The Bravo Company commander took some of his men to reinforce Captain Chancey's side. They're nailing those anti-tank squads and sappers real good."

"Fullback Six called it, Top," Dennis said. "He and Captain Allison knew the attack would come from the south."

"Yeah, he was right. But being right doesn't help much when you're dead. The only thing that'll save them now is that flat trajectory artillery, the flushettes, and the gunships."

Dennis pressed the radio handset tighter to his ear. He had almost gone deaf from the explosions and the snap of bullets. "More jet fighters are due here in a couple of minutes," he said. "They're loaded with anti-personnel bombs and more napalm."

"Those artillery boys are catching hell, too," Eddie informed everyone. "They're fighting like infantrymen, now. We're OK up here; just keep looking and shooting those BMOs."

"BMOs?" Doc Friedman asked.

"Black Moving Objects," Eddie Runge said, laughing.

Dennis switched his radio frequency from the company net to that of the battalion and listened intently, trying to surmise the battle situation. He heard only the rushing sound of radio static. "I haven't heard anything from Captain Chancey in quite a while," he said. "The last transmissions mentioned the fourth platoon. They took some heavy mortar fire. Sounds like Lieutenant Erby and his radio operator have both been hit."

The radio squawked and Dennis steadfastly resumed listening to battlefield reports. "Charlie Company is really catching hell, now."

Between the dozens of messages flying between the commanders, the artillery, gunships, and jet fighters, he heard, "This is Charlie Three Six... Adkins. We're trapped. We're surrounded. The trip flares in front of us are bustin' like popcorn on high heat."

A long period of silence followed Lieutenant Adkins' excited remark and Dennis listened for more. It came quickly and Dennis cringed as he listened to Russell Adkins, A Platoon Leader for Charlie Company, summarize his predicament.

"The illumination is good. The crowd screaming from the brush in front of me looks like a mob at the mall the day before Christmas. My positions are now isolated pockets of resistance. We're being attacked from all directions. We're at close quarters, now... hand-to-hand..."

"That's Lieutenant Adkins, Third Platoon of Charlie Company," Dennis said. "I wonder how Rosey, Jay Cee, and the boys are doing. Jesus, I wouldn't want to be in their boots."

"I don't reckon anybody would want to switch places with Charlie Company right now," Eddie offered. "Those mechanized guys have a patrol stuck out there, too. Here, check this net."

Dennis grabbed the receiver and listened above the roar of big bombs and explosions. The main battle raged south of the perimeter. Dennis instantly recognized the voice. It was Captain Allison.

"Tiger one, this is Charlie Six. What's your situation? Over."

"The goddamn illumination has us exposed, Six. Can we come back in?" the patrol leader asked.

"This is Charlie Six. Negative. It's too bad in here. We'd probably shoot you ourselves. Do you remember the large bomb craters we passed on the way in here? Get to them, crawl in, and lay low."

For more than thirty minutes, Dennis listened to other nets, sometimes monitoring the chopper pilots, and sometimes other ground forces. It seemed like an eternity when, finally, he overheard a transmission from the lost patrol.

"Charlie Six, this is Tiger One. We're in the hole; what do you want us to do?"

"Lay low, be defensive," Captain Allison answered.

"Can't do that, Charlie Six. There's a hundred NVA coming by this hole. They're dragging their bodies right across the lip of the crater."

"Anything you can do, Tiger?"

"Oh, hell yes, there's something we can do. We're going to shoot the sorry fuckers."

"Roger that. I guess that's why we named you 'Tiger One.'"

Chapter Twenty-Five
Heroes from the Sky

Eddie had picked up an aviator net and listened intently to a pilot called "Blackhawk Five Four."

"Here, Three Six, listen to this chopper pilot; he has a doctor on board," Eddie said.

Dennis pressed the handset to his ear and strained to listen through the static. "Blackhawk Five Four inbound with a load of ordnance," he heard. "Got a doctor for you, too. Where do you grunts want us?"

Dennis was amazed that a pilot would attempt a nighttime landing in the middle of the battle zone. He hoped someone would answer and wave him off.

"I say again, this is Blackhawk Five Four... Mr. Wayne 'Crash' Coe. Me and the good Doctor Warden are inbound to your location. Give me a sit-rep. Over."

Silence greeted the aviator, yet his incoming transmissions were clear. Dennis realized that the pilot held an open radio mike and was talking across several frequencies. He listened, spellbound, as the daring flyer and his passenger, Doctor David R. Warden, described the battle from the air.

"Good night, Wayne, look at the firefight going on down there. In this inky darkness, it looks like a fountain of horror, a full-fledged sea of red... tracers going in and out, explosions and fire. There's bullets ricocheting at every angle. It's a real mess. They're fighting for their lives. They need medical help... ammo. Do you think we can we make it in?"

"Hell, yeah, we're going in," came the hearty reply from Blackhawk. "Look out, now, Doc. We're headed into the hottest landing zone in aviation history. Hang on while I try to get radio contact with the ground."

Warrant Officer Wayne 'Crash' Coe raced his aircraft forward through the night. He pressed his mouthpiece closer to his lips. "Ground control, this is Blackhawk Five Four. Over. Someone answer me, baby."

A rushing noise flooded the headsets. Doctor Warden turned to Wayne, smiled, and held up a thumb. "I think you've got somebody; I can hear the noise of the battle. Wait --"

"Blackhawk Five Four. We're under a heavy ground attack. Please stand by. Did you say you have ammo on board?"

"Roger, ground... got beehive and bullets. Get your wounded ready. Doc Warden, flight surgeon out of Cui Chi, is riding with me tonight. He's bringing blood and bandages. Can we come in?"

A long pause ensued and Blackhawk waited patiently. Finally, his headset came alive: "Negative, Blackhawk. It's too hot to land, but we desperately need your ammo and the doc. Please stand by."

Wayne Coe looked at Doctor Warden and shrugged. "Maybe we can find some gunships for cover. I don't hear the 'Rat Pack.' I'll try Stinger. Hey, Stinger, baby, where are you? This is Blackhawk. I've got to get down there... boys need us. Can you help? Fly cover?"

"Blackhawk Five Four, this is Stinger Lead. If you're crazy enough to go in, we'll go with you. What's your location?"

"This is Blackhawk Five Four. Northwest, and about five miles out."

"Roger Blackhawk. Come to the south end of Burt; we'll pick you up and escort you in. Make it fast; there's a hell of a lot of fire down there."

Wayne Coe bit his lip. Powering his bird forward and down at maximum speed, he realized that he had passed the point of no return. He had made promises to the fighting men on the ground and he intended to keep them.

Start a 120-knot approach. OOPS, I passed my gun cover. Flair... slow it down, boy. Ah, there they are... by my side, again. Look at them mini-guns roaring... low-level insanity. I can't see a fucking thing with all this smoke, flares, and tracers.

"Hey, Doc," Wayne Coe shouted. "I see a lone trooper on the ground holding a flashlight. He's waving his arms. I can't believe it. He's exposed to that fire... guiding us in."

"Roger that, Mr. Coe. It looks like every Communist gunner in the world is trying to shoot him. Lord, the bravery of these guys chokes me up. Hey! You're almost down... you are down, now. I see stacks of wounded. Let me out of here."

Doc Warden jumped from his seat into the smoke of battle. He immediately began triage, identifying the most seriously wounded, with the hope that he could save them. Through intense fire, men came out of the dark and unloaded the ammunition. They jerked ammunition crates from the belly of the aircraft, busting them open as they hit the ground. They loaded the wounded into the cavity, stacking them on top of one another.

Doctor Warden bumped into one of the men helping to load the wounded. He had a flashlight in one hand and was shouting orders to the other men. "You the one that guided us in?" Doctor Warden asked. "You got balls, son... big ones. What's your name?"

"I'm Sergeant Mike Pectol," the tall soldier yelled above the roar of the rotors. "We're 2nd of the 77th Field Artillery. No big deal, Sir. You coming back?"

"We won't leave you, soldier. Yes, we'll be back. You going to shine the light?" Doctor Warden grinned as he shook Mike Pectol's hand and climbed back into the helicopter.

"Yeah, I'll be right here... if the VC don't get me," Mike yelled. "You be careful, Doc... and thanks."

Blackhawk Five Four sat patiently, unperturbed by the bullets slamming into his aircraft.

It's only a matter of time before this helicopter will never fly again. Ah, Doc has his load and is back in the right seat. "I'm coming out!"

A pair of gunships covered Blackhawk's ascent, hosing down the outer perimeter with massive bursts of liquid steel. Doctor Warden looked at the writhering mass of humanity behind him. "I better get busy," he said. He jumped over the console and began life-saving treatment for his dying patients.

"We'll take them to the 12th Evac. Hospital at Cui Chi, Doc," Blackhawk Five Four shouted. "Hang on."

In minutes, the helicopter flared "hot" onto the medivac pad at Cui Chi. Corpsman and nurses took charge, carefully removing weapons and explosive devices from the wounded men. Clear of these dangerous appliances, the wounded were rushed to waiting operating tables and into the hands of skilled surgeons. Every move had been practiced many times before.

Someone tapped Wayne Coe on the helmet and he pulled pitch, heading to the ammo bunkers. His total time on the pad was two minutes, maybe less. "How many did you get, Doc?"

"Eight this time. I think they'll make it. Let's go get some more."

Loaded again with ammunition, Blackhawk Five Four and Doc Warden sped back toward Fire Support Base Burt, where the battle continued to rage. It was almost 4:00 a.m.

"Things sound bad, Doc," Wayne said. "Looks like one of the Stinger gunships has been shot down. I can see it burning. Fast movers are laying down napalm out there."

Doctor Warden looked at Wayne and spoke into his mouthpiece. "It sure lights things up... kind of pretty... but it's still deadly. I can't see Burt yet, but the fireworks on the horizon are spectacular."

Several minutes passed. Finally, Wayne shouted, "Hold on, Doc. We're over Burt now. Someone's waving us off. Too hot."

"You're the driver, Wayne."

Several minutes passed. Wayne Coe looked at Doctor Warden and shouted. "I've got a gun team for escort, now, Doc. Stingers, again. One of their birds went down in flames. They're pissed off, big time. Stinger Lead says they'll fly us into hell. Let's go!"

Blackhawk Five Four made no mistakes going in. The ammo crates were again replaced by wounded soldiers. Doctor Warden counted his load and they were away in seconds. Wayne Coe and Doctor Warden continued to fly throughout the night, delivering precious ammunition to the defenders at Burt, and ferrying out dozens of wounded. At dawn, they landed beside the burned-out hulk of the destroyed Stinger gunship. The crew had been badly burned by fire.

Doc Warden set his jaw and went about the grim task of identifying the bodies. As flight surgeon, it was his duty to perform field autopsies and to certify the causes of death. The bodies of the crew were still smoldering hot. Doctor Warden and other somber men placed them into body bags. He turned to Wayne Coe and the silent covey of men who stood there. "Some smells are with you for life," he said.

"War is a bitch, Doc," Wayne offered. "Don't feel bad. Think of the lives you saved last night. Come on, let's get the hell out of here. I'll buy you a beer."

Chapter Twenty-Six
Victory at Burt

"Sit-Rep coming in. It sounds like Mike Balser," Eddie said.

Dennis' thoughts turned to his friends in Charlie Company. *Wally, Jay Cee, Andy, Jackie, and Rosey are somewhere in the midst of this battle. For sure, a couple of them have to be in Mike Balser's group.*

The radio blared. Eddie had rigged a small speaker box to it. An increasingly familiar voice cried out, "Artillery shells ripping across me. Red and green tracers. NVA running all over us. I've got dead and many wounded. I need help."

"That's Mike Balser," Dennis said. "He's getting hammered."

The radio report ended abruptly with the splash of cannon shells to the south. The battle continued to rage in that area. Tactical fighter jets dropped high explosive bombs and small bomblets peppered the woodline. That ordnance, coupled with napalm, locked the enemy inside the battlezone. There was no escape and they chose to fight the Americans at close quarters.

Dawn became daylight and the carnage subsided. The enemy withdrew their pitiful remnants and fled in all directions, the tactical fighters and gunships making a slaughter of their retreat. Medical evacuation choppers began landing. Blackhawk Five Four was still in the air; his doctor reported treating more than one hundred Americans for wounds.

For Lieutenant Mike Balser and his decimated platoon, the dawn brought with it an absolute silence. Mike could see the bleeding wounds of his men and the grotesque postures of the dead. He heard the sounds of an American helicopter landing at Burt. Only then, did he know who owned the battlefield.

Of the sixteen men who had gone out the night before, only two were miraculously untouched: Mike and Sergeant Voltz. Together, they approached Scotty Watson's lifeless body. Scotty still clutched the radio handset. It was connected to nothing, blown free from the radio by the shell that killed him. Mike knelt and pried it from his hand. "I want to remember him," Mike said. He shoved the handset into a baggy side pocket.

He turned then to Sergeant Voltz and said, "Just you and me, Sarge. Let's head toward Burt and get some help. I'll walk point; you bring up the rear."

Sergeant Voltz checked his rifle. He had one bullet left. "You got it, Lieutenant. Let's go."

Captain Allison and the "Tiger One" patrol intercepted Mike Balser and Sergeant Voltz as they walked northward. They all quickly returned to the site of the trapped ambuscade. Many of the men walked on make-shift crutches, but others required stretchers or aid from medical personnel. Captain Allison called over his radio for immediate assistance.

"I'm sorry we couldn't help you earlier, Lieutenant," Captain Allison remarked. He solemnly surveyed the condition of Mike's men and shook his head. "We'll help you now. What happened out there?"

Mike stared at Captain Allison with misty eyes. Choking back the tears, he answered. "We caught hell... all night long. All I've got to show for it is Scotty's handset." Mike pulled it from his pocket and displayed it for Captain Allison.

"I'll keep the telephone for him," Mike said. "Scotty stayed on the radio, warning the perimeter of the mass attack. He called artillery until they got him. I'll be giving this handset back to Scotty, someday... maybe."

Captain Allison put his arm around Mike's shoulder. "I'm sorry, Son. I'm sorry. Let's get you back in, now. I'm sorry."

Back at Burt, Dennis and Allred walked amongst the Third Platoon. They had survived the battle well, and numerous enemy bodies were scattered about. "That's what good fighting positions do for you, Lieu-tenant," Sergeant Allred said. He rested on his rifle, using it as a cane. "Our men had something solid to fight from; the enemy couldn't get to them. God, I'm tired."

Dennis walked his line and told each man how proud he was of them. They were somber in their responses, almost in shock. He contin-ued walking the length of the company. At the command post, he found Captain Chancey conferring with the commander from Bravo Company. By comparison to Charlie Company, Bravo had been only moderately hit, and they had reacted bravely to Captain Chancey's call for help. Dead North Vietnamese lay everywhere and Dennis stepped over many bodies.

American medics worked feverishly on the wounded and Dennis stopped to help.

"John... John Erby, are you all right?" Dennis called to a motionless figure being swathed in bandages.

"Yeah, Dennis, I'm OK. I'm going to be OK. Gave 'em a leg, I think, but I'm going to be... Guess I won't be playing no more football. Look out for my platoon, my boys, Dennis. Take care of my boys for me." Dennis held Lieutenant Erby's hand until his head slumped from a high dose of morphine.

Dennis moved among the poncho-covered victims, then knelt and unwrapped two stiff bodies. He stared into the faces of Jimmy McClendon and Enis Crowley. They looked peaceful in repose and somebody had cleaned the blood from them. Offering a prayer, Dennis became hardened to the death all around him. Looking for a long time at each of Alpha's dead and wounded men, he felt compelled to do something and offered the medics help in preparing and evacuating them.

Carrying one handle of a litter, Dennis merged with a stream of men walking zombie-like. They carried their comrades, dead and wounded, to the helicopter pick-up point. At the center of the perimeter, dozens of men waited for evacuation. Dennis looked across the sea of faces, trying to find his friends. Finally, he noticed Sergeant Beebe, an NCO from Charlie Company.

"Have you seen Dolan or Gerber? Any of those guys?" he asked.

Sergeant Beebe nursed a small wound at his stomach. He spit a stream of tobacco juice and said, "They're all OK, Lieutenant. A couple of them might be wounded, I heard. We got hit real hard. The men fought like old bobcats, all night long. We took twelve killed all total, but your friends are OK."

"Good to hear. Thanks, Sarge. What happened to you?"

Sergeant Beebe rubbed his stomach, thoughtfully. "Oh, nothing much. Some of them beehive shells went off behind us during the night. One of them little arrows went clean through me. In one end and out the other. Didn't touch nothing inside, though. I'll be OK."

Relieved to learn that his friends had survived, Dennis energetically set about helping to load the wounded and the dead. He grabbed the handles of a litter, fumbling with it under the weight. It tilted, and the body dropped to the ground, exposing a muscled, ebony arm as the poncho fell from around it. Dennis screamed in shock. "Oh, my God, not him, too. Please, not him."

"Who's that, Lieutenant. You know him?" Sergeant Beebe asked.

"Yeah. I knew him real good. For a just minute, but we were friends. He was from Greenville, South Carolina. Hell of a man. Jesus."

The dead were loaded aboard a big Chinook cargo helicopter. Dennis brooded as he helped to load all twenty-three of them. *It's a flying hearse. Like Father Tobin said... a stagecoach of death.*

One hundred and fifty-three wounded were evacuated throughout the morning. Many more refused to go, choosing instead to remain in the field with their friends. Dennis walked south until he met with Lieutenant Kelly. Gordon stood with his hands on his hips, glaring across the burned-out hulks of his carriers. Evidence of a terrific struggle lay all about him and Lieutenant Kelly consoled his men one by one. Dennis noticed the drooping machine gun barrels on several carriers. "They fired them until they melted; then my boys took on the enemy hand-to-hand," Gordon said. "What a night."

Incoming helicopters with big stars on the front marked the arrival of "The Brass." The Commander of US forces in Vietnam, General William C. Westmoreland, surveyed the battlefield, rendering his thanks and congratulations to as many men as he could approach. The artillery commander, a patrician-looking Colonel, established a command post and General Westmoreland, along with his entourage, met with him and asked for an analysis of the battle. Dennis edged closer to the crowd, keenly interested in hearing the Colonel's summation.

"Sir, thank you for coming," the colonel began. "Your presence here does much to assuage the anguish that our men feel after this horrific battle."

General Westmoreland nodded his understanding and smiled. "Go ahead, Colonel," he said.

"We call this the battle of Soui Cut. It's just a name on a map, Sir. This fire support base is manned by two battalions of infantry and numerous artillery units. Starting late yesterday afternoon, six enemy battalions had the misfortune to attack us. In the early evening, an intensive mortar barrage and recoilless-rifle fire swept across our perimeter. This was followed by heavy ground fire, and human wave attacks."

The General held up his hand, interrupting the colonel and asking him for specific details.

"We believe they hit us with four battalions, holding two in reserve," the Colonel answered. They were elements of the 271st and 272nd VC Regiments. Their reserves were committed later in the battle. That would be several thousand attackers. At first, we thought the main attack was in the 2nd Battalion, 22nd Infantry sector. Those soldiers, along with fighting artillerymen, gave a damn good account of themselves. The attack was eventually repulsed in their area. Later, we realized that it had been a ruse... a feint. After midnight, the critical area was to the southwest, defended by Charlie Company of the 3rd Battalion. By one o'clock in the morning, the enemy had succeeded in penetrating Charlie Company's bunker line. We were forced to fire flat trajectory cannon fire and beehive rounds at them. This slowed their attack."

"Good, Colonel. Go on. Did you get support? Was it effective? On time?"

"Oh, yes, sir. We had the full range of support. Tactical fighters laid waste the enemy assembling outside the perimeter. Helicopter gunships flooded the area with their rocket and cannon fire. 'Slicks' and medivac helicopters delivered ammunition, flying out the wounded in the heat of the battle. Artillery fire from Fire Support Base Beaureguard, some twelve kilometers to west, joined our own artillery units --"

"What's your casualty count? The enemy's losses?"

"Considering the overwhelming enemy forces we faced, not too bad, General. At this moment, we've counted more than 400 enemy dead. There are plenty more of them out in the brush, I'm sure. I am sad to report that 23 Americans were killed. We have 153 wounded. A few of them might die, also."

General Westmoreland looked around and waved his hand across the perimeter. "This is nothing short of astonishing, Colonel. It is a phenomenal setback to the Communist forces. To what do you attribute your success here? Is there anything we should pass on to other fighting units?"

"Indeed there is, Sir. The successful integration of Infantry and Artillery fires, coupled with the punishing effects of air power, won this battle. I can't praise these fighting men enough. Would you like to meet some of them, General?"

"I'd like nothing better," the General said, smiling.

An official party, led by the artillery commander and General Westmoreland, toured the battle area, paying particular attention to the gun emplacements and praising each artilleryman and soldier that they met. Army Signal Corps personnel scribbled furiously in their notebooks, while photographers snapped pictures of the enemy dead and a large cache of captured weapons.

An assembly of heroes was called for and medals were passed all around. Gordon Kelly received the Distinguished Service Cross for his heroic efforts at defending the south end of the perimeter. His men cheered their approval. Colonel Norris nodded in agreement and put his arm around Gordon.

The commanders departed as quickly as they came. Dennis returned to his platoon where Sergeant Allred informed him of their impending departure from Fire Support Base Burt. By mid-afternoon, the battle-weary elements of the 3rd Battalion were evacuated by helicopter to an American base camp at Katum. There they would rest and reconstitute their forces.

Colonel Norris and what was left of his mechanized unit motored south into friendlier territory, but only after they had buried more than four hundred North Vietnamese Communists in mass, shallow graves. The battle of Fire Support Base Burt was over. Dennis laid his head on his rucksack. He slept for twenty-four hours.

Chapter Twenty-Seven
Taking Command

"Well, Riley, you've now become somewhat of a name in this Battalion," Colonel Taylor said the next morning during an "Officer's Call." "A legend if you will, what with your actions at Burt."

Dennis sat down on a crate. "Thank you, Sir."

"You handled that one very well in spite of your foolish excursion outside the perimeter. Finding your men -- keeping them fighting -- that was smart. Alpha Company held the line and I'm proud of all the men."

The Colonel rose from behind his makeshift desk of ammunition boxes and walked toward Dennis. "Get up on your feet, Riley; I've got something to say."

Dennis did as he was told and stood to meet the Colonel. Instinctively, all of the officers in the tent stood with him.

With one hand on his hip, Colonel Taylor began shaking the big finger of his other hand at Dennis. "I've been giving serious consideration to moving you up, Riley, making you a Company Commander."

"Who, me? Why, Sir?"

"Captain DeMatto here says that your actions at Burt, and on Nui Ba Den, make you a suitable choice for Company Commander. Says you have a certain mettle about you. I rather like that. What do you say? I'm offering you command of Charlie Company. Their company commander will return home soon. I'm taking him off of the line, placing him in administrative duties." Dennis, stunned into silence for a moment, mulled over the Colonel's words. "I'm not sure I heard you right, Sir. You're offering me a Company?"

Colonel Taylor, giving up a token smile, stepped closer to Dennis, placed his hand on his shoulder, and said, "Yes, Lieutenant Riley, you're my choice. Say your good-byes to your platoon and to Alpha Company, then report to Charlie immediately. I expect nothing less than a sterling performance from you. Let's not have any more midnight helicopter rides or 'Lone Ranger' patrols. In spite of your usually rash behavior, the staff and the other commanders have a lot of confidence in you. I'm taking their word for it."

He spun and returned quickly to his chair, sifting through some papers. He stopped suddenly, looked again at Dennis, and said, "I don't like Lieutenants running my companies, but I'll take a chance on you, Riley. Don't screw up. We'll bring you up to date on their situation later this morning. I want you and all the commanders here at zero nine hundred hours for a briefing on our overall operations. I've got quite a bit to tell you."

Dennis' mind began to whirl and he felt no jubilation at the news. Instead, a wave of depression engulfed him. *Now I've got four times the problems I had yesterday. Company Commander, hell. This is crazy. At one time I would have jumped at the chance to command a company, but now...*

Dennis felt weak; impulsively, he sat back down. He recalled Lieutenant Morris explaining his own transfer just a few weeks before the battle at Fire Support Base Burt.

"It's normal to move officers after six months of combat time and give them a nice safe job -- maybe in a headquarters," Lieutenant Morris had said when he left Alpha Company. "After six months as platoon leaders, we deserve to get off the line."

The practice of transfers was done on the pretext that the officer was being groomed for a higher position of responsibility when, in fact, it was a "good old boy" network taking care of its own. The more senior officers lived by the unwritten code; they included junior officers, such as Dennis, to preclude any railing from them.

Dennis' altruistic impulses began to override his reluctance to take command. He knew that his gang over at Charlie Company would gladly receive him as their commander, but he was hesitant to leave the Third Platoon. At that peculiar moment in his young career, Lieutenant Riley made a decision that would alter his life forever.

Standing abruptly, he faced Colonel Taylor and spoke boldly. "OK, Sir, I'm in. I'll do my best. I do have one request, though."

"What's that?" Colonel Taylor said without looking at him. "I'd like to bring a couple of the men from Alpha with me."

"Who? What for?"

Dennis drew a long breath. "My radio operator and Sergeant Allred. First Sergeant Krznarovich, too. These men would give me some key people to get started with. They know me and --"

"Done, Lieutenant," Colonel Taylor waved his hand. He stood and faced the staff and other commanders. "Give them a little position and they think they're a goddamn Field Marshall. Well, I guess you do need some people to lean on, Riley. OK, the Adjutant will make the arrangements. You're dismissed, now. Get to your unit."

The assembled entourage of officers encircled and congratulated him, wishing him well as he snapped to attention and saluted. Apparently, they approved of the Colonel's choice. "Good luck, Charlie Six," someone offered as they dubbed him with his new call sign. They were genuine in their good wishes and Dennis felt a sense of pride.

Damn, maybe I can pull this off. God, after Burt -- after Charlie, Crow and Doc -- I was ready to give it all up. If they only knew how miserable I am about this war. Only Rosey really understands it all.

Dennis decided to get busy. As a new Company Commander, he'd have a hundred things to do in making the transfer. He wanted to properly say good-bye to his Third Platoon. He knew that Eddie Runge and Sergeant Allred would pack up and move to Charlie Company without question. He would have to cajole First Sergeant Krznarovich into joining him, however. Mentally organizing his chores, Dennis surprised even himself. *I've actually taken the job. I must be nuts.*

Dennis nodded to the group, spun on his heels, and rushed to join his new unit.

First Sergeant Krznarovich was already there; he walked out to meet Dennis as he arrived at the Charlie Company perimeter. He extended his big hand, grinned, and offered his own congratulations. "You move fast, Lieutenant. Maybe that's good, maybe not so good. OK, goddamn it, so you got yourself a company and you got me with it. What the fuck for, I don't know. But, here I am. So what's your plan?"

Dennis laughed. He unbuckled his web gear and dropped it on the ground. He looked at the First Sergeant and spoke without hesitation. "Top, I've got to get control of this company real fast. I need your help. After Burt, these guys were badly demoralized. They had twelve men killed and they don't have much good to say about their CO. Something about beehive rounds hitting them from behind."

Krznarovich grimaced. "It's all over the battalion. Some of the men think the Captain called it. Others don't. It don't fucking matter. We'll never know, but he gets the blame. You will, too, if something else like that happens. You sure you want this job?"

Dennis didn't answer him directly. "I talked with the former commander. He says he didn't call it. He blames the artillery. Maybe he's getting a bum rap."

"Yeah. And do you remember our talk when you first got here? Maybe now you see the divide, the big distance between the leaders and the men. It doesn't matter if the story is true, if the men believe it... it is true." The First Sergeant pulled two cigars from a breast pocket and offered one to Dennis.

"Here, Lieutenant, one of my Dutch Masters. It fits a new Company Commander. Congratulations. Let's smoke."

"Thanks, but I don't have much time to celebrate. I want your help, Top. I think this company is about to revolt, they're so pissed off about Burt."

"How about we start with kicking some ass? That's my specialty, Lieutenant. Where do you want to start?"

Dennis grinned. He knew he had asked for the right man to help him. "Troop the line and tell the men to cut out the idle card playing and other crap in these foxholes. Let's whip this company back in shape. I'll start by putting them on alert. You sober them up and get them ready to move out."

"Consider it fucking done."

"By the way, First Sergeant, thanks for agreeing to come to Charlie Company. I need --"

First Sergeant Krznarovich smacked his lips and waved his hand. "Don't worry about it, Lieutenant. We won't let you screw up. You're going to do good, just don't be afraid to stand up for the men. They'll be checking you on that, right off."

"OK, OK, Top," Dennis laughed, reassured by the First Sergeant's attitude. He picked up his rifle and gear, strapped it on, and walked swiftly back to the battalion command post. He was happy that men like Rudolph Krznarovich, for all their stinging rebukes and cursing sarcasms, were still around in the Army to mentor their young officers.

Dennis entered the tent and noticed that it had taken on the aura of a real command post. Folding chairs had been arranged in neat rows. Colonel Taylor was seated behind an old Army-issue field desk and lanterns hummed above him. Dennis was the last to arrive and he quietly took his seat.

Colonel Taylor tapped on his desk for silence. Glaring at the audience for a while, he drank from a metal cup and then began, "Gentlemen, we are about to initiate a major ground operation against the enemy. It's called, 'Operation Saratoga.' It'll begin right after the Vietnamese holidays, just a few weeks away. We're going to end this war. Tell them about it, Captain DeMatto."

The Operations Officer stood and pointed to a large map, resting on an easel. "We move by air to the vicinity of Cui Chi this morning. The entire Division is involved and we have the critical zones of operation. It seems that large concentrations of North Vietnamese Regular soldiers have merged with the depleted ranks of the Viet Cong. They're digging in around the 25th Division's base camp at Cui Chi. We're going to stop them."

Dennis said nothing, but took exception to the term, "we."

Captain DeMatto continued his briefing. "It's also known that they are digging fortifications in and around populated areas, taking over whole villages and using the civilian population as a cover. We think they're hoping for a popular uprising."

He paused for several moments, reading from some papers. Looking up, finally, he said, "This is the 4th of January, men. The Vietnamese holiday of 'Tet,' will commence on the 29th. We'll have a cease-fire starting then. It appears that the tactic is to give them a breather from aerial bombing and the ground battles. That might make them come to their senses and start negotiating an end to this war."

Dennis almost laughed out loud, but his good friend, Lieutenant Dick Prairie, jabbed him in the ribs. Dick was being prepared to take command of Bravo Company soon, and he attended most briefings. Dennis whispered that he couldn't believe that anyone thought that backing off the enemy would make him come to a conference table. He was impatient with the sham.

Standing, Dennis interrupted the monologue. "Sir, begging your pardon, but at Benning we were taught that one of the first principles of war is to, 'Know Thy Enemy.'" He paused for effect and then spoke more forcefully. "We know him now. Weren't we having a truce at Burt? You see what they did, they attacked the hell out of us. This son of a bitch isn't coming to a peace conference because we've decided to accommodate his Tet celebration."

Lieutenant Prairie, always bold in his approach toward tactics and battle, decided to support Dennis. He stood beside his friend. "Begging your pardon, Sir," Dick said, "but Lieutenant Riley is right. You don't score in a wrestling match by letting your man up. You make him say 'Uncle' first. What makes anyone think that releasing our grip will make the North Vietnamese talk peace?"

Having said the obvious, both of them knew instinctively that the temporary truce, the third one they had tried, was more than likely going to end up in one hell of a battle for someone. The hair on the back of Dennis' neck tingled and he shook with emotion as he sat down. Colonel Taylor glared at both of them for a moment, then continued with his message, not bothering to acknowledge their comments.

Dennis leaned into Prairie's ear and whispered, "He's ignoring us, but he knows we're right, huh?"

Colonel Taylor told all commanders to make sure that their forces were pulled inside defensive perimeters on the 29th, "So as not to give the impression that we want to provoke anything," he said. He finished with a court-martial threat to anyone who caused an incident that might be construed as breaking the cease-fire.

Dennis could scarcely believe what he was listening to. "Does he really believe that crap?" he said to Prairie.

"Doesn't matter. We're stuck with it. This nitwit didn't go to the same school we went to. Watch your ass."

The staff officers concluded their briefings and were about to dismiss when Colonel Taylor stepped in front of Dennis.

"I'll overlook your impertinence this time, Riley, but you've got a lot to learn. It will be many years before you are competent enough to question the decisions of our commanders. Until then, I expect your absolute obedience while you're in command. Since this is your first operation as a company commander, I'm giving you the easy one."

"The easy one, Sir?"

"Yes, you'll be securing the engineers along Highway One. That will give you some time to get your feet wet -- to learn your company. Then I'm bringing you down into the Iron Triangle -- the Ho Bo Woods."

Dennis found little encouragement in his remarks, but kept his mouth shut. Without commenting, he saluted, turned, and sped back to his unit.

"Pass the word, Top. We move out in twenty minutes. Get all the platoon leaders and platoon sergeants together for a meeting. Tell them it's a piece of cake for an operation; we'll have supper with the engineers." Dennis declined to tell him about the impending mission in the Ho Bo Woods.

"Oh, by the way, I'd like to see these men for a few minutes after the meeting." Dennis handed the First Sergeant a scrap of paper with Jay Cee's, Wally's, Andy's, Jackie's, and Rosey's names scribbled on it. "They're all in the Third Platoon, except O'Connor, but I'd like to see them all together."

Dennis met informally at first with his leaders. He was not yet ready to issue instructions, using the moment instead to take the pulse of the company and to test his approval rating. From what he could discern, they were all glad to have him as their new commander. They had some foul words for the previous captain and his performance under fire.

"He was a pompous ass," Lieutenant Mike Balser, the Second Platoon leader brazenly remarked. "He fired artillery flushettes directly into his own men to save himself at Burt. Guess I was lucky to be stuck out on that ambush."

Lieutenant Harmon, the First Platoon Leader, looked straight at Balser, then shook his head and extended his hand to Dennis. "We're glad to have you, Lieutenant Riley. Mike doesn't like any commander at first, but, with any luck, you might pass his muster." He laughed and jabbed playfully at Balser.

"You can count on our support," Lieutenant Russell Adkins, the Third Platoon Leader said. "I just wish you had left First Sergeant Krznarovich in A Company." He chuckled lightly and slapped Dennis on the arm. After a hearty laugh and assurances all around that they understood the mission and would begrudgingly accept the Iron Man from Michigan, Dennis dismissed them to their platoons. He waited until they cleared the immediate area, then motioned for the group of men standing in the tree line to come forward.

They stopped in front of Dennis, all of them standing at rigid attention and waving snappy salutes. "Thanks, but you can knock it off, guys," Dennis said.

Wally spoke first, slapping his knee. "Dennis the Lieutenant, boy are we glad to see you. Figured you'd be on your way to the Long Binh stock-

ade by now," Wally said. "How did you get to be the company commander after that midnight chopper ride?"

"Just my Irish wit, Wally. No problem at all."

Jay Cee, Jackie, Andy, Wally, and Rosey seemed awed by the fact that
he was now their commander and they told him so. "Congratulations,
Sir," Jay Cee said, offering his hand. "We're happy for you."

"No more ambush patrols, no more shit burning, huh, Dennis,"
Andy said. "We'll be living the life of --"

"Yes, and will you please approve my permanent transfer to Hawaii?" Jackie asked. "I've had enough of this here vacation."

Smiling at their presumptions and good-natured kidding, Dennis let
them have their fun, then waved his hands for silence. "OK, guys, I don't
know how I ended up becoming your company commander. I certainly
didn't ask for it. I got you all together because I wanted to say hello. I haven't seen any of you for a while. I've been hearing about you, though. I
understand you guys gave a good account of yourselves at Burt. There's
just one thing I've got to ask --"

"I know where you're headed, Sir," Jay Cee said. "We all do. We
talked about how it would be if you ever became our boss. When we got
the word this morning that you were our new company commander, we
held a meeting. Don't worry, Charlie Six. Like some old revolutionaries
once said, "We pledge our honor, our fortunes, and our lives to you.""

"That's almost the truth," Rosey said, pushing Jay Cee aside and
stepping forward. "Except we don't have any fortunes and these guys
have no honor, but we do have our lives. Knowing us, you must have had
second thoughts about coming here."

Jackie Stoner interrupted. "Doesn't matter, Dennis. We're really glad
you're here. Oops, sorry, didn't mean anything disrespectful." Jackie
mockingly placed his hand over his mouth.

"Me and Jackie and Andy here have the machine gun positions in
the Third Platoon now," Wally said. "Don't you worry none, Charlie Six.
We get hit and we ain't going to let our 'Old Man' get embarrassed for
nothing, you hear?"

"Don't do anything foolish, boys. We're friends, but don't do
something that'll get you killed. Rosey -- all you guys -- I know I can
count on you. Thanks for your loyalty. I'll do my best for you."

Jay Cee snapped to attention, the others following his lead. Dennis
gladly returned their salutes in spite of the understood prohibition

against it. Walking randomly, they went back to foxholes along the perimeter. Watching them, Dennis was delighted at the tone of their meeting. *OK, that small matter is taken care of. I've got work to do.*

The next several weeks passed without incident and Dennis had time to assimilate into his command. He understood the company's grief over their heavy losses at Burt, but was not reluctant to issue firm demands.

"They're still reeling from that battle, but a swift kick in the ass sure helps them heal faster," First Sergeant Krznarovich observed.

"Stay with it, Top," Dennis agreed.

The security duty allowed for idle time. Replacements arrived and Dennis relaxed, mingling with his men, playing a card game or drinking a beer with them from time to time. Near the end of January, on a hot and humid morning, Eddie and Dennis lay side by side in a garden of soft grass, resting. Suddenly, the radio squawked. Eddie listened for a moment, then poked the handset into Dennis' chest. "You're in demand, Charlie Six. The party's over. There's big stuff coming across the net."

"I'm sleeping, Eddie. Dreaming about Hamtramck, Michigan. They have the most beautiful Polish girls up there. Tell whoever's calling that I don't live here anymore."

Eddie beat on Dennis' chest with the radio handset. "You better come back to Vietnam, Sir. Wake up, this is some heavy shit I'm hearing."

Dennis listened for a moment and quickly agreed with Eddie's evaluation. "I just started having fun and the damn war heats up," he said. "Operations wants me. Captain DeMatto sounds excited."

Grabbing the handset, Dennis spoke firmly. "This is Charlie Six, over." Always thrilled by his call sign and all that it meant, he spoke confidently into the mouthpiece.

"Charlie Six, this is Falcon Three. I've got a hot one for you. Seems that some major on his way to Saigon got ambushed about two kilometers south of you. There's a small observation chopper flying cover above him. He has no guns. The pilot's firing his pistol, throwing grenades, trying to keep the VC off of the guy. He's hiding in a ditch, and has little cover. His jeep has overturned and is burning. The pilot says that the driver looks dead, but the major shows some signs of life. You're the closest unit to him. You go."

Dennis sat up. "Roger that. Where exactly is he?"

"Straight down that road you've been clearing -- highway QL1 -- near a small village. It's called Ap Cho. Look on your map. It sits alongside the main supply route. You're about two thousand meters northwest of it."

"I got it," Dennis replied.

Captain DeMatto continued. "I've sent an urgent message to the engineer company commander. He'll give you four of his big dump trucks to haul you and your company down there. They should be arriving any minute. Get moving: the chopper pilot reports he took some small arms fire. He thinks there's a squad of Viet Cong holed up in there."

"Roger that, we can handle a squad."

"Falcon Six wants you to get those casualties out and secure the road. Supply convoys might be coming through later. Whatever you do, don't lose that road."

Dennis, excited by his first combat mission as a company commander, stood and paced back and forth, dragging the radio and its operator with him by the cord. Eddie Runge planted his feet, pulled on the telephone cord and forced Dennis to stop his neurotic pacing.

"Sorry, I'm hyper and I know it, Eddie. I shouldn't be. I knew this was coming. I hear the trucks now." Calmer, he grabbed the handset and called Captain DeMatto. "We're on the way in zero five; how about some coordinates on that village, Falcon?"

"X-ray Tango 701088. That's close enough for government work. It's less than a thousand meters southeast of the town of Cui Chi. Quit asking questions and get your ass moving."

Further transmissions were drowned out by the roar of the big trucks as they sped toward his column. Dennis noticed his platoon leaders approaching on the run, their apprehension masked by cold, stony looks. Eddie Runge, privy to the knowledge of the impending mission, had summoned the junior leaders to the command post. "Thank Eddie for the foresight. You know, he could probably run the company himself," he said to Sergeant Beebe, who always attended Dennis' meetings.

"That he could," Beebe said.

Dennis looked at his watch and noted that it was the fifth day of February, 1968. Except for the few enemy mines and the insignificant roadblocks they had encountered, he hadn't noticed much enemy activity. He involuntary shuddered as he sensed that, for Charlie Company, things were about to change.

Dennis called his company to action at about 11:00 a.m. The men of Charlie Company, in good spirits and recovered from dozens of such actions, stirred eagerly from their roadside berths. Chattering and joking amongst themselves, they faced southward, adjusted their equipment, and placed their weapons at the ready.

"Let's kick some ass. Where to, Charlie Six?" one of them called out.

"Ap Cho," Dennis shouted, as if that meant anything to them. "We got Americans pinned down in a ditch there. Let's see if we can help them, boys. It's an easy mission. Let's hope we're in time."

Biting his lower lip, he stole a moment to review the orders he would give his platoon leaders. It would be his first combat briefing as a Company Commander. *I've got to show 'em I'm suited to command. They're all watching me.*

The platoon leaders, hastily gathering in a semi-circle, bent to one knee or took positions sitting on the ground. They silently studied Dennis with calculating eyes. Lt. Oliver Harmon, a tall and lean southerner, commanded the First Platoon. His unerring professionalism as an officer came from the strict education he'd received at an Alabama military college. Dennis couldn't help but notice the explicit and demanding speech he used when addressing his men.

"Lieutenant Harmon, he's a damn good officer," Krznarovich had said of him. Such rare and lofty praise from the first sergeant was reason enough for Dennis to bond with Lieutenant Harmon.

Lieutenant Mike Balser, the Second Platoon Leader, was totally opposite in his demeanor. He combed his light brown hair across his forehead in a style that reminded Dennis of Adolph Hitler. His wispy mustache, cropped square at both ends, reinforced that notion.

"By God, you're right," his Fourth Platoon Sergeant, Bill Walker, confirmed when Dennis jokingly mentioned it. "The men look up to him, though, and he's a fighter. He led a platoon of tanks through sniper fire the first week he got here ... at night." Sergeant Walker's eyes widened as he spoke of Balser's daring.

Balser's unconventional attitude toward all things military brought him considerable scorn, however, from the higher echelons of rank in the battalion. Dennis had been cautioned by Colonel Taylor to, "Watch that damn hippie," when he was initially briefed.

Nevertheless, he liked Mike and concluded that his nonconformist behavior was really an asset. *If he lives up to his reputation, he'll be someone I can count on when things get sticky,* Dennis thought. *Be a good fighter, "Mad Dog." That's all I ask.*

Russell Adkins, a blue-eyed, blonde-haired beachcomber from Portland, Oregon, led the Third Platoon. An OCS graduate, he'd arrived in Vietnam at nineteen. Having spent most of his young life pumping iron and living on the beach, he seemed innocent, even naive about the realities of war.

Considering his youth, Dennis was, at first, doubtful about his leadership skills until Sergeant Beebe reminded him about Russell and his men getting surrounded at Burt. "Got himself snared like a rabbit, he did. Said they were coming at him like hogs for the slop. Next morning, we counted more than seventy dead VC in front of his positions, most of them shot at close range. Don't let them baby blue eyes fool you, Lieutenant. He might look like a kid, but Lieutenant 'Rusty' Adkins -- he's one hell of a man."

"Yeah, I heard him on the radio during the fight. Didn't he say 'coming at him like shoppers at the mall'?" Dennis asked.

"Same thing," Sergeant Beebe replied with a twinkle in his eye.

The Fourth Platoon, the mortar element, worked under the direction of Sergeant First Class Bill Walker. He was a tough and experienced NCO whom Sergeant Allred had appraised as the best mortarman in Vietnam.

Arriving last for the meeting, Sergeant Walker rested his large frame by sitting on his steel helmet, smothering it like a hen nesting on her brood. He let out a big belly laugh at the spectacle of himself suffocating the helmet, then nodded briefly to them all in a form of salute. Dennis instantly felt a sense of trust from the gesture and enjoyed his good humor.

Michael Donnelly, a Second Lieutenant of Artillery, was attached as a Forward Observer. His small frame and innocent-looking features belied his expertise. He had graduated first in his artillery class at Fort Sill, Oklahoma, only two months before. "Get me hot steel on the ground when I need it, Michael," Dennis admonished him as they shook hands. "Glad to have you along."

"Deeds, Not Words," Michael smiled as he repeated the regimental motto and got out a notebook and pen. "What's up?"

Removing his steel helmet, Dennis signaled the others to relax and do likewise. "Let me tell you what little I know," he began. "It seems there's been plenty of activity all around us. The men sense it, I feel it, yet no one has given it a name. The Vietnamese call it 'Tet Nguyen Dan.' It's kind of like our Christmas."

Dennis gestured with his hands. "You've seen all these villagers moving up and down the roads? Supposedly they are going to visit relatives, but, you guessed it, they're using the elbow room to infiltrate villages and towns."

"So what's the word?" Lieutenant Balser asked.

Dennis laughed. "The word, Mike, is that the North Vietnamese Army and the Viet Cong are making a joke out of the cease-fire. They're moving, digging in at critical locations, and attacking everywhere, all over the country."

His rapt audience sat silently, looking at him. Though their eyes told Dennis they trusted him, he felt an obligation to be as clear and honest as he'd ever been.

"We've been doing easy work out here with the engineers. That's over. We have to move right now, soon as our men are on the trucks."

"Where are we headed, Charlie Six?" Harmon asked. "My men say they can tell something big is up. They can't really say for sure, but there are signs."

"Men, the city of Cui Chi was under mortar attack all of last night. You may have heard the explosions. This morning they started receiving small arms fire along with machine gun and rifle-propelled grenades. Delta Company was sent in. I've been listening to Captain Montel bitch about it all day."

"Sounds grim," Rusty Adkins said. "Have I been asleep, or what?"

"I guess we all were," Dennis said. "Seems like everybody's been in a fight during the last twenty-four hours. Now it's our turn."

Chapter Twenty-Eight
The Village of Tears

"Come on, let's get our boys rolling," Dennis said, slapping Mike Balser on the arm. "I'll take the lead vehicle. Load your platoons in numerical order: First Platoon, followed by the Second, and so on. Dismount about a hundred meters north of the village and walk in."

"What are our assignments?" Lieutenant Harmon asked, folding and tucking away his notebook.

"You take the left flank when we get there, Oliver. Balser, use your Second Platoon on the right. I'll go with Adkins's Third Platoon right up the middle. Sergeant Walker, Fourth Platoon will be held in reserve about a hundred yards behind us. Any questions?"

Without waiting for an answer, he ran toward the trucks, shouting, "OK, let's go get 'em, boys." The leaders, feeling his excitement, joined him on the run, waving at their men to follow.

Dennis had only casually explained the extent of enemy activity to the platoon leaders as the reports were too numerous and somewhat unbelievable. They had enough to do in briefing the men and he was anxious to get moving. Besides, he couldn't do anything about the reports flooding his radio. Eddie Runge kept him abreast of matters as they developed.

"First of the 27th Infantry in light contact now," Eddie spontaneously offered as they began loading the heavy trucks. Holding the handset to his ear, he repeated, almost word-for-word, the radio transmissions as they developed.

"Delta Company just killed three VC in the Cui Chi marketplace -- probably holiday shoppers. Bravo Company is engaged somewhere along the supply route and Stinger gunships are flying cover. Sounds like Bravo's taking casualties. Delta is sending reports of two hundred or more enemy moving toward Ap Cho."

"Good God, Eddie, don't spread that word around," Dennis shouted over the roar of the big diesels. "Even I might go the other direction. I'm sure that's another one of Montel's exaggerations."

"The Second of the 12th Infantry is heavily engaged somewhere just northeast of Ap Cho. This cake walk is over," Eddie said. Dennis and Eddie scrambled aboard the bed of the first big truck, pulling and helping the other men aboard.

Dennis chose to ride in the bed of the lead truck with the First Platoon. It pleased the men that their new commander would forsake the privilege of riding in the cab, but Dennis had other thoughts. The roads were becoming more and more heavily mined and the thick steel bottoms of the trucks offered good protection in case they hit one. Also, his radio transmissions were clearer in the open where the antenna could stand erect. He gave Lieutenant Harmon and Sergeant Allred the front seat. The two leaders shared a final cigarette and clambered on board. Sergeant Allred yelled, "Move 'em out!"

Speeding recklessly toward the village, Dennis felt a premonition. Helpless to slow the trucks from his position in the rear, he stood to shout a warning to the driver just as it hit a mine, which blew the right front tire. The vehicle careened out of control and skidded wildly across the road, tottering for a moment as if it were in slow motion, then coming to rest on its side. Dennis, along with his men and equipment, were scattered like puppets into the red dust and gravel of the road. Bruised, but unhurt, he ordered a quick assessment by the leaders. Although they were shaken up a bit, only one man was seriously hurt. "A broken shoulder," Mike Balser said. "After Doc Shiro treats him, we'll send him out in one of the remaining trucks."

The engineers were already trying to right the overturned vehicle with cables and winches, but the first effort failed. The big truck blocked the narrow road and Dennis concluded that it would take too much time to clear or break a trail around it.

"Get your men off the trucks," he demanded. "Get them off and spread out; we'll walk from here." He saw the delay as helpful as he had grown nervous about riding at such high speed into a possible zone of action. "I'd rather be on foot, anyway," he said to Michael Donnelly, who was sticking close to him.

Dennis found Eddie Runge and verified that he was unhurt. He grabbed the handset and called the Battalion Headquarters to report the accident.

"Get walking, Charlie Six," Captain DeMatto ordered. "We've lost all contact with that chopper. He last reported that an enemy force was digging positions in the center of the village. The people are fleeing. How far are you from the target?"

"Probably three or four hundred meters ... no more."

Captain DeMatto agreed with this assessment. Clearing the wrecked truck would delay their movement unnecessarily. He reminded Dennis that his mission was to rescue the trapped Americans and to hold on to the road. Handing the radio handset back to Eddie, Dennis signaled his leaders forward.

"Is everyone off the trucks? We'll hoof it from here," he bellowed. Dennis adjusted his helmet, chambered a shell into his shotgun, and stepped forward. "I'll take the point with Lieutenant Adkins' platoon."

Noting his urgency, the platoons immediately obeyed and fell in behind him. Moving swiftly, but with extreme caution, they spread out onto both sides of the road. The First Platoon sashayed easily to the left, coming abreast of Dennis and the Third Platoon. Looking to his right, Dennis saw that Balser's platoon was on line and he was pleased with their skill.

"They look good," he said to Rusty. "We're a couple a hundred meters out now. Keep your eyes peeled."

They rounded a minor curve in the road and the village of Ap Cho came into view. It looked quiet and peaceful nestled amongst the tropical palms and gardens.

"Holy hell, Charlie Six, it's a lot bigger than a village," Mike Balser exclaimed as he came alongside Dennis. "Might call it a town. It looks quiet enough in there, though."

Dennis reached and Eddie instinctively handed him his field glasses. "Damn, you're psychic, Eddie. Thanks."

He studied the village for a moment, then handed the glasses to Mike Balser. "Take a look-see."

Mike whistled. "Hey, wait a fucking minute, Charlie Six. It's too quiet. I don't see any smoke from cooking fires. No stinky nuoc mam, no people moving, no kids. The Viet Cong are in there, all right." He stared at Dennis as he handed the glasses to Lieutenant Adkins.

Taking the radio handset, Dennis called all leaders and described the village from his prospective. "Looks like maybe ten rows of huts deep and it stretches out about five or six hundred meters. The landscape widens, gets clear, just as you enter it from the north. One Six, Harmon, let's get

First Platoon out to the far left. Move directly into the village. Check for the Americans as you go. We'll keep moving straight down the road."

He grabbed Mike Balser's shoulder. "Get your Second Platoon moving and stay over there on the right. Move out."

His elements fell in behind and Dennis felt an adrenaline flow, a sensation of power. "The platoons react well, Eddie. Just look at them. I'm glad I came to Charlie Company. You?"

"Yeah, Charlie Six, and you're about to get tested. I can feel the shit all around me. My fucking hair is standing up on my neck. The men feel it, too. Wait now --"

Eddie's halting comments were drowned out by the snap of bullets cracking overhead and the roar of nearby explosions. They hit the dirt together. "First Platoon in heavy contact, Sir," he calmly reported to Dennis. "Here, talk to Oliver." He shoved the handset into Dennis' face.

"Six, this is One Six. I'm taking heavy small arms and automatic weapons fire from the front ... anti-tank guns, too. I've got at least four down. We're pinned. Advise, over."

Dennis paused. *Seconds ago I thought I was patrolling a quiet little village, looking for American casualties, feeling too damn good about myself and my rapid rise to authority. Now, I've got wounded men, a platoon pinned down, and they're asking me for direction.*

"Return fire, Harmon. Get your people shooting. I'll get you some help as quick as I can."

"Three Six, Rusty, get your platoon down the road a hundred yards, swing left, and fire across the front of the First Platoon. They're pinned down and have wounded."

With remarkable speed, the Third Platoon moved down the open road faster than Dennis had expected. At one point, he could see Lieutenant Adkins and Sergeant Beebe standing, directing their men into the turn and taking up positions, while bullets rained in upon them. Finally, with the center of the village in their sights, they opened fire with machine guns, light anti-tank missiles, grenades, rifle fire, and any other form of weaponry they could throw across the path of the First Platoon's withdrawing movements.

"We've got them in our sights," Adkins reported. "Tell Harmon to back out of there."

Dennis and Eddie lay in a depression in the earth. They could see little. "What's your situation, Harmon?" Dennis asked.

"I've got maybe two wounded from the reports up front. Doc Shiro is trying to get to them. One man killed, I think. I don't know who. I can't find Jimmy Hollister. Nick Dragon is bleeding real bad right beside me. We've got to get him out. We got hit just as soon as we started walking forward."

"Hang on, One Six. What's their size? What have they got?"

"At least a company," Lieutenant Harmon replied. "They've got heavy machine guns. There's a couple of fifty-two calibers pointed right at us. I'm taking small arms fire and rifle-propelled grenades. There's commo wire strung from bunker to bunker. I can't see it all, but, hell, this is no squad. There's a lot of VC moving around in there, bunker to bunker."

After a short pause, Lieutenant Harmon came back on the net. "I'm hit in the leg, Charlie Six... It's not too bad. Sorry about that, but I'll be OK. Tell Adkins to keep up the fire; I'm pulling back as soon as I find Hollister and have all my wounded."

Seeking better shelter, Dennis moved his command group to the right side of the road amid the palms and irrigation ditches, directing his platoons from there. "Oliver, get your people out, and yourself, too. Pull back a hundred yards and cross the road to my side; there's cover here. Get a landing zone prepared. I'm calling for a medivac helicopter."

"OK, Sir."

"Four Six, move your mortar platoon behind the First Platoon and help them pass through. Shoot forward of them as they go by. Drop some mortars on any targets you see."

"Wilco, Six."

"Rusty, hold these bastards by the nose and kick 'em in the ass. Keep up the fire."

"Three Six, here. We got 'em by the ass; the problem is, they think they got us by the ass."

Oblivious to the sniper and grenade fire now being directed at him and his small group, Dennis stood and watched the fluid motion of his unit fall into accord with his directives. Awed by their courage, he shouted, "Let's go. We're going to join Harmon."

"You're plain crazy, Charlie Six," Eddie pleaded in wide-eyed disbelief.

"They need us, Eddie. Let's go."

"Mother of Mercy. OK, Boss. Lead the way." They stood, and, immediately, a rifle-propelled grenade exploded in the dirt at their feet, showering them both with small bits of shrapnel. The radio protected Eddie's back, but it was blown from its harness and fell, smoldering, onto the ground. Dazed, but unhurt, Eddie still grasped the handset, although it was no longer connected to anything. "Useless," Eddie said, staring at the shattered radio.

Dennis' face was lacerated with small shell fragments. The largest piece split his nose like an overripe melon and caused his eyes to swell to a point where he could barely see. Grabbing a bandage from his first-aid pouch, he swabbed at the blood streaming down his face, then pressed the bandage against the larger wound, slowing the bleeding. Blood ran over his lip and it tasted salty.

Doc Friedman, moving frantically around the battlefield looking for wounded, heard the explosion and came running to Dennis' side. "Lie down, Lieutenant. Let me get a look at that wound." He poured a dark, antiseptic fluid over Dennis' face, then let it dry. Selecting an adhesive bandage from his medical bag, he pressed it tightly against the wound. Finally, he covered it with a thick gauze patch and taped it down.

"That'll stop the bleeding and hold it together, but you're going to need stitches. You'll have to get out of here on that medivac."

"Like hell I will." Dennis held his nose for a moment. "It feels good. Thanks, Doc. Let's get gone, Eddie. Are you OK?"

"Yeah, I've got piss running down my pant leg, but I'm OK. You're a bloody mess, Lieutenant. I'm with you, though, all the way. Come on. I'll be your guide dog. Follow me."

Bursting out of the palms, they raced across the open road, exposing themselves to sporadic bursts of fire from the enemy. Working their way forward in the direction of the First Platoon, they miraculously found a shell hole just as a burst of machine gun fire snapped overhead. Dennis and Eddie landed breathlessly on top of Lieutenant Harmon.

"How nice to see you, Charlie Six. I've been stuck in this hole for fifteen minutes. Got any good ideas?" Harmon asked.

Crossing the road to join his beleaguered First Platoon was a spontaneous act of courage and audacity for Dennis. It was a precursor of how he would perform as a commander. Anesthetized by adrenaline, he had crossed a bridge into a world known only by men who exercise absolute authority over the lives of other men.

He seized the moment. "If you can walk, get your men out of here, Oliver. Pull back across the road and help establish a defensive perimeter with the other platoons."

"I can't leave my boys," Harmon pleaded. "I won't leave them."

"I know. We'll get your wounded... Hollister. Wait until I have some fire coming across your front. Is Nick Dragon out? Let me use your radio for a second."

"Three Six, Adkins, this is Six. Get a machine gun team on the left front of your platoon. We need more fire across our front. We're pulling back. Go."

"Wilco."

The small, embattled group lay silent for a few minutes, waiting for support from the Third Platoon's machine guns. Dennis recalled that Jackie, Wally, and Andy now held those gun positions and the thought cheered him. He knew their spirit.

The rat-a-tat-tat of bullets spewing across their front signaled that the gun crews were in place. With a nod of understanding, Lieutenants Harmon and Riley crawled forward on their bellies to help guide the First Platoon. The enemy fire subsided and they stood, running forward, dodging from hut to hut, seeking concealment behind the ineffectual mud and stucco walls.

"Pull back, pull back," they shouted as bewildered men began to filter past them toward the rear, dragging their wounded with them. Panic and chaos threatened their solidarity as a platoon, yet the evacuation of their bloodstained comrades took precedence over all other considerations. They struggled together as teams, half-dragging, half-carrying themselves and the injured toward safety, evading bullets and shellfire along the way.

Lieutenant Harmon, limping and pumping blood from his poorly-bandaged leg wound, moved methodically forward, firing his M-16 from the hip. Dennis' heart pounded when he saw the weapon jam. Harmon dropped the rifle, then calmly began lobbing grenades to his front. Dennis joined him, rapidly firing shotgun blasts into the enemy positions. Together they advanced, finally stumbling over the motionless body of Jimmy Hollister. He lay still and quiet behind a small mound of dirt. Dennis knelt and he listened intently to his final words.

Doc Shiro arrived and prepared a pressurized can of plasma. "There's nothing I can do; his veins are collapsed." Within moments

Jimmy Hollister was dead. Dennis and Doc Shiro carried his lifeless body to cover in a shell hole. Other men arrived. Mysteriously, the enemy fire ceased. This allowed them to prepare a litter and to begin their trek rearward.

"They're letting us get him out," Oliver said. "They could pick off every one of us, exposed like we are."

Jimmy Hollister lay across the makeshift litter. The small procession of men walked upright, quietly carrying their dead brother across the beaten zone, rearward, into the waiting circle of infantrymen. They laid him in an oxcart which had been abandoned alongside the road by fleeing refugees. In an attempt at civility, they covered his face with his towel. Dennis stood over the body, staring at it.

"I didn't expect this," Lieutenant Harmon said, grabbing Dennis by the shoulder and spinning him around. "Good God, Hollister was everybody's favorite ... the platoon mascot. It's my fault --"

"I'm sorry, Oliver. That's your first one? Don't carry it --"

"Everybody's back and accounted for," Sergeant Allred interrupted. "We've got at least a dozen wounded, a couple of them pretty badly. Doc Shiro and the other medics are stabilizing them now."

"We need a medivac, Top," Dennis said.

"Dustoff from the 'Black Barons' says he'll take a chance and come on in, Sir. 'Blackhawk' and the gun team from the 187th are on the way. I got you another radio from the Fourth Platoon. Battalion is screaming for you to report. Go ahead, while I settle this company down." Without waiting for a response, Sergeant Allred glided back into the ranks of his bleeding men.

"Falcon Six, this is Charlie Six. Over."

"Situation report," demanded the anxious voice of Colonel Taylor.

"We're consolidated on the west side of the road," Dennis answered as calmly as he could. "I've got one killed -- about twelve wounded. We need a Dustoff and some help down here. We took heavy fire from that village. There must be at least a battalion or more of NVA dug in there."

"Your exaggerations don't become you, Charlie Six. You're engaged with little more than a squad. If you can't handle it, say so, and I'll find somebody who can."

"It's bigger than that, Falcon Six."

"Now listen, Charlie Six. Alpha Company should be approaching your left flank any minute. That Commander will take charge of the operation. Also, a platoon of armored personnel carriers are coming up from the south. Coordinate with them and mount an attack against that village. I want it taken by fifteen hundred hours."

"Roger that. Can we get artillery support and gunships? We'll need fire support."

"Gunships are en route escorting your 'Dustoff.' Don't lose that medical chopper. Make sure you are secure before you bring him in. Do you roger?"

"Yes, Sir."

"Your request for artillery is denied. The local Province Chief won't give 'political clearance.' Don't try to control those gunships, either. They are there to protect that medivac helicopter. You don't need it, anyway. Use your soldiers; that's what they're here for."

"Ah... OK. Ouch! Goddamn it." Dennis had unconsciously squeezed his nose. Blood gushed out onto his hand and he wiped it on his shirt.

"This is Falcon Six. Did you curse me, Riley?"

Dennis didn't answer. The denial of a plan for fire support angered him. The cardinal rule for attacking forces demanded tanks and artillery, Dennis knew. Assaulting fixed and fortified positions without such preparations was a summons for failure.

Lying on the ground, resting, Dennis looked at Eddie. "More good men will die today, I think. I wonder how the hell Colonel Taylor can tell the size of the enemy force from his bunker up there at Cui Chi?"

The distant sounds of approaching helicopters distracted him from his preoccupation with Colonel Taylor's message; he shouted instructions to receive the medical evacuation ship. Simultaneously, Captain Chancey and his band of "Alphagators" made contact with his left flank. Dennis exhaled a sigh of relief as he anticipated turning control over to the more experienced captain.

"Oh, no, Dennis," Chancey said as they warmly shook hands. "You know more about the situation. I wouldn't think of pulling rank on you. You're in charge."

"Don't be so damned gracious, Sir."

Chancey, always cool under stress, laughed. "Hell, Dennis, I don't mind taking my instructions from a Lieutenant, especially one I trained. What happened to you? There's blood all over your shirt. Are you hurt bad?"

"Naw, it'll be OK. I'll see Doc Mersack later. I just need a couple of stitches, that's all."

"Good soldier," Captain Chancey smiled. "Now, what's your plan?"

"Damn, Herb. Plan? Hell, I don't know. Well, I guess we'll muster an assault as soon as we get the dead and wounded out and those tracks from 'Tomahawk' get here. I'll go up the center; you take the left. We'll spread out between the tracks and overrun these bastards. What do you think?"

Captain Chancey voiced his agreement over the roar of approaching helicopters and mechanized infantry. Two menacing-looking gunships accompanied the medivac helicopter. They circled low while the badly wounded were loaded. Ambulatory men limped toward the waiting mercy ship when, suddenly, mortar shells began exploding all around them. Men dove desperately for cover. The pilot instinctively lifted the helicopter from the ground in a heroic effort to save her. The fuselage was peppered with shell fragments, yet the aircraft ascended up and away at an amazing pace. Lieutenant Harmon balanced himself on the runners. Holding on to the frame with one hand, he angrily shook his fist at the village with the other. Dennis knew that he'd probably never see him again.

"I've got what I can, Falcon. Red lights are flashing all over the dash. We'll take your men to the Cui Chi field hospital if this sucker holds together. Sorry I couldn't get them all."

Dennis didn't answer as he pulled himself and Captain Chancey off the ground. The mortars had stopped and the two gunships were pulverizing the village where the deadly rounds had originated. In reaction to the mortar attack and the obvious damage to the helicopter, they naturally opened fire without any clearances, political or otherwise.

"Charlie Six, this is Blackhawk ... a 'Rat Pack,' gun team. We nailed that mortar crew for you," the lead pilot calmly reported. "Bad guys are bouncing off the ground down there. We'll stick around as long as the fuel holds out. I'll take the rap for firing. We'll cover you; got any ideas?"

"Thanks, Blackhawk. I hear my tracks coming. Soon as they get here, we're going back in. Can you shoot forward of us as we move?"

"Wilco. I can see ... hell, boys! You've got at least thirty bunkers staring you in the face, maybe more. We'll bust some of them up with rocket fire and mini-guns, but... Oh, well. Good luck, Charlie Six."

Dennis summoned his leaders. Together, they huddled with Chancey and his men, making final attack plans. "We'll put the tracks in the middle and space our men in between them," Dennis said. "The fire-power of their fifty-caliber machine guns ought to get us through. Charlie Company will attack up the middle with Alpha on our left."

Captain Chancey nudged Dennis. "We'll take the middle. Your boys have had enough for one afternoon. My men are fresh; yours are ex-hausted, agreed?"

"Thanks, Sir." Dennis turned abruptly and looked southward. "OK, the APCs are here now. Let me get over to them and make coordination. Get your men ready. Fix bayonets before we cross the road. Start shoot-ing as soon as we're across it." Without waiting for a reply, Dennis raced toward the approaching carriers, pulling Eddie Runge once again by the radio communications cord.

"Hot damn. It's Johnny Knighten," Dennis shouted excitedly as he recognized the platoon leader. He and Johnny had been OCS classmates and competitors for graduating honors.

"It's thick with NVA," Dennis informed Johnny after a brief greet-ing. "We've got orders to attack. I've got two companies on line; you take the middle with Alpha. Start firing those fiftys as soon as we cross the road. The gunships will do their part. We move out in fifteen minutes. Any questions?"

"Let's go get 'em and good luck," Johnny shouted above the roar of the engines. He straightened and climbed atop his command track. Feet spread wide apart, hands upon his hips, he began shouting orders to his men as they scrambled into position.

Dennis realized that he now had a task force of more than two hun-dred and fifty men, complete with armored vehicles and gunships. He optimistically measured their chances for success, concluding that there was better than a fifty-fifty chance of routing the enemy. The gun ship pilot's report of thirty bunkers had sobered him, however.

He and Eddie had only distanced themselves slightly from the carri-ers when he heard a whooshing sound. Dennis turned in time to see an anti-tank rocket slam into the nose of the lead vehicle. Stunned, he watched Johnny's body somersault through the air like a rag doll. Amid the smoke and flames, he came down without legs and was dead by the time Dennis got to him.

"He was our physical fitness champ in OCS," he wailed to the men of Johnny's platoon. "He was my friend ... my friend."

Feeling foolish at his emotional outburst, Dennis fell silent. Quiet settled over him, and, after a few moments, he released Johnny's body to his men. They gently laid him inside another carrier. Revving their engines, they made their way south, in the direction they had originally come.

Watching them depart, Dennis felt an emptiness in his stomach. He hung his head and spoke to Eddie. "I don't know if they had orders to pull out or not, but, without Johnny, they've lost their heart for a fight. I can't say I blame them."

Sending a farewell message as they withdrew, the mechanized infantry turned their heavy machine guns on the village and blasted it indiscriminately. Stucco, mud, wood, tin, and debris of all kinds flew into the air. They left three buildings burning as they defiantly rode off. "It's just us and Alpha, now, Eddie. You ready?"

"Yeah, Dennis. I have a last request, though."

"What's that?"

"Carry your own damn radio, and give me a rifle. I'll walk point for Lieutenant Adkins' third platoon."

"You can't be serious. Why, Eddie?"

"I figure I have a better chance of surviving with them than walking alongside you. Somebody has to do it. Besides, you're going to get us both killed."

Dennis stared at Eddie. He could think of nothing to say.

Eddie smiled. "I can't explain it right now, Charlie Six. I just want to be with the troops for this fight, OK?"

Dennis nodded his approval. Together they walked quickly back to the center of the preparing forces. All eyes were upon him as they emerged from the brush. Eddie assisted him in strapping the borrowed radio to his back. "It's time to rock and roll. Follow me."

"Keep your powder dry, Denny," Captain Chancey said, ushering his forces to the right of Charlie Company. Dennis grinned and gave a thumbs-up sign, showing that he appreciated the older man's confidence in him.

Together, the two companies surged forward into a labyrinth of certain death.

Chapter Twenty-Nine
Night Attack

"Fix bayonets. Move it out, now," Dennis called at exactly 3:00 p.m. He watched as Alpha Company retraced the very steps Lieutenant Adkins had walked only two hours before. *Poor Alpha, they're going to get clobbered.*

The advance progressed well at first. The firepower of the gunships smothered any attempt by the enemy to meet his forces. He marveled at the daring of the pilots and crews as they flew barely fifty feet off the ground. Suddenly, one of the ships quivered in mid-air and Dennis observed the door gunner being blown back into the belly of the beast.

Sergeant Allred, standing beside Dennis, let out an oath. "Holy hell, they took a hit from a mortar or a rifle grenade. I hope they make it."

"Charlie Six, this is Blackhawk. My wingman took a bad hit. They're going down. We're trying to make some distance from the village. We've got to cover him. We're out of here."

Dennis didn't reply as he stood watching the wounded bird disappear into the trees north of his position, the flight leader on his tail. "No smoke, no explosion," he said to Allred. "Maybe they got lucky. Hope so."

"Everybody's moving out, Six." Sergeant Allred reminded him. "Let's keep going."

The snapping of bullets and explosions on his right told him that Alpha Company had barely entered the village before they took fire. So far, he had encountered none.

"Hot Damn, I'm pinned down," Captain Chancey reported. "We didn't get fifty feet across the road. Charlie Six, can you swing an element to fire across my front? I think I've got one KIA and several wounded."

"Roger, Alpha. Doing that. Stand by."

"Balser, Adkins, swing right, firing as you go. Lay down a base of fire across Alpha Company's front. They're stuck just like we were."

Dennis halted and watched as all three platoons made a ninety-degree turn to the right, dodging, running, and firing as they advanced.

Captain Chancey commented by radio that it was working and that fire upon his positions had diminished. The second and third platoons had advanced well beyond the point that Lieutenant Harmon had occupied earlier that day. "No sign of VC yet," Adkins radioed.

"We're making good progress as we advance from the left," Dennis reported to Battalion. "Looks like we're going to --"

His transmission was blotted out by ferocious bursts of enemy machine gun fire that suddenly erupted into the ranks of all three of his advancing platoons. Men began to fall like defenseless puppets and the screams of the wounded shook Dennis to the bone. "Damn it, lay out some firepower," he shouted into the handset. Rushing forward, he found Adkins and Balser excitedly conferring from the safety of a small crater.

"What's the situation?" Dennis said, his voice aflame with emotion.

"They let us walk right up to them before they opened fire," Mike Balser said. "We've got men pinned down up front." His composure in the midst of all the chaos served to calm Dennis and he reacted in similar fashion. On the verge of issuing withdrawal instructions, he was interrupted by the angry voice of his commander:

"Charlie Six, this is Falcon Six. Situation report? Over."

"We're pinned down again on the left flank and I've got casualties up front. Alpha's got the same problem on my right. I need artillery. The gunships took hits. They're gone."

"Artillery denied, Charlie Six. I've already told you that clearance can't be obtained to fire into an innocent village. We have other units in contact. Extract your men and Alpha's; I'm sending them elsewhere. You'll have to go it alone. Collect your casualties and get back here to Cui Chi. Now."

"Roger, Falcon... will comply." Dennis didn't envy Alpha Company, but was relieved to have instructions to evacuate the village. He contacted all platoons and ordered their withdrawal. "Crawl, walk, or run, damn it, but get your men out of there," he shouted into the handset. "Don't leave any dead or wounded."

Dennis glanced at his watch. He was beginning to lose all sense of time and he felt disconnected and dazed. Confusion reigned in his mind. *It's almost 6:00 p.m. The coming darkness would help us break out from the killing field. It seems like only minutes since we started the second assault, but we've been catching hell for more than three hours.*

Collaborating with Captain Chancey, they agreed that Alpha Company would pass through his ranks, leaving their wounded with Charlie Company. They were in a hurry. Dennis, with one platoon, would provide security from the rear in case the enemy attempted to follow. All others would begin the painful march toward Cui Chi.

The bulk of Charlie Company stopped and rested alongside the road about three hundred meters north of the village, waiting on their commander. Dennis and the remnants of the third platoon had no trouble locating them. Out-guards led them in to their temporary bivouac where he expressed sorrowful shock at what he saw.

The men had confiscated three, two-wheeled ox-carts and had laid the dead and wounded upon them. On the bottom, they placed the life less corpses as an uncomplaining foundation. "They can't feel it," Allred said.

On top of them lay the slightly wounded and the next tier carried the more severely injured, about twenty bodies in all. Some squirmed and twisted in pain, calling out for mercy. "Where is Jimmy Hollister?" Dennis called out.

Dennis found him on the bottom of one of the carts. He was bloated and hardly recognizable from the trauma of his death. Dennis touched his cold and motionless hand as it lay outstretched beneath the load of withering bodies. Grateful to be distracted by a greater need, he spoke with all of the wounded and promised them medical attention as soon as he could. Those still conscious cried out for water and Dennis shared the last drops from his canteen, calling for more water from the able-bodied remnants of Charlie Company.

Sergeants Beebe and Allred reported that there were less than sixty men left in fighting condition. "The dead and wounded ain't all ours. We're carryin' Alpha's too," Beebe said. "Cui Chi city is under attack and Cap'n Chancey's been thrown in."

"It's just us, now," Dennis said. "I pity Alpha. It's getting dark."

Sergeant Allred looked at Dennis. "You pity Alpha? Oh, yeah, tell the Colonel we got the Major and his driver. Found 'em both dead in a ditch. They're real dead. They's together there on the first cart. Major has a bullet through his forehead. An execution, if I ever saw one."

"Bastards," Dennis fumed.

"Sir, we've got about three rounds of ammunition apiece," Sergeant Allred said. "All grenades, bullets, anti-tank weapons, water, and food have been redistributed equally among the men. Let them rest here for a while. When it's dark enough, we'll drag these carts and ourselves back to Cui Chi."

Allred watched Dennis carefully, then dug in his pockets and produced a few tins of C-rations. "Here, Lieutenant, eat some chow, and have Doc Shiro look after those wounds on your face."

Dennis had forgotten his lacerations and only now did they begin to pain him. His nose was swollen and his eyes blackened from the trauma. "It ain't nothing," he told the Senior Medic as the corpsman washed his face again with antiseptics and then fashioned small bandages.

"It's bleeding a little bit, Sir. It's a hard wound to bandage," Doc Shiro said.

Dennis thanked him and looked around at the maze of wounded and other confused men. He approached and comforted a wounded soldier, PFC James Dice, bleeding from his face and ears. "These guys hurt a lot more than I do," Dennis said, swabbing James' bloody wounds with a bandage. "God, what a mess you are."

James looked helplessly at his Commander for a moment, then smiled and began gently wiping away the oozing blood from Dennis' face. "It'll be OK, Sir, don't worry. Everything will be all right," he said. Dennis impulsively embraced him for a moment and they bled upon each other.

Dennis patted James on the arm. "Yeah, like you said, it'll be all right, Buddy." He walked away and began a check of his decimated ranks. Moving from man to man, he made an effort to comfort each. His voice carried conviction and he promised them a better tomorrow. Completing his visitations, he squatted in conference with his leaders. "Let's get moving guys; some of the wounded are suffering badly."

"So is the rest of this Company," Bill Walker grimly pointed out. "Boys are pulling at the yokes of the carts now. I'll take the point with the Fourth Platoon. Let's go."

They moved only one hundred meters when the radio crackled with the querulous voice of Colonel Taylor: "Charlie Six, this is Falcon Six. There is a change of plans. Take your company back into Ap Cho immediately. Mount an attack with whatever men you have left. I want a casualty and damage assessment from today's actions. Look for enemy bodies, understand?"

Speechless for just a moment, Dennis drew a long breath and then something snapped inside him: "Take them back into Ap Cho?" he retorted. "Be reasonable, Falcon Six. I've got less than sixty able-bodied men to fight with."

"It must be done, Charlie Six. Are you saying you can't or that you won't?"

"I'm saying we're down to a couple of rounds per man. No water, few grenades. We're out of medical supplies. There are badly wounded men all around me. It's pitch black out here. Do you still want us to attack that place again?"

Sergeant Allred gripped his shoulder and said softly, "Take it easy, L.T. Won't do you any good to get all heated up. Be firm, but don't lose it."

Dennis calmed and he waited for Colonel Taylor's response. Turning to Allred, he pleaded, "He's got to understand our condition. He just can't be that cold-hearted."

"This is Falcon Six. Now you listen to me, Riley. You've been whining all day about trying to take out a squad. You've shot yourself in the foot and squandered your resources. In my view, you've acted cowardly if you've acted at all. Now you have one more chance to redeem yourself -- your last chance. I know full well what time of night it is. I don't care if you are out of ammunition. Fix bayonets and make a night attack. Do you understand me? I said fix bayonets!"

"Roger. Yes, Sir."

Dennis' easy submission to the ludicrous order was formed in a flash of inspiration. In the dark, in this struggle, no one from the headquarters will dare step foot out of their bunkers to verify their movements.

It's time to act on my own, just like I promised myself back there in the hobos. Damn the consequences. The men will follow me and Allred and Beebe if there's any chance at all.

The plan Dennis envisioned would probably cause no injuries, but would comply with the absurd mandate from Colonel Taylor.

"We'll attack under the cover of darkness, silently, not firing," he told Allred. "Stealth and silence will be our weapons and we'll use only that until I can report, truthfully or otherwise, that the attack has failed."

Sitting on the moist earth alongside the oxcarts, Dennis called the few remaining leaders together, informing them of the bizarre order and his own plan for compliance. "We'll take fifty men and feel our way along the right side of the road until we're in the vicinity of the center of the village. From there, we'll crawl on our bellies into the village, maybe a hundred feet, no farther, to the point where we always take fire," he said.

"You're not making this up, are you?" Sergeant Walker asked.

Dennis looked squarely at him. "Let's just comply with the order. You guys know exactly when we'll get hit. On that last step I want everyone down on the ground, behind a building, or in a shell hole. I'll get us out of there after that."

"How?" Lieutenant Adkins said.

"He'll withdraw us or I'll do it myself. I think his ass is on the line at Division. He needs to verify that there are plenty of enemy still left in there. He has to justify the mess he's made of things and he's using us for bait. You with me?"

"Fix bayonets," Allred said. "Give me five minutes to round up the men. Balser is wounded, but he'll be all right. Harmon is gone for good, I think. Adkins is your only officer."

"Jesus."

"I'll act as platoon sergeant. We'll have to leave some ammo and a few guards with the wounded so they can defend themselves. Who walks point?"

"I got it," Eddie said as he stepped forward and fixed his bayonet onto the end of his rifle. "Here, Lieutenant. Guess you'll have to carry your radio again. I need my shooting hands free for the killing I'm going to do tonight. It's payback time for Jimmy Hollister."

Dennis smiled and was heartened by his audacity. "Thanks, I needed that, Eddie."

In the darkness, he could barely recognize the faces of his men. Specialist Patrick Shine, a hardy first platoon soldier, reached out to touch and speak softly to him as he passed. "We're with ya, Charlie Six," he said.

Arriving at the head of the column, he heard the familiar voice of Wally Gerber. "We go where you go, Lieutenant."

Wally, Andy, Jackie, Rosey and Jay Cee stood as a group and would not let him pass. "We take the point, Lieutenant. You and Eddie stay way the hell back," Wally said.

"Wally --"

"Yeah, Dennis. Like I said. Shit for brains... all of us."

Dennis watched as, one by one, they took their places at the head of the line. The phantom column seemed to float along the ground as they crept silently toward Ap Cho. Insisting upon it, Jay Cee went first, followed by Jackie and Rosey. Andy and Wally flanked them on both sides of the road, fingers touching the triggers of their machine guns, a belt of perhaps twenty bullets dangling from each.

In fifteen minutes, they were on their bellies, crawling across the road into Ap Cho once again. His heart raced when, midway through their progress, the familiar loud pop and bang of artillery illumination rounds burst overhead. It flooded the scene with a brilliant, incandescent light. Instinctively the men stood; firing their few remaining bullets, they charged headlong into the enemy. Exposed, it was the only thing they could do. Their well-armed foes were waiting and, with the help of the ill-timed American illumination, the Viet Cong waylaid them with a heavy blast of automatic weapons fire. Sergeant Allred was the first to fall, a bullet slicing across his neck.

Dennis found himself in a shell hole mingled with the torsos, arms, and legs of five or six other men. Someone had shoved him into it and the others piled on top, smothering him with protection from the small arms fire. Finding his radio handset, he bellowed a cursing condemnation to the "Fucking fool," that ordered the illumination. "Shut it off, goddamn it. Shut it off."

No radio response followed and they huddled in holes and depressions, seeking protection from the enemy fire as it grazed inches above their heads. They lay helpless, their ammunition expended, armed only with the bayonets affixed to their rifles. Doc Shiro used the light to drag Sergeant Allred to shelter behind the mud walls of a hut. "He's OK," he shouted above the rattle of gunfire. "He's OK."

As suddenly as it began, the glow of artificial light waned and finally ended. Simultaneously, without clear targets, the enemy stopped firing. Dennis shouted the orders to withdraw. "Pull back, pull back." In the darkness, it took only seconds for the small body of men to reassemble on the sheltered side of the road.

"Get a headcount," Allred ordered as he pressed bloody bandages to his neck. "Give me a report on the wounded. We've got to get out of here fast, Lieutenant. If those bastards realize we're out of ammunition, they'll come up out of those holes and attack us from the rear. We've got a couple of walking wounded, that's all. Let's haul ass."

They reached their cargo of broken humanity at about 2:00 a.m. Fresh water, ammunition, and rations were waiting for them. Apparently one of the rear echelon NCOs had been listening to their plight over the radio. Without orders or instructions, he'd commandeered a jeep and trailer and acquired what stores he thought the company needed. Together, he and another soldier drove without lights down the treacherous strip of road. They delivered the precious cargo just minutes before Dennis and his group arrived.

"'Suds,' brought us what we need, Sir," Mike Balser said. "I don't know where he got it, but it don't matter. We're watered down, got ammo, and medical supplies. Want to go back and take another crack at Ap Cho?"

Before Dennis could respond to the facetious suggestion, Captain DeMatto broke the silence and radioed that they were free to return to the compound at Cui Chi. "Watch for ambushes along the way, Charlie Six. Skirt the city; many of its buildings are burning. Alpha and Bravo are battling it out in there right now. What's your plan?"

"We'll go through the rubber plantation south of the city. I know it's mined in places, but we can't survive out here. We'll take our chances in the rubber."

"Come on in, Charlie Six; we'll meet you at the gate."

The small procession of defeated infantrymen, taking turns at pulling their tormented cargo, methodically plodded northward. In their uncoordinated and inexperienced effort, the stronger men, pulling on the right yoke, steered one cart into a ditch, the weaker men failing to compensate for the yawl. Finally, Sergeant Beebe called a halt to the movement, explaining that it was much like mule teams pulling on a hay wagon; each man had to pull in unison. They nodded their understanding and began pulling together, but not before they had to unload the dead and wounded to retrieve the cart from the ditch. The injured accepted the transfers silently, without complaint. Dennis marveled at the mettle of his suffering men

Beebe walked behind, barking soft commands much as he had done on the hillsides of Tennessee, directing his team of human mules. Dennis pulled occasionally on one of the yokes. The weight of the cargo caused them to walk at a snail's pace. Pulling them was like rowing a boat, the wagons veering right to left. It required considerable coordination to keep them straight. Allred walked beside him, growing weaker by the moment, but refusing to ride atop the bloody mass that was once the pride of Charlie Company.

No words passed between them and the radios remained strangely quiet as if in deference to their plight. By four o'clock in the morning, they had covered the slightly more than one thousand meters, clearing the plantation without incident. They entered the gates of the Cui Chi base camp and fell into a throng of waiting field ambulances, medics, and supply specialists. Dennis and Eddie fell, exhausted alongside the road. Colonel Taylor was notably absent and Captain DeMatto took charge, speeding the wounded to a field hospital and dispatching the dead into reverent hands.

He approached Dennis and stood silently before him for a moment. "I'm sorry for the mess, Riley," Captain DeMatto said. "You handled it as best you could."

"Thanks, Sir. I've lost a lot of men today."

"I've got about a dozen replacements for you. They just got off the plane this morning and they're scared to death. See Doc Mersack. He's got an aid station set up just down the road. Get your wounds tended to. I want your Company to camp here alongside the road. Get some rest, re-supply, do what's necessary to reconstruct your fighting force. Some of your men are only slightly wounded and should return to duty over the next few days."

He paused for a time. Finally, watching Dennis carefully, he announced, "The Colonel blew it in there, Lieutenant Riley. He told Division that there was only a handful of enemy in Ap Cho and he's getting his ass ripped about it now at Headquarters. He never asked for artillery support and never reported the extent of your casualties. I think we've got a new Commander coming."

"Thank God."

"Yes, thank Him and General Philson, the Division Commander. He overheard that stupid order to fix bayonets and that was all it took. He called for Colonel Taylor about midnight and I haven't heard from him since."

"Really?"

"Yes. I intercepted a radio transmission that they were arranging transportation for him to a supply unit in Saigon. I don't think there will be a farewell party for him."

"What am I supposed to do now?"

"Brigade has ordered us to provide a platoon or more to the engineers again. They're busy trying to keep the road open between here and

Trang Bang. The VC have set up road blocks, mines, and barriers of all kinds along that road."

"Good. We need the break," Dennis replied.

"You have little more than a platoon left," Captain DeMatto said, shaking his head. "In a couple of days your Company should be back to fighting strength. Let's see what develops with the new CO. You can rest here until late morning. Move out when you're ready."

Captain DeMatto reached into his shirt. "Here, take a look at my map, then pick your own route. I want to bring you abreast of all the other actions that are taking place. We all know that you caught hell down there in Ap Cho, but for you and your men, it's over. Forget it. I'm sorry about your man, Hollister. Find some time to write a letter to his parents soon. Now, go get your nose patched, then get some rest."

"Keep it clean if you can, Dennis," Doc Mersack said as he washed his hands in a basin. "Took about thirty tight little stitches. It's a real challenge trying to make you look pretty, but it'll heal OK. You'll never notice the scar. Good thing I got you in time." The Doctor laughed, then grew serious. Speaking quietly, he approached Dennis, lying on a litter.

"This wound could get you to Japan, Lieutenant Riley, maybe plastic surgery. I can write it up ... up to you."

Dennis thought about the offer for a moment. "No thanks, Doc. Sergeant Allred, Krznarovich, Eddie. What would they do without me? I owe Jimmy Hollister better than that. I'm out of here. Thanks anyway, Doc." Dennis slapped him on the back, collected his gear, and left the tent.

A glorious dawn burst through and the searing heat upon his face awakened Dennis. He jumped up from the soft earth and grass in which he had slept, his heart racing as he glanced at his watch. *9:00 a.m. on the second of February. ...gotta get moving. Where is everybody? "Fix bayonets!"*

Chapter Thirty
FNG Flint

"Don't panic, Charlie Six," Eddie laughed. "I've been watching over you like your guardian angel. The company is in the tree line, out of the sun, getting a little rest."

"Who's flying the plane, Eddie?"

"Sergeant Beebe took over Allred's duties — he's the Field First Sergeant now. We'll be ready to move out with seventy-five healthy men in about thirty minutes. Here, read these radio logs that Captain DeMatto left for you while I fetch us some coffee and something to eat."

Eddie stood and handed Dennis several pages of reports. "By the way, Allred was only grazed with that bullet, but it was serious enough to get him hospitalized for a few days. He says to tell you 'don't do nothing stupid' and he'll get right back to us. Lieutenant Balser is back with his platoon, too."

Calmed by Eddie's matter-of-fact explanations, Dennis thanked him as he sped off. Glancing at the radio dispatches, he began to study them as an afterthought. A note was attached, instructing him to burn them when he finished. Startled by what he saw, he bolted erect and his heart sank. It was clear Ap Cho wasn't over yet. It was more than a minor incident in the dozens of battle reports unfolding.

2 February 1968: Bao Trai under heavy attack, read the first line of the clipped reports. *D/3/22 receives incoming mortars in their night positions. Gunships react to Bao Trai. Contact ends at 0346. Fixed wing observation airplane is shot down at 0435. 1/27 reacts with A Co. 2/12 Infantry receiving mortar fire. 4/23 Infantry receiving small arms and rocket-propelled grenades into their night positions. Cui Chi ammo dump explodes, scattering heavy shrapnel and tear gas. Report of more than one hundred VC in Tan Phu Trung village. Outpost at Gian Huyuh is overrun and destroyed. Regional Forces retreat. 0830 hours: reports of one hundred plus VC at XT701088, Village of Ap Cho. C/3/22 in moderate contact. Enemy blocks roads and have taken a school house as a Command Post. Hoc Mon bridge collapsed by VC saboteurs during the night. Two hundred VC are spotted at*

XT750234, about 5 miles north of 3/22 Infantry operations, heading south toward Ap Cho or Hoc Mon. All Tropic Lightning elements are engaged finding bunkers, mortar emplacements, mines and roadblocks. A dozen small actions ensue. 4/23 Infantry reports many hamlets flying VC flags along road between Cui Chi and Trang Bang. Tropic Six orders Division priority that Main Supply Route be kept open.

Dennis had read enough. "We're in deep trouble," he said to Eddie as he returned with hot coffee and a tin of scrambled eggs and biscuits. "Looks like the VC and NVA have coordinated a major attack. They're looking for that uprising. Might be getting it, too. These reports scare me."

"Did you read the bottom line?"

Dennis flipped the pages and noted a small comment: *Falcon element, 3/22 Infantry, conducts change of command at 0500 hours 2 February 1968.* Touching a match to the reports, he sat in prayerful thought as the smoke drifted skyward.

By 11:00 a.m., they reached the main body of engineers and fell in alongside them as they methodically swept the roads with electronic and other sophisticated devices. Stopping every fifty feet or less, they investigated suspicious-looking objects, setting charges and exploding them in place. Secondary explosions proved the wisdom of their techniques, but as often as not, it was only a buried metal can or something similar that delayed their progress. Charlie Company was delighted with the snail's pace, being required only once to assist in dismantling a crude roadblock.

Throughout the day, men joked about the effortless mission they had and how they would soon be on the "big bird," carrying them back to "the land of big PXs and mini-skirted girls."

"Encouraging signs, after what we've been through," Lieutenant Adkins said as he removed his shirt and joined the others, lazily sunning themselves.

"Morale's-a-coming back, Lieutenant. We got the fightin' spirit again," Sergeant Beebe added.

"Good," Dennis said. "I think we're going to need it."

Dennis studied this diminutive Staff Sergeant closely for the first time. Sergeant Beebe was from Tennessee. He had spent much of his youth farming with mules along the rocky slopes of the Appalachians. He stood only five feet, seven inches tall, but was solidly built. He sported a bushy black mustache that was always grimy from tobacco juice. At thirty-five, his weather-beaten face suggested he was much older. It was his special savvy, common sense about day-to-day matters, and an easy southern drawl that so endeared him to Dennis.

"Replacements are coming in at Cui Chi, and we're to get back before dark," Beebe continued. "Let's hope it stays quiet. By the way, I got a message for you to report to the new Battalion Commander right quick when we get in."

"Oh, yeah. I forgot about him."

"Size 'em up for us, Sir. I hope he ain't no pointy-headed Yankee like that last guy."

By 5:00 p.m. on the fourth day of February, Dennis stood at rigid attention before his new commander, Lieutenant Colonel Roy K. Flint, OCS, Infantry, 1952.

"Stand at ease, Lieutenant," the Colonel ordered as he stood and extended a firm hand across his desk. His piercing blue eyes suggested he knew their power and they stayed steady on Dennis' face, never blinking.

Remembering Sergeant Beebe's request, Dennis instinctively measured the man: *Pretty tall. Looks physically fit. Lean and wiry. Might be thirty-six years old. That jutting jaw, man he's kinda scary. Doesn't smile too easily, yet his handshake is strong. Aw, hell, he's OK. Those crystal blue eyes remind me of First Sergeant Krznarovich.*

"So, you're Charlie Six?" the Colonel asked rhetorically, snapping Dennis out of his reverie. "Lieutenant Riley, I'm very happy to meet you. Sit down," he said. "Relax."

"Yes, Sir," Dennis said as he sat down on a folding chair.

"Lieutenant, I was in the Division Tactical Operations Center when you first entered Ap Cho." The Colonel paused, folded his hands carefully, and set them firmly atop his desk as he looked Dennis straight in the eye.

"I must tell you, Lieutenant Riley, I listened, spell-bound, to the entire battle. I'm aware of the heroic effort you and your men made down there. General Philson insists that you be decorated for your valor and I agree. It was a hell of a fight you put up. Tell your men -- they should all be proud." He smiled warmly as he verbally applauded Dennis and his men.

Dennis felt vindication at the Colonel's words, grinning broadly and relaxing completely. "Why, thank you, Sir," he said crossing his legs. "I will tell the men. They've recovered well and I wanted to mention how I feel about --"

Switching his demeanor completely, Colonel Flint frowned, swallowed hard and said: "On your feet, now, Lieutenant. That's it -- at attention now. They told me you were a talker and I see what they mean. Sorry, but I don't have the time or patience to listen to it."

Shocked by the radical change in his manner, Dennis jumped to his feet. "Sir, what?"

The Colonel, slowly swiveling back and forth in his chair, stopped abruptly and faced Dennis. Sighing, he penetrated him again with those blistering eyes, boring home an unspoken message. "Lieutenant, one of your Sergeants broke into an ammunition bunker belonging to the 101st Airborne when you were engaged at Ap Cho. He smashed in the door, assaulted and tied up the sentry, cursed the Commander when he tried to stop him, and outran the military police. He was towing a trailer loaded with precious munitions belonging to somebody else. They call him 'Suds,' I am told. Are you aware of all this?"

Dennis' stomach churned and he flared with emotion: "That would be Sergeant Wilson, Sir," he said. "I am aware of it and I'm a bit embarrassed. He took it upon himself to gather the ammunition. I was desperate and I never thought about how he managed to come by it. I'm damn glad he did, though."

"You won't be so 'damn glad' when I dock your pay a hundred dollars for the damage done to the bunker. Also, you'll have to replace the stolen ammunition from your own stores. You and I will personally apologize to the Battalion Commander of the Airborne unit. A gentlemen's code of conduct requires it. So you're a bit embarrassed, huh?"

"Sorry, Sir, but, ah, maybe you don't understand how things were. See, we were in a bloody mess down there in Ap Cho. Colonel Taylor had us make a night attack without ammunition --"

"Cut it right there," Lieutenant. "What I'm telling you, trying to teach you, is that there is no excuse for any one of your men violating laws and regulations. As a Company Commander, you are responsible for everything your unit does. Everything. Get it?"

"I believe I do, Sir."

"The problem with this outfit is that you've been making your own rules because you disagreed with the decisions of your former commander. It has rattled down to your men. If you were really in charge,

Sergeant Wilson -- soon to be Corporal Wilson -- would not have even considered the illegal method he used for getting ammunition."

Rising from his chair, Colonel Flint stepped around the desk, stopping inches from Dennis' face. Poking a finger in his chest, he continued. "Your unit, of all our units, has been picking and choosing what missions they might give their loyalty to. I've looked them over. Your men don't look like soldiers and they don't act like soldiers. You especially -- carrying a shotgun instead of the weapon that was issued to you. What do you think that says to the men about their weapon?"

"I never thought about --"

"You set the wrong example, Riley. Your people perform out of some misguided affection for you. You seem to want to be the good guy. I remind you of what they say about good guys and where they finish."

His voice rising in pitch now, Colonel Flint continued, "For your own good, young man, take back the authority granted to you by that Commission you accepted. These are hard times. Your own survival and that of your men depends on how well you command them, not on how devoted they are to you. Take command, Lieutenant Riley -- seize it -- don't wait for it to come to you."

Dennis' face turned beet red. Colonel Flint paused for a few seconds, sat down behind his desk, and continued in an almost fatherly voice. "Now, I expect a full measure of obedience from you and your men from here on out, understood?" His gaze raked Dennis to the bone. It left him momentarily speechless.

"Yes, Sir."

"Good, Soldier. Now spread this word among the other commanders. I expect absolute obedience and will not tolerate the haphazard methods of fighting this enemy that I've witnessed over the last several days. Get to work tonight on fixing that bunker and getting the ammunition replaced -- legally."

After some hesitation, Colonel Flint cleared his throat and then spoke so quietly that Dennis could barely hear him: "I know you are a hell of a fighter, Riley. I don't know how you survived Ap Cho and that long march the other night. It was horrible, I know, but remember, a pat on the back and a kick in the ass are only about eight inches apart. They always come hand in hand, one behind the other." He swiveled in his chair, turned away, and Dennis glared at his back, fuming in muted rage.

Gathering his emotions, Dennis calmed and spoke with courtesy and confidence, as he assumed Colonel Flint would expect. "Yes, Sir. I'll get the bunker fixed and replace the ammo tonight, but Sir, what are my orders? I was told you had a mission for me."

Lieutenant Colonel Flint, former Master Sergeant of Infantry, had come of age on Heartbreak Ridge in Korea. With deliberate theater, he turned slowly back toward Dennis. Waiting a full minute, he studied his young Lieutenant. The silence thickened, becoming almost intolerable for both of them.

"What, Sir?" Dennis begged. And then he thought he noticed a mist in the eyes of the older man when he finally spoke. "Your orders, Lieutenant? Your orders are to attack Ap Cho at zero six-hundred hours in the morning."

"What?"

"Take it this time. Wipe out that village and everything in it."

"Sir, did I hear you correctly? Did you say --"

"You heard me. Cross the Line of Departure at zero six hundred. Captain DeMatto is at Division Headquarters now, trying to explain the situation in Ap Cho. On my behalf, he's begging for artillery, tanks, anything to help knock that force out. We're spread terribly thin and all of our companies are engaged with the enemy in some way."

Dennis sat down without being asked. "I didn't know."

"When enemy infiltraters blew the ammunition dump at Cui Chi, Bravo Company was unable to retrieve their fighting gear. There are still too many shells and other munitions lying about. It may be a while before they can get back in. They are unable to engage the enemy until we get them refitted. We have only three companies left. They are all short on manpower and they're exhausted. Still, we have a war to fight."

Colonel Flint stood and leaned both fists on his desk, measuring Dennis' reaction to his words.

"It appears that the truce has been irreparably broken. The North Vietnamese Army has invaded the South with hundreds of thousands of men. We're in the middle of the fight of our life. They've attacked the air base at Tan San Nhut and a major battle is taking place there as we speak. Even the United States garrisons, perhaps the American Embassy itself, is, or will be, lost. The only supply route open is Highway QL One, which, as you know better than anyone else, passes directly in front of Ap Cho. If we lose control of that road, all units north of us, including ourselves, are without re-supply. It must stay open."

Dennis jumped up and began pacing the floor. He was overcome by the breadth of information that Colonel Flint related to him.

The Commander continued: "We know from captured documents, prisoners, refugees, and other intelligence reports that there are at least two North Vietnamese battalions dug in at Ap Cho. Their mission is to block that supply route. They have no concept of retreat in their battle orders, no plan for withdrawal. They will fight until they are all dead and that is what I want you and the men of Charlie Company to do -- make them dead."

Colonel Flint pounded now on the desk. "Make them wish they had planned for withdrawal, Riley. You must take that village, and the only way it's going to get done is to kill all of them. For now, at least, keep that supply route open."

"Yes, Sir. Just Charlie Company?"

"We'll get you some help. Your company is all we have at the moment. Now, I ask you, Riley, are you and your boys up to the task? Can you do it?"

His steady voice and burning gaze inspired Dennis. He stopped pacing and faced his Colonel. In spite of the verbal thrashing, Dennis accepted that Colonel Flint was only telling him what he needed and deserved to hear. *That voice, the strength in it... inspiring. Seize command. Yeah, he's my kind of soldier.* Dennis looked directly into the Colonel's stony face, then cheerfully responded, "You bet your sweet ass, Boss. Chargin' Charlie's going to take Ap Cho."

Colonel Flint grinned at his audacity.

"Damn right. We'll take it, Sir. We're going to kick their asses back to -- ."

"Good. Keep me informed by radio of your movements. Hit that bloody village at zero six hundred hours. You'll get five minutes of artillery fire as you advance. Look for a platoon, five tanks, from the Three-Quarter Cavalry unit. They've promised to send something to help you. Any questions?"

"Do you want me to write my apology to the 101st Airborne and leave it with you? I might not see them for a while."

Colonel Flint smiled. "Save your attitude for the enemy, Lieutenant. Dismissed."

Chapter Thirty-One
Back to Ap Cho

"Roger that, Sir," Dennis said as he saluted, abruptly turned, and moved out into the evening shadows. He accepted and approved of Colonel Flint. He even liked him. "Something about his voice -- the muscles in his face," he told Sergeant Beebe and the Platoon Leaders. "He really knows how to chew ass. It made me feel good, then wham, he ate me alive about Suds, and that damn ammunition bunker."

"He's already got Suds' stripes," Mike Balser said. "He moves quick."

"He's all soldier -- by the book, but I think he cares about us. I can't explain it, but maybe we have a Commander we can live with, and maybe fight for."

Without telling them their mission, he recited all that he knew about the significance of Ap Cho and how crucial it had become to their survival. "Maybe I've misjudged everything and everybody above the Company level," he said to his spellbound audience. "Colonel Taylor, his staff, not anyone knew the size of the enemy force in there and this offensive is so sudden, so shocking, that he couldn't believe it. He just didn't know how to react. We're on a World War Two battlefield now. The name of the game is attack."

Lieutenant Donnelly, who had listened intently to the shocking appraisal, demurred politely, then asked the obvious: "Who or what is going to take it out? Air strikes, a nuclear bomb?"

"Funny you should ask that question," Dennis said, making a feeble attempt at humor. "We are, Michael, we are." Without waiting for their shocked reply, he continued: "You all know how bad it is, so let's not waste time bitching about it. Lieutenant Donnelly, contact your artillery people and confirm our supporting fires. We go in at zero six hundred hours. Get me five minutes of hot steel in front of our advance. Tell them to give us all they have."

Adhering to Colonel Flint's admonition to "seize command," Dennis decided it was time to get professional. Standing ramrod tall, he began by addressing his subordinates by their rank: "Lieutenants Balser,

Adkins, all of you. I don't need to draw a map in the dirt; you know the area as well as anybody. We move out at 4:00 a.m."

"What's the plan, Sir?" Sergeant Walker asked.

"We'll cross the road, the Line of Departure, together at 0555 hours tomorrow, the fifth of February. Keep your men low and fix bayonets. I'll work out a scheme for attack and call you later tonight. Any questions?" They were mute, stunned into a silence that unnerved them all.

Suddenly the familiar and confident voice of Sergeant Allred spoke out from the darkness. He had slipped into the gathering of leaders, quiet, efficient, and unnoticed. Dennis' mood brightened as he listened.

"Tell your platoon sergeants to report to me in five minutes," the old soldier ordered. "We've got work to do -- ammo, water, everything. I'll be with the CO in the middle. I've got some payback to do for that bastard trying to kill me the other night. Tell them I'd like some help doing it."

His unexpected arrival back into the ranks relieved everyone and Dennis' spirits soared as he listened to him. Knowing that the others felt the same way, he simply said, "Welcome home, Top; we missed you."

Sergeant Allred bit into a plug of his favorite tobacco. "Glad to be here with you guys. Now, let's get to work," he said. The leadership obediently blended into the brush. Dennis and Eddie sat upright, leaning against trees, forever joined by the ubiquitous radio communications cord. Sleep was impossible; still, out of habit, Dennis shut his eyes for a moment and thought of home.

Asleep for only few moments, something startled him and he jumped to his feet. Eddie pressed a cold can of beer into his neck. "Here, Charlie Six, have one on Father Tobin. He came by visiting the men and slipped me a couple of cold beers. Don't know where he gets them. He saw you sleeping and left you alone. He said he was praying for us."

Fully awake, Dennis sipped the cool refreshment, then decided to move among the men. They were eating from tins and resting in ditches and any place that might afford some protection from shrapnel. Artillery boomed close by and the sky pulsated a dazzling white and red from the glow of illumination flares.

"Good job, today. I'm proud of you. Thanks," he said to each man as he stopped to check his condition.

He called for his leaders at about 1:00 a.m. and they snaked their way through the dark to find him. Dennis, Eddie, Sergeant Allred, and

Lieutenant Donnelly established a command post in a large, concrete pipe abandoned alongside the road. There, they finalized plans for the attack. Summarizing Colonel Flint's analysis of the situation, Dennis convinced them of the need for the early morning charge and all agreed that, with a little help from tanks and artillery, they could rout the enemy soldiers in short order.

Dennis, Eddie, and the others crawled out of the pipe. He watched as his men gathered around him and squatted or sat on the ground, eager to hear his orders.

"I feel sorry for those poor bastards," Mike Donnelly said. "When that artillery hits, it'll flatten that village. They'll run like cockroaches when the lights come on. Nothing's going to live through it."

"Yeah," Lieutenant Balser added. "Give me and Rusty just one fucking tank and we'll punch our way through there in twenty minutes."

"Great, guys, but first we need to see what kind of condition our men are in. Tell me about your platoons. Balser, you first."

"I've got twenty-three men left. A couple of them have minor wounds but everyone is pissed. They've got blood in their eyes. They want revenge."

"Count on me for twenty," Rusty stated resolutely. "I might get three back from the aid station. Third Platoon feels the same way. Let's get even."

"Fourth Platoon has eighteen," Sergeant Walker reported. "We're ready."

"First Platoon has about eighteen that can fight," Sergeant Allred said. "They know where we're going -- no cowards in that platoon. Lieutenant Harmon's leg wound was worse than he let on. I don't think you'll see him again. That young Buck Sergeant O'Connor has taken charge now, the one they call Jay Cee. He'll do just fine. Do you agree, Lieutenant?"

Dennis thought for a moment, then said, "Sergeant O'Connor? He's the ranking NCO? No, not Jay Cee. I don't think he's ready yet. Sergeant Walker, the men know you. Take the First Platoon." Dennis realized that he was motivated by an urge to protect Jay Cee from such responsibility. He hoped that Allred wouldn't notice.

"Whatever's right, Lieutenant," Allred said, "but you know he's good --"

"Not O'Connor, Sarge. Please."

Staring at his young leader, Sergeant Allred spoke quietly. "This ain't Martin again, is it Lieutenant?"

"No."

"Then, whatever's right, Lieutenant. Whatever's right."

Dennis summarized: "The way I see it, we have roughly ninety fighting men left in the company if you count me, Eddie, the Medics and all. We're a little more than half-strength, men. We'll have to be real smart when we go back in. Have your men 'stand to,' at three-thirty. That'll give them a couple of hours' sleep, anyway."

Dennis stood, examining his new M-16 rifle. The leaders watched as he inserted a magazine, chambered a round, and put the weapon on safe. "Sergeant Walker and I will take the lead as we advance down the road," he said. "Are you ready, men?"

"Roger that," Rusty Adkins said.

"You bet your ass," Mike Balser said, slapping Dennis on the shoulder. "Let's go get 'em."

Dennis was heartened. "That's all, men. Meet me on the road headed out of here at zero four-hundred hours."

They departed cautiously into the night and Dennis felt a certainty about their mission, relayed in the attitude of his subordinate leaders. *Damn good men. They'll be kickin' some butt in the morning, I just know it.*

"We said that about Porkchop Hill, too," Sergeant Allred replied when Dennis expressed his optimism. "We thought that we'd take that mountain in a couple of hours. It took weeks and a lot of good men died doing it. My advice is to prepare for the worst."

"I am, Top."

"The artillery isn't going to get those NVA out of them bunkers. Tanks aren't going to do it, either. The only thing that's going to whip those bastards is an infantryman with a sharp bayonet. This Ap Cho, it'll take some real fighting Lieutenant. You get ready."

"I'm ready, Sarge. Scared, but I'm ready."

"See you at four then, Sir." With a parting slap at his shoulder and a nod, Master Sergeant Allred disappeared into the night to nourish and to encourage his Fourth Platoon.

Dennis found a spot inside the drainage pipe and made a final, yet fitful attempt at sleep. He did not even try to imagine the events as they might unfold the following day. Ap Cho was a horror waiting to be taken. The promise of armor support and artillery had given him some hope, yet Allred's words unsettled him. Exhausted, he drifted off to sleep, awakened at 3:30 a.m. by Eddie Runge and the blaring transmissions that flowed from his radio.

"Bad news, Charlie Six," Eddie said. "I've been listening to Brigade and Battalion Headquarters fight it out over who will get tanks and artillery tomorrow -- it ain't us. Seems that the Twelfth Infantry is bogged down in a hell of a fight and the assets have been shifted to them. We'll have to go it alone."

"Damn, Eddie, were they going to call and tell me?"

"Doesn't look like it, Sir. The decision was made about an hour ago and nobody's bothered to call. Guess they're afraid we'll revolt."

"I can understand that. In fact, don't tell anyone yet. Let me talk to Battalion and confirm it before we do. Our guys will crap bricks when they hear this. They expect artillery and tanks."

"Let's get moving, Eddie, it's almost time. See what Lieutenant Donnelly can find out on his artillery net. Meet me on the road in five minutes."

Dennis crawled out of the pipe and stretched his sore muscles. Straining his eyes, he peered into the night, but could see little. His vision focused after a few moments and he could distinguish the shadows of heavily-loaded men, methodically assembling along the road. Impulsively, he moved to join them.

"Good morning, Sir," one of the new men said cheerfully when he recognized his CO.

"Morning," Dennis replied. "How are you? Thanks." He smiled broadly at the innocence of the new man's greeting and was soon speaking to everyone, offering encouragement as they took their positions in the line. "Morale is pretty high," he said to Mike Balser as he stopped to confer with him for a moment.

Dennis made his way to the front of the line, then sat in the moist earth that formed a shoulder for the road. Alone with his thoughts, he fought the urge to light a cigarette and sipped warm water from his canteen, instead. Raising it to his lips, he saw five shadowy figures moving directly toward him in the dim light. He grinned, instinctively knowing that it was Wally, Andy, Jackie, Rosey, and Jay Cee.

"Come to praise me or to bury me?" he said as he stood to greet them. "Good to see you guys. You've been making out OK? Anybody been hurt?"

Jay Cee, always the leader, began: "We've been doing all right; no-body's hurt. Wally got a few scratches from grenade shrapnel, but he won't let the medics touch him. He's too damn proud."

"Holy hell. Wally, you OK?" Dennis asked.

"Yeah, Dennis, I'm cool. We all wanted to see you before moving out today. We wanted to tell you, the whole Company is behind you all the way. Word is, you handled yourself real good in Ap Cho -- with Colonel Taylor and all. You did a lot of crazy things and the men like that."

"Yeah," Andy interrupted. "Our only beef is that you've been em-barrassed by these goons. We don't feel so good about that -- you taking all that heat from that new Colonel. Not today though, Dennis, not to-day." Andy smiled and turned to face the others. "We got something for 'em, don't we boys?"

"Wait a minute ... thanks, Jackie, Wally. Now don't you guys do anything foolish," Dennis said.

Jackie cut him off. "Not foolish, Dennis. It's just that we figured out where most of them bad dudes are. You know where Jimmy Hollister went down? Well, there are three bunkers that stand out like sore thumbs, right where their command post is. We're sure of it. If we can cut off the head of this snake, we'll kick their asses all over China."

"We're in Vietnam, Jackie," Jay Cee corrected him, "but I know what you mean."

Listening to them talk of their personal attack plans, Dennis grew more curious. "Just what do you guys have in mind?"

Andy, who rarely said a word when Wally or Jackie were present, pushed forward and took over the conversation. Dennis could see his gentle features in the dark and thought, *Andy's too smart, too civilized to be here in this cesspool of destruction. He doesn't deserve it.*

"It's like this," Andy said. "Wally and I both carry M-60 Machine Guns. Rosey and Jackie will be our assistant gunners and ammo bearers. Pat Shine will help, some others, too. Anyway, as soon as we hit that vil-lage, we're going forward spraying those bunkers with fire. Don't worry, Dennis, you won't be embarrassed any more after today."

"Now wait a minute, you guys. I know how you feel and I appreciate it. But, I'm telling you, don't try anything like that. You intend to handle this attack all by yourselves, do you?"

"I guess we do," Rosey said. "Let's face it, Dennis. There aren't many of us left to fight with. All the platoons have lost men. Whole teams are broken up. We're the only machine gun crew that's been together for a while and we're still clicking. I hate this war and the killing. I haven't pulled the trigger of my rifle yet, but in this case, every man counts. I say, let's go for it." He sat beside Dennis on the earth and waited for his response.

Stunned by their inspiring bravado, Dennis reflected. *Just a few months ago they were a vagabond band of hitchhikers walking a foggy mountain road in Washington.* A flash of them singing, joking, sharing their lives with him raced across his mind. *They were just innocent boys then. Now, hardened by battle, they're anxious to prove themselves. They'll save the day, they believe, if I'll allow it.*

"Go for it guys," he finally said. "Shoot the fucking hell out of them."

They let out a quiet hoot and slapped hands. "We'll show you, Dennis, don't you worry. It'll be good for you back at battalion tomorrow when they hang a medal on you," Wally said. "Now, we've got to go. Good luck, Sir."

Together they came forward, slapped his hand, and then moved quietly to rejoin their platoon. "See you later," Rosey shouted from the darkness. They left Dennis with a feeling of wonderment at their daring.

Who knows, maybe they'll just do it. I'm sure that Rusty Adkins and Sergeant Beebe will keep them under control, not let them do anything stupid.

"Ready, Eddie?" Dennis asked as his radio operator and the artilleryman, Lieutenant Donnelly, approached.

"Roger that, Sir. Sergeant Walker and the First Platoon are coming up to the front now. Looks like we'll break out of the gate on time. I'll call Battalion and tell them we're moving out."

"Good, Eddie. Any further word on the tanks or artillery?"

"They ain't talking about it, Charlie Six. They're too damned ashamed. No, they haven't said a thing, officially."

"Give me the handset."

"Falcon Six or Falcon Three. This is Charlie Six. We're moving out of the gates now. We expect to hit the Line of Departure -- fix bayonets -- in about an hour and forty-five minutes. Are my big boys and hot steel still a go?"

The radio remained silent and Dennis grew angry at the lack of response. "Damn it, Falcon Six, this is Charlie Six. I say again, is my support still coming?"

"This is Falcon Six. Ah, negative on the support, Charlie. I hate to tell you what has transpired. Just tell your men the tanks and artillery are committed elsewhere. It is necessary. Continue the attack."

Dennis handed the telephone back to Eddie and said, "You're right Eddie, and so is Allred. No tanks, no artillery. Just us and some sharp bayonets. I don't know what I'll tell the men."

"They already know," Eddie said. "Balser and Adkins were bitching about it a few minutes ago. The word spread like wildfire. The men don't blame you, though." Eddie searched his pockets for something and produced a crumpled package of cigarettes. Lighting one, he inhaled, then continued his analysis. "It doesn't surprise anybody. These fuckers always say one thing and then do another."

"Well, maybe we'll get one or two of those other companies to join us later. That would help."

"Don't hold your breath, Charlie Six."

Chapter Thirty-Two
Deadly Enthusiasm

In less than an hour, they were closing on Ap Cho from the north. Dawn arrived and the early light allowed Dennis to survey it from a distance. It looked much the same as the first time he saw it. Not much had changed in two days.

"Get your men on line," he shouted as the company merged into their pre-planned positions. "We cross the road in about thirty minutes. Open fire as soon as we're across; don't wait for them to start it. Get gone."

"The men of Charlie Company, 3rd Battalion, 22nd Infantry crossed the Line of Departure at Ap Cho at zero six-hundred hours on 5 February 1968. They are now attacking fixed positions without artillery or any form of fire support. Put that in your goddamn log at Battalion Headquarters," Dennis radioed with full knowledge of how his sarcasm would be read. "To hell with them," he said to Eddie.

Mortar rounds began bursting to their front and Dennis calmed his men, saying, "That's Sergeant Allred making good on his promise to 'put it in their hip pocket.' We don't have clearance to fire, but the forty rounds we carry will be gone in a few minutes anyway. Too little, too late, but it might just do us some good."

Crossing the road in unison now, the line of men appeared almost perfectly straight. They had advanced about one hundred feet into the village and the Third Platoon was well into the first row of huts. Dennis could see the entire company from his position on the left. "Everyone on line, that's good," he said. "Yeah, there ain't no chickens out here."

A blast of heavy automatic fire caught them in the open just as he finished speaking. Men began to fall while others returned fire, diving for cover. "Two Six, Mad Dog, this is Six," Dennis called. "Lay down fire toward your right front. Third Platoon is getting hit. Looks like they're pinned down again."

To his astonishment, the Third Platoon machine gun crews didn't lie down. Instead, they stood and blasted their way forward, forsaking any cover. Dennis, lying prone alongside Eddie, fretted: *They need to take up defensive positions. Without tanks, a frontal attack into those bunkers is suicide. Enemy firepower is just too great.* "Where are your gun crews, Rusty?" Dennis shouted.

"I don't know where they are. What crews?"

"Wally Gerber and that bunch of his. They had something planned. Oh, good God, they never told you?"

The roar of machine guns lasted for several minutes and then, one by one, they fell silent. Dennis closed his eyes momentarily, fearing the worst.

"Six, this is Three Six. I can see them now -- the gunners. They're all down. It looks like four, maybe five. I can see Rosey Dolan. He's moving, trying to crawl. No movement from any of the rest of them. They're just lying there, 'way forward of the line. They went down right in front of some bunkers. A gook popped his head up and we shot him back into his hole. They're all lying right in front of that bunker. They look dead ... might be playing possum. There's no way to get to them."

"OK, Three Six. I'm coming over to your position. Tell your men to concentrate their fire on the sides of our boys. Keep the enemy off of them, but don't hit them."

Dennis and Eddie crawled a few meters and were soon alongside Rusty Adkins. Several other platoon members joined them, pointing out the downed machine gun crews. Dennis was aghast. Some twenty-five yards in front, the gruesome scene unfolded before him like an appalling tapestry. Rosey had managed to crawl to the side of one the enemy bunkers. He seemed to be out of danger for the moment. Wally and Jackie lay side by side in the open, unmoving, their faces buried in the now-pulverized, gray dirt. Andy lay only a few feet away, face up, his machine gun across his chest.

"They look dead to me," Eddie said. "We've got to get them out. What would the men think if we left them?"

"Right," Dennis said. "Give me a couple of men, Andy. Maybe we can get to Rosey."

With little regard for his own safety, Dennis brazenly stood and ran forward, dodging, jumping, sashaying left and right to escape the onslaught of bullets until, at last, he reached Roosevelt Dolan. Grasping him with one hand by the cloth of his shirt, he found the strength to drag him to a nearby shell hole. Shots rang out, but he never heard them. He cradled Rosey in his arms, oblivious to the battle raging around him. Looking up at him, Rosey pleaded with tear-filled eyes for leniency from anyone. A little mercy, and maybe just one last chance at life.

Rosey tried to speak and Dennis bowed low to listen. He searched for the strength to whisper some last request but couldn't. "What do you want me to do, Rosey?"

"Are you going to get me a Dustoff, Dennis ... get me out of here?" He gasped, his eyes pleading for an answer that might offer some hope.

"No. No, I can't," Dennis answered. "I'm sorry, Rosey, I can't. I just can't."

"Then that's OK, Dennis. Am I going to die?"

"I'm sorry, Rosey, there's just no way..."

"OK, Dennis. Stay with me, please. Pray with me."

Dennis held him and waited. After a short pause, Rosey opened his eyes wide and began speaking in an antiquated Latin tongue. Immediately recognizing the sacred petition, Dennis prayed with him, holding him close.

Their prayers were incomplete, but they seemed to calm Rosey; with misty, confused eyes he beckoned his lieutenant closer. "Tell ma mothrr," he slurred. "Tell her and Vaness...ah. In mah pock-ket, take it, Den-iss..." Unable to speak aloud now, he haltingly whispered his final message into his friend's ear, a request that Dennis promised would someday be fulfilled. Their covenant seemed to momentarily ease his suffering and they waited. Dennis rummaged through Rosey's pockets, salvaging the notebook that he cherished so much.

An unmistakable rapture then swept across his face as he drew his last breath. Shuddering, he slumped and died. "Good-bye, brother. I love you," Dennis whispered, then hugged the lifeless body tightly to him.

Finally releasing him, he clutched the notebook to his bosom as if it were the holy relic of a saint, one that he loved and never knew the full extent of his love until the moment of ultimate truth had arrived. He wept for Rosey and for himself for just a moment, then gave his lifeless body to the others. "Be careful with him, men. Rosey's a sensitive kind of guy."

"Charlie Six, this is Falcon Six. What's your progress?"

"Six, we're pinned," Dennis said, his voice cracking with emotion. "I've got one confirmed killed and three more, maybe four dead. They're lying in the open, right in front of the bunkers. We can't get to them.

Men are throwing grappling hooks attached to ropes trying to snag them, to drag them out. God it's awful. If you move, you get shot."

"Oh, my God," Colonel Flint responded with surprise and shock. "You've got four dead? I'm sorry. Listen to me, Charlie Six, and listen good. I want you to withdraw, to pull back. Line up along the east side of the road. Leave your dead. Alpha is en route; they're about three hundred meters from your position now. They'll join you and do the same. You're in overall command now, Riley, take it!" Colonel Flint stopped talking, but held the radio mike open. Dennis could hear a multitude of voices in the background. In a few moments, Colonel Flint came back on the air.

"Charlie Six, in about twenty minutes a supply convoy loaded with ammunition and other badly-needed materials will pass from the south through your ranks along that road. It must get through to Tay Ninh. Lay down a wall of fire as they pass behind you. Get your men moving, now."

"Roger."

Having overheard the radio call, Walker, Adkins, and Balser, who had all joined him, looked in disbelief at Dennis. "Let's go guys, you heard him. Pull your platoons back now, line up in that ditch that runs alongside the road. As soon as the convoy comes into sight, lay down a wall of fire."

"What about Wally and the others?" Rusty pleaded.

"Stand by. O'Connor, Sergeant Beebe, any of you. What can you see on those casualties?"

A long silence ensued and Dennis grew impatient. "Jay Cee, what gives?" he shouted into the mouthpiece.

"I think they're dead," Jay Cee answered. "Yes. God, they're all dead. Nothing's moved in five minutes. Yeah, all dead. Shit, Dennis." Jay Cee sobbed openly into the receiver, then released it, concealing his torment.

Swallowing, Dennis looked solidly into the faces of his leaders. Choking back his own emotions, his eyes welled with tears and his voice cracked: "Pull your men back, get them in the ditch. Spread them along the road. Leave the dead; we'll have to get them out later. Don't worry, we won't leave them too long."

They voiced their agreement and crawled along the ground, collecting men for the movement rearward. Without further comment, knowing that it was essential, they abandoned the dead and ran, crouched, to the edge of the road. Dennis closed his eyes as they passed.

The company found refuge in a shallow ditch and the ever-increasing number of craters along the edge of the village. Platoon commanders, sergeants, and subordinate leaders spread them out as far as possible and the line covered some three hundred meters.

Alpha Company arrived and, silently, Dennis beckoned Captain Chancey and his men to the south, on line with Charlie Company. They now stretched more than five hundred meters. Every man, lying in silent expectation, with shaking and sweaty trigger fingers, waited breathlessly for something to happen.

Within minutes of their emplacement, the roar and rumble of big trucks blanketed the area. Dennis watched as his men's touchy fingers nursed the triggers of their rifles. Eddie Runge joined him, having survived, untouched, the carnage of the previous assault. "Here they come," he shouted.

The lead truck, heavily laden with precious ammunition and other stores, lumbered slowly into view. Spaced fifty yards apart, dozens of flat-bed and semi-trucks, brimming with wooden crates, ambled into the killing zone. Instantly, the hidden enemy opened fire, only to be met with a surprising onslaught of superior American firepower. Fifty-caliber machine guns mounted on the trucks fired their big bullets over the heads of Charlie Company, directly into the village proper.

Joining the melee, the ground troops fired maximum rates of fire into the flimsy huts and bunkers, sending up a wall of steel and flame. Dennis watched in amazement as artillery rounds began bursting indiscriminately across their front.

"I've never seen such firepower. I guess that political clearance crap is over with, huh, Six?" Eddie shouted above the roar. "That's ours."

"Yeah, but it's hitting right where we left Wally and the others. If they weren't dead then, they sure as hell are now. Good God, Eddie, this is unbelievable."

An anti-tank projectile found its mark on a passing truck, setting it on fire and careening it off the road. Crashing into the ditch, it exploded, killing the occupants. The remaining vehicles stalled dead center in the heaviest sector of bullets and rockets. It blocked any further passage of the convoy. A five-thousand-gallon gasoline truck, the largest and most prominent target, attracted enemy small arms and rocket fire like flies to a dead carcass. The driver, excited and panicky, lurched forward, off the road to the right, bypassing the wrecked and flaming vehicle. He crushed the legs of two men as the huge tanker bounced and floundered through the prone combatants.

Miraculously, he managed to keep it upright and, eventually, found traction again on the main road. Men were waving their arms and shouting above the thunder of the exploding artillery. They directed the other drivers to the left around the burning vehicle. Without orders or directives, volunteers stood amid the clutter and confusion and pulled the two crushed victims from the roadside, dragging them rearward to a safer haven.

Finally the last truck came into view and it sped past them, around the burning vehicle, at a high rate of speed. "That's the last one," Dennis said. "Eddie, tell the men to slow their rate of fire. Conserve ammunition." Before he could respond, the radio crackled with Colonel Flint's calm voice.

"Charlie Six, this is Falcon Six. What's your situation, please?"

"The convoy just passed us," Dennis answered. "They lost one truck and the two men in it. I've got men trapped inside the village and can't get to them. I have at least three KIAs, maybe four. We've got wounded all over the place. A truck ran over a couple of men. Their legs are broken. Advise, over."

"Roger. Ah, you say you have three, maybe four KIAs? Men with broken legs?"

"Yes. "

"Charlie Six, I'm very sorry. We'll get you out of this mess. Pull back across the road, collect your wounded, and start moving back to Cui Chi, it'll be dark soon. We're going to blast that place with artillery as soon as you and Alpha are clear. Can't get your men, can't get those bodies out, you say?"

"That's right; there were five good men cut down in the last attack. We got one man out. There are four more still in there. There's a machine gun bunker right in front of them."

"Understand, Charlie Six. Do as I told you. Gather all you have left and head back this way. Get the hell out of there before dark. Send me the exact coordinates of your KIAs. I'll try to get the artillery to stay clear of them. It's the best I can do right now."

"Roger, but I'd like to take a last shot at getting my men. OK, Falcon?"

"Go for it. You've got about thirty minutes, then get clear."

"Wilco."

Dennis looked at the covey of men surrounding him. They waited patiently for his directions. Dennis stood erect as they knelt before him. "Lieutenant Balser, Lieutenant Adkins, Sergeant Walker. You too, Eddie. You don't have to say, 'yes,' but... will you come with me to get our boys?"

"After you, Sir," Mike Balser answered. "I'll go. I've got a squad looking over them now."

"I'll lead the way," Pat Shine said as he chambered a round in his rifle. "Let's go get 'em." The others agreed; they would make an attempt to get their dead. Near dark, Lieutenants Balser and Adkins, Sergeant First Class Bill Walker, Dennis Riley, Specialist Pat Shine, and Radio Operator Eddie Runge crawled their way to the exact spot where Rosey had died. They lay on their bellies, quietly observing the previous battle scene. The earlier fires of battle had cleared most obstructions and Dennis could easily see the bodies of his pals.

"Hold it, Eddie. There are only three. I thought we had four men lying up here. Sergeant Walker said he counted four. What's your guess, Mike?"

"We've got four missing. I can't understand it. Wait, look, there's someone running toward us. It's one of us -- cover him."

"Don't shoot, GI. Don't shoot, GI," the hysterical figure shouted as he scampered across the arena of death.

Spontaneously, everyone stood, dumbfounded, watching a flood of enemy small arms fire directed at the darting runner. Mike Balser, with open arms, grabbed the fleeing man. Together they fell into a large shell crater. "Who the hell are you?" Mike asked.

Shaking violently, his eyes bulging wide, the man babbled," I'm Donald Evans. Brooklyn, New York. Third Platoon. I just got in the company yesterday. Holy hell, I didn't know what was happening. Wally told me to come with him. When they went down, I took a hit in my leg. See, here? Up by my nuts."

"Calm down, Evans. It doesn't look too bad," Lieutenant Balser said. "Who tied it off?"

"I did. I made a bandage and tied it off with my belt. Then I threw a grenade, but it hit the bunker and rolled back toward me. Brothers, when that fucker went off, the noise put me in another world." Donald Evans wrapped both arms over his head and closed his eyes, reliving the frightening scene. Recovering his composure after a few moments, he continued explaining his personal nightmare.

"I used the smoke and dust from the grenade to crawl into a hole. They kept poppin' rounds at me every time I stuck my head up to see. They couldn't get me. When it started getting dark, I made a run for it. Man, am I glad to see you guys."

"Falcon Six, this is Charlie Six. We recovered one of the men. He's shaking like a leaf, but he's going to be OK. That leaves three still in there. We can't get them right now."

"That's good news about your man, Charlie Six. Pull all your forces out now. Move up the road; I have another mission for you. Call me when you're all together and moving."

They reluctantly complied and a small covey of remaining men tenderly carried Roosevelt Dolan from the edge of the battlefield, placing him in an ox cart as his funeral bier. Jay Cee stood alongside, holding his hand as it stiffened. On top of Rosey they placed Donald Evans, filling him with morphine, and then they stacked many more wounded. Volunteers tugged at the yokes. Darkness swept over them and they raced to escape the light of a rising moon. "Wally, Andy, and Jackie all sleep tonight in the bloodied place where they died, Eddie," Dennis said as they walked.

Eddie turned and walked backward for a few steps. "Don't worry, Sir, we'll get them out. We won't leave our boys."

"I've already left them. Where is Jay Cee? I need to talk to him. Try to explain."

"He's with his platoon now, Charlie Six. That's where you go when you're hurtin'. Jay Cee is a soldier, and you don't need to explain nothin' to nobody."

Chapter Thirty-Three
The Long Walk Home

The grim procession of dead, wounded, and demoralized soldiers had walked less than a hundred meters when Dennis' radio squawked.

"Charlie Six, this is Falcon Six. A commendable job on that convoy. Tell your men. I have another urgent mission for you, now."

"OK, Six, what is it?"

"One of those trucks ran off the road about five hundred meters north of you. It may have been ambushed. It's loaded with thousands of rounds of badly-needed artillery ammunition. Get it and secure it before the Viet Cong do. It could wreak total havoc in our ranks if they get those shells."

"Roger, Six. We're on the way."

They continued their miserable trek northward just as the rush of American artillery shells began breaking the air overhead, screaming toward worthy targets in the mounds of Ap Cho. The force of the blasts made the earth beneath them shudder and their ears ached from the thunderous explosions. Some of the rounds fell short of their mark. Panic and white-hot steel forced Charlie Company into any crevice, crack, or flaw in the earth where they could find some sanctuary. The carts, laden with the dead and wounded, sat unattended, exposed to the shellfire. Fifteen minutes of maximum artillery fires set the village ablaze and Dennis was heartened, knowing that it was payback time for what they had suffered that afternoon.

"There won't be anything left in there; nothing can live through that," Mike Donnelly said, "nothing." He and Rusty Adkins had slipped alongside of Dennis, unnoticed in the dark.

Dennis paced back and forth a few steps, then stopped and gently felt the bandage on his nose. "I don't know what to say, guys. I hope you're right, Mike. I just worry about our boys. I don't know if there will be anything left of them to find and bury."

"My God, Rosey, Andy, Wally -- all dead," Rusty Adkins groaned. "I'd cry, but I'm too damn mad. Ap Cho. It's a village of tears."

The artillery stopped as suddenly as it had begun and the resulting silence was equally deafening to their ears. Only the sounds of Dennis' radio crackling could be heard in the darkness.

"Charlie Six, this is Falcon Six. Have you found that truck? Over."

"Negative, Falcon. Heavy hitters scared the hell out of us. We're spread all over the woods. We're collecting and moving at the same time. Give me time; we'll find your truck."

Charlie Company reconstituted itself in short order. Sergeant Allred counted them one by one, touching each man on his shoulder as they found their way back into the column. The long, dark line of stooped soldiers, silhouetted now against a silvery moon, hastened northward, pulling its heavy load of wriggling humanity.

"Jesus, this is sick," Mike Donnelly said as he stepped directly behind Dennis. "Nobody back home will ever believe --"

At that instant, a single shot tore through Mike's left shoulder. In shock, he slumped into Dennis' arms. "God damn sniper. Donnelly took the round for me," Dennis said as they loaded him onto a cart.

"Keep moving. Watch the wood line. Watch for snipers," Dennis called out. "Everybody keep moving."

They moved another one hundred meters when, suddenly, Sergeants Walker and Beebe, who had been leading the way, each dropped to one knee and motioned everyone into the tree line. The column scattered and obediently took up positions, searching the shadowy forest for targets. "There's your truck, Charlie Six. What do you want to do with it?"

"Stand by.... Falcon Six, we're at the big boy. It's off the road in a small ditch. Ammo is still on board, tied down good. Checking it out now."

"This is Falcon Three. Message from Six. Set up positions and secure that truck. Intelligence indicates a Viet Cong force is moving toward you. Hold on to that truck at all costs. Establish a perimeter around the vehicle and defend it."

Annoyed that the truckload of ammunition meant more to his superiors than his own freight of bleeding and weary infantryman, Dennis looked to Sergeant Allred for counsel. "Be cool, Lieutenant, they're right. If this wagon falls into enemy hands, it'll kill a hell of a lot of us later. Maybe we can blow it in place and cheat them out of it. If we could get it running, we might just get it back to Cui Chi. Think about it, offer the possibilities to the Colonel."

Dennis paced back and forth between the truck and the edge of the road, causing Eddie Runge to spring from his perch and follow. More determined than ever, he squeezed the handset and began: "Falcon Three, this is Charlie Six. There is no way I am going to set up a perimeter around this truck. I've got dead men back in that village. I've got dead and wounded on these carts. My Forward Observer just took a hit from a sniper. They're all around us. We need medical attention and re-supply."

"What are you saying, Charlie Six?" Captain DeMatto responded.

Dennis held the receiver open for several seconds, his head hung low. He suddenly snapped it to his ear and spoke firmly into the mouthpiece. "Now I'm telling you, Falcon Three, what we're going to do. We're going to get that truck running and bring it along with us. If it won't run, we're going to blow it in place. It should make one hell of a firecracker. At least the VC won't get it, over."

"I don't believe you, Charlie Six," Captain DeMatto answered.

"Believe it."

All communications paused for several minutes. Finally, Captain DeMatto answered: "OK. Falcon Six just gave his approval, but says give your soul to God if you don't bring it in. Your ass belongs to him."

In exasperation, Dennis turned to his leaders. "Anybody here know how to drive a truck?"

A tall figure stepped forward out of the tree line. "I can handle it, Sir. I drove trucks for my father's construction outfit in California."

"You sure?"

"Give me a shot, Lieutenant. If it cranks, I'll take it on to Cui Chi. No sweat."

Dennis appraised the big man and felt an instant sense of relief. He radiated composure and spoke in a matter-of-fact way about his willingness to drive the truck. "Where the hell did you come from, John Wayne? I haven't seen you before."

The soldier grinned and shifted the weight of his gear. "I got here a couple of weeks ago. You've been too busy to notice. Asher is my name, James Asher. They call me 'Big Jim.' Fourth Platoon. Do I go?"

"Thanks, James, but I'm having second thoughts. Can you really handle that rig? You might get ambushed a hundred meters up the road. Word is that the VC are moving on it now. It's too damn dangerous. I'm thinking about blowing it."

"Hell, let him go, Charlie Six," Mike Balser said. "If he's willing to take the chance, let him try. If he makes it, we're homebound. If he doesn't, what's going to happen? They send us back into Ap Cho. So what's new?"

"I agree," Sergeant Allred said. He had watched the scene unfold, and only now offered his opinion. "It's our best chance."

Dennis demurred for a moment, then, patting Asher on the arm, he smiled and said, "OK, have at it, James -- Big Jim. Good luck."

"Can I go with him? He's my buddy," a timid voice echoed from the dark. It was Reggie Solomon, another member of the mortar section.

"Asher could use him as a guard. A 'shotgun.' Let 'em both go," Allred said.

"OK, you two, see if you can get it started," Dennis said. "If it runs, take it on up the road and don't stop for anything. The city of Cui Chi is burning and the VC have the ARVN compound. Alpha Company is somewhere up that way. I'll tell them to keep an eye out for you."

Without pausing, Privates James Asher and Reggie Solomon sprang across the road, pulling open the door of the truck, whereupon the lifeless body of the original driver fell atop them, covering each with blood and the remnants of his flesh. He had been shot in the back of the head.

"Executed by the Cong, looks like," Asher shouted. Together they struggled with the bloody corpse, finally delivering it to the carts. "We're out of here," Jim shouted as they raced together back across the road, mounting the vehicle in one step. The engine, groaning and turning slowly, finally coughed and sprang to life. Engaging the transmission, they were quickly away in a huge cloud of black smoke.

"Where do they find such men?" Dennis asked.

"He said he was from California," Eddie replied.

"I meant. OK, Eddie, thanks. I needed that.

"I think they're dead men anyway, Charlie Six."

Huddling in the tree line while the men rested, Dennis sat with Eddie, smoking a cigarette. "I want to give them a little time," he said.

Finally, he picked up the radio telephone and called: "Falcon Three, this is Charlie Six. The big boy is on its way. Tell Alpha to look out for it. Two men are on board. We pulled a dead man from the cab; tell the truckers he's with us, now."

"This is Falcon Three," Captain DeMatto replied. "You better hope that truck makes it. I can't tell you how many people are watching this situation develop. You can kiss your career good-bye, Riley, and don't you ever talk back to me --"

"Break, break, break," interrupted Captain Chancey, somewhat agitated by the acrimonious quarrel. "This is Alphagator Six. Your truck just pulled into the Cui Chi marketplace, Charlie Six. We have them -- everything is OK -- we'll take it from here. Tall skinny fellow says they got ambushed twice after they left you. They drove straight through it. They're some damn brave boys. Watch your step coming home."

Although they were, by circumstances, unable to cheer, Dennis knew that everyone in Charlie Company was rejoicing in his own way. Someone slapped him on the back and said, "Need to hang a medal on those two crazy sons of bitches."

Dennis reacted, "Let's get moving. We've got an hour or more of pulling before we get into the compound at Cui Chi. Watch for snipers and ambushes. We need a point man."

"I got it," Eddie said.

"If you have the point," Dennis said, "that means I've got it, too, Eddie. I'm too tired to carry the radio."

"Let's go, Charlie Six, before something else happens."

Hushed, the company fell in behind them, dragging their primitive conveyances and miserable burden through the night. Not a sound echoed from the wounded, and Dennis realized that they were doing their part to help the company in secrecy and stealth.

Every man, aware of the possibility of further action, kept his weapon at the ready, searching ahead into the wood line. At several points, shots rang out and they instantly returned fire at ghostly, darting targets. Never bothering to check to see if they had hit anyone, they passed the ambush sites with little consideration. Bullets were like pesky gnats to them now. They had grown so accustomed to the sporadic fire that it was little more than an irritant.

"Recon by fire," Dennis said to Sergeant Allred. "Have the men put a burst of six bullets into the wood line every thirty seconds. We'll blast our way home. We've got to make it; we've got to get our men back to Cui Chi. They've been in hell all day."

At about 4:00 a.m., they sighted the burning fires of Cui Chi city. The base camp lay some five hundred meters northeast of there. Dennis halted the column and signaled his approach by radio. "Falcon Three, this is Charlie Six. Lights on in the city. What's the situation in there? Can we move through it?"

"Negative; do not enter the city. It has fallen to enemy forces. Stay where you are. Circle your wagons, dig in and prepare to defend yourselves. There is no way to get through to the base camp."

"Bullshit, we're coming in."

"The only other route is the rubber plantation south of the city and it's held by the enemy. It's heavily mined, too. If you try to enter it now, you will most certainly be ambushed or blow yourself up. You don't have much choice, stay where you are."

Dennis took off his steel helmet, ran his fingers through his hair, and waited a moment before he answered. He boiled inside at his leader's lack of compassion for his men. Snatching the handset from Eddie, he said, "Let me see if I can explain something to you, Falcon Three. This company has been fighting since daylight."

Dennis paused a drew a deep breath, then continued: "We have bodies scattered across the beaten zone at Ap Cho. We've fought our way out of two ambushes. We've been lugging ox-carts filled with dead and wounded and this is the second time this week. Do you really think I can make them stop now, this close to the gates of Cui Chi?"

"You'll do as you're told, Charlie Six," an angry Captain DeMatto replied. Without hesitation Dennis answered, "I'm in command of this outfit, Sir. Not you. We're coming in. We have enough ammo left for one more good fight. I'll take the plantation route. See you in an hour."

He didn't wait for an answer. "Let's go, everyone. Eddie and me, we've got the point."

Selecting their route carefully, feeling for trip wires and watching for disturbed earth, in tandem, the men of Charlie Company passed through the evenly-spaced rubber trees without incident. They entered the gates of Cui Chi Base Camp at daylight. Colonel Flint and a maze of support elements converged upon them as they fell, exhausted and depleted of any strength, alongside the road.

"We made it, boys. Good work. I'm proud of you," Dennis said. He got up after a short rest and walked the length of his column, speaking and checking the condition of each man. Satisfied that they were all accounted for, he sat in a mound of soft earth, burying his head in his hands. He thought about Beverly Ann Jagoda. He thought about his mother and home.

Chapter Thirty-Four
Plan of Attack

"You and your men did superb work, Lieutenant Riley," Colonel Flint said, shaking Dennis' hand. "I could not ask for more, but I must."

Dennis gripped his hand and pulled himself erect. "What?"

"You have men still back at Ap Cho, Lieutenant."

Dennis stood mute for a moment, then asked, "I know, but what the hell are we going to do, Sir? How will we ever get them out?"

"You must go back to get them, Lieutenant. Deliver them to their mothers. You'll find a way; you have no choice. Rest here for a while, take care of your wounded, and replenish your stocks."

Colonel Flint paused and watched Dennis for a moment, then grabbed him by the shoulders and spoke. "At ten hundred hours, Lieutenant Riley, you will take what you have left and go back to Ap Cho. Go back there and get your soldiers."

Colonel Flint released Dennis, then lowered his head and looked at his boots, as if he were grieving. Recovering, he snapped his head upright and stared into Dennis' eyes. "But this time, Lieutenant Riley, you won't be pulling your dead and wounded along these roads by yourself. I'm moving the entire Battalion down there. All companies, the staff, supply, everyone. This is not Charlie Company's fight alone. We'll do it together, Dennis; you just show us the way."

At noon on the sixth of February, the remaining fifty-five able-bodied men of Charlie Company, dirty, tired, immune to fear, uncompromising in their intent, attached bayonets to their rifles. The swollen corpses of Andy Crammer, Jackie Stoner, and Wally Gerber were now the focal point of their labor, their abandonment being a sufficient lure to inspire one more heroic effort at recovering them. Nothing else mattered. At the behest of their young Lieutenant, they gallantly crossed the road and entered the death trap called Ap Cho once again. The attack failed and four more Charlie Company men were wounded in the effort.

Dennis called in his report. "Falcon Six, we got close enough to touch them, but no dice. Four more wounded now. As soon as someone gets within a few feet of one of our KIAs, heavy fire comes raining in from the flanks. It looks like the bodies have been moved. They're using them as bait. They know we won't leave them."

"This is Six. Take the time to develop a sketch map of exactly where the bunkers are. You'll be getting some help. Everyone involved needs to know the lay of the land. We must know exactly where those men are. Pull out before dark. Prepare nighttime ambushes and keep the enemy off your back. More big stuff coming in tonight. Delta Company is moving to join you and should be there by daylight. Hang tough."

Dennis issued his orders. A sketch map was developed. They unwillingly abandoned their dead comrades for another night in the pulverized dirt and ash of Ap Cho. Withdrawing perhaps two hundred meters south and west, they bivouacked for the night, alternating men among early warning patrols.

At midnight, the shelling began. The short distance between Charlie Company and the village was inadequate to protect them from the horrendous effects of the big guns. The earth shook violently. Men foolish enough to stand were thrown to the ground. They complained of earaches and momentary deafness while others vomited in fright. The shellfire continued incessantly, bringing some men to the brink of insanity, testing their nerves beyond all human endurance. One man snapped; using his M-16, he blew half his foot off in an effort to escape the battle.

Dennis heard the shot and came running to his aid. Realizing immediately that the wound was self-inflicted, he spit to show his contempt. "Shooting yourself gets you no priority in this outfit," Dennis said. "You'll be evacuated when we get all our dead out and you'll be the last to go."

Reports that two others had fled into the brush and hedgerows agitated Dennis. "List them as 'Missing In Action,' Top. I hope they get shot or captured. The damn cowards."

By 3:00 a.m., the big guns ceased their deafening roar and Dennis remarked to Eddie, "Thank God they've finally stopped. The men were going crazy."

At daylight on the 7th, Delta Company arrived, boasting a strength of approximately one hundred and twenty fresh and eager fighting men. Unaware of Charlie's dilemma during the past several days, they spoke among themselves of how they might take the village and extricate the dead. They were impatient to try.

Conferring with Captain Montel, Dennis learned that Alpha Company would also join them for the next attack, scheduled for that afternoon. Artillery was guaranteed and a platoon of tanks was a possibility.

"A task force of that size should certainly be able to accomplish what Lieutenant Riley and his men have been unable to do," Captain Montel said to the assembled leaders.

"Bullshit, Captain," Sergeant Allred snapped. "No disrespect to you, Sir, but you ain't seen nothin' but the edges of this battle. There's at least a hundred bunkers in there -- maybe two hundred -- all interconnected, with holes so deep the artillery barely gives them a headache. They might go all the way back to Cui Chi. Last night's bombardment didn't do anything but clear their fields of fire."

Sergeant Allred stepped closer to the Captain, gesturing with his hands. "Charlie Company has about sixty men, you've got a hundred and twenty. If Alpha can show up with a hundred, they'll be lucky. All together that doesn't make two full infantry companies."

Performing now, Sergeant Allred waved a hand above the assembled leaders and pointed toward the village with the other. "I reckon there's four hundred North Vietnamese Regulars in that village. They're a long way from home. They came here to die. They'll try to take as many of us with them as they can."

Captain Montel remained seated, a cynical sneer sketched upon his face. "Your candor is appreciated, Sergeant, but please leave the assessments and tactics to us more experienced leaders. You see, it is well understood that much of your suffering is due to faulty strategies. Perhaps even some shallow thinking on the part of your young Lieutenant Riley, here."

Dennis couldn't believe his ears. He'd heard that Captain Montel was an arrogant man, but he was openly criticizing him in front of his men. "What are you saying, Captain?"

"You know as well as I do, Riley, that Officer Candidate School simply can't prepare a man for the inevitability of a major conflict or battles such as these."

Producing a long-stemmed pipe from his shirt pocket, Captain Montel paused to tamp down tobacco and light it. The audience of leaders waited patiently, tense from the quarrelsome dialogue. Captain Montel blew a large puff of smoke, then seated himself on a log.

"Now, all of you, listen. Upon the arrival of Alpha Company, we will make a three-company attack into the heart of the enemy fortifications. As the ranking man, I, of course, will be the overall commander. The enemy will be routed by suppertime or they will 'all be dead,' as you say, Sergeant. Any comments?"

Sergeant Allred stepped close to him, his face revealing controlled rage. "Just one. Watch how you talk about my Lieutenant, goddamn it." He spat and walked away, shaking his head.

Dennis, inspired by Sergeant Allred's minor insubordination, decided to debate Captain Montel. Wetting his lips, tapping his sore nose, he looked directly at the Captain. "Sir, please forgive the testiness of my good Sergeant Allred. He's a veteran of many battles and has come away a keen observer. I trust his judgment in all matters. Now, we OCS officers, 'Christmas help,' as you have been known to call us, have a particular stake in the outcome of this battle. As you well know, we have dead men lying in there."

"Go on, Lieutenant."

Dennis glared at Captain Montel. "You understand, Captain, that you are the only military school graduate in this battalion. It's a lonely place to be, I'm sure. Beginning with Colonel Flint, all Company and Platoon Commanders are Officer Candidate School graduates. In this war, and in this battalion, they've turned in a good report of themselves. They don't care to change that."

"Touché, Lieutenant, touché."

The words came easily to Dennis now. He felt inspired. "Captain, I accept your invitation to follow you into battle. Perhaps you do have some special plan for eliminating fortified positions via the frontal assault. I suggest you take the middle in this afternoon's attack. When you've cleared the path sufficiently, I and the remnants of my command will be only too happy to deliver to you your afternoon cocktail. I understand that is your custom?"

Knowing he had been bested, at least in the arena of gentlemanly debate, Captain Montel smiled and played his ace.

"Be that as it may, Lieutenant Riley, you will have the honor of spearheading the next attack. You, Sir, will go up the middle. I and my Delta men will secure your right flank. Alpha Company will hold the left. With your excellent vocabulary, I suspect you'll be able to talk the enemy out of their holes, whereupon Delta Company will promptly shoot them for you."

"OK, Captain, let's cut the bullshit. What do you want to do?"

"Agreed, let's get down to business. Falcon Six is preparing the battalion staff, supply, communications, and all other supporting elements to join us by nightfall. He desires that we select a site for his command post. This bivouac of yours will do nicely. You'll have to move and surrender your foxholes to them. They will certainly appreciate it."

"Jesus."

"Ssshh. Alpha Company is approaching now," Captain Montel said. "I understand they are bringing twenty or more replacements for you. That'll increase your strength considerably. They are just in from the States and probably won't lend much to your operations, yet they are fresh, warm bodies."

"The attack commences at 0945 hours," he continued. "Try not to get anyone else killed, Riley. We cross the line of departure at zero nine-four-five. Meet me then."

"Yeah, OK." Saluting Captain Montel smartly as a gesture of disdain, he blended into the brush to summon his leaders. Eddie Runge and Sergeant Allred had already assembled them. "What the fuck's up, Six?" Balser asked impatiently.

"We're attacking again," Dennis sighed, "right up the middle."

"We've got big problems, Charlie Six," Rusty Adkins said. "We don't have much to attack with and our guys are dead on their feet. They're mumbling about that self-inflicted wound during the night and those two cowards that took off through the woods."

"Talk to me, Adkins. What's with them?"

"There's bad feelings in the ranks. Some guys are talking about not going on any more attacks. They're getting damn rebellious, Charlie Six." Adkins showed near panic on his face, explaining the mood of the Company. "What are we going to do?"

"Take it easy, Rusty, all you guys," Dennis counseled. "Come on, let's sit down and talk." Dennis sat on a tree stump while the others knelt or rested on their helmets.

"I can understand how the men feel. Hell, I wish it were different, but this time we do have some help. We've got Herb Chancey on our left and Delta on the right. It'll make a big difference. Besides, we've got to get our boys out; this might be our last chance. Replacements are arriving with Alpha Company. Tell your guys these things. I promise I won't expose them needlessly. We don't want anyone else hurt."

Dennis, completing his instructions, reminded them to assemble at the road by 9:45 a.m. Nodding their understanding, they drifted back to their platoons. Sergeant Allred remained behind, asking, "What will you do if they balk, Lieutenant, if they refuse to go?"

"I'll cross that bridge when I come to it, Top. I don't know what I'll do. Let's hope it doesn't happen; we just have to get our boys out. Today."

Chapter Thirty-Five
Rebellion in the Ranks

At the appointed time, Dennis and his small command group stood back from the road, watching for his company to appear. By 9:40 a.m., they failed to show and he raced back toward their bivouac positions. He was not surprised to find that they had made no preparations to join him. Instead, they were forming into a mob. Rusty Adkins and Mike Balser were trying to calm them. Dennis stood back, watching. Recognizing the forming mutiny, he shouted, "All right, men. Who's going with me?"

Rusty Adkins approached him on the run. "They won't go, Charlie Six. They say they've had enough. There's no hope. They won't listen to us. That young buck Sergeant, Gary Adams, he's the ringleader. He's got them all fired up. We can't reason with him or them. They won't even listen to Allred. I don't know what to do."

"Watch."

Dennis moved closer to the festering insurrection. Stopping at about fifteen feet from them, he ceremoniously loaded a full magazine in his rifle and chambered a round, slow and deliberate. Noting the menacing sounds, their eyes fell upon him. He glared, leveling his weapon at Sergeant Gary Adams.

"Men, we're going into battle now. Pick up your weapons and move to the line of departure or I'll start shooting you, one by one." He paused for effect, glaring at Sergeant Adams, then every man individually.

Dennis waited for some reaction, yet saw none. Holding his rifle at the hip, he waved it back and forth across their front. "Your friends are still lying in there," he said. "Do you want to leave them to the NVA?" He scowled, placed the butt of the weapon on his hip, and flicked the safety off.

"You talk to him, Jay Cee," someone said. "You know him best. Tell him our side of it."

"Yeah, talk some fucking sense into him," another yelled.

Jay Cee, compelled to act as spokesman for his peers, approached Dennis slowly, halting inches from his face. "Will you really shoot them, Lieutenant?" he asked.

"Yes."

"I don't believe you'd shoot your own men, Sir, for a lousy attack that's doomed to fail anyway."

Dennis stared at his friend for a while, never revealing his true emotions or his thinking. "I don't have time to explain all the ramifications of what will happen if your friends cause an insurrection on this battlefield, Sergeant O'Connor, but they are certainly looking at jail time."

"Jail might be a better choice, Sir."

"Jay Cee, go back into that crowd and tell them this; they dishonor their dead comrades. Shame on them. Tell them that they have a better chance of survival facing the NVA across the road than they do me, because I *am* going to kill someone. Tell them anything you want, but convince them that they don't have a chance against me. They might just survive the enemy, but not me. Now go tell them what I said. I start shooting in one minute."

Convinced that his friend was not feigning his intentions, Jay Cee walked back to the center of the crowd. In moments they dispersed, picking up their rifles and walking toward the road. Checking their weapons, eyes downcast, out of shame or fear, they did not look at Dennis as they passed. Only Sergeant Adams and Jay Cee stopped to confront him.

"Would you have really shot us?" Adams asked.

"No."

"Damn, Charlie Six, thank God. Do you know what Jay Cee told us?"

"What?"

"That you were going to shoot him first, then me. I told them that if you were going to shoot Jay Cee, that if he went down, then you must be crazy. We'd all go, too. We believed it."

"Good. You can tell them later what you want. Right now they're doing what's best for them. It may seem ridiculous to say that, considering that we are about to attack Ap Cho for the umpteenth time."

Dennis stopped to light a cigarette. "If our boys quit now, they are doomed. They'll die under somebody else's command or they can die with me. Besides, what would they tell their grandchildren?"

Turning toward the battle, Dennis softened his voice. "Come on, boys. Walk with me to the assembly point, we're ready to move out."

Dennis continued to speak as they walked. "Right now, our men have no faith in their leaders because of the lies they've been told -- because of the lives that have been wasted. We must go on for Wally, Jackie, Rosey, and Andy. We owe this company a win -- some kind of success. Let's recover Wally and our gang today. The men will come to learn that I'd never have shot them. It's just theatrics. I learned it from Krznarovich." They stopped at the edge of the road, the line of departure.

"Theatrics? Krznarovich?" Jay Cee said. "Hell, he'd have shot them first, then started talking."

"I'm real sorry for what I did, Sir," Sergeant Adams said, hanging his head low. "I guess I just let it get to me. You can count on me now."

"It's OK, Adams. Now let's get to work."

Slapping Jay Cee mildly on the back, Dennis watched as he and Sergeant Adams sped off to join their platoons. The artillery preparation was underway and shells screamed, splitting the air, announcing to the enemy that the Americans were coming once again.

Above the roar of the exploding artillery, Dennis shouted into the radio. "Delta Six, Alpha Six, this is Charlie Six. We're on line, ready to cross the road. Say when --"

"Charlie Six, this is the Alphagator. I have a dozen replacements for you. They're green; what do you want to do with them?"

"Send them back behind the line. Top will handle them. No one deserves to die on his first day."

"Roger, Charlie Six. I'm putting my third platoon real tight on your left flank. Their job is to help extract your KIAs. Use them as you see fit. Let's go get it done."

"Alpha and Charlie. This is Delta Command. Please stop revealing your plans in the clear over the radio. Move out in one minute. Stay on line. That is all."

"Who the hell is Delta Command?" Eddie Runge asked, perplexed.

"That Captain Montel. He's leading us into the valley of death. Probably wants a poem written about himself."

"They're moving. Let's go, Six."

Walking stealthily, Dennis evaluated his condition: *it's just me and Eddie now. Mike Donnelly is gone. Sergeant Allred's tending to the new men -- calming them and getting them ready. Mike Balser and Rusty Adkins are the only other officers. Sergeant Beebe's doing his best along with Sergeant Walker to hold the men together. There's no other seasoned leadership except Jay Cee.* "Let's get up front, Eddie," Dennis said. "I want to be the first to see and touch my boys."

"Yo, Boss. I'm with you."

Chapter Thirty-Six
Requiem for the Dead

At exactly ten hundred hours, the three companies crossed the road dividing their own hell and sanctuary. The shellfire had done its job; few buildings or obstructions remained. The lush, tropical trees had vanished along with all other forms of vegetation. Rotting animals lay scattered across the panorama of death. The earth beneath their feet was pulverized into a fine, gray dust and, in places, they sank into it up to their ankles. The black smoke of artillery lifted slowly from the ground, revealing the ever-present protective mounds of the enemy.

Dennis gagged on the taste of cordite. His jaw set, he stood and marched rapidly forward into the graveyard of his comrades. Bullets snapped all around him, over his head, and beneath his feet. He paid little attention. Totally obsessed, haunted, he saw only the living faces of the men he cared about so much. An enemy machine gun rattled directly in front of him. He walked upright, straight into the face of it, the bullets passing to his left and right. At last he came upon the three corpses that, for him, eclipsed all other considerations in this struggle. He knelt to examine the first: it was Wally Gerber, his body mutilated beyond recognition. Dennis knew him by the tattoos on the calves of his legs. The flesh on his arms had been stripped by the enemy. "They skinned him and took his tattoos," Dennis seethed.

A few feet away lay Jackie and Andy. Their arms were entwined across each other's shoulders, in a sort of death hug. Aware that the firing had mysteriously stopped, Dennis motioned Charlie Company forward. In moments, they were at his side, helping to evacuate the dead. No shot or sound emitted from the enemy, yet they all knew and felt that they were being watched. Not commenting on it, they quickly completed their work and scurried to the rear.

Notifying the other units of their success in retrieving the three dead men, Dennis was directed to return to his bivouac to prepare night defenses. He and Eddie were the last to exit the battlefield and they did not speak until they came upon three olive-drab canvas pouches, stretched out upon the earth like quiet children, resting peacefully in their camping bags.

Men knelt in prayer beside them, their voices hushed and their faces wet with tears. Father Tobin draped a purple stole around his neck, opened his Jerusalem Bible, and began his ritualistic requiem for the dead. Asking one of the men to light and hold a candle, he opened his holy oils and approached the zippered bags.

"Wait. Let me, Father," Dennis said. Kneeling, he unzipped the first bundle. He sucked air uncontrollably for a few moments, as he stared into the tortured face of Andy Crammer. Splashing canteen water onto his towel, he washed his friend's forehead, cheeks and lips, removing most of the dirty grime that had caked there. "Father, go ahead. He looks a little better now."

The priest spent his oils, muttering ancient Romanesque canon. Dennis exposed, cleaned, and prepared the other bodies with donated water and towels from the congregation of warriors. Most of the company was assembled now, as were Herb Chancey and other men from Alpha and Delta Companies. Father Tobin motioned them to kneel or sit and he led them in a common prayer.

Finally he spoke: "My friends, Andy Crammer, Wallace Gerber, and Jackie Stoner died as valorous as any men can hope to die. From them we learn and understand, perhaps, the meaning of Socrates' comment: 'Noble deeds from noble men.' They were heroic in the actions that they took for you -- for us -- and it led to their deaths. Do not weep long for them. Remember that God gives life. He does not take it. That is the meaning of the resurrection -- life everlasting. They are in Heaven now, safe from this unholy butchery."

The priest paused, studied his Bible for a moment, then continued his battlefield homily. "Perhaps when this war is ended, we, the living, will all join at some holy sepulcher of peace and talk with Andy and Jackie and Wally again. It is only then, after the many long years have dimmed your rage and softened your hearts, that you will come to know the true glory of their lives and the meaning of their deaths. They will be there waiting for us, these three, and all the others. Now, let us pray."

Their supplications ended, the men moved silently through the shadows to prepare their evening patrols and to dig new fighting positions, pondering all the while the meaning and significance of the good priest's words. He had helped them for the moment, at least.

Dennis and Eddie stayed behind. Dennis asked Father Tobin to hear his confession and to absolve him of any transgressions. Completing that, they fell into general conversation and Dennis reflected on the evil of killing, even in war. "What vice or sin could you possibly commit here, Dennis?" the priest asked. "You are doing only what you must do to keep these men alive."

"But, Wally and Rosey -- what a shame. I should have stopped them."

"Do not assume the burden for the evil acts of greedy men, in places far away from here. It is they who must account for the depravity they provide, they who should suffer the guilt and the shame. Not you, Dennis, not your men. I said that God gives life. It is man who takes it."

Father Tobin produced two warm cans of beer from his pack and handed them to Dennis and Eddie. "Tell me, Dennis," he said, "how did you and your men finally manage to get your friends out? Was the fighting, the killing, as intense as in the past?"

Dennis didn't need to think about it. He answered Father Tobin immediately. "No, Padre, it wasn't. In fact, I knew they couldn't touch me. I sort of had a very strange 'out of body' experience."

Dennis sipped on his beer for a few moments, then continued: "Really, Father, I left my body and it was only my mind that went forward. I just focused on my boys, getting to them. I didn't care if I died, I guess. The bullets were hitting all around me, but some mysterious shield wouldn't let them touch me. I can't explain it, it was just weird."

"Poor Eddie," Dennis said, grabbing his RTO's arm. "I don't know if he had the same feeling, but he was forced to go along with me. The men were only a step or two behind when we finally got to them. Wally was the first one..." Dennis choked. Then catching his breath, he continued. "I noticed that there wasn't a sound on the battlefield as we carried them out. I think they let us get to them -- they gave us a break."

"The enemy -- they're human, too, Dennis," Father Tobin said. "Remember this old Russian saying: 'The only difference between soldiers at war is the brass buttons on their uniforms. I pray for them tonight, also."

They shook hands, the Chaplain explaining that he had other battlefields and other men to serve that night. Eddie reported that Colonel Flint was looking for him at his command post. The Battalion Headquarters was now in place and a Commander's meeting would begin in five minutes. They raced to comply.

Chapter Thirty-Seven
Doublespeak

Arriving late, Dennis noticed that no large tents or other apparatus of command affluence could be found. The Battalion Sergeant Major beckoned them into the tree line with a shaded red light. "Colonel's waiting on you, Lieutenant Riley. All other commanders and staff are present. There they are, under the trees."

"Humph, I like his style, Eddie. Digging in, just like us. Go and tell Allred and the boys. I'll make my own way back."

"All present now," the Adjutant informed Colonel Flint as Dennis merged with the group. He sat on a fallen tree and lit a cigarette. Although it was early evening and not quite dark, a small fire was burning and the flickering light revealed weary exhaustion upon each face.

Colonel Flint cleared his throat and began: "Good. Riley is here; let's get started. Since I've taken command, this is the first time we've all been together. First, let me say how proud I am of you and your men and the way they've performed over the last few days. Second, I have no excuses for the lack of support from our headquarters. You were supposed to have tanks today -- they didn't come."

"No kidding," Captain Chancey said. "Why is that?"

Colonel Flint thought for a moment, then said: "I don't usually explain why things don't happen, but in this case I must, especially since Charlie Six thought we were lying about getting tanks." He smiled at Dennis.

"Men, several days ago I went to the Brigade Commander and asked for a platoon of tanks. I know that, in order to defeat this enemy, you must have them. I literally begged for them, almost on my knees. Do you know what he told me?" No one answered.

"He suggested I read a book. Yes, a damn book." Colonel Flint slammed a fist into his open palm. "The book was entitled, 'How To Attack Fortified Positions With Light Infantry.' I almost cried at first. I wanted tanks, not a book. Then I realized that there probably are no tanks, not for us, anyway."

"Maybe you should have taken the book," Captain Montel said. "I'd certainly like to read it."

"Please, Captain," Colonel Flint said. "The point I'm making is this; the Tet Offensive has consumed almost 90 percent of our Divisions assets: men, tanks, ammunition, supplies of all kinds. Tomorrow is the eighth of February and we have been attacking this bloody fortress since the first. Tomorrow we will end it."

"We're going to throw the book at them, huh?" Lieutenant Prairie said. Laughter erupted and Colonel Flint waved his hands for silence.

"I have good news. Brigade has released a company of tanks for this last assault. Now that Charlie Company's dead are off the battlefield, we can attack without limitations. We start at zero eight hundred hours. You'll have air strikes, 750-pound bombs, napalm, and eight-inch artillery. Several teams of gunships will cover your advance. The tanks, probably eighteen or more, will meet us at the road at first light."

Dennis remained silent. *Yeah ... tanks, airstrikes. It's all just bullshit.*

Colonel Flint turned to him. "Charlie Six, you and your men know more about the terrain than anyone else. Charlie Company will spearhead the attack, anchoring the middle of the line. Delta Company will take the right flank. Captain Chancey and his 'Alphagators' will be on the left. I have no doubt that the battle will be over by noon. Those air strikes will surely destroy most of the targets."

Colonel Flint pointed at the commanders. "Tell your men all of this; it might restore some trust. Tell them it's time to win one. Good night, men, and good luck tomorrow." Colonel Flint started to walk away. Then, as an afterthought, he turned toward the dispersing audience.

"Oh, by the way, Lieutenant Riley. Issue your orders and then take the last supply helicopter back to Dau Tieng. Write the necessary letters and reports on your deceased men, then get some sleep. We have heavy supplies: ammunition, medicines, and rations coming in early. Catch a ride back on that chopper."

Dennis should have been elated and a part of him was. He trusted Colonel Flint and knew that he'd done all he could to get them what they needed for this "last assault." If all of it were true -- the tanks, the air strikes, the gunships -- then there probably was reason for jubilation and hope. Yet, he could not shake the nagging fact that they had been lied to so many times before. *What will I do if it doesn't come? How will I ever face them again?*

Saying "good night," he returned to his post hidden in the brush. Sergeant Allred and the other leaders were waiting.

"What gives, Dennis?" Mike Balser asked. "There's a rumor that we're going back in. We've heard we'll get tanks, air strikes, and everything we need. Is that true?"

"That's right, Mad Dog. We're going back in at zero eight hundred. We've been promised a lot of support, but I don't want you to tell the men anything except that we are going to attack."

"Why's that, Sir?" Allred asked, puzzled.

"Now listen, all of you," Dennis answered. "Do you know the definition of doublespeak?" Without waiting for an answer, he continued. "It's believing two different things at the same time. We're all victims of this kind of thinking. The Colonel doesn't realize it, but they are 'doublespeaking' him and killing us at the same time."

Mike Balser and Rusty Adkins looked at each other, baffled. "What the hell are you saying?" Mike asked.

Dennis sighed. "What will you do if there are no tanks and air strikes tomorrow? Will you join the company in another attempt at mutiny or will you put your bayonet on the end of your rifle and lead your men into that village? I don't believe you'll see any tanks tomorrow."

Dennis stretched to his full height. He was in total command now, making his own decisions. "Let's see how the battlefield develops throughout the night. Don't tell your boys anything about it except that you will lead them across that road and into that village at first light. If you hear the roar of jet engines, the rattle of tank treads, then you can give me hell later. Now, go. Get them ready." He turned and raced to catch the departing aircraft, complying with his Colonel's orders.

Chapter Thirty-Eight
Timidity on the Flank

Dennis spent the evening at Dau Tieng, writing letters to the families of his dead friends. Distraught, he consumed too much alcohol and the nightmare of Ap Cho flooded his dreams. First Sergeant Krznarovich awakened him at first light.

He returned to Ap Cho in the early morning and with him came a thick, heavy fog. The big Chinook landed expertly despite the hazards of limited visibility. "We been here before," yelled the crew chief over the whine of the engines.

His feet on the ground, Dennis met his company and immediately called his commander. "Falcon Six, this is Charlie Six. I'm back from Dau Tieng. We're crossing the line of departure now. I can't see much because of the fog. Are the other elements on line? Funny, I don't hear any big booms from the front. I don't hear any tanks squealing. I don't hear anything other than the sounds of my men sucking in the smoke and ashes of Ap Cho. Is there something that you want to tell me, Sir?"

Without waiting for a reply, he shouted with uncontrollable rage: "Where the hell are the air strikes and the artillery and the tanks, Falcon-Six? Where, goddamn it? Where are they?"

At zero eight hundred hours on the 10th of February, 1968, in the moist and quiet fog that enveloped the village of Ap Cho, only the simultaneous sounds of hardened metal snapping against metal disturbed the serenity of an unusually cool day. The men of the 3rd Battalion, 22nd Infantry, fixed bayonets with poise and intrepidity, certain that this was, indeed, their final assault.

Both sides were ready. Unable to quell foolish nighttime rumors, the junior leaders failed to dissuade the men from believing that soon they would hear and feel the earth rumble under the impact of sophisticated ordnance and would see the bulging hulks of modern tanks.

Throwing the radio hand set to Eddie, Dennis moved up and down his line, urging his men forward. "Stay on line with Alpha and Delta, stay on line, keep moving." Men looked away from him and their eyes told

Dennis they understood now: they should not have relied on the word of anyone over him; if there were to be tanks and air strikes, he'd have told them so himself.

"Falcon Six, this is Charlie Six." He waited.

Finally stopping his men, he listened. It became clear to him that he and the men of Charlie Company were alone at the edge of Ap Cho once again. He could not see or hear the movements of the other companies, so necessary to the advance of his own infantry.

"Falcon Six, this is Charlie Six. I don't see Delta or Alpha. I haven't heard a thing. I can't get them on the radio. Are they with me? What gives?"

"Charlie. Falcon Six, here. The situation has changed. Delta is on your right flank, abreast of you, but have stopped their advance because of the failure of supporting fires. Alpha is in much the same posture. The airmen say they can't fly in this soup. They can't see the targets. Without air cover, the tanks would be very vulnerable. Brigade has canceled them. Continue your assault; the fog should provide good concealment for your advance. Move out."

"Shit. Get me the leaders, Eddie. Now. Tell them to hold their platoons; they don't move one inch."

Eddie slithered into the fog. In moments he returned with Mike Balser, and Sergeants Allred, Beebe, and Walker. Lieutenant Rusty Adkins soon followed.

"You see the fog?" Dennis said. "There ain't no tanks and there ain't no damn air strikes. It's us three companies going at it alone, again. Delta is supposed to be on our right and Alpha on our left. We're committed deep into this attack. How are your boys doing?"

Rusty Adkins spoke for all of them. "They ain't worth a damn, Charlie-Six, but they'll fight. They worked themselves into a fever pitch all night about how they were going to overrun this bitch of a village. Doublespeak you called it, huh? You were right, goddamn it, you were right."

"You guys feel the same?"

"Let's go!" Mike Balser and Sergeant Walker shouted at the same time. "Move em' out."

Allowing time for them to return to their platoons, Dennis checked his M-16 and grenades. He took a long pull on the last of his water, and moved to the center front of his line. The small band of men, now called "Charlie Company Minus" in command circles, lurched forward.

"Falcon Six, this is Charlie Six. We're moving."

PFC Harry Liorete from the Second Platoon volunteered to walk the point. Lieutenant Mike Balser, his M-16 at the ready, walked five feet behind Harry, covering him. Advancing no farther than the third tier of half-destroyed huts, they began taking fire along their right flank. Body fluids and tissue splattered across Mike's face and shirt as bullets passed through Harry's body, killing him instantly. The Second Platoon returned fire as Mike hit the dirt, struggling to find his radio.

"Charlie Six, this is Two Six," Mike called, his voice racked with emotion. "I've got a man down. It's Harry Liorete. I know he's dead. I can't reach him."

Dennis was stunned. Images of Wally, Jackie, and Andy, lying day and night in the smoking remnants of Ap Cho, flashed across his mind. A storehouse of emotions, festering in his belly for days, finally broke free. "Jesus, not again, Two Six," he screamed. "Get him out. Get him out now! We're not leaving another man in this goddamn hellhole. Get Harry out of there." Dennis, lying prone, began to beat on the earth with the radio handset.

Eddie Runge reached and held Dennis' hand steady. Finally, he took the receiver from him. "It'll be all right, Charlie Six. Mike will get Harry out."

Lieutenant Michael David Balser, raised by professional military men, and, for most of his life, feigning open rebellion against them, made a crucial decision. "OK, Commander, I'll get him out, but I'll probably die in the process." Mike rose abruptly from the dirt, stood, and waved his men forward. One by one, several men crawled on their bellies to his side. "Give me the climbing rope," he said.

Silently, the rope bearer handed a long coil of nylon rope to his lieutenant. Mike fashioned a loop, draped it over his head and tied it firmly around his waist. "Cover me, I'm going forward," he said.

"What the hell's the rope for, Two Six?" someone asked.

"Use it to drag my body back," Mike answered. "I figure I'll be dead by the time I get to Harry. If I can get a grip on him, you guys pull us both back."

"You're fucking crazy," PFC Danny Alvis, his radio operator yelled. "We won't let you do it. Why...?"

"My commander insists. I'm going forward. Cover me." Michael turned and walked forward several steps. Unexpectedly, his radio came alive with a compelling message. He stopped to listen to the robust voice of Rusty Adkins, challenging their commander. Mike smiled, then took cover in a shallow depression.

"Charlie Six, this is Three Six, Rusty. If Mike goes up to get his man, I'm going with him. I know you're tormented, but damn it, Mike will die in there."

"Stay where you are, Three Six," Dennis ordered.

"I'm sorry, Charlie Six. This time I have to disobey. I'm going with him. In about two minutes, when we're both dead, then you'll have no Platoon Leaders. You won't have any officers."

"Crazy fuckers will really do it," Eddie said. "You'd better stop them."

Dennis swallowed hard. *Eddie's right. Mike will kill himself and Rusty will sacrifice his life right alongside of him for friendship -- for honor. For Harry Liorete.* "Godamn you guys," Dennis cursed.

"Three Six, Two Six, this is Charlie Six. I've changed my mind. We'll get him out later. I'm sorry, I know there is nothing you can do. I'm sorry for --"

Dennis was interrupted by the snap of bullets. Silence followed, and finally a call came. "Six, this is Rusty. Mad Dog is down. Mike is hit. He's down."

"No. What happened?" Dennis asked.

"He was standing. He took shrapnel in his left leg. He's shot through the right thigh. He's pumping blood, but Doc Shiro has him. I think Mad Dog's out of this fight."

"Mike, this is Six. You're hit? How you doing?"

"It's like this, Charlie Six," Lieutenant Balser said. "They didn't leave me a leg to stand on. Sorry that I couldn't get Harry." Mike gasped, holding open the radio net for a few moments and then there was only silence. Dennis buried his head in his arms, breathing heavily into the earth. Finally looking up, he grabbed his radio receiver.

"Three Six. Andy, find Jay Cee; tell him he's the Platoon Leader of the Second Platoon now. He's got the guts. Get him over there to take Balser's place. Remember, Rusty, you're the only officer besides me in this company now. What's your situation? Can you get to the casualties?"

No answer ensued from Rusty Adkins. Dennis, knowing how totally absorbed he was in commanding his platoon, patiently awaited his response. Finally, the radio static ceased.

"This is Three Six. I thought you said Delta was on our right side? This shouldn't have happened if the sons-of-bitches were there. Harry wouldn't have got hit and Mike would be standing."

"This is Six. Right. I'll check. What's the status on Liorete? Do you have him?"

"He's lying in the open. I can't reach him. I'm taking fire into my right flank. Damn it, Six, if Delta is there, we wouldn't be getting shot at on our right -- they'd be getting it."

The intense tropical heat began an early dissipation of the fog that enshrouded them. Dennis and Eddie moved to the right flank. He could see glimpses of his men but not those of Delta Company. "Delta Six, this is Charlie Six. I have two men down on my right flank. Where the hell are you?"

"Right alongside you, I'm sure, Charlie Six. What are you implying?"

"You lying son-of-a bitch, I ain't implying nothing. I'm flat out telling you that you are not alongside of me. If you had any guts you'd come out from behind your cover and meet me. I have another KIA because of you."

"This is Three Six. He's lying --"

"This is Falcon Six. I don't know what is going on down there, but I'll be over you in three minutes. The air is clearing and I'm in a chopper headed your way. I don't like what I'm hearing. Stay in place and be prepared to mark your positions. Charlie Six, you have a man down? Situation report, over."

"Roger, Sir. I am taking fire into my right flank. I have a man down, possibly KIA. Can't reach him because that flank is exposed. There is no one on my right."

"Another man down. Damn."

Lying on his stomach in a small depression, Dennis found hope in the spontaneous oath of his commander. "He cares, Eddie, but that's all I can say. His bosses and now this Delta Company Commander are bull shittin' him. I hope he sees it. We'll wait right here, and see what develops."

"Ah, Alpha Six, Charlie Six, Delta Six, this is Falcon Six. I want each of you to pop a colored smoke grenade to mark your positions. Do it now."

Dennis signaled Specialist Patrick Shine, the most forward member of his small group to pull the pin and ignite a colored smoke grenade. Soon a highly-visible purple column of smoke streamed steadily through the thinning fog and high into the air.

"This is Falcon Six. I see purple. That must be you, Charlie."

"This is Delta Six and that's a negative. My smoke is grape. Delta's positions are grape."

Over the flap of the helicopter blades, Dennis could hear the pilot and Colonel Flint conferring over an open radio net. "Who is where, damn it?" Colonel Flint asked.

"If Charlie were center, then that smoke came from them," the pilot said. "Tell Delta to pop another, different color."

"Delta Six, pop another smoke," Colonel Flint ordered. "No 'goofy grape'."

Dennis, Eddie, and his entire group watched in awe as three men from Delta Company slithered along their right flank and threw a smoke grenade as far forward as the lead man could manage.

"Damn it," Dennis said. "He sent a patrol forward. Made it look like he's alongside of us. Start shooting over their heads, Eddie. Stop that son of a bitch."

A heavy volume of fire erupted from the ranks of Dennis' small group, directed over the heads of the Delta Company patrol. They quickly vanished, back to the rear of the column where the Delta Commander rested in the safety of Charlie's screen.

"Looks like everyone is on line to me," Colonel Flint surmised. "Move out. Charlie, recover your man and give me a report as soon as you can."

Alpha and Charlie Companies stood and marched forward. No fire from the front impeded their movement. Dennis felt a moment of hope when, suddenly, he heard the rattle of machine gun fire on his exposed right flank. He lay still, waiting for someone to report.

"Dennis, Charlie Six, this is Rusty. Sergeant Walker is dead. Do you hear me? Sergeant Walker is KIA. He got hit trying to get to Liorete. We have Walker. Harry's still in there. I say again, Walker and Harry are dead. This is crazy, man, just plain fucking crazy."

"This is Falcon Six. Everyone pull back to the line of departure. The weather is clearing, and air strikes are due on station at twelve hundred hours. Alpha and Charlie will conduct a simultaneous two-company attack immediately after the strikes. Delta, return to your night position. See me when you get there."

"Delta, here. Will oblige, Sir."

Dennis did not answer and he did not care to answer. He was too busy helping to drag the body of the latest victim of the Ap Cho madness to the rear.

"Six, these bastards are going to get us all killed in here," Eddie said, reaching for Sergeant Walker's limp, warm body. "Somebody's got to do something."

At noon, under the umbrella of two supporting jet fighters, Alpha and Charlie companies attacked, side-by-side. Making meager progress into the fortress, each suffered several more men wounded. Captain Montel was unceremoniously relieved of command and replaced by a new arrival, Captain Jerry White.

"He seems pretty cool, but he hobbles along with a cane," Dennis told Allred. "The Army must be getting damned desperate."

Colonel Flint called no meetings and the chaplain did not appear. Sergeant Walker's body was bagged and placed alongside the road, waiting for the regular evening helicopter ride to graves registration. Harry Liorete rested in the place where he had fallen.

On the morning of the 9th, Colonel Flint organized another futile attempt at overrunning the Ap Cho stronghold. It failed. Charlie Company remained idle that night, licking their wounds. "Maybe they think we've had enough," the men began to say. "Maybe they think Charlie Company can't handle it." They busied themselves cleaning their rifles, sharpening bayonets, and writing letters home to their loved ones.

Daybreak of the tenth day found Charlie Company preparing for yet another assault. Captain Chancey and his Alpha Company faced the agony of Ap Cho with them. Dennis met with him to coordinate their plans. Captain Chancey promised to anchor the left flank.

"I'm lean on manpower and even shorter on junior leaders, Dennis," he said as they squatted in a shell hole with other men.

"I'm using kids for squad leaders and platoon sergeants, like that Specialist Hahn, over there." Pointing, Captain Chancey directed Dennis' attention to a lone soldier, digging in. "The poor boy just arrived from

Germany. I think Hahn was trained as a mechanic; now he's a rifleman. Where the hell have all the soldiers gone?"

"To Canada I hear," Dennis answered. "Fuck 'em. Let's fix bayonets and cross that road. Let's get Liorete and get it over with."

"Yeah, what choice do we have? Let's go."

The line of advancing Infantrymen managed to enter the village farther than they had ever gone before. The rubble of bombed and broken huts offered some concealment and Dennis sensed that they might finally overcome the savage enemy. "We've never made it this far, Eddie."

Explosions and firing broke out in the Alpha Company sector and they bogged down under the many cries for medical attention. Captain Chancey reported several wounded men stretched out across his front. Specialist Dennis Hahn, the mechanic from Germany, raced to assist. He was immediately cut down in a hail of bullets. The incident caused the attack to falter and they became a covering force for motor convoys racing behind them toward Cui Chi. Alpha Company suffered one killed that day, but more than twenty men from both companies were wounded. Their strength continued its downward spiral.

On the evening of the eleventh day, Pat Shine, Jay Cee O'Connor, and Danny Alvis brought in Harry Liorete's body and laid it at Dennis' feet. "It's a bitch." Pat said. "A fucking crazy bitch. It's just all so insane."

On the 12th, two more unsuccessful attacks allowed precious ammunition to move, unimpeded, northward, while Charlie Company sacrificed more Infantry to the North Vietnamese. The other units departed for separate and likewise vital missions. Charlie Company stayed at Ap Cho.

New arrivals and old–timers alike fled on the beds of passing trucks. Men began to pray for wounds that would remove them from the battle. Some wounds were self-inflicted; these men were left to wither in their own pain and suffering. The medics would not attend to them in spite of their pleading. "Let the fuckers die," a senior medic said. "I won't waste my medical supplies on the cowards."

At midnight on the 12th, under a bright moon, Dennis' radio came alive with the steady voice of Colonel Flint. Weary and dazed, he listened.

"Charlie Six. Do not answer this message except to acknowledge that you've received it. You will attack Ap Cho soon after first light in the morning. You will attack it and attack it and attack it, again and again, until it is destroyed. There is no other alternative -- no turning back -- no other mission. You may get some help and you may have to go it alone. Explain this to your leaders and to your men. Make them understand that you are the only American unit capable of keeping our supply lines open."

A long pause ensued and Dennis said nothing in response to the message. He had heard it all before. Colonel Flint came back on.

"If you fail, grave consequences will befall our entire Division. Charlie Company must hold on until we can gather the arms and men it will take to crush it. You can do this, Charlie Six, but it will take great courage and physical strength. Above all, it will be an incredible test of your leadership."

Dennis bolted upright. The tone of the message was unlike anything he had ever heard. "You ought to hear this, Eddie. Our Colonel is on a roll."

"I can promise you nothing," Colonel Flint continued. "You're on your own. Hold that road and take that bloody village. You cannot come out of there until it is done. Kill everyone and everything in it, if it takes all that you have left. You can do this, Charlie Six, but you must rethink why you are a soldier. Are you listening?"

"I'm wide awake, Six."

"Then consign yourself to the obvious and convince your men to commit to the inevitability of a soldier's life. Remember your military history and the Spartans who fought with their swords, and then their hands, until they were slain to the last man. Then you may find the solutions to your fight. Share with your men what I've said. Satisfy their needs. Operations will coordinate your efforts. Coded attack order follows. Good luck."

Dennis waited several minutes before he replied. As he contemplated Colonel Flint's words something curious crept over him: *I understand now, even feel calm about it. This is more than an attack order, it's an order for the death of Charlie Company.* The lesson of the Spartan warriors -- the small band of defenders that committed suicide to deny the Persians the satisfaction of killing them -- was not lost on him.

Dennis lit a cigarette. "Colonel Flint just gave me a history lesson, Eddie. I want tanks."

"How's that, Charlie Six?"

"Ah, he reminded me about the Spartans -- fifth century. They say that a soldier is never the ultimate soldier -- never a complete soldier --

until he has died for his cause -- like a Spartan. I know what the Colonel is saying. We become 'Spartans' in the morning. We're to be sacrificed for a greater good." He picked up the receiver.

"Wilco, Falcon Six. I understand."

Coded orders followed. Dennis deciphered them, passing them on to Sergeant Allred, Rusty Adkins, and Jay Cee. Laying his head on an ant-infested log, he struggled for a few moments of sleep. He no longer dreamed of home and his mother. Only the crush of shellfire and the screams of dying men filled the recesses of his mind.

Chapter Thirty-Nine
The Death of Ap Cho

"Get up, Lieutenant. What the hell are you going to do? Sleep all day?" Jay Cee said laughingly as he nudged his friend hard with the toe of his boot. "The company's moving out. Do you want to get left behind?"

"Moving out? What are you talking about? Where's Eddie and Rusty Adkins?"

"Slow down, Charlie Six, you're still asleep. You called us all together during the night and gave us an operations order that was out of sight: 'Attack at first light; thirty air strikes, flat trajectory howitzers, gunships, two forty-millimeter 'dusters.' Best thing is, we have a company of tanks and two of infantry in armored personnel carriers. Listen, they're pulling into place now."

Dennis jumped to his feet, brushing soggy dirt from his face that had caked there, marking the sorry conditions of his resting-place. "There's ants all over me," he screamed. Reacting to their stinging bites, he thrashed about trying to dislodge them. "I've been sleeping in an ant bed to keep from sleeping -- to stay alive, how much more miserable can I get?" He immediately forgot his personal discomfort as the nearby rumble of heavy tanks and their irritable screeching caused his flesh to tremble and his heart race. "What -- ?"

"Yeah, Lieutenant, we're moving toward the LD now," Jay Cee smiled. "You told us all about it, don't you remember? Well, it doesn't matter. Looks like we're going to take these bastards today. Eddie and I will fill you in. Let's walk. It's crazy, man. A couple of hours ago you were telling us. I guess fatigue has blanked your mind."

"Air strikes are coming in at zero six-fifteen," Jay Cee continued. "There's a Forward Air Controller in a small spotter plane over us now. I've heard him talking to his 'fast movers.' They're in the air. Watch out, here they come now."

Dennis stopped in his tracks and, with his arms slumped, mouth agape, gawked upward through a clear sky. Fast moving Air Force jets of every shape and configuration dotted the heavens. There were at least ten in all, circling wide like vultures at first, then breaking away, one by one, at supersonic speed, plummeting earthward, delivering their deadly ordnance upon the enemy. The impact of their large bombs threatened to lift Dennis and his small group off of their feet. They sought protection among the ditches and palms as sortie after sortie rendered the village beneath them a volcano of destruction.

Nearly kissing the earth as they dove, they disappeared quickly into the upper clouds, reappearing abruptly, delivering their deadly loads upon the hamlet, Ap Cho. Their massive bombs churned it into a wasteland of powdered ash and all life above the ground stood still. Oxen, cows, chickens, and animals of every class burst into flame and bellowed the language of their own special agony. Many were thrown hundreds of yards in every direction, spinning, twirling, and somersaulting violently through the air.

Beneath these plumes of fire and smoke, Dennis could see only a few remaining walls of stucco and mud, their wooden frames and thatched roofs erupting into a hot and savage conflagration. Straining his eyes, peering through the smoke, he saw only nubby bumps -- much smaller in size now -- that were once the impregnable fortifications they had fought so hard to overcome. He choked: "Jesus, help us. The gates of hell have opened --"

Eddie Runge, standing beside Dennis, gazed in awe at this aerial dance raining death and destruction upon the village. He spat, shook his head, then tapped Dennis on the shoulder with the radio handset. "Here, Charlie Six," he said. "Call the main man. Ask for God, not Jesus."

Dennis looked at Eddie, mystified by his comment. "This is no time to be sacrilegious, Eddie."

"Yeah, and this ain't no place for children, either. You know it. We'll be going back in there in a few minutes. They'll be waiting for us. I can still see bunkers."

"You're right, Eddie. We do need all the help we can get. Tell me, you and Jay Cee, what is it we are supposed to do? What did I say to you during the night?"

Jay Cee sighed, "OK, Sir. I guess you're still out of it. Right after Colonel Flint called, you went damned glassy-eyed. You called us into a huddled just as you got a call from operations. We knew it was a coded message. You had to go under your poncho and light your Zippo to cipher it. You came up for air in about five minutes with the biggest grin you could squeeze onto that miserable-looking face of yours."

Dennis, looking mystified by the explanation, motioned them all to sit. "Tell me more."

Eddie interrupted. "You gave us a fifteen minute sermon about how this would be the last attack. You said that after today it would be all over or you would be dead and all the rest of us would be dead, too. God, you scared the crap out of me -- out of all of us."

"You spoke in funny tongues," Jay Cee said. "When we asked what the hell you were saying, you started mumbling about Socrates, Plato and Julius Caesar. You gave us a bunch of other incomprehensible mumbo jumbo, too. You said stuff about the Greeks, the Jews, the Romans, and the Eighty-Second Airborne. You were unbelievable. You stood on an ammo crate and shouted: 'Noble deeds from noble men.'"

Dennis looked at them, his mouth agape. He could remember nothing. "I must have sounded like an idiot."

Eddie laughed. "Naw, you got us all fired up and everybody started whooping and hollering. The boys understood. To the man, they're willing to die right here, for you and for the cause. They know there ain't no turning back from this one."

"It's like this," Jay Cee continued. "Whether we live or die today, Ap Cho will be in American hands by nightfall. Charlie Company would follow you into hell right now, Lieutenant. Dying in Ap Cho is better than living another day trying to capture it." Jay Cee stopped, cocked his ear and grinned: "Listen. Sounds like more tanks coming. Artillery, too: some big stuff."

"I don't believe this," Dennis said, cupping his hands to light a cigarette. "What else?"

"We know we got a company of tanks, maybe eighteen or more," Jay Cee answered. "They're on our radio net now, waiting for instructions. They're 'Saber,' from the Cavalry. We got the 'Tomahawks,' too. They're bringing a company of armored personnel carriers; they'll be here in fifteen minutes. We have tracks from the 1st of the 5th Mechanized infantry and there's three companies of leg infantry from Flame. It looks like a task force of maybe fifteen hundred men."

"Jay Cee, you say I told you all this? I can't remember a thing. Any Artillery?"

"Any artillery? Look at this," Jay Cee said, digging for a notebook. "As soon as these jets are clear, you'll have the combined fires from four whole batteries. Any artillery? Hell, they're all here."

Jay Cee could hardly contain his excitement. He almost broke into a dance as he spoke. "They're sending three Howitzers to fire flat trajectory alongside us as we advance. Some 'Red Leg' officer was here a few minutes ago. He's bringing two 'Dusters' to pick out bunkers and will fire into them with their big shells. We got an 'eight incher,' too."

"It's starting to come back to me, guys. Is there more?"

"I talked with the drivers of two flame-thrower tracks. I told them you'd show them where to go. They're going to stay right alongside of you as we move."

Jay Cee was out of breath and Eddie continued: "Beau Coups gunships on the net. I've talked with pilots from six different assault helicopter companies this morning. They'll be flying cover. We've got continuous gunship fire from overhead. Everybody's on our net now, asking for instructions. Man, I don't know how Colonel Flint did it, but we've got what it takes now. The men are ready, lined up alongside the road, waiting for you."

"Great. I'm coming alive now, but one question. Why are the gunships and artillery and everybody on our company radio net? They should be talking to Battalion."

"Neg-a-tory, Sir," Jay Cee said. "You, my friend, are the Task Force Commander. Don't faint, now. Colonel Flint said nobody knows more about this place than you."

"Yeah, well, I do know something about it."

Eddie interjected: "You know, Dennis, We've made more than thirty back-to-back assaults against this village. The other companies, they came, took their licks and left. Charlie Company has led almost every attack. The colonel says you deserve the honor. Are you ready?"

"There is no honor here, but for the gang: for Rosey, Wally, Andy, Jackie. Yeah, I'm ready."

"Artillery is due in seconds," Jay Cee said. "You need to call everyone, they need a commander. You're it."

Their report was excellent. Bits and pieces of the previous evening's conversation began to filter back into Dennis' war-weary brain. Sucking air, he squeezed the radio hand set and began: "All elements attached to Falcon, this is Falcon Charlie Six. We are Task Force Falcon, now. Place all your big boys along the east side of the road. Infuse your infantry among the tanks -- keep the enemy off of them. Mechanized Infantry, take the south side of the line. Walking Infantry, take the left. Falcon Charlie will anchor the center. Dusters, pick your targets. Send those 'Zippos,' to me. Fix bayonets and begin moving as soon as the arty prep has lifted. Here it comes..."

A series of confirmations from adjoining commanders ensued, but Dennis could barely hear them over the massive wall of exploding artillery. It consumed and eliminated all human sound, destroying any communication between units. He stared at the village, overwhelmed by the molten homicide now streaming into it from the sky. For fifteen minutes, the cannoneers spewed their deadly inferno of white-hot alloy deep into the center of the now-shattered colony. Again, bodies and their armaments were thrown into the air like so many toothpicks, entangled with the human debris of innocent peasants and animals who were now trapped between the two sides.

"It's time, move out," Dennis radioed as he, Jay Cee, and his small crew marched boldly forward. They passed over the spot where Rosey, Andy, Wally, Jackie, and the others had died, and they paused for a moment, seeking evidence of their existence. Looking up from Rosey's grimy deathbed, Dennis thrilled to see young PFC Jim Asher leading, guiding, and commanding the remnants of the First Platoon and Rusty Adkins in front with his Third. Lieutenant Michael Balser had returned during the night and now guided the Second Platoon. He limped badly, but told Dennis he wouldn't miss this fight. Jay Cee O'Connor served as his assistant, moving from man to man, and encouraging them. Sergeant Allred, with only ten mortarmen left in his Fourth Platoon, peppered the front with 60 millimeter mortars, firing them on the move, using their steel helmets as base plates. Besides Sergeant Beebe, these were the only remaining leaders. Dennis surmised that company strength was at about seventy men. "They fight like one hundred and seventy," he said to Eddie.

"Climb aboard, Lieutenant," the mechanized infantry commander shouted from atop his armored personnel carrier. "The view's better up here and you can control things a lot easier." He stood and extended his hand to Dennis, who gladly accepted the lift.

Dennis motioned for them to wait and he reached for Eddie. "Oh no, here we go again, Charlie Six," Eddie said as he accepted the hand and scrambled on board. "I'm a ground pounder. I'd rather be down there."

Riding atop the seesawing monster gave Dennis a thrill. High on this perch, he could see the entire task force as they exchanged bullet for bullet, grenade for grenade, bayonet for bayonet.

Captain Boulanger, the mechanized commander, laughed as he measured Dennis' reaction to his first experience riding the iron beast. He leaned over and shouted into the young officer's ear: "Settle down, Lieutenant, get used to it. It beats the hell out of walking and these fifty calibers will keep anything they got off us."

Suddenly an enemy bunker opened up from behind them with a hail of automatic weapons fire, the bullets nearly missing Dennis' head. He leaped from the track, dragging Eddie with him, shouting "No thanks," to the generous commander. As he rolled through the dirt, trying to gain a foothold, a rifle-propelled grenade penetrated the carrier's hull and began to explode the internal ammunition stores. Men were blown from every exit, but could not escape their horrible fate. Captain Boulanger was crushed beneath the glowing steel along with several of his men. "Jesus," Eddie exclaimed. "Look at that! I'm damn sure glad you got us off that track. I told you, us 'legs' ain't supposed to do stuff like that. What are we going to do with our dead and wounded?"

"We leave them, Eddie. We can't stop. We're too close to finishing this battle. Falcon Six says a graves registration team is trailing us. Medical support, too. We do what we can and move on."

Self-possessed now, Dennis resumed command: "Spread out. Walk alongside and between the tanks," he shouted. "Shoot at anything that looks like VC, kill them all, kill all the dirty bastards." Deranged momentarily by the abrupt death of a man whom he had known for only a moment, all ethical and moral considerations ended for Dennis. He became a merciless and hating killer.

His men, accustomed to such madness, obeyed, and meshed easily with the tanks and mechanized infantry as if they had been born into such tactics. Passing the last of the destroyed frameworks, they broke free into wider and clearer fields of fire. There, Dennis saw the total breadth and magnitude of his command. Huffing and puffing from the excitement, he felt liberated at last from the abortion named Ap Cho. "Look at it, Eddie. Look you guys: tanks and infantry spread out for half a mile."

Revealing its overwhelming power, the multitude of men and machine spontaneously began a total encirclement of the village, wheeling left and right with their heavy tanks and tracks as foot soldiers raced to keep abreast. In ever-decreasing concentric circles, they labored around and around the battle positions of the NVA, blasting their apertures with mighty cannon fire and crushing the fleeing enemy beneath their bloody treads. Infantrymen surged into the open holes, ramming their bayonets into the bellies of those who refused to surrender.

Still, rocket and machine gun fire pelted their ranks and Dennis watched men going down on his left and right. The mechanized infantry stalled before a series of bunkers and several carriers exploded into flames. The NVA brazenly clung to their crushed embattlements. Firing rockets and grenades from beneath the masses of earth and concrete, American tanks began losing their treads and turrets. Pieces of armored hulls twisted through the air like rag dolls as their ammunition racks exploded and the enemy made good their last defense.

Charlie Company joined the melee, firing machine guns, rifles, and rockets from the hip. A lone soldier, calm and methodical in his actions, launched rifle grenades into fleeing bodies with deadly accuracy. Dennis watched as one projectile landed squarely into the shoulder blades of a retreating man. His body exploded, disappearing above the waist.

"That's our Charlie Brown, Fourth Platoon," Eddie said, looking in amazement at the destruction. "He uses 'Kentucky windage.' The boy never misses."

Some men stood, advancing fearlessly while others crawled on their bellies into the hidden nooks and furrows of destruction, seeking the hidden enemy. Mike Balser, Rusty Adkins, Jay Cee O'Connor, and Eddie Runge led the Company effort and Dennis was now forced to trail them. Enemy resistance stiffened in the face of the task force advance, until, finally, the Americans stalled.

Unable to move, Dennis received a frantic call from Rusty Adkins. "Charlie Six, we've got a bunker pinning us down. They've destroyed a couple of tanks. One tank has put a dozen high explosive rounds into the bunker, but the fuckers keep firing ...wait."

Dennis waited calmly. He knew that Rusty needed time to assess the plight of the tankers. Rusty came back on, his voice full of excitement. "The tank is burning, but the commander's still firing his machine gun. He's the only man left alive in that crew. The bunker -- it's the big enchilada -- looks like their command post. Take it, and we've got it all."

"Tell him an infantry platoon will dig them out. Are you game, Rusty? Can you and your men handle it?"

"You bet your sweet ass. Stand by."

Lieutenant Rusty Adkins, almost buried in the pulverized earth, waved an arm, summoning his men forward. Without question, one by one, six men crawled to join him. Drawing his pistol, Rusty said: "We're going into that bunker, men. There's no other way. Follow me!"

Crawling on their bellies, the men followed. Inch by inch, they wriggled and snaked their way forward, right into the sights of the offending bunker. A lone NVA soldier appeared and attempted to poke his rifle out of the porthole. Rusty fired his pistol, forcing the man to duck inside. Within two to three feet of the bunker, Rusty uncorked a concussion grenade, lobbed it inside, and waited.

The narrow walls of the dugout served to magnify the effect of the explosion. The horrendous blast blew Rusty and his men backward a few feet. His ears were ringing and blood oozed from his nose. Turning to look at his men, he gave them a 'thumbs up,' straightened, and then dove, headlong, into the bunker. His men waited in silence. A single shot rang out from deep within the fortification. Sergeant Beebe, who had accompanied the team, didn't hesitate.

"That was a rifle shot," he yelled. "Lieutenant had a pistol. Let's go." Five men followed the brave Tennessean, one behind the other, deep into the hole.

The agonizing screams of men dying in hand-to-hand combat curdled the flesh of other platoon members who had arrived to help. Small bursts of gunfire erupted from within the cavity of death. Finally, silence engulfed them all.

Saber Six, a tank commander, observed the scene from his turret perch. Six infantrymen reappeared, one by one, through the small opening. Two of them turned and dragged a body out onto the ground. Saber Six pressed his hand set.

"Falcon Charlie Six, this is Saber Six. I just watched the most phenomenal act of courage I've ever seen. One of your platoons crawled alongside a bunker that had my tanks in its sights, holding me up. Your young leader, with just a pistol in his hand, entered the bunker alone."

"That's Rusty Adkins."

"I don't know who he was, but the firing from that bunker stopped. Your men are pulling the VC out now. Sorry to say, I think the boy gave his life for it. The men have his body. They'll bring him to you."

"Saber Six, thanks. That was Rusty Adkins. Remember the name. He died too young. He was only nineteen, so young. "

Dennis couldn't breathe for a moment. "Rusty is dead, Rusty is dead," he screamed. He had come to know and to love this beach boy and his guileless courage. In the end, Rusty had become one of Dennis' most trusted Lieutenants and now he, too, lay bleeding upon the ash heap of Ap Cho. "Oh, God, will this ever end?" he begged aloud, unashamed that others would see and hear him.

Barely regaining his composure, he said to Eddie, "Get Sergeant Beebe on the radio; tell him to take the Third Platoon."

"Let me talk to Six," Sergeant Beebe answered when Eddie called.

"You've got to handle the Third Platoon, Sarge. You're Three Six, now," Dennis choked. "I'm sorry about Rusty."

"Now I know you get upset real easy, Charlie Six, but what the heck do you want me to take the 'Third Herd' for?"

"They need a leader. Lieutenant Adkins is dead."

Dennis heard Sergeant Beebe chuckle slightly. "I don't know where in the Dickens you got that idea, Charlie Six. He ain't dead. If he is, I'm looking at the 'second coming.' The boy is wounded, but not too bad. He does look a mite tuckered out, though."

"What? He's OK? Oh, thank God," Dennis yelled into the telephone set. "Let me talk to him."

Waiting became imbearable for Dennis and he shouted again into the handset: "Three Six, Rusty. Let me hear you!"

"This is Three Six. Mission accomplished. What's next, Six?"

Dennis turned to Eddie, Jay Cee, and others who had gathered near him. They anxiously awaited an explanation.

Dennis spoke more calmly now. "Rusty, I thought you were dead. That tanker told me you were dead. I can't believe I'm talking to you."

"I probably am dead. I feel dead. In fact, I think I know how Jesus felt. I've got grenade fragments all through me. I can't hardly walk."

"Why did he tell me -- ?"

"I didn't have the strength left to crawl out of that bunker. My boys dragged me thirty feet. I guess I looked dead to the tanker. I sure could use a beer."

"We'll get you out, Rusty. The medics are coming behind us. They'll police you up. Stay where you are. Give command to Beebe. We still have some fighting to do."

"Roger, Six. See you at my 'sermon on the mount.'" Lieutenant Adkins issued a slight laugh and then the radio fell silent.

Dennis was exhausted. The abrupt shift in emotions from that of profound sorrow to exhilaration dominated his entire physical self. His knees buckled and he knelt in the dirt. He looked at Eddie. "I can't believe --"

Shots peppered Dennis' feet, suspending his message. Eddie ran for cover, dragging Dennis with him. The two flame-thrower carriers came alongside and began to spew a long trail of red-hot napalm directly into the offending bunkers. A flood of enemy soldiers, suffocating from depleted oxygen, scrambled out, throwing their hands into the air and yelling, "Choi Hoi." (We surrender). The American platoons gave no quarter and instantly cut the enemy flesh to ribbons. "There's no Choi Hois in this village," someone said. Buried in his hatred, Dennis did not protest.

Momentum renewed and the task force began to roll forward. Gunships laid down a continuous wall of hot red steel ahead of their advance. Artillery pounded each bunker with flat trajectory fire as they dragged their cannons forward. No enemy position was left unscathed, each being sealed permanently, the occupants either escaping into the flame and bullets of the Americans, or trapped inside to suffocate.

By noon it appeared that all enemy positions had been crushed, burned hollow, exploded, or emptied at the point of a bayonet. The task force, advancing swiftly now, abandoned their encirclement and postured themselves on a straight line, attacking forward into the now-fleeing enemy. Dennis and his men could not keep up; they finally surrendered to exhaustion.

They walked slowly through the village, as the armor had matters well in hand. Passing numerous bodies, some of them American, many of them North Vietnamese Communists, he noticed that several were smoldering from the napalm. Their flesh had fallen in chunks from their torsos and some were seared together, creating a mass of dead humanity.

Dennis knelt to examine one boyish-looking enemy soldier who lay separate and supine amid the waste. A wave of sympathy washed over Dennis and he reached to touch the lad's cheek. Suddenly the male child, dressed in the baggy habit of a North Vietnamese soldier, bolted upright, thrusting his knife toward Dennis' groin. He closed his fingers around the assailant's throat. Together they grappled violently, each determined to hold on to life. A shot rang out and the boy's skull shattered in a hundred pieces, splattering Dennis with blood and a thick, greenish mucus. "His brains," Jay Cee said, unperturbed as he lowered the muzzle of his smoking rifle.

"Thanks, Jay Cee, thanks," Dennis sighed as he dropped his trousers to examine his bleeding thigh. "Just a scratch," he said to the gathering platoons. "Let's keep moving."

By one o'clock they had overcome all resistance in Charlie Company's sector. Only sealed bunkers remained as sizzling hot and airless tombs for the northern enemy. By 2:00 p.m., firing was meager and sporadic. Colonel Flint landed and established a command post dead center in what had been the village of Ap Cho. It was now only a barren wasteland of burning enemy flesh and withering torsos. In places, the dying humanity made the earth itself seem alive. A few survivors cried out for water and aid, but none was forthcoming from the Americans. Stripped naked of compassion, they shot those who dared to show a thread of life. Dennis did nothing to stop it, he hated them so.

At 3:00 p.m., Colonel Flint called for a cease-fire and ordered the combatants to shoot only threatening targets. What few enemy managed to escape fled into the tropical forest that lay well to the east of Ap Cho. The tanks and mechanized infantry gave hot pursuit. Gunships reported numerous kills from their airborne perches and convinced everyone that the battle had truly been won. "The Battle of Ap Cho -- it's over," Dennis said to Eddie and Jay Cee. "Tell the men. It's finally over."

"Cease fire, cease fire," they called. "It's over. It's over." Men looked up from their gruesome foraging and quietly nodded their understanding. No shouts of joy nor whoops of exulted satisfaction emitted from the company of exhausted men. They simply sat down, drinking warm water from their canteens and lighting stale tobacco as their reward.

Chapter Forty
The Aftermath

Colonel Flint called for a meeting, insisting that all of them, seniors and subordinates alike, meet with him atop the former command post of the North Vietnamese. It was an irony that was not wasted upon the men, and they took quiet satisfaction in joining him there. He watched, contented, as they implanted a small American flag.

Standing, hands behind his back, looking out upon the sea of waste, Colonel Flint stared for a long time. The men remained patient; finally, he began: "You've done it men. Congratulations. I am very proud of you. Now, let me share a simple fact. I was proud of you the moment I took command. Now, be proud of yourselves. You've won an extraordinary victory."

Colonel Flint paused and frowned. His voice cracked as he began anew. "I know you men have suffered tremendous losses and you've been ravaged in all areas of your physical self, your emotional self. But, you are the victors, the heroes, and the world will soon know it."

He rubbed his hands together, looked down, then up, and finally smiled at his assembled troops. "CBS news is dispatching a reporter and camera crew to this location. They should be here within the hour. I want you to scour the battlefield. Open those bunkers, dig out the enemy. Lay the dead and their armaments before the cameras. Let the people back home know. Show them how you fought and how your friends, and, yes, even how the enemy died. Hide nothing -- tell them all about it."

"They coming now, huh, Colonel?" someone shouted. "Where the hell they been for two weeks?"

Colonel Flint smiled, waving his hand for silence. "I understand how you feel. Make them understand. Describe this battle, every detail. Maybe your families, someone back home, will see and recognize you. They'll focus on this destruction and then perhaps someone will speak up and act to halt this carnage before it kills more of us -- more of them."

"Fuck them," a man in front yelled. "Fuck 'em all."

"Ah, now. Take it easy, boys. Listen to me: tend to your wounded, evacuate your dead and bury theirs. Consolidate your meager resources and establish defensive positions in preparation for a counter attack."

Someone laughed: "Attack. Who, them?" A chuckle rumbled across the audience.

"Right," Colonel Flint agreed. "I don't think there's much fight left in this enemy. Their Tet Offensive has failed miserably. They've lost at every turn with an astronomical waste of their people. This battle, Ap Cho, may be insignificant to history when compared to the larger fights of Tet. Yet, you and I know how vitally important it was. The credit goes to you men of Falcon who kept the supply lines open and the ammunition and supplies moving forward to those who desperately needed it. Thank you for your courage. You have performed magnificently."

The assembled warriors stirred now. Someone hollered: "We kicked some ass, huh, Colonel?" A cheer erupted up from the crowd. Colonel Flint pointed his finger at them. "You bet your sweet ass you did."

The Falcon Battalion howled their approval, causing Colonel Flint to laugh. The men quieted. Waiting and shuffling his feet a bit, Colonel Flint continued in his exhortation: "Tonight we will camp here among the ruins of Ap Cho -- in this vile desert of death. Reflect and pray upon what you have done here. Tomorrow we will surely move on to other battlefields and other contests of war, but none will be as perverse and as challenging as Ap Cho." He fell silent and stared at them for a long time, seemingly to look into every set of eyes. Finally, as if he were unable to continue, that there was nothing of importance left to say, he called them to attention and shouted: "Dismissed, Falcon."

He moved forward into the throng and shook every hand. "I'm proud of you, boys. Good job. Thank you," he said to the men as he passed through their ranks. Finally stopping in front of Dennis, where he stood with his head hung low, weary and despondent, he reached out and gathered the young hero in both arms, whispering special gratitude.

"Without you and Charlie Company, Lieutenant, this moment would have never arrived. The ammunition and supplies would be burning in massive piles along this road. Had that happened, our Division might very well have lost these provinces. We have you and your gallant men to thank for that."

"I'll tell the men," Dennis replied.

"I know you are weary, Lieutenant, and, perhaps, somewhat bitter. I'm sorry I had to put you through all this. Do you remember the afternoon of our first meeting, when I snapped at you? I was testing your mettle then, your character."

Dennis looked up. "You were what?"

"Yes, I was experimenting with you. Sorry, but your soldierly response satisfied me. I knew that it was you -- you and Charlie Company would lead this battalion through Ap Cho, making these many battles into a final victory."

"Thanks."

"Yes, Dennis. Ap Cho reminded me of a dozen such villages I've seen before. It was very similar to the hamlets we fought for in Korea. I suspected that this was going to be the battle of all battles for us. I'm sorry that it has cost so much. The lives lost. My God..."

Dennis sensed Colonel Flint's own pain. "It's OK, Sir. We won. Whatever that means. What do we do now?"

"Look after your men. Let them search for booty and souvenirs. It may help them to feel avenged. Send your reports every half-hour and be here when that news crew arrives. I want America to see what real heroes look like."

Dennis took little pleasure in the Colonel's words. He felt no redemption, only hatred for the enemy. Lofty praise could not reduce the permanent grief he felt. Turning to Eddie and Jay Cee, he said: "The only thing he didn't do was hold a laurel wreath over my head, but then, he doesn't have to. There is no glory here."

Left to the men of Falcon, the battlefield turned quiet, the tanks, carriers and artillery having departed for other bivouacs. Dennis turned his men loose and they began to forage inside the once formidable bunkers that had cost them so many lives. Near the place where Jackie, Wally, and the others had died, they opened a huge bunker, whereupon they found the mangled torsos of thirty, perhaps even forty, enemy dead.

"They're so tangled up it is impossible to count them," Sergeant Allred said. "Their bodies -- legs and arms -- so tightly laced together from the impact of bombs that you can't tell how many died in there."

Dennis watched as men used sticks and poles from the debris to pry the bodies apart. It was sickening to watch as their bloody intestines and other vital body parts spilled out onto the grimy earth. He felt a strange pleasure in it, though, and fought the urge to believe that the death of any number of North Vietnamese would ever be compensation enough for what they had lost. Yet, he could not escape it.

Surrendering to the emotion, he relished in the satisfaction of seeing the dead enemy, torn and mutilated, unmoving, now being laid in rows. By four o'clock they had dragged more than two hundred and fifty wretched carcasses into a pile. The stench of burning and rotting flesh made it necessary to don protective masks to guard against airborne infection. Bulldozers arrived and began preparing pits to serve as mass graves.

Dennis had seen enough. His rage turned to pity and then he grew sick, vomiting his way back to the battalion command post as a light helicopter began its descent into the village of death.

"Dennis, this is Steve Rorrer from CBS news," Colonel Flint said as he shook hands with the reporter and cameraman. "He's going to do a story on the Battle of Ap Cho. He says it'll be on the five o'clock news. I told him you'd be the best witness to talk to. Go ahead, Lieutenant Riley, tell them," he said, patting Dennis' back.

"Hi, Lieutenant," Mr. Rorrer said, "the Colonel is right. Your folks might even see you. First, I want to get film of the destroyed village, then the enemy casualties, and finally, I'll talk to some of your men."

"OK," Dennis replied, "but I don't think they feel much like talking."

The reporter and his crew unpacked their equipment. Mr. Rorrer unwound the cord of his microphone. "I'd like to interview you first, Lieutenant, and then we'll talk with them. Ready?" The cameraman lifted his heavy instrument to his shoulders and the lights came on.

Dennis, popping gum to remove the taste of vomit and death from his mouth, stared at the reporter and his crew. *I cannot glorify this,* he thought. *Look at them in their clean fatigues, their fat bellies, making a living on the hell of Vietnam. They'll probably be back in Saigon sleeping between cool, clean sheets tonight. He'll send his film on to CBS, collect a fee, and they'll have more propaganda to feed the American people. The destruction of this village and the people who lived in it will become the focus. That's what sells back home. We won't be heroes. He'll show them how we blew this village apart and killed everyone in it. I can tell by looking at him that he's a fraud.*

"Yeah," Dennis said. "Go ahead."

The reporter turned to his cameraman. "Get set," he shouted. "Back up on that small hill. Lieutenant, push your helmet back, hold your rifle on your hip, muzzle up, like the triumphant hunter does. That's it. Now put the camera on me, I'll introduce. Ready? Three, two, one … action."

Placing the microphone at his mouth, Mr. Rorrer began: "Ladies and Gentlemen, we're standing in the aftermath of one of the most difficult battles of the Tet Offensive. Before us is the destroyed village of Ap Cho, somewhere in War Zone C. You can barely tell that it was once a peaceful farming hamlet, with the ruination of it so complete under the ferocious American attack. The 3rd Battalion, 22nd Infantry fought for fourteen days to overcome a tough enemy that had dug in here. Early figures indicate that almost three hundred of them sacrificed their lives in this village as did forty-four Americans. More than two-hundred GIs were wounded."

Mr. Rorrer stopped and the camera panned the battlefield, finally stopping on Dennis. Clicking on his microphone, he began anew. "First Lieutenant Dennis Riley from Detroit, Michigan, led the final assault. Can you tell us, Lieutenant, about the battle? How was it?" He thrust the microphone into Dennis' face and the camera hummed.

Dennis, unmoved by the reporter's clever phrasing, heard only what he was predisposed to hear: "You can barely tell that it ever was a peaceful farming hamlet … ruination so complete under the ferocious American attack … sacrificed their lives." *I know how that'll go over back home.*

Hearing their scuffling feet, Dennis realized that mustering behind him were the men who had fought the long battle. He felt their presence, sensed their anger and understood that he should say nothing to diminish their blood relationship with the dead.

"If you didn't walk the walk, then you can't talk the talk," someone shouted.

"Yeah, tell President Johnson to come and get his own body count," yelled another.

Dennis paced and chewed his gum nervously as he pondered the comments of his men.

They have valid arguments against talking to this reporter; no one would believe it, anyway. There's no benefit to them or their families if they talk to him. Charlie Company has no common citizens anymore. They are no longer the untainted young men who kissed their mothers good-bye just months ago. They're ruthless animals who just spent the afternoon poking sticks into the intestines of men they've been killing for fourteen days. They are barbarous, untamed savages at this point, too crude to put before the camera, but then what about all of our dead friends, who will speak for them? I've got to say something -- tell how they feel. I know their thoughts....

"How was it, Mr. Rorrer?" Dennis finally said. "It was pure fucking hell, man. These bastards decided to stay here and fight to the last man. These communist sons-of-bitches wanted to fucking die and so we did that for them --"

"Cut," Mr. Rorrer said to the photographer as he waved his free hand in a show of disgust. "Stop everything." He glared at Dennis and asked, "Didn't your mother ever tell you that it isn't nice to swear, Lieutenant? I can't use that stuff on TV."

"Fuck you," someone shouted.

The reporter and his man shouldered their equipment and walked quickly in the direction of Colonel Flint who was watching from a few yards away. "Colonel, I guess the boys don't feel like talking. Think you can say something printable for our camera?"

"Sorry, Steve. The men are feeling pretty low. They are deeply bitter about the unnecessary loss of life all around. They are sick of this war, and young Lieutenant Riley there -- he speaks for them."

The Colonel waved his hand. "Look at them. They're haggard, tired and thin from poor rations and overwork. They will recover in time from the physical abuse, but I wonder about their mental health. Some of them will go mad, you know."

Mr. Rorrer set his equipment down and folded his arms. "I didn't realize how tragic this battle was, Colonel. I promise to give the boys some good press, even if they don't want to talk about it."

Colonel Flint patted him on the shoulder. "That's all right, Steve. It's not your fault. You see, it is not common for human beings to kill other humans. These men are now torn with maddening emotions."

"I agree about their emotions, whew. I got scared over there," Mr. Rorrer chuckled.

"Steve, this entire battalion has reached the point of savagery. They are amoral and barbaric. They'll carry a heavy burden of guilt and shame into their old age. Understand that and leave them be. I'll tell you what you want to know. God help them and their families when they return home."

Colonel Flint then gave a remarkable account of the battle and described the heroism of each unit, each man, making sure that his portrayal would satisfy the censorship of television editors and could hardly be manipulated.

"We destroyed this hamlet and the enemy within to save the lives of countless other Americans and South Vietnamese," he said into the camera. "We destroyed Ap Cho to save it."

"Describe the battle, Colonel," Mr. Rorrer said.

"This was part of an operation called, 'Saratoga.' A large concentration of Viet Cong and North Vietnamese soldiers had massed around Cui Chi in late January and early February, digging into the hamlet of Ap Cho. The simple villagers who lived and farmed here either fled, were pressed into service as slaves, or were executed by them." Colonel Flint stopped, sighed and shook his head.

"They built massive concrete bunkers connected by an extensive tunnel complex and interconnecting trenches. This Battalion, the Third of the Twenty-Second Infantry, was called upon to locate the enemy and rout them from their positions."

Colonel Flint removed his steel helmet and cradled it against his hip. Glancing quickly at a notebook he held in his left hand, he paused momentarily, then continued: "The resulting operation amounted to thirty-seven separate engagements, accounting for more than two hundred and eighty enemy dead. We are still counting. The carnage here is so devastating that we may never know the full impact of the battle. How many died it may be impossible to say."

Colonel Flint appeared finished, but then spotted Dennis glaring at him. He nodded and continued. "The greatest part of these engagements were made by one company, Charlie Company. They fearlessly attacked the enemy -- sometimes three, four and five times, each day. They advanced many times alone, through the bullets, trading lives for ground, inch by inch, yard by yard. For fourteen consecutive days they attacked, hacking away at the bunkers and neutralizing the inhabitants. Eventually, they were supported by many other units and today marked the concluding attack."

"It sounds like one heck of a battle, Colonel," Mr. Rorrer said.

"It was. Early on, we knew that the enemy would not give up. They were determined to fight to the death. They did exactly that. That is, they all died before the advance of these daring men."

Dennis and his men gathered around the Colonel as he spoke. They lit cigarettes, chewed gum, drank water, but were absolutely silent.

"This battle was fierce and it was long. Each morning our units would gather along this road, getting on line, attaching their bayonets, and making determined assaults. Although this particular action might be anti-climactic to Tet, the victory marks a major upset to the Communist overall plan for an uprising."

Spreading his arms wide, he gestured above the mass of men like an Evangelist embracing his flock. "Thanks to the robust warriors you see here, the enemy failed. God bless our boys, and ask America to bless them and bring them home."

"Cut; now that's a take," the reporter said. "Wrap it up Billy -- we have got some good celluloid here."

Colonel Flint continued, off camera: "They are the very best that America has to give, Mr. Rorrer. Please tell the people back home about them. Tell them to be proud of their sons, who suffer so much each day that this war drags on. They need to know."

The CBS crew departed and the Battalion moved northeast to the edge of the decimated village. There they found cleaner bivouacs and tried to lay away the sorrow called Ap Cho.

"The village of tears," Dennis reminded Eddie, "was named by Rusty Adkins just before he got hit." He sat silently beside a campfire that night with Eddie, Jay Cee, and Sergeants Allred and Beebe. Under a clear and star-studded sky, he pulled from his pocket a weathered notebook, fat with ragged pages. Unwinding the rubber bands that held it together, he tried to make conversation.

"Let me read to you from Rosey's 'book of wisdom,'" Dennis said. Flipping through the loose pages, he selected one at random. Choking slightly, he read: "If my life has any meaning, it is because you, my friends give it meaning. How will you give me meaning, now? *Roosevelt Dolan*."

Chapter Forty-One
The Catholic Village

Camping that first night out of Ap Cho with Jay Cee and Eddie, they drank warm beer flown in by First Sergeant Krznarovich, who also delivered mail, packages, and other items of comfort and convenience. He moved quietly from position to position, telling the men how proud he was of them. "They're as good as any men I've ever served with," he said.

"You're good medicine for these boys, Top," Dennis said.

"It works both ways, Lieutenant." His crude bravado strangely diminished now, he added, "I've been missing them."

They stoked the fire higher and men came in from their guard posts to spend a few moments with their leader, explaining as best they could their analysis of Ap Cho. Many of them expressed regret over their behavior during the last moments of the attack.

"I shot one right between the eyes," Gary Adams said. "At first I felt real good, like some kind of hero. Then I walked about twenty feet and I started feeling like shit. I still do." Without waiting for an answer from Dennis, he stood and, with shoulders slumped, ambled his way back into the wood line.

"Look after him, boys," Dennis said. "He's carrying a lot. I guess we all are."

"Truth be told, Lieutenant, ain't nobody happy about this battle," Sergeant Beebe observed. "At Burt, we was just defending our asses. Here, we chopped 'em down in cold blood. Ain't nobody ever gonna brag about this one. I know I ain't."

Dennis nodded his head in agreement. He feigned joy at their success, yet he felt a growing agony inside. The violence at Ap Cho exceeded any expectations he had ever had about battle. Killing did not come easily to him, he now knew. He knew also that he would not quickly shed the loss of his special friends. "It'll be a long time before I forget any of them," he told Jay Cee.

"It'll take us both a long time, Sir. I didn't know them before we started on that trip to Fort Lewis, but they were sure some great guys. I'll never forget them. I wonder if they're in Heaven?"

Dennis said little, sometimes deliberately staring past the eyes of his friend as they shared a can of beer. *I'd probably die if anything happened to him,* Dennis thought. *The last one of our gang. I've got to do something to save him.*

"Jay Cee, Father Tobin mentioned that he was looking for a chaplain's assistant to work with him. Says that his man 'Friday' is leaving at the end of the month. You can have the job; do you want it?"

"Are you kidding? Hell yes, I'll take it. You know, Lieutenant, we're more than halfway through our tour. We'll be home in five months. My dad would be glad I'm off the line. Do you think you can swing it? How soon?"

"I'm told we'll stay here and recover for a few days. You have a rest and relaxation furlough coming up: 'R&R.' Why don't you take your leave, and when you get back, I'll have it all arranged? What were your plans, anyway?"

"I'm going to meet my folks in Hawaii, my brother and sister, my mom and dad. I can get a message out tomorrow and meet them at the end of the week. Can we manage it, do you think?"

"Jay Cee, you are as good as gone. Get on the supply chopper in the morning and go make your arrangements. See you when you get back. Your fighting days are over, buddy."

"Hot damn, Charlie Six, thanks." He spontaneously pumped the hand of his friend and commander, then sped off to share the good news with his friends.

At daylight, Jay Cee boarded a chopper and was barely out of sight when a frantic call came from the Battalion Operations Center. "OK, you dog faces. Up and at 'em. You've got a mission." It was the voice of Major Jimmy Johanson, the new Operations Officer. Captain DeMatto had been quietly relegated to a desk job until his rotation home.

Jimmy Johanson was a legend in the Army. He had been a linebacker with the Green Bay Packers' football team. Selected early in the draft, he had been beaten into pieces on the practice field and decided the level of pain required to play professional football was more than he could bear. He activated his ROTC Commission and was now a Major of Infantry.

Dennis was glad to hear his voice. He knew him slightly, having met him on a tour of duty at Fort Benning, Georgia, some years earlier. He was a jolly man, as befit his three hundred pounds of former muscle, now slowly receding into clumps of fat. The troops called him "Tiny Bubbles" after a popular song of the day. Jimmy loved the attention and often hummed the tune himself, sending the name callers into fits of laughter.

"Pack up and move out, Charlie Six. Check your map, and head toward that large village that straddles the Saigon Rver. See that big bend in the river -- the village named Nhi Binh? About a thousand South Vietnamese live there. At least they did until the United States Air Force accidentally put a B-52 bombing run on it last night."

"This is Charlie Six. They did what?"

"Bombed the hell out of it. It's hush, hush stuff right now. You'll provide security for the engineers, medical personnel, and emissaries of all types. Develop day and night patrols to stabilize the area. You're the closest unit; the other Companies will be along in a day or two. Now don't worry, there are no Viet Cong dug in there that we know of. This won't be another Ap Cho."

"Easy for you to say," Dennis replied.

"It's true. Your biggest problem will be the politicians and civilian action workers that don't understand infantrymen -- you in particular. Stay away from them. Damn sure don't talk about this fiasco to the press if they show up, understand?"

"OK, Falcon Three. We'll be moving in thirty minutes. Looks like a nice place for my boys to vacation, eh?"

"No vacation, fella. You'll be working. The village was a French stronghold for many years. Missionaries converted just about everybody in it to Catholicism. Its nickname is 'The Catholic Village.' You got the idea? No 'boom-boom' with the local girls. No booze, no hanky panky."

"The men are going to love you, Sir."

Charlie Company, eager to put distance between themselves and Ap Cho, prepared to move immediately. Airlifted by helicopter, they were deposited near the village of Nhi Binh by noon. A huge, sprawling town, it was surrounded by pineapple groves, rice paddies, and numerous truck plots of beets and grain. Robust cattle grazed peacefully in the fields and fishermen dotted the canals, hoisting their heavily-laden nets into small sampans, almost sinking them. The tragedy of the bombing was evident, however, as hundreds of huge, water-filled craters pockmarked the land.

Dennis carefully selected a defensive position for his unit and, organizing a small patrol, made his way into the center of the village. The devastation wrought by the bombers was everywhere. A wide path of craters began about a half mile south of the town and the trail of holes sliced right through the center of it, extending northward beyond its limits for, perhaps, another mile.

Villagers roamed the dusty streets in shock, still dazed from the bombing. They cried out vainly as they searched beneath rubble for family members and other loved ones. Dennis saw many carrying battered children in their arms and they struggled under the weight of the elderly, dying upon their makeshift litters. American Navy Civic Action personnel and members from a Philippine hospital team arrived in the after noon. They immediately went to work, trying to ease the suffering. South Vietnamese Army units established kitchens and people queued up to receive a meager share of rations.

"It looks like Berlin in 1945," Sergeant Allred said. "This place has been bombed back to the Stone Age."

They met with village officials and members of the American Navy and Philippine Army, to coordinate their missions. From them Dennis learned that almost two hundred people had died in the catastrophic bombing. Finding and burying them was the task of Vietnamese military personnel. The Navy men were engineers, "Seabees." They had already begun rebuilding the dike lines and canals that flooded the land. The Filipinos were to render medical aid and compensation payments to the survivors.

Loaded with bags of American dollars, they set up pay tables, offering five thousand dollars per deceased person as remuneration for their losses. The village mayor himself declared that fifteen family members were killed -- he being the only survivor. Without question or verification, he was promptly paid seventy-five thousand dollars to help ease his despair. Hundreds lined up behind him and the payments went on long into the night.

"Hush money," Dennis told his men when he returned to their encampment and explained what he had learned about the town and its inhabitants. "We bombed the hell out of them. The only way to guarantee their silence is to rebuild the village, the dikes, the farmland, and to make them all filthy rich. Uncle Sam will forever deny that we bombed a friendly village. When the Generals write their books after the war, they'll say they didn't know, or that it never happened. But look around. Someone did and the devastation is appalling."

Dennis rubbed his nose, a recently acquired nervous habit. It had healed well and he no longer felt any pain. "We can relax, men. I don't think we'll have much fighting here; it's not known to be an enemy stronghold. The Village Chief, the Mayor, tells me that the Viet Cong leave them alone most of the time. The people were still friendly to me, in spite of the bombing."

"How friendly?" Eddie asked. "Did you see any pretty girls?"

"Lots of them, Eddie, but you can't touch. I spoke with Vietnamese Army personnel and they'll secure the town. All we have to do is run security patrols around the outskirts of the village. The rest of the battalion will be here in a day or two and the job should be easy. We got lucky, for once."

Dennis paused, swallowing water from his canteen, then continued: "Men, I think we're going to get a real break; we've been told to rest here for a while. Colonel Flint promises replacements over the next few days and wants us to avoid any action that isn't necessary."

"That's good news," Sergeant Allred said. "We need a break, but we still have to defend ourselves. First, dig in. Then we'll rest."

"Thanks, Top, You're right, of course."

Dennis appeared relaxed as he sat in a crude wooden chair someone had confiscated. He thumbed through his notebook, sharing his observations of the village and how they might defend it.

"Our patrols will be small and they'll extend only to the periphery of the village, mainly along the canals. They're flooded so we can't cross them anyway. The dikes, built centuries ago by hand, were broken by the bombs and that's what the Navy is here to rebuild. Let's get at it. Dismissed."

Eddie had already selected an abandoned hut as their command post and was busy digging a fighting position just outside the doorway when Dennis approached. "Piece of cake, this job, huh, Charlie Six? Want a cold beer? I just bought a whole case and some ice from a cute little 'Momma-San.' She had other good stuff to sell, too." Eddie put down his shovel and crawled out of the hole, laughing heartily.

"What's so funny, Eddie?"

"There were four pretty young things trailing behind her, Dennis, but I thought of you. You know, what you said, about no 'boom boom,' so I told her to scram. So this is a Catholic Village? Hell, Six, I think the boys are going to forget Ap Cho real soon. And to think Jay Cee had to go all the way to Hawaii to have a little fun." Eddie laughed again and handed Dennis a beer.

The days following their introduction into Nhi Binh were quiet and allowed plenty of time for relaxation. The men spontaneously formed sports teams, playing football, soccer, and other games. They improvised a hoop and basketball became the highest form of recreation. They bathed and swam in the water- filled bomb craters and lay almost naked in the sun. Two Guamanian boys captured a wild pig and roasted it in an earthen oven. Feasting on pork, fish, fruits and vegetables from local gardens, they washed it all down with large quantities of a local beer, 'Bam-De-Ba,' and 'San Miguel,' a Filipino import. Eating regularly and well, they regained their strength quickly.

Receiving long-awaited mail, they excitedly tore open packages and letters. They wrote obediently to their parents and labored over love letters to their wives or girlfriends. It was obvious to Dennis that they were quickly recovering in physical strength and perspective. He enjoyed little of it, but did take some pleasure at watching his men come around. "At least they're having a good time, Eddie," he said. "I don't want any part of it, though."

"Cheer up, Charlie Six, why so glum?"

"Captain Chancey just called. Remember that kid we met at Ap Cho, Dennis Hahn? He had just come in from Germany a couple of weeks before. He didn't make it. He died on the eighteenth. Chancey was damn near bawling on the radio. Ap Cho just won't go away for me, Eddie. I think of it all the time. I'm just so sick of it all, Eddie, just sick of it."

No hostile actions ensued and they spent the days enjoying their respite from war. Acting with courtesy and compassion toward the villagers, the company soon developed a mutual friendship with them. Dennis allowed small groups to visit the village proper during the day. They returned in the evenings with exotic souvenirs of Vietnamese culture and tales of conjugal friendships that Dennis had forbidden, but was powerless to stop. Replacements arrived daily and Alpha, Bravo, and Delta Companies joined the security effort, sharing patrols and other duties.

Colonel Flint remarked sadly how inherently destructive American military power was as he surveyed the devastation and empathized with the villagers in their suffering. "Just think what an Infantry battalion could do if it used all of its abilities on constructive things, not destructive," he mentioned to Dennis at a meeting.

A few days later, he announced that the battalion would begin building a schoolhouse and would also assist villagers in planting their vegetable gardens. "Our effort will be minuscule compared to what these people need, but it might make our men feel worthwhile to help restore some concern for these unfortunate people."

Sitting in the glow of a small campfire one evening, Colonel Flint showed Dennis how to fold and shape his new Australian Bush Hat. He planted it on Dennis' head and smiled. "Looks good on you, Charlie Six. I think all infantrymen should wear one." Staring at Dennis for a moment, he suddenly became solemn.

"Lieutenant Riley, I'd like to talk with you for a minute. It's personal, about several things."

"You're the boss," Dennis said, playing with the brim of his hat.

"Dennis, I know that you, that your men -- Hell, I guess I'm saying that I know you and your boys left their hearts and souls in Ap Cho. I've been trying to find some way to bring them back to reality, back into the fold, trying to make them a part of the 22nd Infantry again. No, that's not exactly right. I just want to make them a part of life, again."

Colonel Flint paused for a few moments. Reaching into the edges of the fire, he withdrew a can of boiling coffee and set it aside to cool. "Damn, next time I'll use a glove." Blowing on his hand, he looked steadily at Dennis.

"You realize, don't you, that these community action programs are a small part of giving back to your men their sense of self-worth? It just might work. The relaxed atmosphere around here certainly helps. But you, Dennis. I just don't know. You oblige me, follow my orders, but you're distant. 'Way too distant. What the hell is eating you, Son?"

Dennis shuffled his feet for a moment, then looked at his Colonel long and hard. "OK, Sir. You asked, so I'll tell you. Up where the decision-makers sit, it probably doesn't matter much. But fifty men have died in this company since we got to Vietnam. Think of it. Fifty young men. Twelve of them died in one night, you know, up there at Burt. Fifteen of them died under my command."

"It is tragic --"

"This war is going nowhere and you know it, Sir. A whole lot more good men are going to die before it's over. My weakness is that I feel every death. They trusted me. I was supposed to get them back home again. I didn't, I couldn't."

Moisture covered Dennis' eyes and he paused to catch his breath. When he spoke again, his voice cracked with emotion. "I hear them constantly, Colonel Flint. Every night, every waking moment of the day. They call out from their graves. They ask me, 'for what?' I can't answer them, Sir. Can you?" Dennis bawled unashamedly now and Colonel Flint reached out and wrapped an arm around his shoulder. He squeezed him for just a moment.

"It's not your fault, Son. They don't blame you. You did your best. It's not your fault."

Dennis blew his nose on an old kerchief that Colonel Flint handed him. He dried his eyes, snapped to attention and said: "Sorry, sir, I was having a moment. I haven't had a chance to tell anybody. I don't think I was cut out to be a soldier. Thanks for listening. I'll be OK, now."

"It's good to cry, Dennis," Colonel Flint said. "But, it's not good to cry alone. I can only tell you that the greater your ability to grieve -- and you are grieving -- the greater your capacity will be to love. In fact, you cannot love these men, the memory of them, until you have agonized over them fully. You can come to me anytime you want to talk."

They sat silently for a while, sipping coffee from tin cups. Colonel Flint reminded him of an eight o'clock meeting he had called for in the morning. "Be there on time, Dennis. I have a lot to tell all of you."

Dennis returned to his hut and slept fully for the first time in many days. In the morning, he was the first to arrive at the command post. The other leaders quickly assembled and Colonel Flint began with an appraisal of their circumstances.

"Gentlemen, we haven't had any action to speak of and the men are getting complacent and bored. We could find ourselves right back in a fight at any time. They should realize that we're not going to stay here forever. As soon as this battalion is healed and back to strength, Division will surely throw us into a fight, if they can find one." He shuffled through some papers he held in his hand, then looked up.

"These reports from higher headquarters indicate that everything is quiet within our zone of action. We kicked their butts during Tet. We destroyed the cream of the North Vietnamese Army. The remnants, the stragglers, they're running northward, getting slaughtered on every parallel."

"Good, I got here just in time," Captain Jerry White said.

Colonel Flint laughed. "These are exciting reports. The Viet Cong virtually cease to exist. They were wiped out, men. I believe that the war is substantially over. You won. Yet I can't help mentioning that peace never came in Korea and it might never come here. See to it that your men understand this and remain 'good soldiers.'"

Colonel Flint's voice rose with excitement. "I've thought of something that will keep our men busy. Every day your companies will provide a platoon each to work on human relations projects while we continue patrolling and defending our area. I think it'll help these villagers, but it'll certainly help us, too."

"Yeah, it might help somebody," Dennis said under his breath. The meeting was dismissed soon afterward and Dennis returned to his duties. The experience of Ap Cho would never wane for him and the memory of his lost friends captivated his every waking thought. He didn't talk about it to anyone but Colonel Flint. He could not let go and he thought of them constantly, writing letters to their parents and friends.

Vanessa, the teen-aged sweetheart who had stolen Rosey from the seminary, wrote that she was carrying his child and would give birth in a few weeks. "He never knew," she wrote sadly, "that he would soon be a father. That I'll have our child."

Dennis wrote back, telling her of Rosey's dying words and assured her that: "he did indeed know that you would carry his child. He told me so in his dying breath."

Delta Company began to probe farther out from the village and had a minor skirmish with a band of well-armed Viet Cong. No injuries resulted, yet Captain White felt obliged to comment to all the officers and Colonel Flint. "They're not all dead and gone, Colonel. Those bullets were real. They're recovering and rebuilding their units just like we are. This war isn't over yet."

Colonel Flint accepted his analysis and issued strict instructions regarding security. Social visits to the village were suspended and larger and more frequent patrols foraged into the night. Other units began to encounter Viet Cong moving ammunition and supplies by sampan and the battalion quickly established river ambushes to intercept.

Delta Company, under the careful direction of Captain White, invented armed flotillas, binding two or three old fifty-five gallon fuel drums together. They were able to place a machine gunner and a rifleman into them, creating curious-looking "duck blinds." Camouflaging and hiding them among the reeds and grasses of the canals, they floated them along the banks of the rivers.

The ingenuity of such devices soon revealed their worth. Colonel Flint ordered all companies to build them. Late one afternoon, Bravo Company intercepted a squad of Viet Cong moving supplies and riflemen by sampan. Waylaying them in a surprise and violent ambush, they killed all of the occupants. Day after day, more and more boats came sailing down the river. Each of them were easily intercepted and destroyed by the Americans.

High praise befell the battalion for their cunning employment of the duck blinds. Gathering vital intelligence, they forewarned the Division of enemy movement and impending battles.

"Captain White was right, the war ain't over yet; they're up to something," Major Johanson remarked.

"For me," Dennis said depressingly, "it'll never be over." He remained downhearted and dispirited. Colonel Flint chastised him when Navy personnel complained that Dennis refused to recover and bury a Viet Cong body that had been floating in the river.

"That guy is a screwball," an angry and unbelieving Navy commander reported to Colonel Flint. "There was a body floating in the river. It kept bumping into the pilings of the bridge we're building across the main canal. My men were distracted, despondent, and finally fished the body from the river."

"Where does Riley fit in?" Colonel Flint asked.

"I didn't know your protocol, what to do with it, so I asked your Lieutenant to dispose of the body. 'Bury it please,' I said, 'you should be used to it.'"

"He jumped up and almost attacked me. He said, 'Fuck him, throw the son of a bitch over the bridge and let him float out to sea where he can rot in the open water.' He refused to help, so my engineers had to dig a grave. Your Lieutenant is a mental case, Colonel. He needs professional help."

"Yes, Commander, you're right. He has turned bitter and cynical, but he has good reason. He's been through some terrible savagery -- the worst of battles -- many times. You wouldn't know about that. He'll be transferred to a staff position in a few weeks and perhaps he can get his bearings then. I'll deal with it, and please explain his personal hardship to your men."

"Yes, Sir. In the future I'll try to treat the enemy dead with a little more respect," Dennis responded coldly when Colonel Flint admonished him for his unsympathetic behavior. He seemed disinclined to talk further and Colonel Flint left him alone for a while, assigning few missions to his company. "Don't give Lieutenant Riley any tough ones, if you can help it," he told Major Johanson. "Use him only if you must."

Chapter Forty-Two
A Prophesy of Death

Early in the morning on February 26, 1968, Dennis received what seemed to be a simple operations order. It would serve to compound his ever-growing hatred for war and the men who made it.

"Operations wants you at the command post, Lieutenant," First Sergeant Krznarovich said, shaking him awake. "You're moving out right away."

Rubbing his eyes while trying to untangle the mosquito net and find the floor he asked, "What the hell time is it, Top?"

"Three a.m. Major Johnson wants you in five minutes. You got a hot one. A Regional Force outpost near the village is being overrun. Let's go, get your skinny ass up." With a flashlight waving in his face, Dennis sensed the urgency and he bolted upright.

"You awake now? You'll be glad to hear Sergeant O'Connor is back from R&R. He came in last night, so you have a senior squad leader or a platoon sergeant if you need him. Sergeant Allred is limp with a planter's wart. You have to leave him back. Get the goddamn lead out, Lieutenant. Move." He left the hut as quickly as he had come.

"Yeah, yeah, yeah," Dennis shouted after him. *Top will be busy now, getting the company ready for action. Three o'clock in the morning. What the hell is this? Did he say Jay Cee is back? Good, I can't wait to see him.*

Sleeping in his clothes, boots included, he didn't need much preparation. Outside the hut he splashed stale water on his face from a wooden wash bucket, shaking himself awake. Racing toward the Battalion command post he again felt a moment of elation at the First Sergeant's words, "O'Connor is back."

In spite of Dennis' promise to transfer Jay Cee to a chaplain's assistant job, he had neglected to do much of anything about it. Jay Cee was second in rank now to Staff Sergeant Beebe. Sergeant Allred had been grooming him to take command of a platoon.

Dennis couldn't wait to tell him that he was now a permanent Platoon Sergeant, up for a field promotion. "I wonder what he'll say," he asked Eddie as they met, entering the headquarters tent. "Will he still want the chaplain's assistant job or will he jump on the chance to become a platoon sergeant?"

"He'd be nuts to accept," Eddie said, "so don't even ask him. They'll call him an idiot if he stays here."

"I don't see it that way, Eddie. Jay Cee's been on the line for almost six months and seen his share of battle, especially at Ap Cho. He's been awarded the Silver Star for his gallantry, but doesn't know it yet. He's a damn good choice for Platoon Sergeant. Don't you agree?"

"Damned idiot, I said."

In deference to Eddie's reluctance to agree with him, Dennis thought carefully about the matter. The men naturally rallied around young Sergeant O'Connor. His two-week rest and relaxation furlough had left a void in the company that they all had felt. Unsure of themselves without him, they anxiously awaited his return. *He's back. Good,* Dennis thought. *He'll give us that shot in the arm that we need, especially after he hears about his promotion and his Silver Star.*

Major Johanson, standing beneath a flickering lantern, was pointedly quick with his instructions. "The enemy, possibly one-hundred-and-fifty men, has been attacking a regional force outpost near the edge of the Catholic village all night. The defenders have put up a terrific struggle, but they're outnumbered and out-gunned."

"Lieutenant Riley," he said, pointing at Dennis, "your mission is to foot march directly into the besieged compound and destroy the Viet Cong. Colonel Flint is at Dau Tieng on business. He directed by radio that Charlie Company take this mission. All other units have platoon ambush patrols out and they're split up. We can't gather them fast enough in the dark."

Dennis had never seen the Major so serious. He shuddered as Johanson pointed to a red dot on his tactical map.

"The Cong may already have this compound," he said. "The rest of the battalion will move out behind you at first light, Riley. You're at full strength now, so get them together and be out of here in fifteen minutes. That's all. Now get." He stood and waddled his hulk from the dimly-lit tent.

Running in the dark back to his hut, Dennis could hear Sergeant Allred and Jay Cee assembling the company, giving them a final equipment check. Calling for Jay Cee to join him in his hut, he wanted to greet him and then give him the plan for movement.

The compound under siege was about a mile northwest of the perimeter of Nhi Binh. They had passed it many times in daylight as they entered and exited the village on routine patrol missions. Dennis had the location and the route well fixed in his mind and was certain they could find it in the dark.

Jay Cee entered the hut cautiously and Dennis began by vigorously shaking his hand, then spontaneously patting him on the shoulder. "I'm glad you're back, Jay Cee. Man, I missed you, we all missed you." They stood facing each other and, in the dim light, Dennis noticed something in his friend's eyes. He asked pointedly, "What's the matter, Jay Cee, aren't you glad to be back?"

Without waiting for an answer, Dennis gave him instructions for movement, explaining his approach to the objective. "We'll move in three separate platoons. Attach machine guns to the first and third squads. It's easier to move at night as small units, don't you think?"

Jay Cee, shuffling a foot across the plywood floor, said nothing.

Dennis continued: "I want one machine gun up front with me. You'll take the Second Platoon and bring up the rear. Sergeant Allred's staying behind. He has a bad foot."

Dennis looked at his friend and smiled. "You and me and Eddie, up front again, just like old times. We'll head straight down that dirt road leading to the compound. Let's get outside and tell the others," he said, pulling Jay Cee along by the arm.

"Men, you know the drill," Dennis said to the assembled company. "We've been lying on our butts for a while, so pay attention. The ARVN compound at the edge of Nhi Binh is under attack. We're going to go save it." Dennis elaborated for a few moments on his plan, then hurried back to his hut to gather his own equipment.

Jay Cee followed, entering the shack behind Dennis, watching quietly as he fumbled for canteens, extra ammo, and grenades. Securing them to his webbed belt, Dennis searched his frequency handbook for the Regional Force radio net. "I don't want them to shoot us as we come storming to their rescue," he said.

Jay Cee recoiled as Dennis reached out to touch him once again, then stuttered. "Can I talk with you a minute?"

"Sure. What's up, Jay Cee?"

"I was just wondering, Sir, if I couldn't stay back on this one? You know I just got back from R&R last night and I haven't quite got my stuff together yet. I've got to get my feet back on the ground. I'll come out with the other companies later in the morning."

A certain pleading in his voice alarmed Dennis. He had never heard it before from any man, but it was unmistakable begging. Knowing Jay Cee's reputation for courage, however, he shrugged and let it pass.

"I've got to have you, Jay Cee," Dennis said. He shifted his eyes from Jay Cee's, and adjusted his heavy web belt to his waist. "Besides, Jay Cee, Sergeant Beebe is too overloaded with responsibility. Hell, he's the only field NCO we have besides you and Allred. I thought I told you, Sergeant Allred has a bum foot."

"I don't want to go, Sir."

"We need you, Jay Cee. I need you," Dennis said, playfully waving his arms in an attempt to end the discussion. "You'll have to tell me all about your trip as soon as we get some time. How's your family? Anybody tell you that your Silver Star has been approved? General Philson and Colonel Flint want to present it to you this afternoon, right out here in the boonies." The lantern burning above their heads cast an eerie shadow across Jay Cee's face and Dennis saw no joy in it. His chiseled jaw grew more prominent in the pulsating yellow glow and his steely eyes bore in on Dennis as he spoke.

"Jesus Christ, Lieutenant, have I ever asked to stay back on a mission before?" His voice quivering in exasperation, Jay Cee groused openly: "I've been everywhere and done everything for this company, for you. I've always been the 'good soldier.' I just have to have a little more time."

"What's so important, Jay Cee?"

"Please, Sir. I've got to get a letter off to my dad and mother and get some other stuff straight."

Dennis was shocked at his attitude and the intensity of his pleading. *He sounds like a wounded child. I can't believe it. Jay Cee O'Connor, my friend, the last of our gang, the best soldier among them. Now he's begging for special consideration. I've never doubted his courage or his loyalty. There's some other reason he doesn't want to go.*

Although time was growing short, Dennis sighed and invited Jay Cee to sit on the edge of his cot. Dennis remained standing, looking into his eyes to see if he could find any explanation for Jay Cee's reluctance.

"What's really bothering you, Jay Cee?" he asked. "This is a simple mission. The Viet Cong will probably be gone by the time we get there. All we have to do is be careful and not get ourselves ambushed along the way. I plan to leave you and the Second Platoon outside the compound anyway as a blocking force. We'll be back here drinking cold beer this afternoon."

Dennis reached out and placed a hand on his friend's shoulder: "Besides, Sarge, these men look up to you. They'll be disappointed as hell without you and Allred. Scared. After this one, I promise, I'll get you sent up to Father Tobin. He's agreed to accept you as his assistant. Says on the first of March you can join him. Come on, what do you say?"

"Yeah, yeah, I know, Lieutenant. I heard it from the others and I appreciate your trying to help me," Jay Cee said, dropping his head. "It's just that I've found something while I was away." He looked up and Dennis noticed that his tanned face had turned ashen white.

Jay Cee spoke now as if he were a little boy begging permission from a stern parent. "Please, Sir, you don't understand; I fell in love in Hawaii. She's a gorgeous girl. I promised her I'd come back as soon as I could. She's waiting for me. I've got to get off the line, Sir. If you could just see her. She's beautiful. I can't get her out of my mind."

Jay Cee became testy now. He stood and faced Dennis.

"Besides that, I made a deal with my dad. When I get back to the States, I'm going to law school and my dad said he'd help me. Don't you see Charlie Six? Everything is different now. I almost didn't come back. I thought about going AWOL, but I had to talk to you first."

Jay Cee knelt on the wooden floor, the plywood sagging and creaking beneath his weight. He grabbed Dennis' pant leg in his right hand and pulled against it, tugging and pleading. "Just this one time, Dennis, I'm begging you, please don't make me go. Please, please," he cried, and tiny tears dropped intermittently down his cheeks.

Dennis ached, looking down at him and at his tears. He watched, speechless, as one glistening drop fell slowly, cutting a channel across his friend's face to his lower lip. Jay Cee dragged a sleeve across his eyes to conceal the wetness and sniffled as he wiped moisture from his nose.

Dennis quickly weighed the consequences of leaving his friend out of combat for one more day: *He needs to be with us. He just lost his nerve during that R&R. He's got to get his feet back on the ground. It'll do him more good to come with us than it would if he stayed back here alone.* Swallowing hard, Dennis wet his lips, then spoke sharply: "Get up, Jay Cee. You're going with us. It's best. Now move out."

"Please, Sir, please let me stay back. I'll come out in a couple of hours, I promise. I just need a couple of hours." He gathered the loose cloth of Dennis' pant leg in his fist and tugged, waiting for an answer.

Jerking his leg from Jay Cee's grasp, they both stumbled from the hut: "Get your act together, Sergeant, and get in front of your platoon," Dennis said. "We're moving out and you're going with us. If you're not in position in three minutes, I'll have your ass 'busted.' You'll lose your stripes."

Jay Cee sighed heavily and, without looking again at his Lieutenant, surrendered to his demands, quietly taking his place in the column.

Dennis pondered Jay Cee's strange display of emotion. *I hate myself for what I've done -- been forced to do. Ah, hell, it's best for Jay Cee. He'll come around later in the day. I can't wait to pin that Silver Star onto his chest.*

Dennis could feel dry spittle forming around the corners of his mouth and he washed it with warm water from his canteen as he merged with the waiting company. The confrontation with Jay Cee had unnerved him. "Move out, damn it," Dennis snapped unnecessarily. The company automatically began to advance forward as soon as they saw their leader.

Trading speed for caution, they raced along the sides of the road. Dennis was aware that his mood had soured. He felt that he was right to hold his ground against Jay Cee's unreasonable begging. *I don't enjoy playing the hard-line commander or issuing threats. He'll get rid of the shakes as soon as he gets back with his platoon.*

The thought of their disagreement continued to nag Dennis as they speed-marched down the road. *There's that odd look in Jay Cee's eyes; I've seen it in other men. Does he think he's going to get killed? Is that the real reason he's afraid of this mission?* "Naw," he said out loud while Eddie looked at him in amazement.

"What's got into you, Charlie Six?"

"My man, Jay Cee. He's come back different. Guess he fell in love in Hawaii."

"Yeah, everybody does," Eddie said.

Jay Cee's professed love for family and a new girlfriend was obvious, understandable, but his unwillingness to lead his platoon, Dennis could not accept. His reasons, Dennis felt, were 'way out of proportion to the scene he'd just put on. "I think he's lost his nerve, Eddie."

"Too bad; that could get a good man killed."

Chapter Forty-Three
Outpost X-Ray

Staff Sergeant Jay Cee O'Connor died from a bullet wound through the heart at about noon today, February 26, 1968, Dennis wrote in his journal. It was a neat, clean little wound, and he died like the man he was.

"Jay Cee didn't know when or how," Dennis told First Sergeant Krznarovich, "but he guessed it pretty close. He knew, I knew, but it was too late to help him."

"Some men know they're going to die," Top chewed at Dennis. "You ain't God and you couldn't have stopped it even if you tried. They fight it for a while, then realize they're powerless to stop it. They finally accept. Letting him stay back wouldn't have helped. Don't beat yourself up about it; he'd have cashed in anyway. Be glad that you got to know him at all."

Slamming the journal down on a makeshift desk, Dennis got out clean writing paper and an ink pen. Struggling for words, he wrote the tragic news to Jay Cee's parents. *Looking at Jay Cee earlier, listening to his pleas, I thought I was helping my friend recover his manhood. I didn't know I was looking into the eyes of a man about to die -- who knew it, felt it, and didn't understand why his time on earth was so limited.*

Late that night, through his tears and aching heart, Dennis drafted the last of several letters to Jay Cee's parents.

HEADQUARTERS
Co C, 3 Battalion, 22nd Infantry
APO San Francisco, 96249
26 February 1968

Mr. And Mrs. William O'Connor and Family
Route 7, Box 276-A
Dearborn Heights, Michigan 48127

Dear Mr. and Mrs. O'Connor and Family,
    By now you have received the shocking news that your son, Sergeant Jay Cee O'Connor, was killed in action today. I wish to express

my profound sympathy and assure you that the prayers of the entire company are with you tonight.

My first letter to you, which you should have received by now, was admittedly a superficial accounting of the circumstances that caused Jay Cee's death. As his Commander, I am required to write such a letter, knowing full well that a survivor's assistance team has already contacted you. I wish to reconstruct the events of this terrible day while they are fresh in my mind, in the hope that knowing the episode completely will somehow help diminish your pain.

Follow-up letters such as I am writing are prohibited by regulations. I guess the Army thinks that we junior grade officers are not competent in our writing skills, or perhaps they fear we'll be too graphic in our descriptions. Regardless, in respect for the memory of Jay Cee O'Connor, I am compelled to violate such restrictions. I trust that you will keep this information in confidence.

Early on the morning of February 26, our Company, of which Jay Cee was a senior and principal leader, was dispatched hastily to rescue a Republic of Viet Nam outpost. It was named "Compound X-ray." An American Captain, advisor to the Vietnamese soldiers there, had been seriously wounded and he reported by radio that his position was being overrun by Viet Cong Communists.

Although we had little time for preparation in the dark, Jay Cee assumed his duties as Platoon Sergeant in a masterful manner. Organizing men for movement -- for combat -- in total darkness is a formidable task. Your son handled it exceptionally well. He was everywhere, up and down the line, checking canteens, ammunition, and the condition of the men as well.

He offered words of reassurance to all and they took comfort in the fact that such a gallant and courageous leader would guide them on this hazardous mission. They were unafraid because of him. As always, he led by example.

I knew that Jay Cee had just returned from a quick visit with you in Hawaii. We spoke briefly about his trip just as we were preparing to move out. During that conversation, he confided to me his most intimate thoughts about you and his brother and sister. He not only loved you, he had a consuming passion for you all. His family was his life and he didn't care who knew it.

During that conversation, I sensed that Jay Cee's visit in Hawaii caused a rebirth in his affections for you; he had come to terms with his position as the "good son." He confided that he intended to leave the Army after Vietnam, building a new life for himself and Lannie, his lovely new girlfriend. He wanted your respect and he wanted "to be a family again," he said.

Although these thoughts were heavy on his mind, he did not cringe when the alert sounded. He shouldered his responsibilities as the senior enlisted man in his platoon with boundless enthusiasm and professionalism. He loved his men and he would not let them down.

We departed our bivouac at about 3:45 a.m. in total darkness. Jay Cee and his platoon brought up the rear, acting as a security force. Actually, he moved up and down our column as we raced toward the besieged compound, offering advice, encouragement, and giving confidence to the twenty-nine men under his command. They were fearless under his direction.

Within minutes, we were in sight of the objective. The sky was brilliantly illuminated with artillery flares bursting over the stormed compound and we had no trouble finding it. The American advisor inside responded quietly and calmly to my radio inquiry as to his situation. He reported that his position had been completely overrun and that most of the defenders had been either killed or captured. He had taken refuge in a ditch against the western wall, himself wounded, where he lay silently watching the enemy strip the dead of their weapons, ammunition, and valuables. I optimistically promised that we'd get him out.

Halting the advance, I called for a quick conference with our leaders. I decided to divide the company into three attacking elements. We were approaching the target from the west. The American lay not more than one hundred meters directly in front of us. I would take the lead platoon and attempt to scale the low wall. Another platoon would quietly slip around to the opposite side of the compound, the eastern approach, where the main gate stood. Jay Cee chose to lead that effort in spite of the fact that he was to have been only a backup. A third platoon would create a diversion on the south side, firing as they advanced.

I had hoped that our superior firepower would cause the Viet Cong to flee toward the gate where they would encounter Jay Cee and his men. The diversionary platoon was charged with doing just that, scaring them into evacuating the complex. I planned on rescuing the American Captain while attacking the retreating enemy from the rear.

In minutes, everyone was in place. While issuing radio instructions to begin the attack, I heard your son's steady voice acknowledge my order from his position with the ambush platoon. Hearing him, I was automatically filled with hope.

As the diversionary attack began, they immediately ran into trouble. A Viet Cong security force was lying in wait for them. They were only a few, but they managed to stall the advance and entangle that platoon in a standoff. We instantly found ourselves at the edge of success or failure. The enemy within the compound were now alerted and had time to plan and react aggressively. I had already begun my own march and there was no turning back. I expected to meet the enemy head-on as a consequence of the failed diversion.

Suddenly, there erupted a horrendous firing from the vicinity of the main entrance. Sergeant Jay Cee O'Connor, your brave son, sensing the collapse of the effort, seized the initiative and mounted an attack directly into the compound. Survivors tell me that he led his men at a run straight through the gate into the confused and disorganized enemy. Fighting immediately fell to close quarters.

In the chaos, I could only guess at what lay in wait as I and my men scaled the walls. I had no clue as to where the American lay hidden; I hoped he would call out or somehow signal to us.

The battleground became a mass of confusion. Grenades exploded everywhere, sweeping men off their feet and pitching them through the air like playthings; machine gun and rifle fire rattled around us and the defiant screams of men engaged in hand-to-hand combat curdled the very air we breathed. I was momentarily blinded by an explosion and fell to clear my head and rub my eyes. Through foggy vision, I looked up to see Jay Cee standing over me. With pistol in hand he fired randomly at darting figures. Behind us cowered the wounded American Captain.

He continued firing as he knelt to assist me. I was dizzy from the blast and lay there, defenseless. I am convinced that Jay Cee's intent was to give his life for mine. Helping me up, we stumbled upon the American Captain and the three of us began a hasty withdrawal. Jay Cee pushed me over the wall while he tugged at the wounded Captain with his free hand.

We huddled about twenty meters to the rear of the action while Jay Cee attended to the Captain's wounds. My vision cleared and I quickly realized that the battle was over. My radio operator found us and, through sporadic communications, I learned that we were in control of the compound. We had taken some casualties, but had succeeded in routing what remained of the enemy. I can attest that their losses were greater than ours.

Your son, Sergeant Jay Cee O'Connor, led the way and saved this day. He rescued me and that American Captain from certain death.

Unfazed, he continued to function as the overall leader during my temporary incapacitation.

At daybreak, we began a consolidation of our forces. The remainder of the battalion arrived and our commander ordered us to return to our bivouac. They would secure the battle area. I asked Jay Cee to lead the way. Following him, I realized that I'd never seen a man walk so tall as Jay Cee O'Connor did that morning. We were within a half-mile of our bivouac when a retreating remnant of the enemy force ambushed us. Our answering fire scattered them quickly. I raced forward to find that Jay Cee had been hit with the first bullets from their automatic weapons fire. I was with him in the final seconds of his life.

These are his exact words: "Are you OK, Sir? How's that Captain doing? Tell everybody not to worry about me now. Tell them I'll be OK."

With that, he smiled and life passed from his body and his soul was commended into the hands of the Lord. I am convinced that he did not suffer. He showed no anger or agony. He was at peace when his spirit left him. I cradled his head in my arms for the longest time, with the company gathered around, until it was no longer appropriate.

A field ambulance arrived to carry his body the rest of the way, but the men would have none of it. They took turns carrying him those last few hundred yards, they loved him so.

Tomorrow morning, Father Tobin, our Brigade Chaplain, will conduct a memorial service to the men who died at compound X-ray. Jay Cee will be foremost in our hearts and in our minds. I've asked the men to write to you; those who knew him best surely will. Others have started a scholarship fund for his brother and sister, but I fear the effort might falter because of heavy demand. Don't be saddened if we fail.

Finally, Mr. and Mrs. O'Connor, please do as Jay Cee asked: don't worry -- he is at peace. He rests snuggled, warm, and safe in the bosom of his Lord, I am sure. He was more at peace with himself at the moment of his death than any of us have a right to expect. I knew his frustrations, his agony over what he should do with his life. I understood his desire to be with you, to marry Lannie, and to work for a better life for everyone. He surrendered all of that to save the life of that American Captain and me. He died as he lived, serving his country and his fellow man.

Sergeant Jay Cee O'Connor has been recommended for the
Medal of Honor, our nation's highest compliment to a soldier, for his
heroism at compound X-ray. He well deserves it.

May he rest in peace and may the love of Jesus Christ be with
you always.

Dennis J. Riley

Dennis put down his pen and thought of Jay Cee's parents, his
brother and sister, how saddened they would be. *I wonder if his high
school pals will give him a good Irish wake and a proper Catholic funeral?
He's back with the gang: Wally, Rosey, Andy, and Jackie. He was the last of
that wonderfully innocent troupe of boy soldiers that wandered the foggy
roads of Washington state. Surely we were brought together by some strange
element of fate, for some purpose. I wonder what?*

Calling up the faces of each man, Dennis categorized what he knew
about them: Rosey, the timid hero who loved life and God so much he
could hide from neither. Vanessa, his teenage sweetheart, now carrying
his unborn child. *I hope her baby will be just like him. Yeah, it's got to be.*

*Rosey, Jackie, Andy, and Wally and all the others who have lain still
and stiff in those death tents, feeding parts of their bodies to a sewer. How
many more will lie there before this nightmare ends?*

He searched his soul for a prayer that would release his bond with
them, but it would not come. *Who were they? Why do they affect me so?
Why did they have to die?*

Laying his head in his arms, Dennis envisioned each of his friends
and each experience he'd had with them, each conversation, each laugh,
every cup of coffee, and every shared piece of bread. He wept, and when
he could no longer produce tears, he waited for something, someone, to
erase the agony in his bones.

In his semi-sleep, the answers suddenly came, as if their spirits
sensed his struggle and they were there, shepherding him. They were
good Americans, living their lives to the extreme. *They're free now from
society's demands, yet not so free. Vietnam took all that.*

Dennis raised his head and took a long pull from a bottle of sour
whiskey. He was calmed by the effect and he continued his meditations.

*There was such abundant life in all of them. Rosey knew what having a
soul meant. Wally knew what hearty living was, what fun was, what war
and death and hate were. Jay Cee had more courage than any man has a*

right to have. They all knew what love and laughter and friendship was, and they spent it freely, sharing it with me.

They knew what was sacred about life and what was wonderful about life -- it came so naturally to them all. They knew what to hate, who to love. None of them ever cried for having been born, for having been sent to Vietnam. They understood that men are brothers, that they could love one another. They had no vices.

Who were they? Ah, they were just sacrificial lambs, unwitting guides, teaching through their own courage a reverence for life, a revulsion for war. They were only five, but they led the way for a generation of lambs who are now dying by the thousands. For what?

Shivering, Dennis felt their ghostly presence and rose slowly from the desk. *Peace: where is it?*

Throwing his shoulders back, he grabbed his rifle and walked outside into the night. He could not live in a world without them. They were his essence and, when they left this world, his soul left with them. Chambering a round, he prayed a simple contrition and uttered softly, "I'm sorry, Mom." Without hesitation, he placed the rifle into his mouth, held it with his left hand and pushed hard against the trigger with his right thumb.

Chapter Forty-Four
Too Much to Bear

The rifle clicked harmlessly, the round having never been chambered by Dennis' fumbling in the dark. He cursed, pushed the bolt back and tried to load another bullet, but the first had not ejected, causing a malfunction that rendered the rifle useless. "Damn this piece of crap they call a rifle," Dennis said. Slumping down to his knees, he began to cry uncontrollably. Eventually depleted of all tears, he laughed at the foolishness of his act. It was not the rifle, he surmised. It was not God -- it was his gang: Jackie, Rosey, Jay Cee, Andy, Wally, and all of the dead men of Charlie Company. Acting from their nearby spirit world, they had taken control of his fate. He surrendered to them then, deciding that he should live or try to live. "I hear you," he shouted loud into the night, "I hear you guys. Rosey ... Wally." He called each name and they came echoing back from the jungle wall. Sucking in the night air, he fell silent, listening to them again.

Back inside his quarters, he sat drinking the rest of his cheap, foreign whiskey. Gradually, he penetrated the contradictions of his puzzle. He could not face his future without them, but they would not let him die and go to them. *I must have work to do,* he concluded. *They want me to live for some reason. I wish I knew what it was.*

Feeling refreshed and strengthened by these spiritual discoveries, Dennis went, unarmed, down the muddy road leading to the Catholic village.

In the shadowy candlelight of a small church sanctuary, he reached into his baggy pants pocket and pulled out Rosey's treasured notebook. Reading all of his simple and gentle prose, he offered it as a prayer. In Rosey's crisp and unhurried penmanship, he discovered many of the secrets for living.

"In whatever arena of life one may meet the challenge of courage, whatever may be the sacrifices he faces, if he follows his conscience -- the loss of his friends, his fortune, his contentment, even the esteem of his fellow men -- each man must decide for himself the course he will follow.

Without belittling the courage with which men have died, we should not forget those acts of courage with which men have lived." (John F. Kennedy). *It was just like Rosey, always humble, honest, to give credit where it was due.*

Dawn crept quietly through the stained glass of the little Vietnamese chapel. Dennis rose from his pew to go. Having spent the night in conversation with his friends, he was stronger now. The demons that possessed him earlier were gone and he sensed a relief that only the truly redeemed know. Throwing his shoulders back, he stepped from the church into a bright, sunny day and walked briskly back to Charlie Company.

"Where the hell you been all night, Charlie Six?" Eddie asked. "Colonel's called for an eight o'clock meeting. Something's up."

"Been to church. What's the poop?"

"I'm not sure, Charlie Six, but the radio's been humming all night. I think we can kiss Nhi Binh good-bye. We're moving out. We got choppers inbound around noon."

"Good riddance; I'll be glad to leave this --"

"By the way, here's your rifle. I found it lying on the ground. Shells all around. I cleaned it up for you. Want to tell me about it?"

Dennis folded his arms and stared at Eddie. Finally he whispered, "No, Eddie, not now, not ever. It's passed. Just let me be."

Dennis and Eddie, passing the time until the commander's meeting, built a small cooking fire. After punching holes to release the pressure of heat in several cans of C-rations, Eddie placed them along the edge of the flames.

"What are you cooking, Eddie? Smells good."

"Ham and mammy jammers."

Dennis laughed at Eddie's mocking reference to the meal of ham and lima beans. It was a common one and he had heard it before. Somehow it seemed the cliche epitomized all that was wrong this moment in his life -- everything that was wrong with the war in Vietnam

"You just said it all, Eddie. Ham and mammy jammers. Yeah."

"Good to see you laugh again, Charlie Six. It's all going to work out, you'll see. Let's eat up, almost time for the Colonel's meeting."

"You look fit, Charlie Six," Colonel Flint said, smiling his welcome to Dennis and the other officers at the circle of commanders. "That's good because we have a busy day today. Everybody take a seat, on a log or a case of ammo or something. Get comfortable; I've much to tell you."

Colonel Flint opened his notebook, thumbed through several pages, then looked across his commanders' faces, analyzing their circumstances.

"I'd say I'm looking at four of the best field commanders in Vietnam, men. I want you all to know how much I appreciate your service. Now, I must ask you for one more big performance before some of you leave your commands. Soon, a few of you will be transferred -- some of you will be going home. I'm sure you're looking forward to that."

The leaders sat up straight, listening carefully to the upbeat remarks of their Colonel. "Who gets out of this hell hole first?" Lieutenant Prairie asked.

"Not so fast." The Colonel laughed and waved a hand. "Captain Chancey, Lieutenants Riley and Prairie -- you'll be getting staff assignments before too long. Captain White will stay on for a while as the CO of Delta. He's managed to really get a handle on that company. It couldn't be in better shape. The battalion is nearly full strength. Division headquarters knows it and they're sending us out again to do what the third Battalion always does best."

"What's that?" Captain White asked.

"Kill people and break things," Lieutenant Prairie answered. "I thought we'd already whipped the VC. What's left to break?"

Spontaneous laughter erupted from the gaggle of men. Colonel Flint sipped from a canteen cup of hot coffee as he calmly surveyed their boisterous behavior. Waving his cup in a call for quiet, he continued: "You're right, Dick. As crude as it may sound, that's what we're expected to do. Intelligence tells us that the Viet Cong and North Vietnamese have merged their depleted ranks. They're infiltrating northwest, toward sanctuaries prohibited to U.S. forces: Cambodia and Laos. If they're allowed to muster there through the coming spring, they'll be back in force this fall and winter. We may be able to end this thing if we can intercept and destroy them. We've got him down. Now let's make him cry, 'Uncle.'"

"Go for it, Colonel!" Lieutenant Prairie shouted, jumping to his feet. "Kick some ass."

"Delta Company is ready," Captain White added. "What's the mission?"

Dennis shook his head at the swagger of his comrades, but said nothing. *They don't feel the same way about the men or about war. I don't think I can do another mission. I've got to tell him, but I don't have the guts. Maybe after this one, maybe tomorrow.*

"Settle down, men. We move out by helicopter at noon today," Colonel Flint said. "Let me give you some background. Listening to the Division operations orders this morning, I was reminded of General Sherman's march across Georgia during the Civil War." Standing, Colonel Flint crossed his arms and stared at them for a moment.

"Nothing will be left standing: no one left alive. Not an animal nor a grain of rice will remain in his sanctuaries. We've got him down now and we're going to end this war. There's even talk of foraging across the border into Cambodia."

"That'll never happen," Captain Chancey said.

Colonel Flint nodded his head in agreement. "Yes, we're not going there. We've got another mission. Division G-2 reports some enemy activity about thirteen miles north of Dau Tieng. They aren't sure what it is. We'll be airlifted into that remote jungle area today to take a look."

The Colonel sipped his coffee and invited the men to do likewise. The meeting took on an air of blasé and Dennis became unsettled. "May I say something, Colonel?"

"Sure, Lieutenant Riley. What's on your mind?"

"Just a word of caution, Sir. Our men are rusty -- they haven't dug a foxhole in weeks. More than half the battalion consists of new arrivals and they have yet to face the enemy in a hard fight. Maybe you all don't see any immediate action, but --"

Major Johanson interrupted. "Let me give them their orders, Sir, before Riley spins us a war story."

"Go ahead, Major. Sorry Charlie Six, but we get the picture."

"Captain Chancey, Alpha Company stays back on this one," Major Johanson began. "Bravo, Charlie, and Delta Companies will 'Airmobile' into a position about seventeen kilometers northwest of the Michelin. It's a large clearing surrounded by jungle. Charlie Company goes in first. The Battalion Reconnaissance Platoon is already out there. They report no enemy activity, and say it's a dry hole. They'll protect Charlie Company's landing so we'll forgo the usual artillery and gunship preparations."

"Speaking of the recon platoon," Colonel Flint said. "As much as I hate to do this to you, Charlie Six, I'm taking Lieutenant Balser from you, assigning him as the platoon leader of the reconnaissance platoon. I spoke with him earlier and he's eager to take the job. He wants to take your Sergeant Asher with him. What do you think, Dennis?"

"You hit me where it hurts, Colonel. You want both of them? Do you have to take both of them? Are you sure you want to take Mike to recon? He'll give you gas pains once in a while, maybe even a heart attack. No, I don't want to see him go, but I don't want to hold him back, either. Jim Asher is good anywhere; he'll make a great recon platoon sergeant."

"Then it's done. You still have Lieutenant Adkins. The rest here in Nhi Binh has been good for him. His wounds are healed and Doctor Mersack says he is fit for duty."

"Yes, Sir," Dennis answered. "That leaves me with only one other officer, besides myself."

"Oh, I've thought of that, Charlie Six," the Colonel said. "We do have a new Lieutenant, a replacement for Lieutenant Balser. He just arrived this morning. He's right out of OCS. He's Second Lieutenant Francis Williams. I'm assigning him to you. Make a soldier out of him, Dennis."

Major Johanson waited patiently for the leaders to finish their discussion. Finally, he cleared his throat. They fell silent at the obvious demand for attention and listened.

"Now, to continue our operation order," Major Johanson said, "tonight we'll dig in and establish a defense." He squatted, smoothed the earth, then drew an arc with his pencil. "Shape it like a semicircle, facing west. Bravo Company takes the center. Charlie goes in on the right flank and Delta occupies the left, facing west and south. The recon platoon and the Battalion Headquarters sections will hold the rear."

"Have you checked it out, yet?" Captain White asked.

"It looks very quiet from the air. I flew over the site just a few hours ago. There is a narrow trail, you might call it a road, running north to south, right in the middle of the clearing. We'll land on that. It looks like it hasn't been traveled in years. I didn't see any animal movement, no smoke from cooking fires, no people. It is isolated and I don't expect any trouble going in. Any questions?"

"Yes, Sir. What's for supper?" Lieutenant Prairie quipped. "I'm on strike against C-rations."

The assembly of men laughed at Lieutenant Prairie's outlandish question. They had all been eating well in Nhi Binh, dining on the abundance of fresh fruits and vegetables from the gardens of that village. Each day a hot meal had been delivered by helicopter or truck and many of the men enjoyed Vietnamese food, purchased from children loitering along their perimeters. Dennis had been eating wild bananas and pineapples along with nuts and berries to temper his hunger. He could no longer eat the starchy and heavily salted tins of C-rations.

"Actually, your question isn't so facetious, Lieutenant Prairie," Colonel Flint remarked. "Today is the 11th of April. Tomorrow is Good Friday. Considering that we'll be up there over the Easter weekend, I've asked for some special comforts for the battalion. A hot meal will be flown in each afternoon. That might replace the need to consume too many of those ham and whatever you guys call those lima beans. Chaplain Tobin has promised to join us and provide an Easter Sunday service. I'm having some cold beverages brought in, too."

"Maybe we can have an Easter egg hunt," joked Captain White. "Charlie Six here can play the rabbit."

Good humor abounded. Eventually, the leaders dispersed to inform their men and to make preparations for the movement.

"It's a piece of cake," Lieutenant Balser said while Dennis explained the mission to his assembled leaders. "Too bad. Thought I'd show our FNG, Lieutenant Williams, how to skin a VC."

"Get real, Mike," Dennis replied. "You know we'll only be a few miles north of the Michelin. When you're anywhere near that plantation, you'd better take it seriously."

Gesturing toward a young man about his height, Dennis grinned. "Men, meet our new man, Lieutenant Francis Williams. He's taking over for Lieutenant Balser. Mad Dog is going to recon; we're going to miss him."

Applause interrupted his explanations as each soldier knew how prestigious a position command of the reconnaissance platoon could be. The recon platoon leader often operated on his own, conducting long-range reconnaissance patrols and occupying distant outposts as the eyes and ears of the Battalion. They served at the commander's pleasure, sometimes defending the command post or breaking trail ahead of advancing columns.

"Lieutenant Williams will take the second platoon," Dennis continued. "Lieutenant Balser will orient him as best he can in the time we have remaining. Let's get behind Lieutenant Williams, and help him get his feet on the ground."

The gathered Charlie Company leaders nodded or voiced their assent, shaking hands with the departing officer and welcoming Lieutenant Williams through queries about his hometown and his marital status and his education. Finally they quieted, waiting for further orders.

"Sergeant Asher is going with Lieutenant Balser to recon," Dennis said, "but he won't go until tomorrow. For this operation, he'll work with the Fourth Platoon. Lieutenant Adkins' wounds have healed and he'll stay with his third platoon. I'm glad you're back from the dead, Rusty."

Lieutenant Adkins and the others laughed. Rusty let out a wary cry. Dennis called for silence.

"Lieutenant Donnelly will provide artillery fire if we need it. Doesn't sound like we will, so Mike, watch over that mortar platoon in your spare time, OK? Sergeant Allred, you're the field first sergeant. Is your foot healed?"

"Yes, Sir, it is, and I'm ready. May I add something to this little bullshit session?"

"Go ahead, Top."

Sergeant Allred scanned the audience of young leaders and waited a full ten seconds before he spoke. "I don't like preaching to the choir, men, but I think you need to change your attitude a bit about this operation. You're all smart soldiers now and, Lieutenant Williams, I expect he'll get initiated real soon. Don't none of you fall for this crap that there ain't no enemy up there. 'A piece a cake,' somebody said. 'Don't think we need artillery.' That was you speaking, Lieutenant Riley? I thought I'd trained you better."

Dennis crushed the empty can of soda he had been drinking. Chastised by Sergeant Allred, he looked down at his boots. "You're right, Top. Go ahead, chew my ass."

"Have you forgotten Burt? Ap Cho? We didn't think there was much of anything there at first, either. Maybe this company's been a laying on its fat ass too long and gotten lazy. Or maybe you've just gone dumb. I think you'd better light a fire under these young bucks, and get them ready. There ain't no other way."

"We hear you, Top," Dennis replied. "How do you propose we 'light that fire?'"

"Well, dad gum it, Lieutenant, you use the last page of the book. You know, the one where there ain't nothing written. That's why they put it in there. First off, tell the men to double up on ammo, grenades, claymores, trip flares, water, rations. Everything they can think of. Get real loud, act excited. That usually gets their attention. Have them clean their rifles, then inspect them. Then make them clean them again."

"That'll do it," Lieutenant Adkins agreed.

"Not quite," Sergeant Allred said. "Tell them they aren't going to eat until their foxholes are neck-deep. Oh, yeah, tell them to bring a lot of toilet paper. They'll get the message."

"Good advice, Sarge," Dennis said, patting him on the shoulder. "You heard him, men. Go back to your platoons and do like Sergeant Allred says. Get them in the mood for a fight. Meet me at the pick-up zone at 1145 hours. Put ten men to a chopper. That's it. I'll tell you more when I figure it out myself."

The group dispersed to follow their commander's instructions. Dennis felt a sense of release from his growing depression.

"It's good to have something to do again, Top," he said to Sergeant Allred. "Even if there is nothing there, we can act like soldiers once again."

"I don't usually cuss too hard around officers," Allred replied, "but goddamn it, Lieutenant, I wasn't kidding about being ready. We aren't going to act like soldiers, we are soldiers. Let's stay on our toes and keep the men that way. We might all live a little longer."

"OK, Top. Seems like everyone else thinks the war is over, or like we're going out on a picnic. I'll watch my step."

Preparations for movement took the remainder of their morning. Leaders checked each man's weapons and supplies. There remained ample time for a rehearsal of their actions after landing. It was obvious to Dennis that Charlie Company had accepted the implications of a serious battle occurring and the men zealously went about their preparatory duties.

"I'm satisfied," Sergeant Allred reported at 11:30 a.m. "We're good to go."

"You amaze me, Top. You got us ready in spite of ourselves. Thanks. I hope nothing happens, but at least we're organized. It's time to go; let's get them out to the PZ."

Like tiny black spots in the distant sky, a flight of helicopters approached Nhi Binh at low level. Coming out of the sun, Dennis squinted as he watched the specks grow larger and larger with each passing second.

"They're going to touch down right on time, Top," Dennis said. "Amazing how they do it."

"They's just kids flying them machines," Sergeant Allred observed. "I have a lot of respect for them. I don't care for flying, myself."

Dennis was always thrilled by the sight of choppers and he now held the pilots in high esteem. His earlier displeasure with the gunship performance in the Ho Bo Woods had passed. They had since flown him into and out of many dangerous spots. He often thought of the door gunner who had gone down at Ap Cho and he wondered who he was and if he'd made it. He remembered, too, Blackhawk Five Four and the doctor who had flown into the heat of battle at Fire Support Base Burt. He accepted now that these aviators would risk their lives, day or night, to help a foot soldier, or "grunts," as the pilots and crews called them. From an aviator, "grunt," was a title of respect.

"Charlie Six, this is Crusader Three. We're inbound with a flight of twelve. Beautiful day up here. You ready for some air conditioning?"

"Roger, Crusader. Come in east to west. We're in groups of ten, watch my smoke."

"Roger, Charlie Six. I see yellow. Do you copy?"

"Correct. Any instructions?"

"Tell your boys we don't like to sit on the ground too long. Let's see how fast they can load these birds. Same thing on the other end. Have them jump and run, OK?"

"You got it, Crusader. Nice day for flying, eh?"

"Yeah, nice day all around. I hear the landing zone is cold; what's your impression?"

"That's what they tell me. I believe it because I don't know any better."

"Roger that, Charlie Six. We're short final, now. Easy does it. Touchdown. OK. Load up, you smelly-ass grunts."

Chapter Forty-Five
Holy Days

The pilots turned their aircraft a hard, 180 degrees under a brilliant noonday sun; simultaneously, the aircraft nestled lightly onto the ground. From the air, Dennis could see that they were landing on the trail Major Johanson had described. In seconds, the infantrymen of Charlie Company spewed from the jump seats, sprinting into the wood line as they'd done a hundred times before. Flesh-eating ants, bees, and thousands of other species of insects attacked the soldiers. They'd been stirred by the powerful wash of the propellers and it gave stimulus and energy to their race for the woodline. In spite of the irritants, Charlie Company fell quickly to the task of establishing their defense. By four o'clock in the afternoon, all elements of the Battalion were delivered into the clearing and the last helicopter left for its home base.

"It's all been routine," Eddie commented as he handed the radio handset to Dennis. "Colonel Flint is calling for another meeting. He said not to hurry, though."

Dennis was the last to arrive at the command post and he noticed a large campfire being stoked by other officers. "Why the big fire, Dick?" he asked Lieutenant Prairie.

"Oh, no particular reason, Dennis," Lieutenant Prairie said, nonchalantly stirring the embers of the fire. Looking up at Dennis, he grinned. "Since there's nothing happening up here, I figured we'd build a bonfire tonight, give the damn VC a neon light, then they could come chase us for once. You know, we act really careless, make noise, bait the fuckers."

"Please let that fire die down," Colonel Flint said, crawling out from his foxhole. "Just because you men think it's quiet up here, doesn't mean we can violate every rule in the book. Put it out, now, I said."

Dennis and Lieutenant Prairie, reacting to Colonel Flint's agitation, quickly smothered the fire by scraping dirt on it with the soles of their boots.

"Gather around, now," Colonel Flint said, taking a seat on a five-gallon water can. "Let's make our plans and get ready for the night. Choppers will bring in extra ammunition later. They'll also bring in the evening meal, keeping it hot in the Thermos cans. Have any of your patrols or listening posts developed any signs of the enemy? Any trails? Have they discovered any camp sites or the like?"

"The only enemy out here is these blasted ants and bees. I had to evacuate one man he was stung so bad," Lieutenant Prairie reported.

"No, nothing in my area," Dennis added.

"Looks the same in Delta's sector," Captain White said, leaning comfortably on his stick cane.

"I just don't know what we're doing 'way up here," Colonel Flint mused. "I don't mind at all that there is little expectation for a fight, but I'd have rather kept the battalion in Nhi Binh over the religious holy days. I've heard reports of actions 'way to our south, but I think the Regulars have been dumped into the middle of nowhere. Nevertheless, be vigilant as always."

Colonel Flint's face beamed. "I've got a surprise for you men. As a morale booster, I've arranged that each man be issued a cold can of soda and a cold beer. That ought to lift their spirits a bit."

"What kind of beer?" Lieutenant Prairie asked. "The last time we did this, Delta Company got Budweiser and we got Carlings. 'Embalming fluid,' the men call it. You should have heard them bitchin'."

"Yeah," Dennis chimed in. "How about some Coors?"

"Oh, good Lord, Bravo Six, Charlie Six. All of you. This is a hell of a war when all we've got to do is complain about the quality of the beer. Let's be grateful for what little we have; now get on back to your companies."

The leaders stood in preparation to move, when Colonel Flint added, "By the way, Father Tobin will fly in tomorrow for Good Friday services. He's coming early. He says he's got too many units to visit. Tell your men about it, and let them attend if they wish. A final word of caution: I know we got in late, the ground is hard, the men haven't eaten -- all of that -- but, I expect an adequate defense. Dismissed."

In unison, the commanders dispersed, all of them eager to get back to their units before darkness completely surrounded them. They knew well the mysteries of the jungle and how they were amplified by darkness.

Dennis said little at the meeting. He couldn't seem to join in the joviality that often characterized these sessions. A void had settled into his psyche and he remained somber most of the time. Returning to his position, Eddie Runge greeted him with a howl.

"Damn, Six, glad you're back. The ground is like digging through iron. I've been chopping away with my entrenching tool and look at it. The tip is bent. How about some help?"

"Wow, you said it, Eddie," Dennis confirmed, testing the earth with Eddie's shovel. "It is damn solid. Mike Donnelly, Doc, Sergeant Allred, and I will all help. Is it the same everywhere? What if we moved a couple of yards?"

"Umm, maybe, but I don't think it makes no difference. The platoon leaders have been in and out looking for you. That's their biggest complaint: 'The ground is too hard.' Troops are bitchin,' but they're not too worried, and they don't think anything is coming down tonight."

Dennis' gaze froze on Eddie's face for just a moment. It seemed that all of his intuition and Vietnam battle experience coalesced at the sound of Eddie's voice. *Don't think anything is coming down tonight? Platoon leaders complaining? Troops are bitchin'? Krznarovich would kick my ass.*

"Sergeant Allred, get your divining rod and find us a soft spot," Dennis said. "We need a hole. A big one. You're always good at picking positions. Move around a little. Set up about twenty-five yards behind our front line, if it's possible. I want to be up close. Dig deep, and build overhead cover. Do it all."

"Yes, Sir," Sergeant Allred answered, peeling off his shirt.

"Eddie, call all the leaders; I want them here in five minutes."

"OK, Charlie Six."

Mike Balser was the first to arrive with his new protégée, Lieutenant Williams, in tow. The young buck, Sergeant Charlie Brown, fondling his grenade launcher, arrived soon afterward. He conversed at length with the old soldier, Sergeant First Class Alfred Beebe. Charlie, spitting tobacco juice far and wide, laughed at one of Beebe's jokes, then turned and asked, "What's up, Six?"

Mike Donnelly, penciling figures on large graph paper, wandered nonchalantly into the gathering. "Hey, Boss, what's happening?"

Dennis looked at Sergeant Allred, hesitated for a moment, and then exhaled dramatically. "You guys just don't get it, do you? Don't answer now, just be quiet and listen to me. All day long I've been hearing about how soft a mission we have: no enemy ... lots of cold beer ... church services. The ground is too hard to dig a decent foxhole, you say? Bullshit, men." Dennis paused for a moment, then wagged his finger at them.

"Let me tell you how it is and how it's going to be. You get up alongside of your men. You tell them that there will be no hot meal, no cold beer, no religious services, nothing -- not a goddamn comfort known to man until I see some foxholes. I don't care if it's ten o'clock at night when they get finished. When I walk that line, I want to see soldiers dug in up to their necks. Understand?"

"Yes, Sir," the leaders said in unison.

"I want overhead cover, booby traps, trip flares, listening devices, cleared fields of fire. Put in aiming stakes and barbed wire to our front. I want each platoon's machine guns deployed in pairs, firing across our front and I want physical contact with the other companies at the limits of our sector. Cut paths behind the lines so that we can move from position to position without getting shot by our own men in the dark. Get down on your knees and crawl forward. Chop away at the underbrush, channel the enemy into our guns. Look in front of you for depressions in the earth. Cover those dead spaces with booby traps and flares. Do everything you know how to do. I want a goddamn solid defense." Dennis grew excited delivering his orders. His leaders shuffled and looked away, rebuked by his tone of voice.

"Lieutenant Donnelly, we're going to walk the limits of our perimeter. Plot artillery defensive concentrations all across our front and to the rear. Let's have a marking round, hot steel on the ground at each concentration to verify it. Tell the artillery to plan fires within fifty meters of our lines. Lay on illumination, too."

Dennis took a long pull on his canteen, staring at his men as he did so. "You platoon leaders, get your listening posts and patrols organized. Sergeant Brown, the Fourth Platoon has the ambush tonight. You and Asher put it together. Move out right after dark. We'll have a continuous mobile defense until then. Am I clear on all of this?"

"Yes, Sir," a chorus went up.

"What then, Charlie Six?" Sergeant Brown asked. "It'll be midnight before we get finished."

"Then you can eat, take a shit, drink a warm beer, but you'll be ready for an attack. And there will be an attack. I want a 100 percent alert after midnight. Every man will be up, looking down range through his sights."

Lieutenant Francis Williams, on his first combat operation, summoned the courage to speak. "Excuse me, Lieutenant Riley, but I just have to speak out. I heard that you -- they say that ever since Ap Cho, you make your own rules. I know that the Colonel said one third alert tonight. Every other company is taking it easy and you want to work us like mules. I don't think it's fair."

"Fair -- fair? There ain't nothing fair about men dying, Lieutenant Williams," Dennis said, throwing down his web gear and rifle in an act of rage. "Dying in this goddamn jungle is even worse. Now you listen to me. You're a fucking new guy -- you have little to say about my methods. When you've walked the walk, then you can talk the talk. You do as I tell you and you might survive the night."

"Whoa, hold on Dennis," Mike Balser interrupted. He picked up Dennis' rifle and handed it to him "What the hell's going on here? Williams will do like you say. He doesn't get to ask questions until he gets his dick wet, or cuts the nuts off some dead Communist. But, tell me something, how the hell do you know we're going to come under attack?"

"More than a couple of things. The first one is called Sergeant Allred. He smells it and I'm getting a whiff of it, too. The second thing is my guts and the hair on the back of my neck. I haven't felt this way since Ap Cho. Did you guys look at that trail we landed on? It's beaten down. It's been used recently. Those choppers told everybody in Vietnam that we're here. G-2 is right -- there is enemy movement up in this area and we're just the bait."

Dennis turned away, lighting a cigarette. "There's no more discussion. Let's go get our positions made. Lieutenant Donnelly and I will walk the perimeter, check it out. Top, see if you can find Eddie some softer ground."

Dennis and Mike Donnelly began at the right limit, where the Third Platoon had laagered. Apparently word of his agitation had spread and the men were vigorously building their positions. In spite of the difficulty in digging, the depth of the holes was satisfactory and men busied themselves cutting logs and stringing barbed wire. Dennis was pleased at the activity.

"Good job, Lieutenant Williams," he said, approaching the Second Platoon sector. "I'm sorry I barked at you. I just don't want you to make the same mistakes we've all made. These soldiers expect you to lead. They want a hard-ass Platoon Leader -- they deserve one -- because they know that he'll get them home. That's all that matters, Williams. Get them home alive, if you can."

"No, Sir, Charlie Six; it's me that should apologize. I was out of line. I'm sorry; it won't happen again. What about these positions?"

"Some things are standard procedure in Charlie Company. Digging in is one of them. Get out in front of your lines and look in toward them. Ask yourself what you see. Take a machete and cut some underbrush to channel the enemy into your guns. Get your men to show you how. Do it all. Get ready."

"If you'll excuse me, Sir, I will. There's not much time left before dark. Besides, I've got to get busy digging a hole for myself."

"Dig a hole for yourself? You've got to dig a hole for yourself?" Lieutenant Williams looked at his commander with curious eyes. "Yes, Sir. I've got to have protection, too."

"Yeah, better get busy then, Lieutenant. Dig yourself a good hole."

Shaking his head, Dennis returned Lieutenant Williams' salute and walked the length of his line, speaking to each man, patting him on the arm or shoulder and encouraging him to work harder. At the left flank limit, he met Sergeant Beebe, stripped to the waist and helping a soldier carry several heavy logs. Smiling, Sergeant Beebe laughed and said, "They be a-looking mighty good, eh, Charlie Six? When do we chow down? I could eat the ass out of a mule."

Dennis agreed with Sergeant Beebe. "Yes, they are taking shape, Sarge. Good work, but we'll eat when these holes are finished."

His artillery concentrations plotted, Dennis dismissed Lieutenant Donnelly and walked the final steps of his line of defense alone. At the Bravo Company sector, he continued to walk ahead into their ranks, alarmed at the meager positions he saw there. A few men lounged beside their small holes, consuming their evening meal from paper plates. Several waved beer cans toward him in a form of friendly salute.

"Where's your CO, Lieutenant Prairie?" Dennis asked a Senior NCO.

"Right behind you, Dennis," Dick Prairie said from out of the brush. "What the heck you doing over in Bravo's sector?" He approached Dennis from behind.

Dennis turned. "Just 'checking the tie-in,' my friend. I notice your guys have eaten already. How was it? How's the beer?"

They stood toe-to-toe. "Hey, Dennis, kiss my round ass," Lieutenant Prairie said. "If you want to work your boys to death, go ahead. Bravo Company earned their hot rations and the cold beer. I don't intend to deny them."

"Dick, we've been friends since OCS. I didn't mean anything. Oh, what the hell, Charlie Company digs in before it eats, that's all."

A loud explosion burst just outside the perimeter, interrupting them. Both officers, seasoned to the sounds of battle, never flinched.

"Mike Donnelly," Dennis explained. "He's putting steel on the ground and confirming his artillery shots. Good man."

"Yeah, OK, Dennis." Dick backed away. "Sorry I was touchy with you. I've been catching hell from a couple of my sergeants about eating first, but this is the first break Bravo has had in a while. You were laying on your ass back at Nhi Binh while we were out chasing bad guys up and down the rivers."

"Yeah, I know." Dennis turned to hide his eyes, but Dick Prairie touched him on the shoulder, gaining his attention.

"Don't worry, Dennis. After they eat, they'll keep digging. They'll work all night if that's what it takes. C'mon, Dennis, let me show you where our machine guns tie in."

"That's OK, Dick. It's getting dark; I saw your guns. See you later." They shook hands and Dennis walked away, struggling through the thick vines and heavy undergrowth to find his own command position. *I hope I don't have to do any digging and that damn, snot-nosed Lieutenant Williams catches me at it. What the hell are they turning out at OCS these days?*

Stumbling out of the brush, Dennis was pleasantly surprised to see a large hole, about fifty feet behind the main line of defense. It was big enough to hold himself, Eddie Runge, Doc Shiro, Mike Donnelly, and Sergeant Allred. Everyone was gathering logs to lay across the top. The thermal cans, keeping the evening meal warm, sat in neat rows alongside cans of water and boxes of extra ammunition.

"Top, it's almost dark. The positions are coming along fine. They look real solid. Have the men come and get their rations and water. Sorry I took so long."

"They've been by, Lieutenant. After you passed each hole on your inspection, I had one man from each foxhole come in and collect the plates for himself and one or two more. The last man just left here. The listening post has been watered and fed, too. I told them to eat with one hand and dig with the other. You've got to have some balance, Lieutenant."

"That's OK, Top," Dennis said, sitting down on a mound of earth. "I knew you'd have it all under control. Actually, I'm satisfied with our positions. Bravo is still working on theirs. Lieutenant Prairie says they'll finish during the night."

"The hell you say," Sergeant Allred spat.

"This is a terrific-looking foxhole, Top," Dennis said.

"Yeah, and he worked our fannies off digging it, too. C'mon in, Charlie Six." Doc Shiro beckoned from beneath the logs

"No thanks, Doc. I think I'll string my hammock between these two trees and leave my boots on. I can just roll over into the hole if something happens." Dennis arranged his nylon hammock while he, Eddie, and Sergeant Allred evaluated the day's events.

"Charlie Company is looking good, Lieutenant," Sergeant Allred said. "If they come, we're ready. Thanks for backing me up on this one."

"No way in hell I wouldn't support you, Top. Now let me see if I can get into this contraption and try to get some sleep. Eddie, wake me if anything exciting happens. Goodnight."

Chapter Forty-Six
The Battle of Good Friday

Dennis, as was his custom, slept with one boot on and one boot off. His rifle lay across his chest, his hand around the pistol grip and his finger resting on the trigger. Although he was absorbed by the possibility of battle, he was exhausted and sleep came easily to him. Near midnight, Dennis awoke suddenly.

"What the hell was that?" he asked, jumping from his hammock.

"Sounded like a couple of shots from one of the LPs. Bravo's maybe," Eddie whispered. "Might be accidental. The listening post from Delta claims it has movement, but, after a lot of chatter, they decided it was an animal. Go back to sleep, Lieutenant."

"Nothing from our LPs, Eddie?"

"Not a thing. It's all quiet on the Western front."

Dennis put on his other boot, then climbed back into the hammock and tried to sleep. Instead, he lay awake, thinking about his past and his future. *If I ever get out of here, get back home, I'm going to join the nearest monastery and get away from people. ...find some peace. Come morning, I'm going to talk to the Colonel, and ask for that staff job.*

At 2:30 a.m., a short burst of small arms fire erupted from about two hundred yards out, directly in front of his positions. Dennis rolled from the hammock and crawled into the bunker, calling his outposts. They could not identify the firing except to say that it sounded like AK-47 rounds.

At 3:00 a.m., probing rifle fire occurred in front of Bravo's positions. Finally, it showered in upon Delta. Colonel Flint, from his shallow dugout, was quick to react.

"Bravo, Charlie, Delta -- this is Falcon Six. What's your situation?"

"Probing fire, trying to pinpoint our positions," Dennis answered.

"Got that right," Bravo Six replied. "My listening post estimates two or three men, trying to find us and draw fire."

"Can't say," Delta Six said. "I've got an ambush patrol out there and they took some fire. They've scattered. It's dark as hell. I'm trying to get them together now. I'll let you know."

"All units, this is Falcon Six. I've called for standby support. I think we've been fooled. I'll have artillery flares on the way in a couple of minutes. They've promised gunships standing by and tactical air cover as well as a lot more. I've notified Fullback Six of the probing activity. They're about five miles away. They'll stand by for us. Keep me informed."

Dennis sat still in the bunker. "What do you think, Charlie Six?" Sergeant Allred whispered.

"It's too early to jump and run, Top. If the VC are going to hit, it'll be about an hour before daylight. They'll do as much damage as they can in the dark and then run as soon as it gets light. I'd say four o'clock. Funny, how I can almost predict these things now."

"You had a good teacher."

"Yeah."

At exactly 3:55 a.m., Dennis recognized the first sounds of enemy mortars popping out of their tubes from several hundred yards out. "Oh shit, here they come," Eddie shouted.

The mortar rounds fell indiscriminately within the circle of men. Dennis stopped counting after one hundred and twenty-five rounds had exploded. He was not immediately concerned for his men as he knew they had good positions with overhead cover. Although frightening in their awesome explosive power, these mortar shells were scattered and many fell harmlessly in open areas, unoccupied by troops. Several fell behind Dennis in the vicinity of the Battalion Command post, but most had been directed toward Bravo's positions.

"The VC will be coming right behind the mortars, Charlie Six," Sergeant Allred commented.

American heavy artillery soon answered the attack, exploding forward of their positions. Lieutenant Donnelly crawled from the hole to direct it.

"Get your ass back in here, Mike," Dennis yelled above the roar.

"Can't call it from down there," he said. "I've got to see the splash and hear the boom. I'll see you."

"Shit. He's walking right toward it. Ground attack coming," Eddie yelled.

"Charlie Six, Bravo Six, Delta Six, this is Falcon Six. What's happening? Give me a situation report. Over."

"This is Delta Six. My ambush is catching hell out there. The enemy are all around them. They're in close contact, and holding their own, but they're stuck between our artillery and the VC. I've told my platoon leader to hold his positions; he can't get back in. He says, 'Beau Coups VC coming our way.' We're taking fire all across my front, but we're shooting back. We're all right for the moment."

"Bravo Six, here. I've got no time for bullshit. They're coming in on top of me now and swarming across my men. I've got to go. There's a radio operator from the listening post trapped out there -- needs my help."

Dennis hesitated as enemy bullets spewed across the perimeter, brilliantly lighting it with their green tracers. "Holy hell, look at this, Sarge," he called to Allred. "It makes Burt look like a Sunday School picnic. The whole perimeter is lit up like a Christmas tree, just from the tracers. Anything standing is going to get cut down. Don't move from here. Stay in the hole."

"We've got to get up there with the men, Lieutenant."

"Stay in the hole if you want to live another day, Top."

"Charlie Six, this is Falcon Six. What's your situation?"

"We're taking heavy rifle and machine gun fire all across our front. From recoilless rifles, too. We can't move an inch at the moment. Illumination is coming in real good now. I can see them pouring across my left front. Bravo's taking the main attack, and getting hit hard. The enemy rate of fire is increasing now. They're shootin' their wad. It ought to slack off in a few minutes."

"Charlie Six, I haven't heard a word from Bravo since that last transmission. If he needs help, reinforce him where you can. Delta Six, do the same. I'm sending a section of recon up there, too. What's your situation?"

"This is Delta. I'm hit hard in several places, but I think we're only a diversion. Bravo's the main target. I'll take a squad up there and some ammo. My positions are about gone now, anyway. Troops are fighting from isolated pockets."

"This is Falcon Six. Charlie Six, If you're not in the jam that the others are in, I need some help."

"How's that, Sir?"

"Seems like they've broken through at some points. There's one VC or more on top of my bunker. Major Johanson is trying to get them, but he only has a pistol. They're trying to roll grenades in, but he pops a round and they dodge it. It's a cat- and-mouse game. I can see VC foraging through our supper cans and other supplies. We're stuck in this hole. We need help. Can you do anything?"

Dennis couldn't answer for a moment as reports flooded in from his forward platoons. "The men are holding on, we still own the property," he told everyone. "It sounds like the Battalion CP is overrun. Falcon Six is cool as hell, but they're in trouble. Let's get 'em some help, Top."

"Charlie Six, this is Falcon Six," Colonel Flint spoke into the radio, his voice cracking with emotion. "Did you hear me?"

"Roger that, Six. We'll get the bad guys off your bunker. We're coming. Don't worry. Remember that old phrase; 'I think the poor bastards got us surrounded?' That's us."

"I don't believe you, Charlie Six. How many beers have you had?"

Dennis didn't answer. "C'mon, Top, Eddie -- let's go. The Battalion CP has enemy on top of it. They're trapped. What the hell is that?"

"Be cool, Charlie Six. It's me," Mike Balser said, slamming onto the ground beside Dennis. "I've got a couple of men with me. I can't see shit. What's up?"

"Mike, thank God. Who's that with you?"

"Francis Williams. He's getting his dick wet."

"There's VC on top of the Old Man's bunker; can you help?"

"You bet your ass. We're out of here. Tell the Colonel recon is on the way. Tell him we're going to place machine gun fire across the top of his bunker and tell him to keep his head down."

"Go get 'em, Mike," Dennis replied.

Dennis relayed the message, then instinctively crawled out of the foxhole, Eddie and Sergeant Allred following. Crawling on their bellies, they began wriggling forward toward the main thrust of the attack. Bullets snapped inches above their heads, yet they plodded their way forward, feeling their direction with outstretched arms. Within fifty feet of the point where Charlie and Bravo Company joined, they froze, halted by the intense, grazing fire. Dennis could hear the drum beat of helicopter rotors and knew that help was on the way. Illumination flares lit the battle area and he could see dozens of men engaged at close range, firing their weapons indiscriminately at any moving object. Molten shards of white-hot steel from artillery bursts whistled across their heads and they pressed their bodies into the earth.

"Holy hell, look at those sons-of-bitches coming," a voice cried out.

"Get your ass down, Asher," Eddie yelled. "What are you doing out here?"

"I was checking on my men. I heard that recon was supposed to reinforce Bravo. ...thought I'd help. You guys all right? I've got a couple of men with me and a machine gun team. What do you want to do, Charlie Six?" The enemy fire slackened and Dennis squatted on one knee. Jim Asher knelt beside him.

"OK, big Jim, let's pick up a few more men and then attack the bastards. Are you with me?"

Before Jim Asher could answer, several more men dropped alongside the assembling reaction party. Dennis counted twelve men, prone, stretched on a line, nearly shoulder-to-shoulder, facing the area of greatest penetration.

"Who've we got here?" Dennis asked, unable to recognize all their faces in the glimmering shadows of the artillery flares.

"Romeo Six and Rusty Adkins. We have Francis Williams with us, too," Lieutenant Balser yelled. "We cleaned off Falcon Six's bunker and came back up. The Colonel is OK. We'd better do something fast. They're coming across Bravo's center like a herd of wild elephants."

The battle zone was now a mass of confusion. Unable to distinguish Americans from Viet Cong, Dennis stood to survey the action. Finally, he shouted his battle instructions.

"Let's get on a line. Place all your fire across Bravo's positions. That's where they're coming through. Wait a second –"

Dennis grabbed the handset. "Bravo Six, this is Charlie Six. I can put some fire across the front of your bunkers, and slow the advance. Where are you? Where are your men?"

"This is Bravo. Quit asking questions and start shooting. I've lost most of my positions. Everybody that could move has pulled back twenty yards. Put your fire across my lines. We'll mount a counterattack as soon as you start."

The volume and intensity of the illumination flares increased, allowing Dennis to observe the figure of a lone man, squatting, throwing belts of machine gun ammunition and other items to small pockets of American soldiers. Under his arm, he clasped tightly to a walking stick.

Bullets and shell fragments cracked all around him, yet he worked unperturbed, redistributing ammunition to every man within his reach.

"Delta Six is passing out ammo to Bravo," Dennis said. "Watch out for him. Let's go for it now. Follow me!"

Dennis was the first to move forward and simultaneously the small band of warriors rose, spread themselves out, and, firing from the hip, joined Dennis in his gallant foray. Step by step, they walked deliberately into the enemy ranks. Mike Balser and Rusty Adkins stood side-by-side, M-60 machine guns pressed against their hips, belts of ammunition being consumed by the guns.

Jim Asher took a position at the far right with three men. His machine gun blazed red-hot bullets across Bravo's positions. At Dennis' constant urging, the line surged forward, spewing thousands of rounds of machine gun and rifle bullets into the advancing enemy. The air spilt with the snap and crackling of projectiles crossing their front, likewise directed into the surging mass of Viet Cong attackers.

"That's Delta's men on the other side. We've got them in a crossfire. Pour it on, men," Dennis screamed.

A crimson sea of American tracer bullets formed a liquid vee as enemy bodies fell on top one another, caught in the deadly cross fire of blazing steel. Several feet from Bravo's original positions, Dennis halted his team. Their fire became more effective as they took up stationary positions. A supersonic "whoosh" broke the air overhead and the first of a dozen napalm canisters splashed scarlet death across their front, delivered on target by low-flying Air Force dare-devils.

Gunships circled like vultures, spewing death from their doors. A lone aviator landed in the center of the mass, his crew kicking out badly needed ammunition.

"We've brought you some goodies, boys. We know you can use it. This is Blackhawk Five Four. When the hell are you guys going to let me get some rest? Hang on, now. We've got more good stuff inbound. Give my birds some protection. This is Blackhawk Five- Four, I'm outta here."

A glimmer of daylight greeted them and Dennis watched as men from Bravo Company fought to reclaim their bunker line. Lieutenant Dick Prairie led them. Dennis and his ensemble of heroes rushed forward and merged into their ranks.

Engaging the now-disjointed assault column, one-on-one, they exchanged bayonets and rifle butts, man for man, selecting their foes at random. The rumble and whine of approaching armored personnel carriers echoed through the jungle. Their heavy, fifty-caliber bullets broke limbs from the trees as they blasted their way through pockets of the enemy. At full daylight, the Viet Cong stopped suddenly and ran in the opposite direction, Americans bravely followed and showered them with horrendous bursts of deadly fire.

"We've got 'em on the goddamn run, Charlie Six. The mechanized boys got here just in time," Eddie Runge shouted, a wide smile glued upon his face. "We've got to stop Fullback; they don't know where we are," he reminded Dennis. "I think I have them on the radio now."

Eddie bent forward and pressed the handset hard against his ear. "Yeah, listen. It's Fullback Charlie. It's your buddy, Wild Bill Allison."

"You guys stay with Bravo and finish the job," Dennis ordered. "Top, check our own lines, I'm going to try to stop Fullback from shooting us when they break through."

"Fullback Charlie, this is Falcon Charlie. You're almost on top of us now. Stop your firing ... cease fire, cease fire."

"I hear you, Falcon," Captain Allison answered. "We're taking fire from the trees and pockets of resistance as we go. From the sounds of our guns, how far do you estimate that we are from your positions?"

"About a hundred meters. Shut it off."

"My communication is not so good with the lead tracks, Charlie Six. Five miles of jungle takes its toll. Get a man out in your clearing and pop a smoke grenade. The lead track will see it and they'll know what to do. What's your situation?"

Dennis ran toward the center of the clearing, dragging Eddie behind him. Attempting to talk as he ran, his broken transmissions were enough to clarify the character of the battle zone.

Dennis stopped and spoke into the telephone: "When you come in, Fullback, spread your tracks west, all across our front. Get between the holes. The center has the most damage. The enemy is in retreat, running like hell."

Handing the radio handset back to Eddie, Dennis broke into a full run. He leaped over and around bodies, many of them mangled Americans, mixed with the smoldering carcasses of Viet Cong. In some pockets, fighting continued at close quarters; the enemy was trapped and fighting to the death.

At fifteen meters from the confluence of the jungle and the clearing, Dennis stopped and frantically waved his arms. The armored vehicles were only moments from breaking through and still firing their guns. Large shells exploded at Dennis' feet, yet he stood firm, waving, stopping only long enough to ignite a purple smoke grenade.

A final shot blasted from the big fiftys and missed Dennis by inches. He ran toward the menacing hulk of the first carrier. The driver nodded his recognition. The gunner released his grip on the trigger.

"We're here. My name's John Marts. Where the hell are your lines?"

Chapter Forty-Seven
Leaving Command

Dennis shouted instructions and the vehicle commander relayed them by radio to his column. In synchronized motion, the big tracks pushed through, encircling the perimeter, ensuring the defeat of the now-scattered enemy.

"Good to see you, Charlie Six," Captain Allison shouted to Dennis as he halted his command vehicle beside him. "Climb on board and show me the front. Where were you hardest hit?"

"The center, Bravo Company," Dennis said, clambering up the front of the carrier and pointing the way. "There's still some fighting going on up there. Bravo took the brunt of the attack. We've got plenty of casualties. Thank God you got here. How's the Colonel?"

Captain Allison spoke calmly, as always. "Colonel Norris left for the States a week ago. We've got a new commander. He's unsettled ... hesitated too long trying to decide whether to send us so I just took the company on my own. We couldn't let you down, Dennis. They'll probably send me home as punishment. What the heck, there are worse rewards."

"Glad you did, Sir. Those fifty calibers scared the hell out of the VC; they're running now."

They sped across the perimeter directly into Dick Prairie's decimated ranks. Scattered shots in the distance rang out, while gunships, flying at tree-top level, vomited showers of bullets upon the now-vanishing enemy.

Artillery continued to burst along the path of their retreat, causing incalculable death and destruction. Passing Bravo Company's most forward positions, Captain Allison stopped his track. Instantly, the mounted infantry jumped from the vehicle, dispersing among the foxholes.

"What the heck is this?" Captain Allison shouted, stunned as he surveyed Bravo's positions. In one small hole lay two dead Americans. Around them were the bodies of eight Viet Cong, most of them dead from multiple bayonet wounds. Across the entire front, similar macabre scenes of violent death unnerved both commanders. They walked forward of the line to search for listening posts or Americans still too frightened to move.

Captain Allison spotted a lone Viet Cong and froze. The soldier peered through the sights of his AK-47 rifle, aiming directly at the Captain's head. Slowly, the soldier squeezed the trigger. The weapon clicked harmlessly and he died in a hail of American gunfire and grenades as Wild Bill's troops surrounded him. They admonished their commander for his careless foray.

Relinquishing command to his lieutenants, Captain Allison and Dennis walked to the center of the perimeter, in search of Colonel Flint. They found him walking among the waste of human lives, stopping to speak with wounded and praying over the many mounds of dead.

"Seems like the perimeter is all secure now, Sir," Captain Allison reported. "Your guys put up one hell of a fight."

"Yes, and so did the enemy," Colonel Flint replied. "They were desperate. Thanks for coming so quickly, Captain. I'm grateful to you and your men. Listening to the radio, I thought you were being held in check and not going to react."

"There was some delay. My God, look at the piles of dead. It doesn't look as if you needed us."

"Nevertheless, I'm grateful, Captain Allison. I think your tracks finally scared them off. We're getting a count of the death toll now. Let's walk."

Soldiers from both units worked tirelessly, dragging the mangled bodies of the enemy dead to the center of the perimeter. They separated them by some distance from the neat rows of lifeless Americans. At one point Dennis noticed smoke from beneath the poncho coverings of several dead Americans. He knelt beside them and threw back the flimsy shrouds. Aghast, he recognized the smell of napalm as it continued to char the flesh of its dead victims.

"Help me put it out," Dennis pleaded with those standing near the bodies. "We'll have to cut off the air. Nothing else works. Pack dirt on the burns."

Dennis and several men worked feverishly as they dug dirt with their bare hands, pressing it against the smoldering sores. Father Tobin appeared and, decked in his purple stole, he bent to assist. Gagging from the stench, Dennis sobbed as he smothered the groin and abdomen of a dead soldier.

"This is sick," he blurted out. "Packing dirt into the open wounds of dead men."

"Take it easy, Dennis," Father Tobin replied. "The men will finish. Come on, walk with me as I anoint and pray for the dead. Here, hold these oils for me."

"How the hell do you know who is Catholic? Who to anoint?"

"I don't. I just anoint and pray over all of them. They never complain."

"Jesus."

"Yes, Dennis, and when I'm finished I'll pray over the enemy. I won't be too obvious, but they need prayers, too."

"Like hell. By the way, where did you just come from? How did you get in here?"

"Oh, I hopped a ride with a chopper pilot. A guy named Blackhawk something or other. Scared the devil out of me. I've been busting open ammo boxes and loading magazines all morning."

"What?" Dennis said, putting his hands on his hips. "A Catholic priest distributing ammo? Are you allowed to do that? I thought you guys had rules about not getting involved in the fighting."

"Yeah, well, I believe they're still debating that in Rome. Judge not, Dennis."

Dennis left the smoldering bodies as he and the priest continued administering to the ranks of deceased soldiers. They came upon scores of wounded and other men who stared blankly into the wood line or sat with their eyes tightly closed. The injured were prepared for evacuation and the priest stopped to comfort them. White bandages concealed the ugly stumps of amputees. Doc Shiro and other medics filled the wounded with liquid painkillers.

Near the center of the perimeter, Dennis spotted his friend, Dick Prairie. He stood alone, propped against a single tree, his rifle slung low. He was obviously deep in thought.

"How you doing, Dick? It was a hell of a night, eh?"

"I ain't doing worth a damn. Most of the dead and wounded are mine. The VC came through us like fuckin' diarrhea. Those two boys in the middle, they had eight dead VC around their foxhole. We stumbled over them. They were already dead when we went up to get the radio operator. Hell, that guy was fighting off ten VC by himself. I'm mighty proud of my men. They fought a hard fight."

Dennis and Lieutenant Prairie sat and shared a cigarette. "Yeah, they did the job, Dick. And they paid a hell of price. You, too."

"Thanks for your help Dennis. Tell Balser and Adkins, and all your guys I said I owe them. Maybe next time we'll eat a late supper. Dig a little deeper."

"I didn't say anything, Dick."

"You don't need to."

"What happened here?" Father Tobin asked. "I've never seen such carnage in such a small and confined spot."

"I think they were starving," Dennis answered, stooping to roll over an enemy body. "These are North Vietnamese soldiers, trying to make their way home or into other sanctuaries after Tet. Look at the bodies. They're skinny, they need haircuts, they have badly colored teeth. I think they were desperate." Dennis stood and shook his head.

"I agree," Father Tobin commented as he examined and organized the contents of his bag. "I'm almost out of candles and oils."

Dennis watched him, hesitated, then spoke: "Father..."

"Yes, Dennis?"

"Aw, nothing."

"No, go ahead, Dennis. What's on your mind?"

Dennis sighed. "We almost lost it during the night, Padre. Bravo Company, Charlie, Delta; they fought like savages, but now look at the dead and wounded. What's it all for? It's all so unnecessary, Father. I hate it. I want out of here."

"We all do, Dennis. I'll speak to the Colonel for you."

Colonel Flint and his headquarters' staff walked the line of dead and wounded. Spotting Dennis, he beckoned for him to approach. "You and your men fought a hell of a battle last night, Charlie Six," he said shaking Dennis' hand. "I understand there are dozens of bodies in front of your lines. Thank the men for me." Turning back toward the piles of the dead, Colonel Flint waved his hand across the butchered landscape. "Just look at all this hell," he said.

Shell holes still held the bodies of dead Americans and Viet Cong, intertwined in death, without consideration for whose dogma they had fought for. Rescue teams checked them to confirm their deaths, then dragged them out of the craters by the feet.

"We have terrible casualties here," Colonel Flint said, "but the enemy paid dearly. One hundred and fifty-three of them died within the perimeter. Most of them were killed by that cross fire that Charlie and Delta created. Seventeen Americans are dead. We have, perhaps, forty-seven wounded. All of our boys, every man here, is a hero today. I wish the Americans back home could appreciate the Americans here the way I do. There are a lot of real heroes here. You can't find better men than this."

Interrupted by the sounds of approaching helicopters, Dennis gazed into the sky and recognized the shiny red panel of stars mounted on the nose of the bird. General Philson pinned the Distinguished Service Cross on Jerry White before the battle smoke had cleared and Delta Six walked without his cane thereafter. Dick Prairie was commended for his bravery and received the Silver Star along with six other men. Mr. Al Chang from the Associated Press wrote a story for the newspaper *Pacific Stars and Stripes*. He mentioned that, although bayonets were fixed, ammunition had been quickly delivered by air.

"It proves what everybody already knows," Major Johanson said, reviewing Mr. Chang's notes with him.

"What's that, Major?"

"Hell, our rifles swallow up all the ammunition we can carry in twenty minutes. If that pilot hadn't had the guts to fly in here and deliver ammo during the height of the battle, you wouldn't be standing here, none of us would be."

Mr. Chang left in the General's helicopter, satisfied with his war story. Dennis wandered alone amongst the dead. Their torn and mangled bodies, stacked-side-by side like cordwood, disgusted him. He silently raged inside. Late that afternoon, he asked Colonel Flint to be relieved of his command.

"I can't stand the killing any longer," he said. "You're probably disappointed in me, Colonel, but I've had it. Do with me what you will, but I'll never pull the trigger of a rifle again. I can't call artillery on anyone or even imagine sending these men on patrol. I just don't believe in it anymore. I can't bring myself to take part in it."

Colonel Flint nodded his understanding, and placing his arm around Dennis' shoulder, drew him alongside. Together they paced the length of the clearing, the older officer conversing quietly to his lieutenant.

"Are you sure, Dennis? I can understand your displeasure with all of this. I am probably more disgusted with it than you are. The total destructiveness of it all, the waste of lives. You've lost many good men along the way -- good friends. At your level, you are forced to be so close to your men. ...can't avoid it."

"That's been my problem all along," Dennis said.

"I know," Colonel Flint said. "I can stay at arm's length, thank God, but I feel the death of each and every one of them. I am a parent, too, you know. I can just imagine how those mothers and fathers will feel when they get the news back home."

Nearing the end of the perimeter, at the jungle wall, they turned and looked back across the cluttered battlefield. Colonel Flint folded his hands behind his back and stood silent for a while, seemingly deep in thought. After several minutes, he spoke. "We live in a fatalistic environment, Dennis. It seeps into your psyche and then finally swallows you. Yes, I agree, you've had enough. I'll reassign you to administrative tasks back at Dau Tieng."

"Thanks."

"Don't think, however, that the reassignment is of your doing, Dennis. I decided during the night that if we both lived to see Easter Sunday, I'd take you out of command. You've been a courageous and faithful soldier. It just wouldn't do for anyone to think that you had yielded to timidity. You carry every death with you. Too bad. I'm afraid you'll suffer more." Spontaneously, they both began walking back across the clearing, the Colonel continuing his evaluations.

"Would it surprise you to learn that you have been one of my heroes, son? Ever since that first night when I heard your voice along the road at Ap Cho. I took courage from your character as you displayed it there. We draw our strength from many places, don't we? You say the damnedest things sometimes."

Stopping, Dennis turned and faced the older man. "Why do you say that? Did I irk you with that comment about the poor bastards having us surrounded? I only had two cans of beer."

Colonel Flint chuckled and said, "On the contrary, Dennis; at the moment you made that audacious comment, I was about to sacrifice my life to a Communist from North Vietnam. When you made that remark, it filled me with optimism. 'How could we lose the battle?' I asked myself. How could we lose with men such as you leading the way?"

Colonel Flint reached in his pocket and withdrew a package of Winston cigarettes, offering one to Dennis. Lighting both on one match, he blew smoke and grinned. "I had quit smoking until last night; I guess it's time we both get out of here. I'll be going home soon, too."

"When are you leaving, Sir?"

The colonel paused and chuckled again. "In a couple of months or so, before any more damned holidays, I hope. But, you, Dennis, you've fought your final battle. I was thinking that maybe you are subconsciously pursuing a death wish. I am aware of your attempt at self-destruction after Compound X-ray, after that young Sergeant died. Were your actions last night motivated by bravery, or were you trying to get it over with? Don't answer, just think about it."

Dennis shifted his feet and cast his eyes downward. "I'm ashamed of that."

"Don't be. I can understand your state of mind; let's trust that it has passed. I hope to save you for greater service, Son. You'll be a Captain soon. There is college in your future and Military Service Schools. You can reach the highest levels of rank and make great contributions to your country. That is the highest honor: to serve your country."

"Yeah?" Dennis said, looking at Colonel Flint quizzically. "You see any honor in all of this?"

"Yes, and you'll see it later. Right now I want you to go back to Dau Tieng, and await further orders. Go back with your head held high. You have performed well. Behave yourself and stay out of trouble. If it is true that you are trying to join your friends, maybe this will give you time to think about how tragic that would be. Good luck, Soldier."

They shook hands and the Colonel's firm grip remained with Dennis for a while. By nightfall on March 14, 1968, Easter Sunday, Lieutenant Dennis Riley became a noncombatant. He went quietly back to Dau Tieng.

Chapter Forty-Eight
A Soldier's Despair

Dennis busied himself with administrative duties when he was sober, speaking to no one except out of necessity. He cloistered himself in a small room inside the Battalion headquarters. In spite of all that Colonel Flint and his friends had said, he could not dispel the depression and guilt that consumed him. His remaining days passed quickly. He managed to get Eddie Runge transferred to a radio operator's desk job at Dau Tieng, because he thought one day he had seen "that look" in his eyes.

Minor actions in and around the Michelin plantation caused the death of two more Charlie Company men. Sergeant Beebe was severely wounded, taking several bullets in the chest as he tried to rescue one of the men. Dennis wrote more letters to the families of those killed in action, but he was inoculated against any feeling, and the letters were bland and hollow.

As promised, his promotion to Captain came through. At a small celebration hosted by friends and staff officers, Dennis seemed unimpressed as they "pinned" him. He spoke little except to murmur appeasing platitudes.

"No big deal," he said to Dick Prairie who sincerely complemented him for his achievements.

Sipping drinks and enjoying their short respite from war, someone told a bawdy joke. The group roared with laughter, but Dennis found no humor in it. Laughter was beyond him and he turned away. Father Tobin noticed his stony-faced silence and cautioned Dennis against his obvious self-pity.

"You'll heal someday, Dennis. Give it time. Pray," he counseled.

On July 4, an enemy attack penetrated the defenses of Dau Tieng, and they infiltrated as far as the steps of Dennis' quarters. He took no defensive or evasive action, never arming himself or seeking shelter. Sitting on the floor in the dark, he drank putrid whiskey straight from a bottle, waiting for fate to deal him the final hand.

The enemy was repelled and Dennis did not ponder his individual fortunes. He received his second Silver Star award at a modest ceremony in Dau Tieng. Colonel Flint boasted to the small gathering of Dennis' gallantry. "See here," he said, pointing to the inscription on the back. "It says, 'for gallantry in action.' You certainly deserve it, Dennis."

"It belongs to the men, Sir, but thanks, anyway."

Dennis returned to his room and threw the medal into his foot-locker. He sat on the edge of his bed and thought of all those who had gone before him. He sobbed openly for a while, but no tears flowed. He no longer cared if he lived or died and he had no emotion left to spend.

There were few people left in the battalion that he knew. Colonel Flint had departed for the United States a few days before Dennis was scheduled to return home. Sergeant Allred and many others had left, also. A few stopped by to say farewell, but most avoided him. They felt un-comfortable in the shadow of this shell of a man.

"Lost his balls. He's a fucking wimp," the new men said of him. Eventually, Dennis boarded a plane for the United States. He carried gov-ernment orders rolled up in his hand. They defined his future, but made no mention of any Service Schools. They were discharge papers.

As the huge aircraft spread its wings against the night sky, Dennis could see the red-hot streaks of tracer bullets in the jungles below. Three hundred men aboard the plane roared their approval as the "stretch eight" lifted off the runway. Dennis sat silently with his eyes tightly closed. An endless sea of faces rushed passed him and he wept inside, shaking uncontrollably. Others around him assumed he was stricken with a fear of flying and they smiled at his obvious timidity.

In San Francisco, Dennis lounged for a week in a shabby hotel room, drinking himself into a stupor. "My folks are coming to get me; I don't know how I'll act," he said to a resident prostitute who had befriended him. "They're flying here to get me and take me home."

"What are you going to do, Baby? Will you stay in the Army?" she asked.

"No, I'm getting out. This war might go on for years. Many career men are already going back on their second tour of duty. I've had it; I'm not going back."

Without a second thought, before departing Vietnam, Dennis signed the necessary discharge papers, leaving the Army he had loved for so much of his youth. *I'll never see Colonel Flint or any of them again. What the hell do I care? I'm glad to be done with it. Fuck it, just fuck it. It don't mean nothing.*

His mother, weary from the strain of worry and flying across the country, hugged him many times and kissed him dearly over and over again. For a moment he felt safe and then the feeling crashed when she said: "God has kept you safe for us, Dennis. We must get to a church soon and give Him our thanks."

Fuck Him, give Him thanks for what? Sending me to Vietnam. For killing my friends? All those people? "OK, Mom, we'll do that real soon," he said.

Finally settled into his parent's modern garden home in suburban Detroit, Dennis began to relax. He called Beverly Ann and learned that she had married.

"You didn't write. Sorry we couldn't ever get together, Dennis. I would have liked that."

He visited his old school and stared from across the street at Saint Anthony's church, but he would not enter it. He took long walks into the night and abstained from drinking out of respect for his mother.

Lying, he would leave the house early on Sunday morning, telling his mother he had attended Mass before she arose. Proud of Dennis, overjoyed that he had returned from war safely, she boasted to her parish friends, "Some mothers are not so lucky; their boys come home damaged. Dennis is OK, thank God."

Dennis' father, a veteran of World War I, had little sympathy for him. "You look shell-shocked, boy," he said. "Why don't you get a job and get out of the house on your own? It's no good to lie around collecting a government pension for being 'a loony.' Hell, if you'd lost a leg or an arm, I could see it. You need to get busy, forget the war. It wasn't like the big ones, you know."

Dennis looked away. He loved his father, but the constant scolding drove him farther into his personal humiliation. He had not come back a winner and his father knew it.

"Hell, four hundred men died in the Hurtgen forest in World War Two," his father continued. "You should a been with us during the Great War -- at the Marne -- then you'd know what fighting is all about. What did you guys lose, three, maybe four a day?"

His mother presented him a cigar box on his birthday. It was filled with savings bonds, deducted from his pay over the years, perhaps ten thousand dollars in value. Dennis thanked her, but didn't count it. The following day he redeemed the certificates for cash at a bank, bought a second-hand car and began planning his flight toward a future he could not see.

An attempt to explain his emotional suffering to his mother that night fell on sympathetic ears. He was leaving in the morning to seek "more peaceful pastures."

"Without God in your life," she said, "you'll never find peace. I'll pray for you always," and then she kissed him long on the forehead and cheek.

The following morning, with his few clothes in a cardboard box, he drove west until long after the sunset. Continuing his aimless journey the following day, he stopped finally, out of gas because he had neglected to buy any.

Unconcerned, he simply took up living in a Texas rest stop somewhere along the highway. He stayed there for a month or longer, sleeping in his car. A cold and smelly rest room met his other needs. He begged for scraps of food, sandwiches, fruit, and drink from travelers and spent his days and nights talking to truckers and prostitutes.

Dennis experimented with drugs, drinking himself into perpetual unconsciousness. He was robbed by vagabonds of his savings as he slept in the grass behind his car. The few dollars remaining in his pocket fed him for a day or two. Finally, his only sustenance was the acidic and putrid water from the rest area spigots.

At the point of starvation, he begged gasoline from a family of travelers. He started the car and drove toward a nearby town. Stopping on the outskirts, he straddled the double tracks of the Union Pacific railroad. Sitting there in the sweltering heat, he hummed a line from an old Hank Williams' song, "Just a-waitin' on a train."

He closed his eyes and was drifting into sleep when the blasts of a loud horn startled him awake. Looking in the rearview mirror, he saw a pickup truck moving slowly up behind him. Matching bumpers perfectly, the driver pushed him off the tracks just in time to escape the heavy steel of an oncoming train.

"Damn, screwed again," he said.

Chapter Forty-Nine
Angel of Mercy

Sitting motionless in the seat, he watched as the driver got out and walked briskly up beside him, wearing perplexed anger on her face like she was born into it. A stunningly beautiful and petite young girl: about twenty-one, Dennis surmised. Her golden locks fell to her shoulders from beneath a wide-brimmed cowboy hat and they underlined the beauty of her youth.

She wore cowboy boots and tight-fitting blue jeans with a Western-style shirt, sparkling with tiny purple and red rhinestones. He stared at her pretty blue eyes and pouting red lips as she shouted: "You damn idiot! Do you know you could have got yourself killed, sitting there on those tracks? What the hell is wrong with you, pilgrim?"

Dennis sat motionless in the car. "That's what I was fixin' to do, Lady. Hitch a long ride on the Union Pacific. What's it to you?"

Stunned, she impulsively reached through the open window to touch him. She shook him on the shoulder and then grabbed his neck, rubbing it slightly. It was the first human touch he had felt in weeks and he succumbed to natural emotions. He began to cry softly.

Speaking tenderly now, she murmured: "C'mon, mister, get out of that car; it probably won't run anyway. I think the transmission snapped when I pushed you off the track. You look pretty bad; in fact, you look terrible. Hungry? Come on, get into my truck. I'm going to take you someplace and feed you."

Opening the car door, she continued her hold on his neck, forcing him to get out. Like a lamb he obeyed her and soon found himself riding beside one of the friendliest and prettiest women he had ever seen.

"So, you're going to save me, huh?" he asked. "Better let me out of this truck; you have no idea what you are doing."

"At ease, Soldier," she said. "Shut up, we're going into town. We're going to go see somebody."

The familiar command to be still quieted Dennis and he submitted to her control. "I don't want to trouble anybody, Lady. Your boyfriend's the Sheriff, I'll bet, or are you married to the town shrink?"

"No, but I'm fixing to get that way and my great big boyfriend will kick your butt if you try anything funny, so stay over there on your side and keep your hands to yourself. We're going to see him."

Her voiced softened and she turned toward Dennis, offering her hand. "My named is Barbara Jo. My honey, Johnny, runs a small restaurant here in town. He'll give you something to eat. I'll bet you're a Vietnam veteran, huh?"

"How did you know, Barbara Jo?" Dennis said, accepting the handshake.

"Johnny has been back a year now. You get to know the look. I can tell one when I see one. It's in the eyes. What's your name and what were you doing out on those tracks?"

"I'm Dennis Riley. I don't know what I was doing there. I'm down on my luck. Guess I was just waiting for something to happen. It did -- you."

She looked at him quizzically, shrugged and asked where and when he had served.

"I've been back from 'Nam a couple of months now," Dennis answered. "I've just been wandering, living in rest areas and other places. Got robbed a couple of days ago and I guess I just wanted to end it all. Thanks for caring."

She reached over and patted him on the arm. "It'll be OK, Mr. Dennis Riley. Talk to Johnny; he has a good handle on these things. He went through a lot, too."

Dennis thought he noticed tears in her eyes and a husky thickness developing in her voice as she talked. He liked her. He hadn't thought of a woman as a friend for a very long time and she awakened long-buried feelings within him.

"Hi, Guy," Johnny said. He wiped his hands on an apron and extended a friendly handshake to Dennis. "You look like death warmed over. Ever heard of a bath and a shave? C'mon, I know you're hungry; Barbie never brings a healthy stray in here."

Dennis took a stool at the end of the lunch counter as Johnny began preparing a breakfast of ham, eggs, and fried potatoes. It smelled delicious and he fidgeted on his seat, thinking only of the moment when he could devour it. Johnny seemed very friendly and paid little attention to Dennis and Barbara Jo, concentrating on his cooking and serving the few customers sitting in booths.

They stared for a moment at Dennis when he arrived, but soon turned their attentions elsewhere. Apparently they were used to his kind and knew of Barbara Jo's fondness for vagrants. Standing beside Dennis, she leaned close and kept touching his arm or hand as she pumped him for information about himself.

"Where are you from, Dennis? Do you have a family? See much action? Where were you in Vietnam?"

He vaguely answered her questions about home, but kept his Vietnam experience to himself. *She'd never believe me,* he thought. Becoming somewhat tense at Barbara Jo's closeness to him, he worried that Johnny, in a fit of jealousy, might refuse to feed him. Starving and eyeing the cook, he gently pushed her away.

Johnny turned, noticed Dennis' nervousness, and laughed. "She's not my girlfriend, Dennis, she's my little sister. She brings a couple of drifters like you in here every month. A lot of our local kids served in Vietnam, including me. Some were wounded pretty bad and a few were killed. Tommy -- he was her high school sweetheart -- First Cav Division. Died in the A Shau valley."

Dennis cringed and looked at the floor. "I'm sorry to hear that."

"Yeah. It tore her up. She wrote to Tommy every day he was over there; she got such an obsession with it after he died."

Busily working the grill and serving food to customers, Johnny still found time to jabber. "If you're a vet, she's going to bring you in here to talk about it."

"I'm lucky," Dennis said.

Johnny's back was toward Dennis, but he continued. "She tells everybody at first that I'm a big guy who could knock your block off. If she begins to trust them, then they get a free meal. Sometimes she never tells them the truth." He smiled at his sister and pointed: "We call her Barbie cause she looks like the doll, doesn't she?"

Barbie, blushing at the revelations, moved even closer to Dennis. "Tell me all about Vietnam, please. Did you know Tommy?" She picked up his steaming plate of food and carried it to a booth, ushering Dennis into it. Sitting across from him, she rested her chin on her hands, staring into his eyes. He could not escape hers. "I'm sorry about your friend," he said. "How old was he?"

For more than an hour, she sat, spellbound, as he told her about his life with the 22nd Infantry. He did not tell her about Rosey, Jay Cee, and the others. He never mentioned Sergeant Allred or Colonel Flint or Colonel Taylor. He described Nui Ba Den, the rice paddies of Hau Nghia, and the jungles of war zone "C." He did not tell her about Ap Cho. Surprisingly, he grew more comfortable and he told her more about the war, but nothing of what he felt. "You know, Barbie, talking to you I feel a little bit better about it all."

Barbie stared at him, listening, interrupting only now and then with a cooing sound, signifying her sadness at Dennis' vivid descriptions of war. "I do that when I'm sad," she giggled. "I do it when I'm happy, too. Crazy, huh?"

Late that evening, with Dennis finally out of words, she smiled and asked politely, "What will you do now, Dennis? Just be a rolling stone? I think it's time to get your life in order."

"You might be right."

"Johnny is looking for some help. If I talk real sweet to him I know he'll hire you. At least you can eat free and maybe make a few bucks. What do you say?"

Captivated more by the wholesomeness of her youth than her offer of employment, Dennis nodded his agreement to the idea. He didn't know it, but he had surrendered totally and completely to this woman. "Yeah," he said, "I'd like that."

Johnny agreed and soon Dennis was working as a handyman around the cafe. He received a few dollars a week, but took most of his payment in meals. He lived inside the cafe during the night, bathing in the large utility tubs in the kitchen and sleeping in a booth or on the floor. Barbie stayed with him on many nights and they talked until they both fell asleep, their heads touching from across the table.

Months passed and, in the spring of 1969, Johnny made Dennis a permanent member of his staff, with decent pay and benefits.

"It doesn't look like you're going to go anywhere, Dennis, and I don't think Barbie will let you. Why don't you find yourself a place to stay? We'll help you fix it up."

He was ready now and Barbie found a quiet, one-bedroom apartment not far from the restaurant. She decorated it with pretty embellishments and Dennis loved to watch her as she worked, trying to make him comfortable.

She's so damned innocent, he thought. *So completely different from me, yet we are much the same. We both lost what we loved to Vietnam.*

He knew he was physically attracted to her and she to him, but he did not want to spoil their relationship with amorous advances. *She's good medicine, but we need the separation of souls. I ache too much inside to have any more friends, even a woman like her.*

She spent most of her evenings with him, reading, watching television, cleaning house and cooking delicious meals. Often they went on late-night walks, holding hands, not speaking for long periods of time and enjoying the broad, star-studded Texas skies.

On an especially cool spring evening, as they celebrated her twenty-second birthday, they fell asleep on the floor after drinking too much wine. For warmth, they snuggled closer together and, impulsively, he kissed her cheek. She responded by pressing her femininity tight against his groin. Wrapping her arms around his neck she drove her tender young tongue deep into his mouth, kissing him violently.

They engaged in a fit of burning lovemaking and Dennis told her that he loved her as he lay his head between her supple breasts and cried. She rubbed and kissed his head and cooed sweetly to him in the darkness. They married in the fall.

With Barbie's constant affections, Dennis' life began a period of healthy restoration. Giving up drinking and smoking, he enrolled in a small college and, before long, he held a teaching position in the local high school. He and Barbie still helped at Johnny's restaurant on nights and weekends. He was hopelessly in love with her and she with him.

He had moments of regression, several times choosing to sleep on the concrete floor of the garage in their new house. The Sheriff called once to ask her to come and get him out of the local jail. He'd been put there for safekeeping after they found him riding up and down the freeway with a large K-Bar knife in his hands and an olive drab bandanna around his forehead. "They call it flashbacks -- some kind of stress disorder," the Sheriff said. "Better get him some professional help."

"He has professional help, Sheriff," she said with a wink and a giggle as she led her lover from the jail. They made gentle love that night, and as always, he laid his face between her breasts and wept uncontrollably while she petted him to sleep.

Chapter Fifty
The Healing Begins

By 1971, she had presented him two children, a boy and a girl, both blessed with inherited good looks and he loved her even more. She was a natural and loving mother and he a devoted father, but always she carried his agony for him, personified in the aftermath of their lovemaking. He always cried. She cooed sweet nothings to console him.

Vietnam became less and less a reality for Dennis as the years passed. Watching television as the Communists captured Saigon on television in 1974, he never flinched when the commentator declared: "The only war America ever lost." He turned it off and walked outside to cut his grass. Barbie watched him through the window for an hour. Out of love and pity, she joined him, finally dragging him back inside the house to their bedroom.

Deeply involved in his work, he never spoke of Vietnam. Flourishing under his wife's loving tutoring, his children prospered, finishing high school and entering college.

Except for one minor difficulty in his life, he was happy. Still, he could not make love to his beautiful wife without being reduced to the infantile condition of a bawling baby. It remained a persistent blot on his psyche. Ashamed, he tried to control it, but always failed.

Enjoying an evening at home, around the fire in the winter of 1989, some twenty-one years after Vietnam, he felt the urge to wrap his arms around Barbie's shoulders and tell her once again how much he loved her. As he reached out for her tender body, the phone rang, jarring him into reality.

"Dennis Riley?" a vaguely familiar voice asked.

Thinking it was telephone solicitation, an offer to buy something, he abruptly told the caller, "Yeah, I am, and what do you want?"

"Are you Charlie Six, Lieutenant Riley, who served with me in Vietnam?" the voice asked.

Dennis fell speechless, collapsing into the nearest chair. He turned to Barbie for help and handed her the phone, bending forward and placing his head into his folded arms. "It's Eddie, Eddie," he cried as the past came rushing across his buried consciousness. All the names, all the faces, all the battles. The ghosts had never gone away. They were back.

"Who are you?" Barbie asked.

"I'm Eddie Runge. I was Dennis' radio operator in Vietnam. Is he OK? I've been looking for him. A lot of us have; can I talk to him?"

"Just a second, Eddie, he seems to be having a moment, you know."

"Yeah, I know. I've had few of them myself."

Dennis looked up into her face and she motioned with the phone for him to take the call. Reluctantly he obeyed, slowly pressing the instrument to his ear. He said nothing, but his heavy breathing and little sobs told Eddie that he was listening. Finally, he said, "Hello, Eddie. Long time, no see."

"Charlie Six, this is Six X-ray. I just wanted to say hello. Where the hell you been hiding, man? Did you know that Charlie Company formed an association a few years ago? We've found over three hundred of our guys. We hold reunions every two years and this year I was asked if I could find you. Your mom gave me your phone number."

"Really?" Dennis asked. His eyes brightened and he smiled at Barbie. She pursed her lips and blew him a kiss.

"We're putting Charlie Company back together again, Dennis. If you want to be a part of it, I'll give you my number and you can call me back. You'd love it."

"Ah -- yeah -- maybe."

"I just saw Sergeant Allred and Beebe," Eddie continued. "Sergeant Beebe made it, you know. Lieutenant Balser was there too, and our old artilleryman, Mike Donnelly. Jim Asher came and many of the guys you know: Gary Adams, Nick Dragon, Pat Shine -- lots of them. They miss you, Charlie-Six, they want you back. Please say yes, and I'll send you our newsletter and some other stuff in the mail. What do you say, Dennis?"

"OK," he whispered, "OK, Eddie -- and thanks." Hanging up the phone, he took his wife into the bedroom and stormed her with his sexual appetite. They melded into each other, becoming one soul, one spirit, at last. He did not cry when they finished; instead, as he quietly absorbed her affections, he thought of Eddie, Allred, and all of the living and the dead from Vietnam. Sleep came easily. The next day he attended to his students with a new exuberance for life and for living.

Barbie watched the mail box every day and it took little more than a week to arrive. Finally, a large brown envelope came addressed to: "Charlie Six, Lieutenant Dennis J. Riley." She longed to open it, but waited for Dennis to arrive home from work. Casually mentioning that Eddie's promised package had arrived, she waited for his reaction.

"Later -- thanks," he said, then laid it on a coffee table and went out into the garage to service his lawn mower and to cut the grass. Finished, he stood idle by the machine for several minutes. With his body glistening with sweat, he came back in and said, "OK, Honey, open it and read it to me."

She put on her reading glasses, smiled, and began: "It's from Eddie Runge, Chico, California." He says, "Dennis, this is Eddie. How the hell are you? I know you almost had heart failure the other night when I called. You should have seen me when they found me. I was a babbling idiot. I hope I haven't left you in the same shape. Sorry if I did.

"About three years ago, a fellow out in Oregon, named Bill Schwindt, spotted someone in a store that he thought he'd served with in Charlie Company; it turned out that it was. They went over together back in '65. Between the two of them, they knew about six vets from around the same time. They got together at somebody's house and held a small reunion. From that little beginning, they searched, and, during the last three years, they've found about three hundred guys. Everyone looks for someone else. They figure there are about a thousand or more they'd like to find. We call our group: 'Charlie Company, Third of The Twenty-Second Association.' Right now, we write a newsletter (copy enclosed), and hold reunions every two years."

Barbie paused and looked at Dennis. He sat on a sofa with his eyes closed tightly. She smacked her lips, moved to him and stood, touching his neck. "Should I go on?"

"Yes, Baby. I'm just thinking."

"Tell me. About what?"

"About the way it used to be."

Barbie smiled and continued reading. "I've included a mailing list that has the addresses of everyone we've found plus the families of some of our KIAs. There are a few names in there that will really interest you.

"Now, the reunions are what it's all about. I went to my first one last month. I cried like a baby. You couldn't know it, but I stayed drunk for ten years after I got back. I was a real mess. Since I got hooked up with this association, I've found the love of my life and she has rules. Melissa won't let me drink and I don't want to.

"I believe it has something to do with the experience I got from attending the reunion. Father Tobin was there and he asked about you. I promised him I'd find you.

"Well, anyway, there you have it. C'mon and join the gang. It is a super bunch of guys, the best men that ever poured piss out of a combat boot. Ha, Ha.

"Say hello to the Missus; she sounded as sweet as a petunia on the phone. Can't wait to meet her. I hope you'll join up with us. We need you. You need us. Bye, ole' buddy. Call me, OK?"

Barbie lay the letter on a table. Her eyes filled with tears. She picked it up again and held it in front of her face.

"He signed it, Charlie Six, X-ray and Melissa."

Dennis asked Barbie for the letter and, after recognizing Eddie's handwriting, he began to peruse the crude collection of thoughts they called a newsletter.

"Printed with an old mimeograph machine on sheets of different colored paper," Dennis said. "It's an obvious modest effort at journalism, pieced together by one man, but I'm thrilled reading it."

Reading and rereading the pages, he found little tidbits of interesting information and recognized many names on the mailing list. Several in particular almost stopped his heart: Mike Balser, Herb Chancey, Allred, Beebe, Krznarovich.

The list went on and he grew more and more excited. "I want to be a part of this," he told Barbie. "I don't know where it's headed, but I need to belong."

That night, he composed a letter to one of the C/3/22 Association officers, the man Eddie called Bill Schwindt. Attaching a check for his small dues payment, he completed a short questionnaire, and thus, was propelled upon a course that would carry him once again across the battlefields of Vietnam.

In the late evening, he and Barbie sat on their patio, sipping wine, eating cheese and fruit as he poured out for her his awesome and terrible experiences at war. By daylight she knew the hero, Eddie Runge. She knew also Dennis' unusual relationship with Jay Cee, Wally, Andy, Jackie, Rosey, and a host of other brave men. Holding her husband's hand all during the night, she kissed him when he finished. "I didn't know," she said. "Nobody knows, I guess. Just you guys."

He thanked her for being patient, "for understanding me," he said. Then he dressed and prepared for work, eager to see his young students. *Maybe I could explain it to them someday -- they might understand.*

Returning home that evening, he went straight to his garage, searching for and finding several old, battered shoeboxes.

"Yeah, c'mon. I'm looking for something special," he said when Barbie asked if she could help. They spent the evening digging through the old letters and documents his mother had saved for him. In one lay the notebook that Rosey had given him on the day he died. Reading some of it, Dennis gave it to Barbie to examine while he sat down at his desk to pen a special letter.

"Who are you writing to?" she asked.

"There are other people besides me that have to close the door on Vietnam, Barbie. I'm going to write to the first one now, then all of them."

> *Dennis J. Riley*
> *2129 Greentree Dr.*
> *Pilot Point, TX 76258*
> *15 December 1989*

Deacon Justin R. Dolan
The Pontifical University
Maynooth, Ireland

Dear Justin,

   You don't know me; however, we are connected by past experiences which I feel compelled to relate to you. Your father, Roosevelt N. Dolan and I were together in Vietnam, more than twenty years ago. I was his platoon commander and with him on the day he died. I spoke to your mother recently by phone and she concurred in my plan to write to you.

   I do not wish to disturb your life or to reacquaint you with sad occasions, long since past, and perhaps better forgotten. Vanessa tells me that she and you buried all emotions about this dreadful affair long ago; "We had to get on with our lives," as she put it.

   As for myself, unfortunately, I have been unable to do that. Daily, there occur incidents which remind me of your father. Not the terror of his death, but of himself, his life, and how he lived it.

He knew more about the ways of man and God at the conclusion of his young life than I will ever know. He was the teacher, and I the student.

Approaching the mid-century point in my own life, I more and more come to understand that your father was correct in his definition of God: that He is manifest in all things, that we are all brothers and we are all born free, free in our thinking, free to act as we will. He made difficult choices based on these beliefs, but they were, ultimately, correct ones, and they satisfied him.

He was the bravest of us all, trying to be Christ-like in everything that he did, in a place that can only be described as a living hell.

While the rest of us sank deeper and deeper into the tragic excesses of that war, he openly professed his hatred for what we were doing. He suffered inside, yet carried it with great dignity, a dignity that I've tried to learn as tribute to our friendship.

I never visited your mother or grandparents in Detroit as I had promised. Forgive me; as the war dragged on, I became lost in a sea of death and destruction. Evil won out over good for a time and I lost my way. When I returned home, I could not bear to open these old wounds of the heart, they heal so slowly.

Several weeks ago I had the occasion to meet a young man about your age in a place of business. As he negotiated my purchase I felt him staring at me and without any hesitation he asked, "Did you serve in Vietnam?"

Startled by his spontaneous inquiry, I immediately answered, "Yes." His eyes held a pleading that I could not refuse and I asked him, "Why?"

As customers lined up behind us he quickly related that his father, whom he never knew, had disappeared in Vietnam. He had been searching for someone who might have known him -- anyone who could tell him the things a young man should know about his dad. The time of his father's disappearance did not correspond with my tenure there. I said so and we parted company. He was visibly disappointed and I promised to return later and tell him about the war.

I lay awake that night thinking of your father and you. The following morning I renewed acquaintances with your mother and

she seemed pleased that I had called, telling me of your own strug-
gles with the perplexities of life and how you were beginning to
doubt the authenticity of your calling. I resolved then that I would
draft this letter.

Enclosed are the pages of a notebook I have been safeguarding
over the years. The cover was lost long ago and the pages are
brown and curled at the edges. Whenever you doubt who you are
and what you should understand about life, refer to this simple
collection of prose. His poetry. It holds the wisdom of the ages and
will sustain you through many trials.

It will nourish your soul. Cherish it, as it is rightfully yours.
In a whisper your father willed it to you at the moment of his
death. Read it and you will come to know him and all that you
ever wanted to know about him.

In parting may I say that Rosey would be extremely proud of
you and the vocation you have chosen. Pray for him and me and
all of those who lived and died during the dreadful episode of
Vietnam.

Sincerely,
Dennis J. Riley

Laying down his pen, he took his wife into arms and they made love. Both slept well that night. Within a month, Barbie handed Dennis a thin letter decorated with colorful overseas postage stamps. He tore at the edges and, glancing over the handwriting, recognized that it was a duplicate of Rosey's neat and careful penmanship.

Dennis sat down and carefully laid the letter on a table.

"What's the matter?" Barbie asked.

"It's Rosey's -- Justin's penmanship. I thought I was closing the door on Vietnam, but I've only opened it wider."

Barbie squeezed his hand. "What do you mean?"

"The next of kin. How do we explain to them?"

Barbie moved directly in front of Dennis and raised his chin with her delicate fingertips. "It's not your fault, Dennis. I'm sure they don't blame you or any of the other guys."

"OK, Baby. Give me the letter. Let's see how he feels."

Deacon Justin D. Murphy
The Pontifical University
St. Patrick College Chapel
Maynooth, Ireland

January 15, 1990

Dennis J. Riley
2129 Greentree Dr.
Pilot Point, TX 76258

Dear Dennis,

Imagine my sheer delight as I examined the contents of a small package that arrived yesterday from the United States. I haven't finished reading all of it. I want to go slowly and get to know him.

Mother always said that we would hear from you -- that you were too good a person to just forget us. I can understand why you might want to avoid anything that would bring back these terrible memories. It must be difficult even today to relive those times.

Yes, lately I've been struggling with matters of the soul and of the heart, wondering if I have true vocation. Sometimes I think I'm only following the wishes of my grandfather and my mother. That matter is now resolved, thanks to you.

Reading my father's innermost thoughts clarifies my own thinking. I feel at peace for the first time in my life and I believe I can now pursue my calling without misgivings. Thank you, Dennis, for helping me to know him, for freeing me.

Chapel bells now summon me to vespers: I will devote my evening prayers to you and all of the men who still suffer the experience of Vietnam. In parting, I offer these words from Dante's Paradiso III. Perhaps they will comfort us both: "In la sua voluntade e` nostra pace." "In His will is our peace."

Yours in Christ,
Deacon Justin Dolan

Chapter Fifty-One
The Absolution

Having overcome his long-avoided contact with Vanessa and her son, Dennis threw himself into the fray. Each evening he and Barbie would scan the mailing list, calling others that he knew and asking for information on those not listed. Eventually, he volunteered to write and publish the newsletter as his contribution to the ongoing reunification of Charlie Company.

The list swelled to more than five hundred names due to the constant searching by dedicated men like Bill Schwindt. By telephone and letter, Dennis came to know them all as well as any men he had served with. In 1991, a reunion was scheduled for San Antonio, Texas, but Dennis could not bring himself to attend. He lay awake at night, cradled in his lover's arms, reliving his personal agonies, knowing that, emotionally, he was not ready, the healing not yet complete. "Will I ever be ready?" he asked Barbie.

"You'll know when, Dennis, you'll know," she answered.

In 1993, another reunion was scheduled and the mailing list now topped seven hundred. Dennis knew that if he attended, he would see many friends. Some of them called or wrote, giving him special reasons to go. Horacio Dos Santos begged him to come.

"Dee was the machine gunner who carried the day when Jay Cee attacked the front gate of Compound X-ray," he told Barbie. "He still calls me, 'Sir.' He sounded as if he were standing at attention when we spoke on the phone. I promised him I'd give some serious thought about going to the reunion."

In mid-June he loaded his small car and struck out for Las Vegas, the site of the Charlie Company gathering. Almost two hundred men with their families were scheduled to attend. Dennis stood in the lobby of the hotel, fighting the urge to run when, finally, a big fellow came over and draped his arm across his shoulder.

"You're one of us, ain't you?" Bill Schwindt asked as he introduced himself. "I've been watching you, Buddy. The first one's hard, but it gets easier, then it becomes fun. Come on, let me introduce you to some folks." Bill whisked him immediately to the "hospitality room," where dozens of his former comrades mingled with each other, talking about and laughingly reliving the experience of Vietnam.

Eddie Runge was the first to grab him and he held on to him for what seemed like an hour. Dennis beamed unashamedly at the loving hug and then there were more: Mike Balser, Father Tobin, Sergeants Allred and Beebe, a dozen or more of the men who walked beside him at every turn in Vietnam.

Charlie Brown stepped forward, placed a finger against the inside of his cheek and produced a popping sound identical to that of an M-79 grenade launcher. Dennis feigned alarm and he ducked slightly as Charlie shook his hand.

A low growl emitted from the corner of the room and Dennis spun excitedly to stare again into the face of First Sergeant Krznarovich. Almost seventy-nine years old now, he still carried himself with soldierly bearing. They watched each other knowingly for a few fleeting moments, then, shaking his hand, the top soldier asked, "Want a fucking beer, Lieutenant?"

Late the next evening a banquet was held, and each man read the name of a fallen comrade. It was a memorial to the men who could not be there and many families participated.

Children read the names of their fathers as did mothers and brothers and sisters. "Taps" echoed from a recording and Dennis ran from the hall. Telling Eddie to excuse him, he said that his mother had fallen ill and he was summoned home on an emergency basis. *A damn lie, but I've got to get out of there. I'm suffocating. I need air.*

The long drive home gave him time to think and he stopped at a pay phone to call his Barbie. She cooed him into silence and he drove on, feeling, but not understanding, the healing process he had embarked upon.

In 1995, he attended another assembly at St. Louis, Missouri, feeling much more comfortable with the crowd. He even joined the club of dedicated officers and volunteers who worked to hold the organization together. From the podium, at their business meeting, he told them of his desires for the direction of their newsletter. It had become a popular piece among the men and they commented favorably upon his work. Many said that they waited eagerly for each issue, consuming every word. When he finished speaking, they gave him a long, standing ovation and he beamed, knowing their applause was not solely because of his newsletter.

Searching for some normalcy, he sensed a beginning restoration of his damaged soul and spirit. Pleased and comfortable among his friends, he called Barbie and she said she understood.

"Write down every detail and don't forget to take lots of pictures."

Almost the entire Fourth Platoon was present this time and Jim Asher acted as Platoon Leader. He and Pat Shine organized a midnight patrol and they collected every man from Dennis' time to pose for a company picture. He was filled with joy and gratitude at their honest high regard for him.

"Let's hold the next reunion at the Vietnam Veteran's Memorial, 'The Wall,' in Washington, D.C.," someone suggested and it was unanimously agreed upon. They would gather there in July of 1997, some thirty years after Dennis' arrival in Vietnam.

Still, fleeting ghosts and demons rummaged through his mind and he could find little comfort with the thought. "Looking at the wall might be too much for me, Eddie. I don't think I'm ready yet."

To Dennis it was a symbol of the useless squandering of lives and he hated unknown men for it. Explaining his reluctance to stand before a monument that represented so much death, he asked Barbie if she would come with him. "I'll need you," he said.

"It's about time you included me," she said. "Will I go? I've been waiting for eight years for you to ask. I want to be part of a 'whole you,' Dennis. This might just make it happen. You need to come home from Vietnam."

Eagerly loading their car for the trip to Washington filled Dennis with delight. That his beautiful wife would be there to support him meant everything. She was the only one who really knew his fragile soul, nursing it for almost thirty years in the quiet of their bedroom. Barbie was the only thing he loved on this earth besides his children, his mother, and his Charlie Company. It was now time to bring closure to Vietnam -- they had both waited long enough for the day.

Like giddy teenagers, they put the car in motion, hugging as they backed out of the driveway and began their journey to the famous wall, America's black granite symbol of gratitude to the Vietnam Veteran.

Arriving at the reunion hotel early, they saw the many families already gathered there. Eddie and Melissa greeted them first, congratulating Dennis on his excellent choice for a wife. Melissa and Barbie became instant soul mates. They went shopping and sightseeing while Eddie and Dennis merged with the crowd to find friends and to drink toasts to everyone and everything.

Jim Tobin hailed them in the lobby. He was retired, but promised to say something at the ceremony by the wall the following day. Colonel Flint, now a retired General, introduced his wife and children. From Privates to General, they were all there.

Jim Asher hugged him as always and introduced his father, saying: "Dad just doesn't believe the stories I tell him so I thought I'd bring him along to hear for himself." John Asher's eyes glistened, looking at his son.

"Mississippi," was there, Steve Rye. He had given a leg to the infamous mountain, Nui Ba Den. Donald Evans, in good humor, reminded everyone about the night he was abandoned in Ap Cho.

"Don't shoot, GI," he laughed. "Don't shoot." James Dice talked about the horror of "carrying men on a stick," and he stroked his former commander's arm as he reminded him of how they had bled upon each other at Ap Cho. James had lost most of his hearing forever that night. Dee Dos Santos stood at perpetual attention as they collaborated on machine gun tactics.

General Flint told Gary Adams how proud he was of him and the boys cheered and applauded. Then he reminded them how special they all were, shaking hands and patting each on the back. On and on it went into the night. Man after man, telling Dennis stories that had been nightmares for almost thirty years. Now, they were only memories, things to boast about, to laugh about, and to cry about.

In the early evening, the men assembled in the huge banquet hall of the hotel. General Flint served as guest speaker and was seated on the dais beside his wife and children. After dinner, he spoke eloquently and with passion, enthralling the men with a clear explanation of the causes and the consequences of the war. He paused, choking several times as he described how the war had affected all Americans, but especially the men who were seated before him.

He praised them for their courage, their loyalty and their devotion to their country. The audience stood and cheered, roaring their approval. General Flint then invited other men to the microphone, and some accepted, telling of their personal pain and expressing gratitude to the association for having "found them -- bringing them home from Vietnam."

Pat Shine, Eddie Runge, and Jim Asher, seated at the table with Dennis, urged him to speak. "Come on, Charlie Six, get up there and tell them about Ap Cho, Good Friday, and the other hell we went through," Eddie urged.

"Yeah, speak for us," Pat Shine begged, grabbing Dennis on the arm.

"What the hell will I say?" Dennis asked, reluctant to speak publicly and perhaps expose his fragile soul.

Nick Dragon, Steve Rye, and Dee Dos Santos approached from another table. Dee took his arm, forcing Dennis to stand.

"Tell them about Rosey and Jay Cee. Do it for them -- for all the guys," Dee said.

"Don't worry about it," Steve Rye exhorted. "Go for it, Six. Just talk from the heart. Tell them about Charlie Company."

Forcing him to stand erect, they thrust Dennis forward. The audience noticed the commotion and some laughed. Suddenly Dennis felt the urge to oblige, a need to explain. He strode quickly to the dais, took the microphone in one hand and stepped forward, facing the congregation. He rubbed his nose between his forefinger and thumb for a moment, then tapped it. "Still sore," he said, smiling. Those who knew of his injuries in Ap Cho responded with a polite chuckle.

Dennis cleared his throat and scanned the audience. He stared directly into the eyes of the men who had persuaded him to speak. Examining their waiting faces for just a moment, he smiled and began: "Ladies and gentlemen, fellow soldiers, thank you for the opportunity to speak. My guys seem to think that I have some special insights into the business of war -- Vietnam. I don't, but I'll try for them. I'll try for the guys who didn't come back and I'll try for all of you."

He gazed at the floor, thrusting his left hand in his pocket, then drew a long and audible breath. Looking across the sea of faces, Dennis sensed that they waited in quiet anticipation for something special from him, some explanation, something that would undo their thirty years of agony. He was still their commander, he realized, and they expected it.

"You're the man, you'll always be the man," Pat Shine called out.

Making a modest attempt at humor, Dennis mentioned something about the Association of Retired Persons chasing him through the halls. He called the names of the men he knew, seated there, telling brief anecdotes about their war experiences and their individual heroism. Sensing that the audience was sufficiently warmed, he straightened his tie, inspected his congregation and said, "Yes, my friends want me to speak to the Vietnam Veterans, those who are gathered here and those who cannot be here, the living and the dead."

Dennis paused, then gestured broadly, sweeping the room with his arms. "My name is Dennis Riley. I was born in Conemaugh, Pennsylvania, near the end of World War Two. Now, my little hometown was a smoky little coal-mining borough in the 1940s. But, even as a small boy, I realized that the major event of the day was World War Two. Ah yes, I remember the times: to sacrifice for one's country -- to be a soldier. It was a wonderful and glamorous thing to be.

"One afternoon, barely five years old, I stood on the creaky wooden porch of our home watching soldiers pass by in parade. Sirens wailed and drums beat. There were flashing lights and little flags waving. It was led by our only fire truck, a military jeep and old Mr. Lehman, riding on his police motorcycle. Yes, my earliest impressions of life came from watching soldiers. My mother explained that it was VJ Day. 'The war is over,' she said. 'Peace has come at last.'

"I became so excited, I broke from her grasp, dashed from the porch, and joined the parade of victorious men, falling in behind them, carrying my own little wooden stick at right shoulder. Yes, tramp, tramp, tramp, we boys went marching.

"She wasn't too happy about my escapade, but I didn't care about the scolding; I had been in the company of soldiers and that was reward enough. It still is." Dennis closed his eyes for a moment, then suddenly opened them wide, his voice becoming powerful and resonant.

"The years passed and it seemed that I was always in the company of soldiers. Our neighbor told me how his brother, Charlie, and some other fellows had raised the American flag at a place called Iwo Jima, and he showed me the Medal of Honor Corporal Charles Strank got for that.

"The Korean war came next. I remember my big brother, Joe, so splendid in his Marine Corps uniform, teaching all us younger kids how to sing 'The Halls of Montezuma.' Joe never came back from the Choson Reservoir. I heard he froze to death."

Dennis stopped, fighting tears that seeped from his eyes. The audience, sympathetic, sat spellbound at his revelations, waiting for more. Regaining his composure, he cleared his throat and wiped his eyes on the sleeve of his coat. "So why did we, you and I, why did we go to Vietnam? I suppose, based on these kinds of childhood experiences and family traditions, it was only natural that we would grow to love our country. We'd fight and die for it, if necessary. That's why we joined up, why we accepted the draft, and went to Vietnam -- because it was the right and honorable thing to do."

A burst of applause erupted from several corners of the room and Dennis raised his arms to still them.

"In the late 1960s, you and I, we found ourselves on a jungle floor in Vietnam. Infantrymen. Riflemen. The tragedies and excesses of that war are well documented by authors and speakers much more qualified than I. I cannot explain the reasons for the war. I cannot speak for the spineless men in high places who made the war -- whatever their reasons. But I can tell you about the men, the soldiers who fought and sacrificed their lives and bore the painful wounds. That's what I do know.

"You boys, you were as wholesome in your beliefs about America as any soldier who had ever passed before you. You and me, we were all eager to serve our country, to save the people of Southeast Asia from the yoke of Communist enslavement. At least that is what we believed at the time. So we marched off to Vietnam, honorably motivated, to serve our country.

"It is no secret that the war became a quagmire of political ineptitude. My God, college kids getting shot down at Kent State." Dennis smacked his lips, looked at the floor and shook his head.

"Whew, you all remember the assassinations: Doctor Martin Luther King, Bobby. How about the 'Chicago Seven?' You remember all that?

"Young people, with flowers in their hair, circled the White House, chanting: 'Hey, hey, LBJ. How many kids did you kill today?' American flags were burned and draft cards torn apart, sometimes soaked in blood."

Dennis lowered his voice. Looking at them, he knew that he was in command again. "Gradually, there surfaced a certain level of despair in America over Vietnam -- disenchantment with our leaders, a sense of guilt for being there. All that guilt, men. It was somehow transferred by the American people to your shoulders. They needed someone to blame, and it became you, the soldier, the only symbol of that misguided government that people could see.

"Many in our society turned against their sons, and you boys -- you felt it -- deep inside your hearts and in your souls. Yes, they made us feel guilty for having served, for having been there. For fighting their war.

Can you believe it? They blamed *us* for the war. Some men were so ashamed they ducked into airport restrooms and changed into 'civies' before they made their way home."

Dennis glared at the audience through misty eyes, then shrugged. "But what the hell, there wasn't any parade to go to, anyway, was there?" Dennis waited, letting the audience chew for a moment on his question. Then he continued speaking.

"The ultimate indignity occurred when those same spineless men handed Vietnam over to the Communists -- because they had made such a mess of it. It became fashionable -- common and trite, to say: 'The only war *we* ever lost.'

"The same television commentators and news writers who worked so hard to undermine your honor, coined this biased phrase, this lie. I agree that the war was lost. Damn right, but *they* lost the war. Not you."

The audience stirred and Dennis could hear murmuring here and there. He waved his hand above them for silence and resumed speaking, his booming voice reverberating across the room.

"You men who fought the battles, hacked away at that formidable jungle, held off the hordes of Viet Cong that tried so hard to kill you, you never lost a damn thing! You hear me? You didn't lose nothing!" Dennis lingered for a moment on the echo of his words, then calmed.

"Oh, yeah, you might have lost a leg, an eye, some body tissue, perhaps. Worse yet, you might have lost your best friend, lying there beside you. But, *you* didn't lose the war." Dennis stopped, a perfect silence now filled the room.

"For almost thirty years I have carried in my heart this belief: that someday, somewhere, somehow -- our absolution -- a forgiveness for the guilt that was wrongly forced upon us, would come to pass. A good priest told me long ago that it would happen."

Dennis reached for a glass of water from a nearby table, then thought better of it.

"In America today," he continued, "there are those prominent media personalities. You know them, the ones who won't let this tragedy pass into history. They continually rehash the depravities of that war, such as the massacre at My Lai, that beastly atrocity that had nothing to do with you. They do this, I believe, because their agenda is to justify, to authenticate, their own shameful and inept reporting on the war.

"Realize, my friends, that each and every time they belabor the excesses of that war, they include you in their broad brush condemnations. They acknowledge no responsibility for the war, so they blame you. They keep the myth alive. We lost the war. Vietnam was a national failure. So therefore, you and me -- we are failures.

"I know better. You are the finest fighting men that America ever sent onto a battlefield and that vindication you so rightly deserve is right around the corner. They call it the Vietnam Veterans Memorial -- 'The Wall.' There, tomorrow morning, you and me, we'll see our friends again, relive our personal hell, and, with our tears, we'll wash away these lies. Come with me to the wall, men. Let's all come home again."

Lieutenant Dennis Riley laid down the microphone and strode briskly between the tables. He tried to leave the room, but the standing ovation and the throngs of men and women embracing him prevented his flight.

"I've been waiting thirty years to hear that. Thank you, Charlie Six," someone said.

Eddie Runge hugged him. "You said it all, Dennis."

Retired Sergeant Major Rudolph Krznarovich shook his hand vigorously, then said, "Like I told you thirty years ago, Riley, you can really sling some crap. Damn good job. Come on, I'll buy you a fucking beer."

With his arm around Dennis' shoulder, the old soldier led him from the hall. They, along with dozens of the men from Charlie Company, sat around the tables of the hotel bar, drinking modestly and analyzing the evening's events. They talked endlessly about Dennis' remarks and their impending visit to the wall.

"Hold me up when we get there," Jim Asher laughed.

"It'll be you doing the holding, I think," Dennis replied.

"Have you ever been there before?" Nick Dragon asked. Dennis stared at him, holding a terrible vision of Nick's wounds at Ap Cho. He shuddered and answered, "No, this will be my first experience."

"Me neither. I'm scared." At three a.m., Dennis crawled into bed. "It's like it doesn't matter anymore, Barbie," Dennis said. "They're shedding their own bad dreams. The hand clapping, the laughter, and the tears are their medicine." He sighed. "There's one last step to take, though, and everybody's anxious about it, especially me."

Charlie Company slept restlessly that night and Dennis snuggled closer to his Barbie. She lay awake and held him tight until the dawn.

Epilogue

Led by General Flint and other prominent men of the association, they boarded rented busses to ferry them to the wall. The temperature approached ninety degrees, humid and hot like all Washington summers. Gathering on a grassy knoll about two hundred yards east of the magnificent symbol, they wondered aloud how they'd behave as they gazed upon it from a distance. It represented everything about their lives and whatever pains they carried home from that Asian experience.

Waiting for their favorite chaplain, they milled around, sweating profusely. Thousands of summer tourists passed the wall and Dennis smiled as troop after troop of boy scouts and other caring citizens reached up to touch the chiseled names of heroes.

Finally, Jim Tobin arrived. Motioning his flock into a semi-circle, he smiled: "My friends, it is good for us to be here. I know that 'The Wall' has so many different meanings for each of you. Many are apprehensive about being here and it will take some of that special Charlie Company courage to visit there today. But let me tell you a little bit about it, about why we are here, why we have this wall.

"Many years ago, along a dusty road in Vietnam, I witnessed one of the most loving and merciful acts I have ever seen. A young Lieutenant, a commander at the time, insisted upon washing the faces of his dead soldiers before he'd allow me to place holy oils upon their foreheads. I was stricken, awed by such devotion, such love for men. I knew then that the day would come when we would gather at some obelisk, some shrine, because of that kind of love.

"That young Lieutenant asked me for absolution from his sins that night and I gave it, muttering some mumbo jumbo Latin words, but I knew that a greater forgiveness was due him, one that I couldn't give. That acquittal, that exoneration is due him now and far overdue for all of you."

Father Tobin fiddled with the volume knob of the portable speaker, hanging from his shoulder. He took his time adjusting it, letting his words sink in.

"Men, that amnesty you seek, that vindication you so rightly deserve, stands majestic and imposing right there, in front of you."

Turning, he pointed dramatically at the wall and said, "There, just a few yards away is your absolution. Go to it, touch it. It is your wall, built for you and for the men who forfeited, sacrificed, and gave away their young lives.

"I know looking at it might be troublesome for some of you. Your eyes will be awash with thirty years of stored-up tears and emotion. Some of you might feel confused and others of you may want to leave early. Run if you must, but you'll come back." Jim Tobin paused, looked over his crowd, stepped closer to them and chuckled.

"Let me tell you about that wall and my own first visit. When it was being built, I worked just a few blocks away. I'd take my lunch here on a park bench and watch the workman place those black stones together. I was skeptical, unsure if I ever wanted to see it. I had said prayers over so many of them and I, too, still see their faces in the night.

"Finally, when the wall was finished, out of curiosity I drew closer, just to look at it. It intrigued me so much that I came to visit it every day.

"Eventually, something came over me: I vowed to read every name on that wall. It took me fifteen months of lunch hours, but I read and prayed for every name on that wall. Yes, every name. In a sense they were all mine, you know.

"Not long after I began my litany of readings, an amazing thought occurred to me. I felt that I was actually speaking to my friends. Yes, a peace settled over me when I finally realized that I *was* talking to my friends. I had no reason to be shy about approaching them. One doesn't hide from his friends, does he? They are more your friends than they are mine -- you knew them best." He waved his arms and gestured toward the wall.

"Now, go on over there and visit with your friends. They have been waiting there for you, waiting for so long. Talk to them; they will help you chase away those little demons that run wildly through your night dreams and your daydreams. Talk to them out loud. If you believe in a power greater than ours -- in a God -- in a Deity of some sort, then you must believe your friends are with Him now, and that they hear you. Yes, go on over there and talk to your friends. They will listen to you and answer you and help you close the door on Vietnam, forever. Go --"

The audience was mesmerized by the sincerity of his speech and his sage explanation of the significance of the wall, none more so than Dennis. He remembered washing the faces of Wally, Rosey, Andy, and Jackie, and his desire for an absolution that night.

He felt the thirty-year clutch of despair fleeing his soul as Patti Schwindt led the group in sweet verses of "Amazing Grace." At the end of the song, Eddie took Dennis' arm. Together they walked the few yards to the wall, their women holding hands and trudging along behind.

"Look, Eddie!" Dennis shouted in amazement. "There's Crow and come here, over here. There's Jimmy Hollister and Martin. My God, there's Doc Shiro. Arishiro, I didn't know." He reached out to touch them and the throngs of passing people stopped to watch. Dennis knelt while Donald Evans stood on his back to reach a name high up and make a graphite rubbing.

"For his mother," Evan moaned.

Dennis swelled with emotion and choked back his tears. He placed a small guidon at the base of one panel where he found Doc Johnson's name. "He died coming down off Nui Ba Den," he whispered to the General.

Free now from any embarrassments, Dennis called out loudly to his men, resting there at the wall, asking them how they were and chatting with them in frank conversation.

They are present here. They're alive again. There's Bill Walker and Harry Liorete. Ap Cho. I'd run if Eddie wasn't holding on to me.

The tourists and the Scouts stood mute as they watched the survivors of Charlie Company pay amiable respect to their unforgotten dead. Almost a thousand people were passing the wall at that moment and, in awe of the veterans, they stayed hushed, whispering only to explain to children the meaning of the moment.

The silence overcame Dennis and he called out in distress: "Where are Jay Cee and Andy and the rest of the guys?" he asked as he drifted and searched. "Where are they? I can't find them."

"Whoa, Charlie Six," the strong, but gentle, voice of Jim Asher said as he reached out and grabbed him by the arm. "Come this way, Dennis. Come with me. This is what you came to see, who you need to see."

Walking a few steps back along the path, he pointed. "See, here they are, waiting for you." Then taking Dennis' first finger in his big hand, he helped him trace the granite etchings of Roosevelt Dolan, Jackie Stoner,

Wally Gerber, and Andy Crammer. Finally, he pressed Dennis' hand fully over the name of Jay Cee O'Connor and they remained there together, hand upon hand, weeping softly.

"I agree with Father Jim," Dennis finally said. "It wouldn't do for me to be emotional in front of them." He turned to the crowd that had gathered behind him. "I'm OK now, guys. Thanks. No more tears." Calm, in control of his emotions, he sojourned the length of the wall alone, until he had touched and spoken with all his sleeping friends. For Dennis, they were alive and would never die. They were happy he had come to see them, the heroes of Vietnam. They had waited much too long.

Dennis turned and smiled broadly at Jim, Eddie, Melissa and Barbara Jo. "I'm finished, now. All done. Let's go home."

Glossary

Airmobile: A method of transporting combat units by helicopter.

AK-47: Automatic or semi-automatic Assault Rifle. Soviet or Chinese man u-facture. Principal firearm used by Communist's forces in Vietnam.

APC: Armored Personnel Carrier. Sometimes called a "track." An armored vehicle assigned to "mechanized" infantry units.

ARVN: Acronym for Army of the Republic of Vietnam.

AWOL: Acronym for Absent Without Leave.

Beaucoups: French word expressing many, a large number, or a great amount. American mispronunciation and misuse: "Boo Coo."

Beehive: An artillery round filled with thousands of small metal arrows or darts (Flushettes). Designed for "flat-trajectory" fire against attacking perso n-nel.

Big Boy: Slang expression for any large vehicle. i.e., a tank or large truck.

Busted: A slang expression describing a reduction in rank for enlisted persons.

Choi Hoi: (Chew Hoy or Choy Hoy) A Vietnamese expression declaring su r-render. Often mispronounced and construed to become a noun by American solders. Choi Hoi(s) were enemy personnel who had surrendered to Ameri-can or ARVN forces.

Claymore Mine: An aboveground, anti-personnel mine, detonated by an electrical charge. Although this explosive device originated in the US., in Vietnam the name was used to describe any aboveground mine, either d o-mestic or foreign-made.

Click: A slang expression indicating a distance of 1000 meters on the ground.

CP: Command Post. Physical location of military leaders in the field.

C-Rations: Canned foods with condiments. Basic rations for soldiers.

Dustoff: A medical evacuation helicopter.

Field First Sergeant: Senior Enlisted Man (NCO) of an Army unit in the field.

Final Protective Fires: Pre-planned fires of all weapons available to a unit in a defensive position. Initiated as a last resort to stop enemy soldiers from attacking.

Flair: A helicopter pilot's description of the attitude or position of his aircraft in relationship to the earth, and his landing approach.

Flame Thrower: A mechanical device, a weapon, that emits flame, fueled by thickened or jellied gasoline. Backpack units are the most common; however, armored personnel carriers (APCs) are designed to perform the same function.

FO: The forward observer for artillery units. He calls for, and adjusts, fire.

Grunt: Slang expression for an infantry soldier in Vietnam.

Gunship: An armed helicopter. Usually carries a variety of rockets and fast-firing machine guns.

Huey: Acronym for a utility helicopter. The name derives from the manufacturer's model number: UH-1.

KIA: Killed in action.

Laager: A South African word describing a camp or encampment arranged in a circle. Used frequently in Vietnam to describe overnight defensive positions.

LP: A listening post. Two or three soldiers, occupying a position, slightly forward of larger units, in a defensive position. An early warning element of a larger unit. Listening posts are employed at night, observation posts during daylight.

LZ: Landing zone for helicopters. Usually refers to a clear or open location in which to land troops.

MIA: Missing in action.

M-16 Rifle: Automatic or Semi-automatic rifle issued to most soldiers in Vietnam. Capable of firing 750, 5.56mm rounds per minute. Early on, it experienced serious malfunctions in the hands of combat soldiers. It became a source of much controversy during the Vietnam war. It is a much-improved weapon, today.

M-60 Machine Gun: A bi-pod mounted, or hand-held automatic weapon. It fires a 7.62-mm bullet, at a sustained rate of 750 rounds per minute. It proved to be a worthy weapon in Vietnam, and continues to be the primary machine gun used by US Army infantry units today.

M-79 Grenade Launcher: A single shot, short barreled, "shotgun" type of weapon that fires a 40-mm explosive grenade. Variations of ammunition are available, such as tear gas. Its primary purpose is to launch explosive grenades a greater distance than the infantryman could throw by hand.

Napalm: Thickened or "jellied" gasoline. Delivered in canisters, or metal casings, by aircraft. Explodes and ignites upon impact with the ground.

NVA: An acronym for the North Vietnamese Army. Regular army soldiers from The (Communist) People's Republic of North Vietnam.

OCS: Officer Candidate School. Formal training whereby enlisted persons are commissioned as officers.

PZ: An acronym for a pick-up zone, a physical location where helicopters load personnel.

RTO: An acronym for a (field) radiotelephone operator.

Regional Forces: Identification for local militia units of the Army of the Republic of Vietnam. Might be characterized as National Guard-type units.

RPG: An acronym for Rocket Propelled Grenade. A shoulder-fired, anti-tank or anti-personnel weapon. Can be compared descriptively to the "bazooka" used in previous wars. Employed by NVA and Viet Cong forces

S&D: Search and destroy. A tactical method of searching for enemy soldiers in a forested environment, and engaging them in combat, with the ultimate goal of destroying them. In late 1967, public opinion in the United states rendered the term too offensive, and it was replaced by a more palatable expression: "Reconnaissance in Force," or RIF.

SitRep: Situation report. Expression of tactical or non-tactical circumstances of a military unit. A frequent update on conditions rendered verbally, usually by radio.

Stand To: A state of preparedness. A military term designating the precise time a unit will prepare itself for battle. It usually refers to the period immediately before dawn.

TOC: Acronym for a Tactical Operations Center, a command post for the commander and staff of units, battalion size or higher.

"Top": An unofficial term reserved for the First Sergeant or "top" enlisted man in an infantry company. An expression of respect for that position. Often used to identify the senior enlisted man in a field situation, where the official First Sergeant is not present.

VC: Viet Cong. Indigenous, Communist guerrilla forces, operating in South Vietnam. Principal foe of American soldiers until 1968, when the North Vietnamese Army (NVA) dominated the battlefield.

WIA: Wounded in action.

Bibliography

More than four thousand books are now available on events concerning the war in Vietnam. The list will surely continue to grow. Using modern electronic means, library databases, and traditional paper research, it is now an easy task for anyone to make a thorough and critical examination of America's involvement in Vietnam. The titles listed below represent those books which relate most notably to the events depicted in the book, *Absolution*.

Adams, Sam. *War of Numbers: An Intelligence Memoir.* Introduction by Colonel David Hackworth. South Royalton, VT: Steerforth Press, 1994.

Amter, Joseph A. *Vietnam Verdict: A Citizens History.* New York: Continuum, 1982.

Anderegg, Michael, ed. *Inventing Vietnam: The War in Film and Television.* Philadelphia: Temple University Press, 1991.

Arnett, Peter. *Live From the Battlefield: From Vietnam to Baghdad, 35 Years in the World's War Zones.* New York: Simon & Schuster, 1994.

Baker, Mark. *Nam: The Vietnam War in the Words of the Men and Women Who Fought There.* New York: Berkley Books, 1983. William Morrow & Company, 1981.

Bergerud, Eric M. *Dynamics of Defeat: The Vietnam War in Hau Nghia Province.* Boulder: Westview Press, 1991.

Bergerud, Eric M. *Red Thunder Tropic Lightning: The World of a Combat Division in Vietnam.* Boulder: Westview Press, 1993.

Bilton, Michael and Kevin Sim. *Four Hours in My Lai.* New York: Viking, 1992.

Brennan, Matthew. *Brennan's War: Vietnam 1965-1969.* Novato, CA: The Presidio Press, 1985.

Broughton, Colonel Jack. *Thud Ridge.* Philadelphia: Lippincott, 1969; New York: Bantam, 1985.

Bui Tin. *Following Ho Chi Minh: The Memoirs of a North Vietnamese Colonel.* (Vietnamese original Hoa Xuyen Tuyet). Translated and adapted by Judy Stowe and Do Van; introduction by Carlyle Thayer. Honolulu: The University of Hawaii Press, 1995.

Buttinger, Joseph. *Vietnam: The Unforgettable Tragedy.* New York: Horizon Books. 1997.

Caputo, Philip. *A Rumor of War.* New York: Holt, Rinehart & Winston, 1977; Ballantine, 1978.

Del Vecchio, John. *The 13th Valley.* New York: Bantam, 1982.

Downs, Frederick Jr. *The Killing Zone.* New York: Norton, 1978; Berkeley, 1983.

Ebert, James R. *A Life in a Year: The American Infantryman in Vietnam, 1965-1972.* Novato, CA: The Presidio Press, 1993.

Edelman, Bernard, ed., for the New York Vietnam Veterans Memorial Commission. *Dear America: Letters Home from Vietnam.* New York: Norton, 1985. Paperback, New York: Pocket Books, 1986.

Esper, George and The Associated Press. *The Eyewitness History of The Vietnam War, 1961-1975.* New York: Ballantine, 1983.

Fall, Bernard. *Hell in a Very Small Place: The Siege of Dien Bien Phu.* Philadelphia: J.J. Lippincott Company, 1967.

Fall, Bernard. *Last Reflections on a War.* New York: Doubleday, 1967.

Fall, Bernard. *Street Without Joy.* 4th ed. rev. Harrisburg, PA: Stackpole, 1964.

Flynn, Robert. *A Personal War in Vietnam.* Texas A&M University Military History Series, No. 13. College Station, TX: Texas A&M University Press, 1989.

Gelb, Leslie H. with Richard K. Betts. *The Irony of Vietnam: The System Worked.* Washington: The Brookings Institution, 1979.

Gibson, James. *The Perfect War: Techno War in Vietnam.* Boston: Atlantic Monthly Press, 1986. Paperback *The War We Couldn't Lose and How We Did.* New York: Vintage, 1988.

Grant, Zalin. *Facing the Phoenix: The CIA and the Political Defeat of the United States in Vietnam.* New York: Norton, 1991.

Hallin, Daniel C. *The "Uncensored War": The Media and Vietnam.* New York: Oxford University Press, 1986.

Hearden, Patrick J. *The Tragedy of Vietnam.* New York: Harper Collins, 1991.

Heinemann, Larry. *Close Quarters.* New York: Farrar, Straus & Giroux, Inc., 1977.

Heinemann, Larry. *Paco's Story.* New York: Penguin Books, 1989.

Hemphill, Robert. *Platoon: Bravo Company.* Forward by Joseph Galloway. Fredericksburg, VA: Sergeant Kirkland's Press, 1998.

Herr, Michael. *Dispatches.* New York: Knopf, 1977; Vintage International, 1991.

Herrington, Stuart. *Silence Was a Weapon: The Vietnam War in the Villages.* Novato, CA: The Presidio Press, 1982.

Isaacs, Arnold. *Without Honor: Defeat in Vietnam and Cambodia.* Baltimore: The Johns Hopkins University Press, 1983.

Kahin, George M. *Intervention: How America Became Involved in Vietnam.* New York: Knopf, 1986.

Karlin, Wayne, Le Minh Khue, and Truong Vu. *The Other Side of Heaven: Postwar Fiction by Vietnamese and American Writers.* Willimantic, CT: Curbstone Press, 1995.

Karnow, Stanley. *Vietnam: A History.* New York: Viking, 1983.

Krepinevich, Jr., Andrew F. *The Army In Vietnam.* Baltimore: The Johns Hopkins University Press, 1986.

Levine, Alan J. *The United States and the Struggle for Southeast Asia, 1945-1975.* Westport: Praeger, 1995.

Lac, Hoang and Viet, Ha Mai. *Blind Design: Why America Lost the Vietnam War*. Self-Published: Sugarland, TX, 1996.

Lomperis, Timothy J. *From People's War to People's Rule: Insurgency, Intervention, and the Lessons of Vietnam*. Chapel Hill: The University of North Carolina Press, 1966.

Maurer, Harry. *Strange Ground: An Oral History of Americans in Vietnam 1945-1975*. New York: Henry Holt, 1989.

MacPherson, Myra. *Long Time Passing: Vietnam and the Haunted Generation*. Garden City, NY: Doubleday and Company, 1984.

Martin, Andrew. *Receptions of War: Vietnam in American Culture*. Oklahoma project for discourse and theory, V. 10. Norman, OK: The University of Oklahoma Press, 1993.

Mason, Robert. *Chickenhawk*. New York: Viking, 1983.

Moore, Lieutenant General Harold G., and Joseph L. Galloway. *We Were Soldiers Once and Young: Ia Drang: The Battle That Changed the War in Vietnam*. New York: Random House, 1992.

Morrison, Wilbur H. *The Elephant and the Tiger: The Full Story of the Vietnam War*. New York: Hippocrene, 1990.

Moss, George D. Vietnam: *An American Ordeal*. Englewood Cliffs, NJ: Prentice Hall, 1994.

O'Ballance, Edgar. *The Wars in Vietnam: 1954-1980*. New York: Hippocrene, 1981.

O'Brien, Tim. *Going After Cacciato*. New York: Dell, 1989.

Oberdorfer, Don. *Tet*. New York: Doubleday, 1971; DeCapo: 1984.

Palmer, Jr., General Bruce. *The 25-Year War: America's Military Role in Vietnam*. Lexington, KY: The University Press of Kentucky, 1984.

Palmer, Laura. *Shrapnel in the Heart: Letters and Remembrances From the Vietnam Veterans Memorial*. New York: Random House, 1987.

Pentagon Papers: *The United States Congress, House Committee on Armed Services. United States-Vietnam Relations, 1945-1967: A Study Prepared by the Department of Defense.* Washington, DC: U.S. Government Printing Office, 1971. 12 Volumes.

Podhoretz, Norman. *Why We Were in Vietnam.* New York: Simon & Shuster, 1983.

Prados, John and Ray W. Stubbe. *Valley of Decision: The Siege of Khe Sanh.* New York: Houghton Mifflin, 1991.

Puller, Lewis B. Jr. *Fortunate Son: The Autobiography of Lewis B. Puller, Jr.* New York: Grove Weidenfield, 1991; Bantam, 1993.

Race, Jeffrey. *War Comes to Long An.* Berkeley: The University of California Press, 1972.

Scarborough, Elizabeth Ann. *The Healer's War.* New York, Bantam Books, 1988, 1992.

Schulzinger, Robert D. *A Time for War: The United States and Vietnam, 1941-1975.* New York: Oxford University Press, 1997.

Scruggs, Jan Craig, Esq. President and Founder of the Vietnam Veterans Memorial Fund. *The Wall That Heals.* The Vietnam Veterans Memorial Fund, Inc., McClean, VA, 1992.

Scruggs, Jan Craig, Esq. President and Founder of the Vietnam Veterans Memorial Fund. Compiled by Jan Scruggs. *Why Vietnam Still Matters.* Vietnam Veterans Memorial Fund, Inc., 1996. Paperback: write to The Vietnam Veterans Memorial Fund at 1360 Beverly Road, Suite 300, McClean, VA 22101-3685.

Shafer, D. Michael, ed. *The Legacy: The Vietnam War in the American Imagination.* Boston: Beacon Press, 1990.

Shaplen, Robert. *The Road from War: Vietnam 1965-1971.* New York: Harper-Colophon, 1971.

Shay, Jonathan. *Achilles in Vietnam: Combat Trauma and the Undoing of Character.* New York: Athenaeum, 1994.

Sheehan, Neil. *A Bright Shining Lie: John Paul Vann and America in Vietnam*. New York: Random House, 1988.

Sheppard, Don. *Riverine: A Brown-Water Sailor in the Delta, 1967*. Novato, CA: The Presidido Press, 1992.

Short, Anthony. *The Origins of the Vietnam War*. New York: Longman, 1989.

Smith, Winnie. *American Daughter Gone to War: On the Front Lines With an Army Nurse in Vietnam*. New York, Morrow, 1992.

Summers, Colonel Harry. *On Strategy: The Vietnam War in Context*. Novato, CA: The Presidio Press, 1982.

Thayer, Carlyle A. *War by Other Means: National Liberation and Revolution in Vietnam, 1954-60*. Cambridge, MA: Unwin Hymin, 1989.

Turley, Colonel Gerald H. *The Easter Offensive*. Novato, CA: The Presidido Press, 1985.

Turley, William S. *The Second Indochina War: A Short Political and Military History, 1954-1975*. Boulder, Colorado: Westview, 1986.

Van Devanter, Lynda, and Joan A. Furey, eds. *Visions of War, Dreams of Peace: Writings of Women in the Vietnam War*. New York: Warner Books, 1991.

Westmoreland, General William C. *A Soldier Reports*. New York: Doubleday, 1976.

Wexler, Sanford. *The Vietnam War: An Eyewitness History*. New York: Facts on File, 1992.

Wintle, Justin. *The Viet Nam Wars*. New York: St. Martin's Press, 1991.

Young, Marilyn B. *The Vietnam Wars, 1945-1990*. New York: Harper-Collins, 1991.